Metaphors, Narratives, Emotions

Consciousness Literature & the Arts 24

General Editor:
Daniel Meyer-Dinkgräfe

Metaphors, Narratives, Emotions

Their Interplay and Impact

Stefán Snævarr

Amsterdam - New York, NY 2010

Cover illustration: Ólafur Þórðarson, *Escargot*, clock in black rubber. Copyright/TM 1997: Olafur Thordarson.

Cover design:
Aart Jan Bergshoeff

The paper on which this book is printed meets the requirements of "ISO 9706:1994, Information and documentation - Paper for documents - Requirements for permanence".

ISBN: 978-90-420-2779-4
E-Book ISBN: 978-90-420-2780-0
ISSN: 1573-2193
© Editions Rodopi B.V., Amsterdam - New York, NY 2010
Printed in the Netherlands

Table of Contents

Foreword and Acknowledgements

The manuscript of what became this book was a rather loose collection of articles when I sent the book proposal to Rodopi. Much to my surprise, Daniel Meyer-Dinkgräfe, the editor of this series, accepted my proposal. In the meantime, the collection of articles has changed into a book with common themes. Whether it has transformed from an ugly duckling into a beautiful swan I leave to others to decide.

I am indebted to several colleagues for having read earlier versions of some of the chapters and giving me excellent advice on how to proceed. They include Kristján Kristjánsson, Richard Eldridge, Albert Rothenberg, Sigríður Þorgeirsdóttir, Peter Goldie, Paul Knutsen, Robert C. Roberts, Ronnie de Sousa, Mark Johnson, John M. Kennedy, Kendall Walton, Anstein Gregersen, Harald Grimen, Kjell S. Johannessen, and Ingmar Meland. Meyer-Dinkgräfe gave me valuable advice on the book as a whole as did Rodopi's anonymous referee. Steven Connolley has most ably corrected my broken (?) English and given me advice on all sorts of things, including the correct translation of ancient Greek. Rosemary Knutsen has corrected one chapter. Gro Vasbotten has been of invaluable assistance in preparing the pdf-files of the manuscript. And thanks to Olafur Þorðarsson for the beautiful picture on the cover.

The foundations for some parts of this book were laid in articles, books and papers, written and given in Icelandic and Norwegian. Of greatest importance is my book in Norwegian, *Fra Logos til Mytos. Metaforer, mening, erkjennelse* (*From Logos to Mythos. Metaphors, Meaning, Cognition*). That book was published in 2003. A year later, I published a volume of essays in Icelandic, some of which discuss the themes of the book you are now reading.

Some of the chapters of this book have roots in papers I have given at conferences: "Metaphors and Meaning: The Alethic Theory", *XV World Congress of Aesthetics*, Makuhari, Japan, August 2001; "The Heresy of Paraphrase Revisited", *The World Congress of Philosophy*, Istanbul, August 2003; "Understanding Metaphors: The Alethic Theory", invited paper, *Department of Philosophy*, University of Oslo, May 2004; "The Cogito of Don Quixote", The Annual Conference of *The Nordic Aesthetic Association*, Uppsala, Sweden, May 2004; "Metaphoring and Emoting", *XVI World Congress for Aesthetics*, Rio de Janeiro, July 2004; and "Emotions as Texts", a conference on *Emotions, Others and the Self*, Åbo, Finland, August 2005. The audiences of these presentations deserve special thanks for their comments.

I am also grateful for the permissions to reprint material from some of my own articles: "The Heresy of Paraphrase Revisited", *Contemporary Aesthetics*, Vol. 2, 2004, "Emoting and Metaphoring. On the Metaphoric Structure of Emotions", *Sats. Nordic Journal of Philosophy*. Vol. 7, No. 1, 2006; "Don Quixote and the Narrative Self", *Philosophy Now*, Issue 60, March/April, 2007; "Poetics and Maieutics", *Contemporary Aesthetics*, Vol. 6, 2007. Faber&Faber kindly allowed me to reprint parts of Ezra Pound's poem *Cantos 1*, Direction Press and Carcanet press have been kind enough to allow me to reprint William Carlos Williams' poem *This is Just to Say* in its entirety.

Introduction: A Book Of Mosaic

1 Themes of this book

At first glance, this book might seem like an amalgam of ideas and arguments, but a closer look shows that these ideas and arguments are like pieces of mosaic that form a picture. It depicts the way metaphors, narratives, and emotions hang together. But do they really share any interesting common features? My answer is yes. There are certain features that deserve our appreciation and scholarly attention. Until relatively recently, none of the three has usually been regarded as vehicles for argumentation or cognition. The threesome was traditionnally banished beyond the pale of reason or even seen as its antithesis, its Other. While metaphors were thought to be ornaments of speech and writing, literal language alone was seen as the proper vehicle for argumentation. Narratives were not considered to be cognitive tools but rather devices for aesthetic enjoyment or pure entertainment. Theories, preferably those that are confirmed by experience and that satisfy the canons of formal logics, were privileged as our main cognitive devices. Emotions, furthermore, were viewed suspiciously, as something subjective and irrational, a world away from cool, objective reason. However, over the last decades, a different picture has emerged. It has become commonplace to say that emotions have a cognitive content, that narrations can provide rational explanations and that metaphors can perform cognitive functions. And yet, as far as I know, nobody has tried to articulate the implications arising from this new picture of all three concepts for our conception of reason, much less whether there are important logical links between them.

Articulating these implications and showing where these logical links are situated are my main purposes in this book. But I must emphasise that uncovering these links does not imply an attempt to find an essential definition of the threesome by locating some features that all and only narratives, metaphors, and emotions share. Such a search might prove futile for several reasons, one being the possibility that all three concepts might be *fuzzy concepts*, i.e., concepts with blurred edges (unclear limits); it is debatable, for instance, whether or not similes are metaphors.[1] Rather, this work focuses on non-trivial similarities and connections in fields that matter to human life, such as the fields of rationality and meaning.

There are a number of these similarities and connections, which I shall now mention cursorily. To begin with, all three are constituted by *aspect-seeing*, i.e., *seeing-as* or perception of Gestalts. Now, there are thinkers like Max Black who have insisted that metaphors are constituted in this way, and others such as Louis Mink who have held that narratives are. Additionally, Paul Ricœur has led the claim that metaphors and narratives share this feature, and Robert Roberts, among others, has claimed that emotions are constituted by aspect-seeing. However, as far as I know, I am the first theorist to maintain than *all three* are constituted by aspect-seeing.

Secondly, all three are *meaning-endowing* devices; they help us furnish our world with meaning. But while metaphors and narratives are nothing but such devices, emotions have in addition biological and experiential dimensions.

Thirdly, the cognitive roles of the threesome point towards a richer conception of rationality than we Cartesians are (or were) wont. Rationality has metaphoric, narrative, and emotive sides (There are those who have argued that rationality has metaphoric or emotive sides, but to my knowledge nobody has said that it possesses all three.) We can talk about *emo-narra-ana-logics* (ENAL), that is, ways of reasoning whereby analogies, metaphors, stories and emotions play an important role, owing to the narrative, emotive, and metaphoric properties of reason.

Fourthly, the threesome is a trinity. By this specification I mean that emotions have both a narrative and metaphoric structure and that we can analyse the concepts of metaphors and narratives partly in terms of each other. Further, the concept of narratives can partly be analysed in terms of that of emotions. And if emotions have both a narrative structure and a metaphoric one, then the concept of emotions must to some extent be analysable through the concepts of narratives and metaphors. Further, metaphors (not least poetic ones) are

---

[1] The issue of the relationship between similes and metaphors will pop up now and again in the first section of this book.

important tools for the understanding of the tacit sides of emotions, perhaps because of the metaphoric structure of emotions. (This observation shows how metaphors can have a cognitive function.) But I confess that I have not found any way to analyse the concept of metaphor in terms of the concept of emotions.

The notion that narrations can be tools for understanding emotions follows from both the fact that narrations are devices for explanation and the fact that emotions have a narrative structure. Because of the explanatory nature of narratives and the narrative nature of emotions, narratives can help us explain emotions.

There is, then, a complex logical and epistemological interplay between emotions, narrations, and metaphors. Our recognition of this interplay should not, however, blind us to the differences between the three, especially with regard to the special qualities of emotions, which obviously have certain ontological aspects quite distinct from those of narratives and metaphors.

2 An Overview of this Book

The book is divided into three sections: the first one is devoted to metaphors, the second to narratives, and the third to emotions. Every section comprises a number of chapters and a conclusion. At the end of the book there is general conclusion.

I open the first section with a chapter on the nature of metaphors by route of a critical evaluation of such thinkers as Donald Davidson and Max Black. I criticise Davidson's contention that metaphors have no cognitive content and endorse a very cautious version of the idea that metaphors involve interaction between their subject and predicates. In the second chapter, I introduce and critically evaluate Paul Ricœur's theory of metaphors. In the third chapter I propose my own theory of metaphoric understanding whereby I argue that an apprehension of a metaphor requires a grasping of its cognitive content. The cognitive content in question is not truth, but rather a truth-like content, just like a caricature can have a cognitive content but that content cannot be truth. In the fourth chapter and the fifth chapter, I ask whether our language and thinking is soaked by metaphors and whether metaphors have some kind of transcendental status. While agreeing with those who think that metaphors play an ineliminable role in language and thought, I shy away from granting metaphors a transcendental status. The thinkers discussed in the third chapter include Friedrich Nietzsche, Jacques Derrida, and Mary Hesse. Hesse's theory of analogical reasoning has provided great inspiration for me. I further try to show that there are no clear limits between literal and non-literal language, and that it is therefore difficult, if not impossible, to privilege any of them, say, for instance that language is essentially literal or essentially metaphoric. The fifth chapter examines the cognitive semantics of the Lakoff School. I express doubts about the soundness of the empirical foundation of this brand of semantics while lauding it for demonstrating the limitation of a one-sided focus on linguistic metaphors. I also commend them for their conception of imaginative rationality, i.e., a kind of rationality that makes great use out of tropes and analogies. In the sixth chapter, I try to rejuvenate the old idea that poems and metaphors are not paraphrasable. As an instrument for that endeavour, I perform a thought experiment, showing that in a world where all poems were paraphrasable, the concept of poetry would become empty. The reason why typical poems are non-paraphrasable is that our knowledge of them is essentially tacit; poems are in many ways like complex Gestalten. In the conclusion of this section, I introduce what I call '*ana-logic*', i.e., thinking by means of metaphors, analogies, and similes. I propose that ana-logic is as just as central for our thinking as deductive logic.

The second section is a consideration of stories and narratives. In the first chapter, I briefly discuss the concepts of narratives and stories, besides introducing my own concepts of narrative structure and storied structure. In the second chapter, theorists of historical narratives take the centre stage. I focus on the concept of non-fictional narratives with the aid of such theorists as Arthur Danto, Louis Mink, Donald Polkinghorne, Jerome Bruner, and W. B. Gallie. I aim to show that narratives can have cognitive functions, including an explanatory one. The third chapter is a discussion of the relationship between fictional and non-fictional narratives, using Hayden White's theories as a point of departure. I stress the complex interaction between them; we cannot separate them clearly. At the same time, I discuss briefly the concept of imaginative literature and try to show that cannot be defined essentially. We can, however, talk about 'indicators of literariness': the more such indicators a text possesses, the better reasons we have for calling it 'a work of imaginative literature'. I explore further the issue of fictional and non-fictional narratives in the next chapter, concentrating on Paul Ricœur's seminal analysis. I maintain that he sees both fictional and non-fictional narratives as 'factions', even 'docudramas'. The fifth chapter also features Ricœur along with Mark Turner. Both theorists have shown that metaphors and narratives are interrelated in various ways. In agreement, I put forth a theory about there being N-Ms, symbolic structures that combine elements from metaphors and stories. The sixth chapter deliberates the theory that our lives and cognition is permeated, and even created, by stories and narratives. I argue in favour of both our thinking having a storied structure and the existence of spontaneously created non-told stories (dreams, fantasies, reveries, scenarios that somehow overwhelm us and so on). Stories and narratives, then, certainly are all-pervasive in our lives and cognition. Finally, in the conclusion I propose my notion of *narra-logic*, i.e., the analogue to ana-logic in the realm of stories.

Emotions are the focus of the third section. The first chapter begins with my discussion and endorsement of the view that emotions can have cognitive import. I criticise biological, reductive naturalism concerning emotions and defend the view that subjectivity is an ineliminable factor in emotions. I agree with the 'construalists' who think that emotions have their basis in aspect-seeing. I try to wed this idea to Charles Taylor's hermeneutic view of emotions, developing my own *hermeneutic construali*sm in the process. In the second chapter, I endorse the view that emotions have their basis in narrations, i.e., that they have a storied structure. In the third chapter I introduce my view of emotions imbued with meaningfulness. This means that emotions are partly constituted by interpretation, that they have illocutionary aspects and have a metaphoric structure as well as a storied one. I introduce in the fourth chapter my thesis that ana-logic is often required to disclose tacit sides of emotions and that poetic metaphors are important tools for that endeavour. At the same time, emotions have a disclosive function. In the conclusion, I advance the notions of ENAL and emo-logic, the latter one being the emotional analogue to both ana-logic and narra-logic, the former the product of all three 'logics'. The importance of ENAL and emo-logic is one of the reasons for me maintaining that our cognition and existence are imbued with emotivity.

3 Being Post-Analytic and somewhat Pro-Wittgenstein

I do not doubt the keen reader may already suspect that I am a philosophical opportunitist, using whatever tools are convenient for my purposes - and indeed, her suspicions are well founded. I use Continental tools whenever required and analytical tools when they are convenient. I employ analytic tools more frequently, which; this is why I call myself 'a *post-Continental* philosopher'. In other contexts, I stress that I am post-analytical, and so I happily deconstruct the purported analytical-Continental distinction! It is not by chance, therefore, that I quote approvingly philosophers who disregard this distinction, most notably Charles Taylor, but also thinkers like Michael Polanyi and Mark Johnson. I sometimes refer to them as the *go-betweeners* (or even *in-betweeners*). Moreover, Taylor has been under the strong influence from Ludwig Wittgenstein, and I have been as well. It is unsurprising, then, that Max Black has influenced my thought on metaphors, Louis Mink my conception of narratives, and Robert C. Roberts my ideas of emotions - all of whose works are deeply imbued with Wittgenstein's ideas. The Norwegian philosopher Kjell S. Johannessen counts as another; his interpretation and articulation of Wittgensteinian thoughts has inspired me profoundly. But, as we shall see, I am quite critical of certain aspects of their thinking, and the same holds for some of Wittgenstein's own ideas.

Seven of Wittgenstein's main ideas are central for my project. These are the analysis of aspect-seeing; the idea of there being no rule on how to apply a rule; the idea of family concepts; the idea of the separation between saying and showing; the argument against the possibility of a private language; the idea of the plurality of language games and the implicit argument in favour of there being tacit knowledge. I shall return to the last argument in a later chapter but I shall now briefly sketch the other six arguments.

I have already mentioned the first idea, that of aspect-seeing or seeing-as. The paradigmatic example of aspect-seeing is our seeing an ambiguous figure as something rather than another. In the case of the duck-rabbit figure, we see it either as a duck or a rabbit. The concept of *aspect-dawning* is of great importance here; first I see a puzzle picture merely as collection of lines but all of sudden it dawns upon me that it is a picture. I notice a hitherto unnoticed aspect of this collection of lines in the same way as I can notice an aspect of the duck-rabbit figure, which I previously perceived as a duck, and, in virtue of the new noticing of an aspect, I suddenly see the figure as a rabbit. I also become aware of an aspect when I contemplate a face and the all of sudden notice its likeness to another face. As Wittgenstein says in no uncertain words "…the flashing of an aspect on us seems half visual experience, half thought" (Wittgenstein 1958: 197). Seeing an aspect is not a question of interpretation but rather of sensation. We do not infer from dots and lines that what we are seeing is a rabbit or a duck; we simply see it (Wittgenstein 1958: 195).

We shall later see that the idea of seeing-as has been successfully articulated in various domains, including the ones of metaphors, narratives, and emotions. There have also been some highly thought-provoking attempts to articulate the concept in the fields of aesthetics, theory of science, and philosophy of psychology.[2] The strength of these expositions plus the strength of Wittgenstein's own arguments count in favour of the fruitfulness of the concept of seeing-as. Furthermore, the convenience of being able to unify various fields under this single concept also enhances its attraction. I am alluding to the virtues of using Occam's famed razor.

I take issue, however, with the contention that the operation of seeing-as does not have any moment of interpretation. Interpreting A means understanding A as A1 rather than A2; seeing a duck-rabbit figure as a rabbit rather than a duck also involves the choice of one alternative understanding while other alternatives are disregarded or rejected. The analogies between interpreting and seeing-as are so strong that I think we are talking about an analogous kind of process, a process not of interpretation but of *semi-interpretation*. Seeing-as is usually a spontaneous, more or less subconscious interpretation, perhaps rooted in tacit knowledge, but it has interpretative moments nonetheless. We know that there are such moments from the fact that people can be persuaded to see Jastrow-figures in certain ways. Similarly, in the aesthetic realm, one can use directive reasoning to get people to see artwork X as being Y. These persuasions involve drawing attention to certain features of the artwork. We can for instance draw attention to the fact that the witches in Goya's painting

---

[2] For such an articulation in philosophy of science, see for instance Hanson 1958. For one of many articulations in aesthetics, see Wollheim 1980. For an articulation in philosophical psychology, see Mulhall 1990.

The Witches' Sabbath can be seen as forming one, round whole, thus underlining their stupidity and gullibility which also can be seen in their facial expressions. They are just flock animals who do not think and are therefore easy pray for the devil's manipulations. But notice that we do not have to see the witches as forming a whole; we could just as well focus on them as individuals and perhaps then not seeing them as flock animals. Perhaps we infer from our beliefs about the painting which of these ways of seeing the witches is the most fruitful one, while these ways of seeing them in their turn shape our beliefs. The interpretative moment in this ought to be obvious.

Now, British Wittgensteinian David Best has coined the expression 'interpretative reasoning', a way of reasoning strongly involving seeing-as. He asks us to consider a psychological test: we see figures which at first appear as a meaningless jumble of lines, but in which, when pointed out, we can clearly recognise a face (notice that one is trying to make us see the lines as something). The reasons offered in support of the judgement that there is a face would consist of drawing attention to the relevant features in the drawing (Best 1992: 35). I basically agree with Best's analysis, which strengthens my contention that seeing-as has interpretative moments. But he does not differentiate between interpretation proper and semi-interpretation; he even talks like the latter is the former. That goes against the grain of my thinking; Best goes a bit too far in the right direction.

In my view, seeing-as is *half-interpretation* (compare "half-thought") and half-sensation. In some cases (such as directive reasoning), the interpretative moment dominates, in others the sensation half. I do not rule out the possibility that there are different kinds of seeing-as, some semi-interpretative, others not.

My conclusion is that Wittgenstein's conception of interpretation is too narrow. It goes against the grain of his thinking to talk as though interpretation has clear, given limits. My hunch is that the concept of interpretation has blurred edges, and it is perhaps a family concept, a prototypical one or even an open-textured concept. (I shall explain these expressions later.) There is more between interpretation and sensation than Wittgensteinian philosophy could dream of!

The second Wittgensteinian argument is the contention that there is no rule for how to apply a rule, and, therefore, rules *in abstracto* do not give us any guidance for action: "This was our paradox: no course of action could be determined by a rule, because every course of action can be made to accord with the rule" (Wittgenstein 1958: 81 (§ 201).

Obeying a rule is a custom or a practice and cannot be understood as a mechanical application of abstract rules (Wittgenstein 1958: 81 (§ 202)). He says in no uncertain words: "Not only rules but also examples are needed for establishing a practice. Our rules leave loopholes open, and the practice has to speak for itself" (Wittgenstein 1979: 21 (§ 139)). This argument will appear in various contexts in the course of this book, most prominently in my attempt to allot analogic an important and ineliminible place in the world of reasoning.

The third Wittgensteinian idea is that of *family concepts*. Wittgenstein noted out that there is a host of concepts we use with somnambulistic certainty without being able to define them. His solution to the problem was that our finding of necessary and sufficient conditions for defining concepts is not always the precondition for using them correctly. Take the concept of game, which we have no problem using but which we find hard to define. Not all games are made for entertainment, though many are; not all games have winning as a goal, though many do; not all games involve more than one participant, though most do (e.g., patience only involves one participant). To make a long story short, we do not find any qualities that all games must share in order to count as games. We only find a host of similarities in the same way as members of a family might have. John has brown eyes like his sister Judy; Judy has red hair like her sister Joan; Joan in her turn has a big nose like John. Judy has a small nose like her brother Jim; Jim has blue eyes like Joan, and so on. Here we see, in Wittgenstein's own words:

> ...a complicated network of similarities overlapping and criss-crossing: sometimes overall similarities, sometimes similarities of detail.

> §67. I can think of no better expression to characterise these similarities than "family resemblances"...(Wittgenstein 1958: 32 (§66-67).

Games are thus connected with each other through strands of similarities. We can find a somewhat similar idea in the works of Eleanor Rosch. Her empirical investigations led her to believe that our understanding and use of most of our concepts are drawn from our knowing *prototypical* examples of the phenomena, which are subsumed under the concept. An apple, for example, is a prototypical fruit but a tomato is not, and a comprehension of what apples are is the key to understand the concept of fruit (Rosch 1973: 111-144).

There is no lack of criticism directed towards the notions of family resemblance and prototypicality.[3] Yet, whatever the merits these lines of criticism may have, it does not exclude the possibility that some of our most important concepts are somehow fuzzy or open with blurred edges and elusive to definition. We may note that Wittgenstein and Rosch tried to explain the purported fact that there are concepts of this kind. It may well be that their explanations were wrong, but that does not mean that there is a set of necessary and sufficient conditions for the application of every single concept. Indeed, I am convinced that there are concepts that cannot be defined essentially, or at least have unclear boundaries. Concepts that cannot be defined in essentialist manner can be called 'family concepts', 'prototypical concepts', 'fuzzy concepts', 'open concepts' or whatever you want. I refer to them as *amoebaean* concepts because they are elastic and can easily divide themselves into further concepts, in a manner similar to these creatures. My guess is that the concepts of metaphors, narratives and emotions are of this kind or even belong to the class of what Friedrich Waisman has called '*open-textured* concepts'. Their definitions are always corrigible or amendable (Waisman 1951: 119-124). It seems to me that their definability distinguishes them from family concepts in a decisive way. Even though an open-textured concept has blurred edges, it has a common denominator of sorts that stands in contrast to family concepts.

The open-textured concepts are in-between amoebaean concepts and essential concepts. We may perhaps find an essential definition of the meaning of open-textured concepts, but not their reference, even though Waisman never discussed this possibility. As with family concepts, there is no rule for how to employ the rule for using open-textured concepts due to their unclear boundaries. The concept of biological motherhood is a case in point. Before the advent of test-

---

[3] For criticism of the idea of family concepts, see for instance Mandelbaum 1965: 219-228.
I shall later briefly discuss Kristján Kristjánsson´s criticism of the idea of prototypicality as applied to the concept of emotion.

tube fertilisation, this concept was a precise one. But nowadays, 'mother' is ambiguous between 'she who was the source of genes' and 'she who gave birth'. The concept did not, of course, become open-textured with the invention of test-tube fertilisation; rather, it always was so, which became only apparent through these new, unforeseeable conditions.[4] Perhaps, something similar holds for my threesome. If there is any way of finding anything resembling common denominator for each of my three concepts, my educated guess is that such a definition would be open-textured. As Noël Carroll points out, we cannot know *a priori* whether a given concept cannot be defined in an essentialist manner (Carroll 1999: 10). He seems to think that we can learn much from mistaken attempts to find essential definitions, and I agree.[5] I am also open to a pragmatist way of looking at concepts whereby we might treat a given concept as essentialist in one context, open-textured in another context, and amoebaean in the third context. The purposes of our activities determine which approach is the most fruitful (for such an approach, see Shusterman 2002: 175-190).

The fourth argument concerns saying and showing. A true proposition shares logical form with the facts that it is true about, but it cannot express the relationship between itself and the facts. Any attempt to express this relationship in propositions leads to an infinite regress. The relationship between the proposition in question and the facts can only be shown, not said, i.e., expressed in a proposition (Wittgenstein 1922: 79 (§4.12-4.1212). Consider a curve showing the development of fever in a given patient. This curve and the fever share logical form. But we can neither incorporate the form itself into the curve nor express it in the curve; it can only be shown.[6] This argument is vital for my analysis of the disclosive role of poetic metaphors that show rather than say.

The fifth argument is the famed private-language argument. Wittgenstein maintained that there is no way we can identify thoughts or

---

[4] I borrowed this example from the definition of 'open texture' from *The Oxford Companion to Philosophy* (Honderich 1995: 635).

[5] Carroll is actually one of the many non-Wittgensteinian analytical philosophers who have influenced this project. Arthur Danto is another one, Nelson Goodman a third one and Kristján Kristjánsson a fourth.

[6] For a systematic introduction to Wittgenstein's seeing/showing argument, see Harward 1976)

feelings just by looking into our own minds. He asks us to consider the following: what would happen if I tried to invent a language for my own sensations? This language of mine is supposed to be completely private, not intelligible to anybody but myself. Accordingly, I have to invent some symbols for my sensations with the help of ostensive definitions. I now write the symbol **S** whenever I have a certain sensation. I cannot, then, give an intersubjectively understandable definition of **S** since it denotes my private sensations. Have I succeeded in inventing a totally private language for my sensations? No, Wittgenstein replies, I cannot even know what my own symbol **S** means. The reason is that if I ask myself whether it is right or wrong to write **S** down in a given situation, I have no possibility of checking whether it is appropriate to write it down or not. The trouble is that I use **S** every time I feel a certain sensation, and I have no other definition of that sensation than that is the sensation which occurs whenever I use **S** correctly. So I am actually moving in logical circles when I try to invent a totally private language for sensations. We need an outside perspective in order to be able to judge whether **S** is being correctly used or not. To make matters worse, memory is of no help when it comes to ascertaining whether or not I use the symbol to denote the same phenomena at different times. Maybe the private phenomena keep changing constantly, while my memory systematically misleads me.[7]

Wittgenstein thought that the use of language is a rule-following activity. Rules are, so to speak, woven into our linguistic practices. We cannot follow rules that are essentially private; others must be able to test our attempts to follow them. The reason for this is that believing that one is following a rule is not the same as actually following it (Wittgenstein 1958: 81 (§ 202)). If we pretend to follow a rule nobody else can follow, then we cannot discriminate between believing that we are following the rule and that we are actually doing so. We cannot be said to follow a rule if others cannot control whether our behaviour can be subsumed under that rule or not; hence our difficulties in establishing a rule for the use of **S**.

---

[7] Wittgenstein introduces this theme in the § 258 in Wittgenstein 1958: 92. See further, Wittgenstein 1958: 93-94 (§ 265) and Wittgenstein 1958: 207.

Even more problematic for the inventor of the private language is the fact that we can ask what reasons we have to call the symbol **S** a sign of a sensation. "For 'sensation' is a word in our common language, not of one intelligible to me alone. So the use of this word stands in need of a justification, which everybody understands" (Wittgenstein 1958: 93 (§ 261)). We cannot, therefore, identify sensations solely by looking into our minds. The same holds for thoughts; Wittgenstein went so far as to say that only other people could know our thoughts, but not we ourselves (Wittgenstein 1958: 222). His point seems to be that we can only be said to know the truth of a given proposition P if there are ways to doubt the truth of P, which means that he was a fallibilist of sorts. There is no way, however, that we can doubt the existence of whatever thoughts we are thinking at the very moment we are thinking them. It makes no sense, therefore, to say that we can know our own thoughts. The same holds for such raw feels as pains. If I were to say in earnest, "I am in pain", I am actually making an avowal and not stating anything about my inner state. I could as well have cried "Ow!", and that exclamation (or indeed any exclamation) is neither true nor false. Utterances such as "I am in pain" really only replace exclamations of the aforementioned kind. These exclamations are part of pain-behaviour such that pain is not only an inner state but also a part of public behaviour. Avowals of pain can be judged as being either sincere or insincere, but neither true nor false. Only one's subsequent behaviour can show whether one was being sincere or not. The only way to find out whether a person is sincere in giving a promise is to find out whether he kept the promise, given the opportunity (Wittgenstein 1958: 89 (§ 244) and elsewhere).

Thus, Wittgenstein abandoned pure *mental philosophy*,[8] that is, the idea that the solitary consciousness is the corner-stone of our knowledge and being. We know our inner experiences (thoughts, sensations) with absolute certainty and any knowledge of what is outside our mind is inferential. According to mental philosophers, consciousness is the centre of the world, and questions of its nature and its relation to the rest of the world are the most important of all philosophical questions. Thus, they are subjectivists. But owing to the private-language argument, Wittgenstein belongs to the group of

---

[8] This is an English translation of the untranslatable German expression *Bewußtseinsphilosophie*.

theorists whom I call *intersubjectivists.* They focus on such intersubjectively existing phenomena as language and society, believing that analysing them is more worthwhile than studying the solitary subject, usually thinking that the subject is constituted by intersubjectivity and that inner experiences are functions of something intersubjective, for instance language. But even if Wittgenstein was an intersubjectivist and did not seem to regard subjectivity as being paramount, he certainly was neither an eliminativist nor a reductionist when it comes to subjectivity. Actually, many analytical philosophers suffer from a kind of horror of the subjective; they perform an exorcism of sorts, trying to exorcise the ghost of subjectivity out of the machine. Wittgenstein perhaps did not feel horrified by the subjective but he tended to ignore it.

Wittgenstein's private-language argument is of major importance for my project. It figures perhaps most prominently in my discussion of the concept of emotion. I think that the argument is basically sound and that is one of the main reasons why I call myself an intersubjectivist, albeit of a moderate sort. Nevertheless, I have qualms about some aspects of it, and these qualms temper my intersubjectivism, making me allot a somewhat bigger place for subjectivity than Wittgenstein seems to do. One of these aspects I have qualms about is the strange contention that others can know our thoughts but not we. As I see it, knowing our thoughts means that they must be able to think about our thoughts. But according to the argument, they cannot know their own thoughts, and so they cannot know their thoughts about our thoughts! Therefore they cannot know whether they know our thoughts. Someone else must be able to know their thoughts but in order for that to be possible, still others must be able to know their thoughts. It is easy to see how we land in an infinite regress.

Secondly, there are some noteworthy arguments against the idea of the indubitability of inner states. Gareth Evans has, for instance, pointed out that a person could see ten points of light arranged in a circle but would report (and would firmly believe) that there are eleven points because he made a mistake in counting. This mistake can occur again when the person re-uses the procedure in order to gain knowledge of his inner state. He reports falsely, "I seem to see eleven points of light", and obviously he is mistaken about his inner state. He erroneously thinks that it looks to him as though there were eleven points of light. It could be added that even if he just imagined ten points of light, he could make exactly the same mistake, wrongly believing that he imagined eleven points (Evans 1982: 228-229). I should not, however, be the judge of whether the British philosopher was right. Thirdly, most of us have the intuition that indubitability is the hallmark of at least some kinds of knowledge. Why should this intuition be ignored? Wittgenstein wanted to defend common sense and ordinary ways of using language, but in ordinary language we refer to indubitability as one of characteristics of true knowledge. Fourthly, could not there be several types of knowledge, some fallible, and others not? Such recognition would be more in harmony with the Wittgensteinian pluralism concerning language games, each with its own logic[9] as part and parcel of the practices of the language-game. At the same, the logic of each language-game is related to the logics of other language-games in various ways. Perhaps there are particular 'private' language-games that we play in our head, which we call 'thinking', 'imagining', and not least 'feeling'.[10] These games are made possible by our taking part in various practices and by their having their own logics, closely related to the logics of some intersubjective language-games. That could mean that as a part of the logic of the 'private' games, which are played in our heads, it might be misleading to say that we know our thoughts. Regardless, it would be correct to say that there was a cognitive content involved and that its function is directed by the particular logic of the private language-game. As I shall try to show later, there is such a private cognitive content involved in a typical language-game of emotions and this cognitive content is subjective by nature.

Be that as it may, if there is a paradigm of cognitive content, such content cannot be private but must instead be a function of actual or potential intersubjectivity. In most, even all cases, the content must be

---

[9] 'Logic' should not be understood here as meaning 'formal logic', but rather 'constitutive rules and the way they ought to be applied, given the context'.

[10] Richard Eldridge pointed out to me that Wittgenstein allows for some kinds of private experiences, just not of the Cartesian kind, as can be seen in Wittgenstein 1958: 190 and elsewhere (email from Eldridge, 27th of May, 2008).

woven into our public practices.[11] What we can learn from Wittgenstein's private-language argument, then, is that inner experiences of indubitability can neither be a paradigmatic kind of knowledge nor be the foundation for knowledge in general. We should do well to consider whether the Austrian philosopher might have thrown the baby out with the bathwater.

He was not engaged in any such dubious activities when he introduced his idea of the plurality of language-games.[12] Language games are woven into practices and forms of life, the rules embedded in the language games being only applicable in the context of practices. This makes meaning and cognitive content something contextual. The threesome, i.e. language games, practices and forms of life, create (or are) this context at the same time as cognitive content and meaning are parts of the threesome.[13] As we have seen, he did not think that we could define the concept of language in an essentialist manner. No particular form of the use of language is primordial. Therefore, the activity of asserting has no privileged place in the employment of language, in contrast to what the pundits seem to think. Other linguistic activities, such as the use of declarative sentences, expressing emotions with the aid of words, etc., constitute language-games of their own with their particular standards for right and wrong, just like the language-games that involve assertions. At the same time, there are complexes of criss-crossing family resemblances between the different language-games (Wittgenstein 1958: 11-12 (§23) and elsewhere).

---

[11] On the communal interpretation of the private-language argument, it must be woven into actual public practices. For an exposition of this argument, see for instance McDowell 1989: 285-303.

[12] He introduces the notion of language-game in §7 of the Investigations (Wittgenstein (1958): 5).

[13] Experts in Wittgenstein's later philosophy might not be impressed by this rough sketch. It could added that Wittgenstein sometimes writes like the concept of a form of life is of a greater importance than the other two, even primordial, for instance when he says that what is to be accepted as the given is form of life (Wittgenstein (1958): 226 (II, xi). This also points in the direction of the communal interpretation of the private language argument being the correct one. Forms of life are communal, intersubjectively shared and structured; if they are the given, then it does not make any sense to believe that there could be a solitary subject with its own language, which is potentially shared by others but not necessarily actually so.

I am not going to judge the quality of this analysis, only inform that it has been a great source of inspiration for my brand of cognitive pluralism and my moderate contextual approach. When I talk about 'ana-logic', 'narra-logic' and 'emo-logic', I am talking about the logics of various fields of human existence or language games that only make sense contextually. Needless to say, emo-logic is woven into emotional practices or language games, narra-logic into narrative games.

But why do I call my contextual approach 'moderate'? The reason is the fact that I think that there are cases were contextual analysis is not of any greater importance, hence the emphasis on being moderate. One might say that I have a somewhat more 'logocentric' approach than Wittgenstein, stressing the subjective dimension and the concept of interpretation a tiny bit more than he, context and practices somewhat less.

4 Alethetic Values

My cognitive pluralism is central for my arguments in this book because I hold that metaphors, narratives, and emotions have their own yardsticks for rightness that are not necessarily reducible to the truth-conditions of propositions. But in order to understand my theorising, the reader must get familiar with a couple of my neo-logisms; the first one is *symbolic structures*, i.e., 'meaningful entities'. I use 'meaningful' here in a broad sense, and the same holds for 'symbolic'. 'Symbolic structure' ranges over sentences, discourses, texts, symbols, depictions, metaphors, narratives, and so on. Symbolic structures do not have to be of a linguistic nature; a meaningful picture or a gesture can also be symbolic structures. Need I say that such structures can only be applied and can only make sense contextually?

The second one is *alethetic values*, the word 'alethetic' being a derivation from the ancient Greek word for truth, *aletheia*. But alethetic value covers more than just truth-values. As I see it, each different symbolic system has its own set of alethetic values, besides being an integral part of practices (compare the Wittgensteinian idea of the plurality of language games). As Nelson Goodman correctly points out, there is a host of relations of rightness, and truth does not monopolise such relations. Maps and pictures have their own relations of rightness to reality but they cannot be called 'true' or 'false' (Goodman 1978: 19).

Inspired by Goodman (as well as Joseph Margolis, Paul Ricœur, and, of course, Wittgenstein), I use my concept of alethetic values as ranging over both truth/falsity and truth-like values[14], such as 'the correctness/incorrectness of a map', 'the degree of a picture's resemblance/lack of resemblance to certain objects', 'the appropriateness of an interpretation', 'the validity of a sketch (a sort of paraphrase) of a metaphor', 'the correctness of metaphors' and so on. Alethetic values have, in other words, to do with the way symbolic structures referentially relate to reality. Among such structures are pictures, models, maps, theories, propositions, sentences, and, last but not least, metaphors. The values in question are the yardsticks for our cognitive efforts. These efforts in their turn are parts of practices and those practices are the lifeblood of the alethetic values. The echoes from Wittgenstein's idea of practices and language games are easy to hear. However, I will not focus much on these echoes now but instead take a closer at the various types of meaningful entities (**M.E.**s) and their corresponding alethetic values. It is obvious that those **M.E.**s that have a predicative structure normally have truth-values.[15] They are typically expressed in words or mathematical formulas, or both. Let us call these **M.E.**s 'predicative symbolic structures' (**P.S.S.**). The class of **P.S.S.** includes propositions, sentences, theories, etc. There is another important sub-class of **M.E.**, the class that I call 'visual symbolic structures' (**V.S.S.**). As the expression 'symbolic' indicates, the structures in question symbolise or represent objects. This means that the class of purely decorative ornament, like those to be found in mosques, cannot be a sub-class of the class of **V.S.S.** This class ranges over diagrams, maps, caricatures, pictures, etc. They do not have truth-values, at least on the face of it. A map is either correct or incorrect, but neither true nor false. A map showing a volcano in southern Sweden is incorrect but it is not false.

But matters are not quite that simple. It would be tempting to say that the reason we can understand these **V.S.S.** is that they can be

---

[14] I think it was Joseph Margolis who invented the expression 'truth-like values' (Margolis 1991).

[15] To be sure, there is no lack of predicative sentences without truth-values. But surely the institution of predication was created in order to discover truths.

translated into sentences, which possess truth-values. If this were the case, then knowing the truth-conditions of these sentences would be sufficient for us to understand the **V.S.S.** There are indeed certain simple **V.S.S.**s that can easily be translated into words. We can choose between using the red light as symbolising 'don't walk' and simply use the words. But I am not even sure whether or not maps can be converted into **P.S.S.**s. It would, of course, be a most cumbersome translation; one would probably need several volumes of books for a translation of a map of any big city. Maybe there could be a superbeing that could handle such translations easily. But would we ordinary mortals be able to decide whether the translation is really successful? What kind of criteria would there be for the success of this translation? That the superbeing says so? But maybe this superbeing is a superliar. Then again, it could be superhonest. How are we to know?

Most importantly, there is no doubt that we can ascertain the alethetic values (the correctness) of the map without such a (super)translation. As we have seen, it is not probable that we can translate maps into sentences with truth-values. There is no doubt that complex **V.S.S.**s resist any conversion into **P.S.S.**s. We can also be pretty sure that such **V.S.S.** as caricatures cannot be thus converted. How one can translate a caricature by David Levine into a finite number of propositions? Asking the superbeing to help us will not do. Let us compare this to the case of the maps. Perhaps I could describe the caricature to an ordinary person who has never seen it in such a way that the person could draw the same caricature on basis of my description. That seems extremely unlikely, but possibly our superbeing would be able to do that. Still, this does not solve the problem. For what do I know when I know that **D** is an accurate description of the caricature **Ca**? Is the criterion the ability of the superbeing to draw the caricature? Can the superbeing and we really discriminate between the causal effect of the description and some other cause? Could that other cause be our superbeing's ability to read minds (in this case mine), an ability of which the superbeing has hitherto been unaware? Being a superbeing does not necessarily mean that you know everything about your own superpowers. Further, just postulating that a superbeing must know everything about its powers is not going to help us much either. Maybe my description was not good enough; the hidden superpowers actually did the job, but the being did not tell us. We certainly are in no position to know whether hidden powers were at work. The superbeing could have used his superpower to delude us. Superpowers or not, I cannot see how one can reduce caricatures and stylised (non-realistic) pictures to a finite number of propositions. At the same time, caricatures and stylised pictures are meaningful entities. It seems tempting to think that in order to understand a given caricature or stylised picture, we should have to know how much it possesses of its own particular brand of alethic value. We might also have to know the truth-values of some sentences that describe or explain, or both, the caricature, but our knowing them alone will not do the trick. Analogously, in order to understand a given map **M**, we must know under what circumstances **M** maps an object correctly. (As in the case of the caricatures, we might also have to know the truth-values of certain sentences.) A good map has the alethic value of mapping something correctly, and so caricatures and stylised pictures might have their own conditions of correctness or aptitude. We shall discover that their conditions of correctness are closely related to the ones of metaphors. As for narratives and emotions, there is a host of particular alethic values involved in our dealings with them. We shall discover their nature later in this book.

5 Being Rather Post-Continental and Ana-logical

The Continental streak in whatever passes for my thinking shows itself in the way by such Continental thinkers as Paul Ricœur, Martin Heidegger, Friedrich Nietzsche, Wilhelm Schapp, and David Carr have influenced my project. Ricœur plays by far the biggest role in this book, primarily because of his attempts to show the interconnections between metaphors and narratives and to analyse analogical thinking. These attempts have been a tremendous source of inspiration for me, and so I have devoted two and a half chapters to his thought.

The inspiration from thinkers like Ricœur is not the only Continental element of my project. Another is my Continental inclination for synthesising. This synthesising can show how that certain views that seem either to contradict each other or to lack anything in common can be fused together in a powerful synthesis. This is a tradition of Hegelian provenance; I often call Continental philosophy of this kind '*synthesising* philosophy', in contrast to the notion of analytical philosophy. Indeed, I think that there is a synthesising moment in at least the key texts of Continental derivation; these texts must be understood as totalities, something more than merely sums of arguments.

Owing to my synthesising tendency, I do not just reconstruct different actual or potential views but also discuss actual thinkers, often using some space to present their theories. I offer these descriptive passages partly as a matter of practicality; this book is a multi-disciplinary endeavour, and few of my readers will know the best-known theories in the three main disciplines I discuss, the studies of metaphors, narratives and emotions. These descriptions (sometimes sort of reconstructions) also have their basis in certain theoretical justifications. The first one is my aforementioned Hegelian-dialectical tendency. The second one is that philosophical texts often have a life of their own just like works of imaginary literature; they cannot always be regarded as just another way of solving some given philosophical problem.[16] This holds clearly for the two philosophers who have inspired my project the most, Wittgenstein and Ricœur.

The third reason is an analogical one; by comparing different views, I hope to set in motion a rewarding metaphoric process, just like the way we can compare different conceptual domains and create new cognitively productive metaphors thanks to these comparisons (for instance, THE MIND IS SOFTWARE). The fourth reason is a rule of thumb that I bombastically call *the principle of philosophical quasi-induction*: if more than one set of premises lead the same or similar conclusion, and if the premises seem reasonably plausible, and if the deduction from them appear to be in order, then one should regard this, *ceteris paribus*, as an argument in favour of the conclusion and the premises. The more different sets of premises we can find, the more prepared we ought to be to accept the theory. The ceteris paribus clause is of importance; if there are strong arguments against that which is stated in the conclusion or it is blatantly wrong, then no quasi-induction can save it.

---

[16] I confess being inspired by Stanley Cavell, who does not regard philosophy as a set of problem, but as a set of texts (Cavell 1979: 5). My Solomonic judgement is that it comprises sets of both.

This approach is reminiscent of the situation in natural sciences. If two natural scientists use different kinds of technologies in testing a certain theory and the results of both tests confirm the theory, while no tests speak against it, then that is a sign that there might be a grain of truth in the theory. As I hinted at, I think that philosophical quasi-induction is roughly similar to this way of thinking inductively in natural science. The success of this kind of science ought to add some support to my rule (despite my epistemological pluralism, the fields of knowledge are not isolated from each other so cognitive success in science can spell success in philosophy). Now, consider the case of there being a possibility of arriving at conclusion C with the aid of premises p1, p2 and also by route of non-p1 and p3, while all the premises seem plausible and the conclusion too. Employing our rule, we regard C and *some* of the premises as having an increased plausibility. Obviously, given the law of contradiction, we cannot think that both p2 and non-p2 become more plausible in this case, and, therefore, only some of the premises acquire increased plausibility. So we need to try to find some arguments that help us decide between them. But whatever we do, we must not forget that theories cannot be proven with the aid of induction; it is debatable whether or not their plausibility can be increased that way. There have been many excellent attempts to prove the existence of God, but chances are that he or she does not exist or that it is not given unto us human to prove his or her existence.

The reader can also see my dialectical, synthesising approach in my attempt to synthesise metaphors, narratives, and emotions, to show the hidden connections between them. To this it might be added that bridging the gap between the Continental and the analytical as I do is yet another example of my synthesising activity.

Yet another Continental trait is my tendency to paint with a broad brush like Continental thinkers tend to do. The very undertaking of trying to find important interconnections between narratives, metaphors, and emotions is in itself painting with such a brush!

Further, I sometimes write in a somewhat literary way as certain Continental philosophers do. Writing in a literary fashion is not only for the sake of ornament or fun and games. I firmly believe in the redeeming power of *les bon mots*, the well-turned phrase, the well-told tale, the striking poetic image, and the original metaphor. Their power increases vastly if authentic emotions are expressed with their aid, these emotions having redeeming power in their own right.

Continentally inspired or not, I like to view this book as a choir of different voices – and hopefully not a cacophony of voices. Some of them belong to me, others are the voices of various thinkers, and most of them sing much better than I. But I certainly try to silence some of these voices, or to put it more prosaically, "I try to show they are wrong". All the same, I entreat the reader to try to hear these voices as singing in harmony, to understand this book as a totality, and not only as a series of disparate arguments that do not really form a whole.

I believe that asking new questions without necessarily finding any answers is often more stimulating than answering old questions. The Leibnizian question "why is there is something rather than nothing?" can hardly ever be answered. But it opens up a new horizon of possibilities, the possibility that 'somethingness' is radically contingent; the question discloses the world anew.

I have accordingly put forth several questions in this book without necessarily answering them conclusively. My preferred manner of thinking and writing is hypothetical; "what if...?" is my favourite expression. I want to increase the number of possible ways of thinking, of possible solutions to problems, possibly contributing to a non-existing *possibilology*!

However hypothetical my leanings are, I am too much of an analytical philosopher to accept that philosophy is only the proliferation of possibilities and a brand of imaginative literature, or both. Lenin is supposed to have said that Machiavelli was an antidote against stupidity, and, *mutatis mutandis*, analytical philosophy is an antidote against sloppy thinking. Philosophy must *also* be analysis.[17] But the particular type of analyses that I perform is often more in keeping with the canons of ana-logic rather than formal logical analysis. It is already likely that the reader is eager to know what I

---

[17] I do not exclude the possibility that the object of investigation can determine the method. Perhaps a phenomenological approach is necessary when one is scrutinising consciousness, a formal logical approach when one is dealing with the philosophy of mathematics, a pragmatist approach with epistemology, and a Wittgensteinian approach when one is philosophising about art.

mean by 'ana-logic'.[18] For now, let it suffice that I take this term to mean a sort of analogical or metaphoric kind of reasoning (compare what I said earlier about comparing different philosophical views). Metaphors and narratives are among the most important tools for this analysis (which is where the literary and the analytical side of my undertaking meet). The fruitfulness of making thought-experiments with the aid of fictional stories ought to be well known among analytical philosophers. I employ this method a couple of times in this book. More important is my attempt to understand the nature of a given concept with the aid of metaphors and analogies, which help me to compare different concepts. This comparison is a way of finding out which important aspects of the concepts are significantly similar or dissimilar to certain other concepts. In a manner of speaking, I situate the concept in a network of similar and dissimilar concepts. Thus, I have found out that in order to understand the concept of emotion, it is important to situate it in relationship to the concepts of narrations and metaphors, to show the non-trivial similarities and dissimilarities between emotions, on the one hand, and narrations and metaphors, on the other. Of course, I bear in mind the fact that everything is similar or dissimilar to everything else in the universe. After all, the biggest dinosaurs ever and the biggest painting of all times have in common the fact that they were the biggest objects of their kind! I stress, therefore, that the attempt at finding non-trivial (dis)similarities to be a Herculean task indeed, one that demands a cautious approach of the analytical kind. But basically, it demands an informed judgement, for there is no formula for assessing the triviality and the non-triviality of (dis)similarities. The degree of triviality in similarities and dissimilarities is partly a function of our interests and the goals of our inquiries.

This method arguably reveals its greatest worth when we discuss amoebaean concepts, and as I said earlier, it could very well be the case that the concepts of metaphor, narrative, and emotion are of the amoebaean kind. If that is the case, then narratives of different kinds are required. We have to relate stories about the typical ways people tell stories, have emotions or use metaphors. Thus, in order to

---

[18] I fully acknowledge the fact that the idea of ana-logic owes much to both Ricœur and Wittgenstein, and even Hans Vaihinger, a theorist whom I shall introduce shortly in the first section.

understand metaphors and narratives, I have to use metaphors and narratives! Emotions play also a role in my approach (the reader should bear in mind that I defend a cognitivist view of emotions). One of them is a strong feeling or intuition involved in my theorising that we humans are co-authors of reality or at least some segments of it. We write the real with the aid of narratives, metaphors, and emotions; they play a part in constituting our reality.

Wittgenstein, the family-concept man, emphasised the use of metaphors, analogies, thought-experiments and concrete examples in analysis. That man was a true master of ana-logic, and so was Paul Ricœur who saw the world in an ana-logical fashion.

Whether or not I myself am a master of this kind of logic is not for me to decide but for the readers of this book.

I. METAPHORS AND MASKS

I.1. Introducing metaphors (and masks)

Are metaphors anything but masks we put on sentences at the masquerade of language? What do we see when the masks fall off at midnight? The ugly reality of literal meaning? We shall see in this section that the theory of metaphors as masks is not very convincing; metaphors are much more than ornamental; they also have cognitive functions.

When we talk about metaphors, we usually think of them as tropes, just like metonyms, synecdoches or irony. In tropes the meaning of words is turned or even twisted, they are not used in their literal fashion. When we say metaphorically that Man is a wolf, we are 'twisting' the meaning of the word 'wolf', not using it in a literal way. We so to speak transfer the meaning of 'wolf' from its ordinary use to unusual, even bizarre, kind of use. It is often that metaphors involve comparison or analogies, that they even are shorthand for comparison. That view goes back to Aristotle (Aristotle 1965: 61 (Chapter 21)). Another old, perhaps venerable, idea is the one of metaphors involving mental images, that using and understanding a metaphor meant having a mental image of, say, Man as a wolf. Yet another idea is the one of metaphors enabling us to understand one thing in terms of another. Janet Martin Soskice defines metaphors in the following fashion "...*metaphor is that figure of speech whereby we speak about one thing in terms which are seen to be suggestive of another*" (Soskice 1985: 15).

In contrast to her I am not going to put forth any clear-cut definition of 'metaphor'. Instead I shall try to find some background conditions and some necessary conditions for the employment of the concept. The reason for this approach is that I am not sure whether it can be defined in any worthwhile manner. In fact, Soskice has noted that there are 125 different definitions of metaphors, some of which contradict each other (Soskice 1985: 15). As hinted at, my intuition is that it is an amoebaean concept, even though I do not exclude the possibility of it being an open-textured one. One of the reasons for my thinking it is amoebaean is that its boundaries seem blurred. It is not clear whether or not similes and metaphors belong to the same class of objects.[1] It is also unclear whether or not metonyms and metaphors are one of a kind[2] or whether metaphors are only linguistic. I shall discuss the possibility of visual and behavioural metaphors later in this section.

I think we can discriminate between the following modern schools of theories about metaphors. a) There are the *iconoclasts* who deny that there is such a thing as a particular figurative meaning or even doubt that metaphors exist. Metaphors are nothing but masks (Davidson, Searle). Now, my use of the expression 'iconoclast' in this context needs clarification. It is a Byzantine Greek expression, meaning 'image-breaker'. I am alluding to the fact that we tend to regard the use of linguistic metaphors as ways of conveying images through language. Those who are iconoclasts of metaphors do not regard these images as having any greater cognitive worth, and so we might as well destroy them.

b) Another group is the *interactionists* who think that metaphoric meaning arises out of interaction between the topic and the vehicle of the metaphor (Richards, Black, Glucksberg, Sovran, Way, Ricœur).

c) There are also the *iconodulists* who think that metaphoric meaning is the primordial form of meaning, so that literal meaning either is an illusion or is a function of the metaphoric one. They also tend to be *metaphorists*, believing that our lives, thought, and cognition are soaked with metaphors (Nietzsche, Hesse, Lakoff). 'Iconodulist' is, not surprisingly, another Byzantine Greek word to designate the 'worshipper or server of images' who opposed the iconoclasts. Theorists who are iconodulists of metaphors regard the images, presumably conveyed by metaphors, as being of great cognitive and even existential worth.

Most of the theorists in categories b) and c) believe in the cognitive theory of metaphor, i.e., that metaphors have cognitive import. It must be emphasised that, technically speaking, one can be both an interactionist and an iconodulist, even though most interactionists try to steer a middle course between a) and c). Ricœur, for one, comes

---

[1] For a short discussion, see Cooper 1986: 8-9.
[2] For a discussion of these problems, see Fishelov 1993: 14.

close to being both an interactionist and an iconodulist, besides being
a sort of a metaphorist. He, like most of the theorists in categories b)
and c), also believes in the cognitive theory of metaphor, i.e., the
theory that metaphors have cognitive import. I shall introduce my own
brand of this theory at the same as I criticise the iconoclasts quite
harshly while being sceptical to radical iconodulism. I shall try to
show that there is a grain of truth in interactionism. I also support the
view that metaphors (at least prototypical ones) cannot be paraphrased, even though there can be that which I call a *quasi-
paraphrase* (a rough, sketchy paraphrase) of metaphors.

1.1 The Iconoclasts

a) Donald Davidson, a prime iconoclast, thought that metaphors
express neither ideas nor thoughts. Metaphors, he said, belong fairly
and squarely to the pragmatics of language. He famously defended a
truth-conditional semantics; we know the meaning of a sentence if and
only if we know under which conditions it would be true. Metaphors
are more than often untrue, and, if they are elliptic similes, then their
meaning is simply literal and their truth trivial. The reason for their
truth being trivial is that everything can be said to be like something
else in some respect. The words in a metaphoric utterance like "Man
is a wolf" mean exactly the same as they mean in literal contexts but
they are used in a peculiar fashion. No one would say that we use
words in a different sense when we lie, speak ironically or tell jokes,
so why on earth should the use of words in metaphoric utterances give
them a special sense? The fact that an utterance like the one about
humans and wolves can cause associations and reflections is a
psychological, contingent fact and therefore without interest for the
theory of meaning. The 'systems of association' of words like 'wolf'
is contingent and thus have no implication for the meaning of
sentences. To be sure, a metaphor cannot be paraphrased, but the
reason is that there is nothing to paraphrase. An attempted
'paraphrase' is just an attempt to make a list of the thoughts and
associations a metaphor can cause, and their number is, in principle,
infinite. Davidson even goes so far as to say that it is a
misunderstanding to believe that the basic role of metaphors is to
convey ideas. A metaphor can certainly make us discover facts, but
not because it symbolises (represents) facts; in the same manner,

jokes, lies or a good cup of coffee can inspire us to discover facts (Davidson 1984: 245-264).

The crux of Davidson's arguments is that meaning is literal, non-contextual, and not determined by interpretation; metaphors can only be understood contextually through interpretative efforts. Therefore, they cannot have any special meaning. But Eva Feder Kittay has put forth some notable arguments against this view. She says that Davidson does not realise that context also plays a role when we understand a sentence in a literal fashion. If Davidson is right about context being a determining factor when we interpret a sentence as conveying a metaphor, then it follows that the understanding of a sentence as being literal must also be partly determined by context. Context helps us to determine it as being not non-literal, and without such a determination we cannot understand the sentence literally. Besides, Davidson does not see how ambiguous a large part of the sentences of language is. Think about "the men are pigs". Usually, such a sentence is used metaphorically, but we can think of cases where it is literally true. For Ulysses this sentence was true when Circe had changed his men into pigs. At the same time, he could have understood it metaphorically as well if he also thought that his men were metaphorically pigs. Not only are sentences often ambiguous, Kittay notes, every sentence can actually be interpreted metaphorically. We may even take her own writing on metaphors metaphorically. Suppose we lived in a very oppressive society; we could then conceivably understand her essay in its entirety to be a metaphoric criticism of the political system. We could also interpret her arguments for the context-dependency of literal language as a call for our mutual interdependency in our struggle for freedom. This means that context and interpretation always play a role in determining whether a given sentence ought to be understood literally or metaphorically (Kittay 1995: 81-82).

I find Kittay's criticism of Davidson pretty convincing but the question is whether she is not going too far in arguing as though every discourse can be intended or interpreted as being metaphoric. Is not her imagination really running wild in the example of her own writing? By the same token, we could interpret the telephone directory in its entirety as a metaphor for the mechanistic society of our times – and that is certainly going too far. Moreover, we cannot exclude the possibility of some kinds of sentences being quite resistant to metaphoric interpretation. Along this line of criticism, Max Black pointed out that there were sentences that we can hardly use metaphorically, for instance, "a chair is a syllogism" (Black 1993: 23). But this objection does not help us much either in trying to discover the limits of metaphoric interpretation. Black did not think about the possibility that it could be our lack of imagination that makes us blind to its potential metaphoric use. Perhaps we could think about the chair as having three parts, just like a syllogism. At the same time, the chair is something cold, prosaic, and given, in a similar fashion as a correct logical deduction. But maybe this is going too far, just as the example with the directory.

Jerrold Levinson is somewhat more cautious than Black and restricts himself to saying (as I do) that some sentences are almost metaphor-resistant. Levinson has in mind sentences in which things from the same category and at the same level of specificity are treated as equivalent. Consider sentences like "a fox is a wolf", "a man is a woman" or "gold is lead" (Levinson 2001: 21-22). I do question, however, whether these examples are good enough. It does not require a great deal of imagination to interpret or use the last sentence metaphorically if we understand gold, say, as something as lethal as bullets, and bullets are made of lead. We know that people kill each other over gold. We can understand the first sentence metaphorically if we think about a fox as metaphor for a sly person and a wolf for a cruel person. Then, "a fox is a wolf" means that the sly one is also cruel. As for the second, we could interpret it metaphorically as meaning that, despite the differences between the sexes, we share a common humanity or that men have a feminine side. Still, the problem might only be an unfortunate choice of examples on the part of Black and Levinson. Nevertheless, it is clear that some sentences are easier to interpret metaphorically than others; in all probability there are sentences that prototypically lend themselves to metaphoric use and the examples Black and Levinson give are not among them. I am indeed certain that the line between those sentences or discourses that can be interpreted or used metaphorically and those that cannot is not clear. This means that we require interpretation and knowledge about the context to find out whether a sentence lends itself to metaphoric use.

There might be, however, a simpler way of demonstrating Kittay's point that knowing the context and interpreting sentences are essential for knowing whether they have truth-conditions and what these conditions might be. Ironically, we can use some examples from that arch-iconoclast, John Searle.[3] He points out that the sentence "the cat is on the mat" is only meaningful in the light of a host of implicit assumptions. We must presuppose, for instance, that the cat is within a certain gravitational field, for outside of such a field words like 'on' or 'below' have no designation. Would it make sense to say that the cat is actually lying on the mat if we saw the cat and the mat outside a window of a spaceship in outer space? Even if we were to see the cat and the mat on solid ground, we would still have to presuppose that the cat is not somehow glued to the mat, that it is not hovering a few millimetres over the mat, and so on *usque ad nauseam.* The number of these implicit presuppositions is in principle infinite, and so we have no chance of explicating them all (Searle 1979: 85 and elsewhere).

Searle is actually not only an iconoclast; he is also in favour of a strict separation of pragmatics and semantics. Nevertheless, Kittay, and I for that matter, can profit from his analysis. It strengthens Kittay's contention that we cannot determine the truth-conditions of sentences without invoking context and interpretation (Kittay 1987: 104 and Kittay 1995: 83). I think that she is quite right about this: we cannot throw context and interpretation into some limbo, banishing them from the heaven of semantics. Determining a sentence as having a literal meaning also requires knowing the context.

Like Kittay, Samuel Guttenplan doubts the possibility of a neat separation between semantics and pragmatics. He quite correctly points out that discussion about a semantic account of metaphors as opposed to a pragmatic one is not very fruitful as long as semantics is not clearly circumscribed. We just do not know precisely what semantics and pragmatics are (Guttenplan 2005: 8). He also doubts that we can paraphrase metaphors; he even says that it is inappropriate to

---

[3] His iconoclastism is based on a differentiation between utterer's meaning and sentence meaning. When someone says, "Man is a wolf" and means it metaphorically, his (the utterer's) intended meaning is something like "Man is lonely and evil", while the sentence meaning is something very different. There is no place for any particular metaphoric meaning, not least because Searle denies that anything resembling interaction has to take place in a metaphor (Searle 1993: 83-111).

paraphrase metaphors. Theorists tend to confuse the paraphrasing of metaphors with the elucidating or explaining of them. But we must distinguish sharply the notion of paraphrasing an utterance from saying or telling what it means. Now, suppose that someone utters the sentence "the cat is on the mat" and that he is actually using a code: his fellow gangsters know that he means, "the money is in the bank". But this does not mean that they have paraphrased "the cat is on the mat" as "the money is in the bank". Paraphrase, at least in the strict sense, is a re-statement of the sense of a passage using other words, and the words "the money in the bank" cannot be used to re-state "the cat is on the mat" (Guttenplan 2005): 16-18).[4] Now, consider whether the following can be called a 'paraphrase' of the metaphor JULIET IS THE SUN: "Juliet is necessary to my (i.e., Romeo's) existence" and "Juliet is responsible for my (i.e., Romeo's) seeing the world right". Guttenplan's answer is "no": these may be explanations for Romeo's metaphoric assertion about Juliet, but they are not expressed in the assertion (Guttenplan 2005: 132-136). I find this criticism rather compelling, because there is no doubt that a re-statement is a paraphrase in the strict sense, which does not, of course, exclude the legitimacy of using 'paraphrase' in a somewhat wider sense, including the sense of quasi-paraphrase, to be discussed in a short while.

Let us look again at Davidson's contention that metaphors do not represent facts any more than jokes and lies do. I do not find his view convincing, not least because it does not quite square with my linguistic intuition. In ordinary parlance, we say "what is **M** a metaphor for?" not "what is **J** a joke for" or "what is **L** a lie for?" It is

---

[4] I am setting to the side his fascinating semantic *descent* theory of metaphor, the treatment of which would require another book. According to this theory, the meaning of metaphors is partly determined by non-linguistic objects ('object' is used in a wide sense, covering states of affairs, events, and words). These objects can play a sort of predicative role which Guttenplan calls 'qualification'. Every metaphor has a hybrid predicate partly consisting of words, partly of such objects. Thus, the object 'sun' qualifies 'Juliet' in JULIET IS THE SUN and conveys information about Juliet in similar way that a predicate would do. In order to understand the metaphor, we must 'descend' semantically from the words in the sentence, expressing the metaphor, to the object in question, i.e., the sun. Guttenplan points out that if metaphors have a non-linguistic component, then it makes no sense to say that they can be paraphrased in the strict sense (Guttenplan 2005: 129). But has he really succeeded in showing that objects can play this predicative role unless mediated or constituted by symbolic structures? I have my doubts but need another book to express them.

intuitively difficult to see how **M** can be a metaphor but for nothing in particular, which might be an indicator that metaphors somehow represent facts. Of course, our intuitions and habits of speech are not infallible; I certainly cannot refute Davidson's analysis just by evoking intuitions and habits. Nevertheless, they should not be ignored. It is fortunate, however, that there are some thinkers, including Frank B. Farrell and David Novitz, who have dealt severe blows to Davidson's arguments. Farrell is quite right when he points out that Davidson is inconsistent when, on the one hand, he says that sentences are the smallest meaningful entities of language, and yet, on the other hand, when discussing metaphors, he talks solely about the meaning of words used in metaphors (Farrell 1987: 625-642). Both Farrell and Novitz maintain that Davidson is on the wrong track when he says that metaphors only nudge us into noticing differences and similarities between phenomena. He does not understand that we can put forth statements with the aid of metaphors.[5] Farrell and Novitz say that metaphoric utterances can have truth-conditions. Novitz uses as an example an utterance by Anthony in Shakespeare's *Julius Cesar*, "authority melts from me". Given contextual evidence and a use of the principle of charity, we can construct the following **T**-sentence on the basis of Anthony's metaphor: "authority melts from me" is true when uttered by Anthony at time **t** if and only if Anthony was losing his power slowly but surely at or around time **t**". The fact that such a **T**-sentence hardly has the liveliness and impact of the original metaphor does not matter because Davidson regards impact as belonging to the pragmatics of language. Novitz concludes that if we know the truth-conditions in question, then we know the meaning of the metaphor (Novitz 1985: 101-114).

Given truth-conditional semantics, then, we can say that meta-phoric utterances can be meaningful in their own right. This analysis has its faults, however. I think that it really just shows that a quasi-paraphrase (a rough and tough, inexact paraphrase) of a metaphor can have truth-conditions. If the truth-conditions of such quasi-paraphrases were all that there is to metaphoric meaning, then the following would be true: "authority melts from me" means the same

---

[5] Notice that if we can put forth statements with the aid of metaphors, then we can also express beliefs with their aid.

as (the paraphrase) "I am slowly but surely losing power". This obviously makes no sense.

Now, we cannot paraphrase (at least prototypical) metaphors in any satisfactory manner, even though they can be given a quasi-paraphrase, or, in Kittay's terminology 'an *exposition*', i.e., a rough paraphrase (Kittay (1987): 37). Keeping to my terminology, a quasi-paraphrase is a *sketch* of a metaphor. *The* correct sketch does not exist even though some sketches are invalid. Sketching MAN IS A WOLF as "rabbits are nice" is invalid because it is hard to find any context in which the sketch is not absurd. On the other hand, several different sketches of the same metaphor can be equally valid. Sketching MAN IS A WOLF as "human beings live in packs" is equally valid as "human beings are wild, selfish loners"; the context determines which sketch is most fitting. I shall return to the issue of paraphrasability in a later chapter.

So the iconoclasts' attempt at 'crushing the icons', that is, 'debunking' metaphors, has not been very successful. We have no reason to believe that metaphors are masks. This brings us to the interactionists who certainly do not see metaphors as masks.

1.2 Black's brand of interactionism

Even though I. A. Richards is the founding father of inter-actionism, Max Black has had a much greater impact. He has almost single-handedly made metaphor a subject worthy of the attention of analytical philosophers. And almost nothing I say about metaphors can be intelligible unless one knows both the basic outlines of his thought on metaphors and his terminology. Think about the metaphor MAN IS A WOLF. Black calls WOLF, which makes the corre-sponding linguistic string metaphoric, the *focus* of the metaphor; the rest is the *frame*. The expression 'Man' is the *principal* or 'the *primary* subject of the metaphor' because the metaphor is supposed to tell us something about Man (Black 1962: 28). 'Wolf' on the other hand, is the *secondary* or *subsidiary* subject of the metaphor.[6]

---

[6] In his earlier writings, he used the terms 'principal subject' and 'subsidiary subject' (Black 1962): 25-47. Later he started to use the other expressions (Black 1993: 19-41). The reason for this change of terminology is unclear.

According to Black, "The metaphorical utterance works by 'projecting upon' the primary subject of 'associated implications' comprised in the implicative complex, that are predicable of the secondary subject" (Black 1993: 28). As an example, he uses MARRIAGE IS A ZERO-SUM GAME. The implicative complex to the secondary subject (zero-sum game) can be:

(G1) A game is a contest
(G2) between two contestants
(G3) in which one player can only win at the expense of the other.

How these implications can be projected on the primary subject is decisively dependent on the interpretation of such terms as 'contest', 'opponent', and 'winning'. We can imagine the following projection on the primary subject:

(M1) A marriage is a contest
(M2) between two contestants
(M3) in which the rewards of one contestant are gained only at the expense of the other.

G2 and M2 seemingly predicate the same about two-person games and marriages, while G1 and G2 predicate something similar about them. In M3, 'gain' must have an extended sense in contrast to its sense in G3. After all, marital "battles" usually do not end in clear-cut 'victories' in the conventional sense of that word. The relations between the meanings of the corresponding main words of the two implicative complexes can be classified as, for instance, identity, extension, and similarity. (Black mentions more dimensions.) There are structural similarities between the complexes; they are *isomorphic.* But, in contrast to mathematical systems, the two complexes are not linked by a single projective relation but a mixed lot of such relations.

Armed with this conceptual apparatus, we are now in a position to understand Black's criticism of the theory of comparison, which holds metaphors to be abbreviated assertions about similarities. According to this theory, a metaphor has the form "M stands for something

Black's great source of inspiration, I. A. Richards, called the primary subject 'the tenor', the secondary one 'the vehicle' (Richards 1936: 96). As we have already seen, I adopt the modern way of using his term 'vehicle', while substituting 'topic' for 'tenor', also an accepted modern terminology.

similar to that which L stands for". But the followers of the comparison theory do not understand that there is no such thing as objective, absolute similarity. In the first place, similarity is always a question of degrees and perspectives. When we ask a question like "is A more like B than C?", we had better reformulate it as "is A more like B than C on such and such a scale of degrees of P?" Secondly, we bundle together a variegated set of relations, which we call 'similarity'. When we apply it to the explication of metaphors, then 'is like' is not as sharply contrasted to 'looks like' as 'is taller than' is with 'looks taller than'. The imputed relations in a metaphor have a subjective as well as objective aspect. Thirdly, everything in the world is similar or dissimilar to everything else in some respect and this fact certainly undercuts the theory of absolute similarity.[7] Saying that metaphors record similarities, then, does not say very much. It is more informative in some cases to say that metaphors create similarities rather than to say that they formulate some already existing similarities (Black 1962: 37 and Black (1993): 36). George Lakoff and Mark Johnson agree with Black's contention and provide us with even better examples than Black does. Love and collaborative works of art do not seem to share many similarities. Nevertheless, LOVE IS A COLLABORATIVE WORK OF ART is a potent metaphor because it creates new similarities. In light of this metaphor, we see an experience of frustrated love as being similar to frustrated efforts to create an artwork together (Lakoff and Johnson 1980: 151). This does not mean that Black thinks that the theory of comparison is worthless; indeed, every metaphoric statement may be said to implicate a statement about similarity. But, as Black says, "Implication is not the same as covert identity: looking at a scene through blue spectacles is different from comparing that scene to something else" (Black 1993: 30). Metaphors cannot, therefore, be paraphrased in literal language. Certainly, we can paraphrase parts of the relations between the two subjects of the metaphor literally (Man and wolf in MAN IS A WOLF), but one should not expect too much of the paraphrase. One reason among others is that a paraphrase would present the implications of the metaphor as being of equal importance while the metaphor itself gives the receiver (i.e. reader or hearer) the

---

[7] Similar thoughts on similarities can be found in the writings of several thinkers, for instance, Popper 1959: 420-422.

opportunity to weigh the importance in his or her own fashion. To my mind, this is a strange argument because there is no reason why the receiver should not be able to judge the importance of the paraphrased implications. But, if Black is right, then we are on the way to an understanding of why we should see **A** as being metaphorically **B** even if it is not literally **B**. Conceptual boundaries, Black also says, are usually not rigid but elastic and permeable. He must mean that there can be cases where we can see **A** as **B** metaphorically simply because there are no clear-cut boundaries between them. Black adds that the literal resources of our language are often insufficient to express our sense of the rich correspondence and analogies of domains that are conventionally separated (Black 1993: 33).

How does this all relate to the term 'interactionism'? Black introduced his brand of the interactionist theory of metaphoric meaning by route of an example, THE POOR ARE THE NEGROES OF EUROPE. Our thoughts about Negroes and poor people are active together; they *interact.* The expression 'negro' gets a new meaning, which is not entirely its literal meaning and not entirely the meaning of any literal synonym. We ought to think about metaphors as filters. Take again the metaphor MAN IS A WOLF as an illustration. The receiver does not only have to understand the ordinary dictionary meaning of the word 'wolf' but also our common associations with the word. In our culture, at least, we tend to associate wolves with loneliness, ferocity, etc. According to Black, these properties are parts the system of associated commonplaces of the subsidiary subject of metaphor (Black 1962: 40). Now, if Man is a wolf, then Man is a loner and a predator, at heart a solitary marauder, and so on. If we use this metaphor on humans, then we highlight certain aspects while ignoring others. The metaphor organises our picture of humankind by functioning as a filter, i.e., by extracting out certain aspects of Man in order to make others more discernable. At the same time, thanks to the metaphor, we see wolves in a new light, perhaps as having a somewhat human dimension. This is how the expressions 'wolf' and 'Man' interact in the metaphor.

It must be added that Black emphasised in his later writings that he was talking figuratively when he said that the two subjects interacted. This interaction actually takes place in the consciousnesses of the speaker and hearer. Further, the change in meaning due to interaction is a change in the way speakers and hearers understand the expression in given circumstances (Black 1993: 28).

In order to illustrate his idea of filters, Black says that using metaphors can be likened to viewing the night sky through a screen of smoked glass in which some lines are clear (such a screen is more than little like a filter). You only see those stars that shine through these clear lines. In the metaphor of the wolf, the expression 'wolf' is the screen and the lines represent the various qualities with which we tend to associate wolves. In Black's view, the metaphor transforms its object in certain ways, and in this case, MAN IS A WOLF, there is a sense in which human beings 'become' wolves. To help us understand this point, Black asks us to see what happens if we use the vocabulary of chess to describe a battle. This diction would lead to the highlighting of certain aspects of the battle while others would be downplayed or even downright ignored. The vocabulary in question filters and transforms the battle, perhaps showing us aspects of the phenomenon that would have been obscure without this particular set of terms. For instance, the strategic and tactical aspects of the battle might stand out in sharper relief in this metaphor while the emotional aspects of the battle recede into the background (Black 1962: 41-42).[8] Thus, a metaphor like A BATTLE IS A GAME OF CHESS transforms the object, but this transformation is not a free creation of the imagination; it is constrained by facts about the battle. The metaphor creates objects, but not *ex nihilo*; the chess metaphor changes the pre-existing battle into a chess-like phenomenon. It is "changed, changed", but not utterly, in contrast to Ireland in William Butler Yeats' poem *Easter 1916*. This example shows that metaphors are indeed co-authors of our reality.

I think this analysis of metaphors is magisterial, which, among other things, suggests that metaphors can have cognitive import. We probably learn something new about battles thanks to this metaphor and the way it 'transforms' reality. It could be useful to liken this metaphoric 'transfiguration of the commonplaces (topoi)' to the way mathematical models transform non-mathematical reality. In the

---

[8] Strangely enough, Black forgets to mention which aspect of the battle the chess metaphor might show us in a way that nothing else would. As hinted at, my educated guess is that the metaphor would show us something illuminating about the tactical and strategic aspects of the battle.

process, these models filter out those aspects of non-mathematical reality that escape mathematisation. Again, we see a transformation that consists in the casting of objects into a new mould, in our case a mathematical one constrained by the facts about the objects. Needless to say, this alleged transformation has become indispensable in the physical sciences, making mathematics the co-author of physical reality. It has vastly improved our knowledge of the physical universe (that is, if we are not labouring under some gigantic illusion about it). If the analogy between mathematisation and the work of metaphors is fitting or fruitful, then we have found support for the cognitive theory of metaphor or, for that matter, my theory of co-authorship.

Black has his own way of arguing in favour of the cognitive theory. As so many other theorists of metaphor, he uses similes and metaphors in order to understand metaphors. We have already seen some of them, and we shall now get to know the way Black likens metaphors to slow-motion appearances. He points out that such appearances did not exist before the invention of cinematography, unless some mutant children were born with the ability to see in slow motion with one eye. If there have never been such beings, then we can safely say that slow-motion appearances are man-made but have become part of reality at the moment someone had perceived them. Just like the relations we can see in a slow-motion appearance have become a part of reality once perceived, certain relations become part of reality once they have been created by certain metaphors. The chess metaphor creates new relations, but, at the same time, they can tell us something important about the nature of war. There is nothing strange about this, given that we take seriously the fact that the world is necessarily this or that under a certain description or one from a certain perspective. The point is that it does not make sense to talk about the world as it is *an sich*, not tainted by description and seen from nowhere. Perspectives are all we have; metaphors can create certain perspectives, and, therefore, metaphors can have cognitive import.

Nobody would deny that maps and diagrams have cognitive import. According to Black, linguistic metaphors have more in common with maps, models, and diagrams than with descriptive statements. Metaphors, just like maps and diagrams, are *isomorphic* to their objects and are not equivalent to finite numbers of propositions.

They cannot, therefore, be translated into literal statements that simply substitute them (i.e., they cannot be paraphrased). Metaphors are cognitive devices *without* having truth-values, just like maps, models, and diagrams. Maps and diagrams can be adequate or inadequate, correct or incorrect in many ways but hardly true or false. They are correct or adequate when they are somehow isomorphic to their objects and the same holds for metaphors (Black 1993: 36-39).

This does not mean that Black thought that metaphors are kinds of linguistic or mental maps. The basic cognitive function of metaphors consists in their enabling us to see (understand) things as something else (which maps hardly do). We understand Man as wolf thanks to the tired, old metaphor (Black 1993: 31-33). In a similar fashion, when we all of a sudden see a cloud as a clock, then we see connections between elements of the clouds that were hidden before (compare the screen-metaphor). To use Wittgensteinian language, an aspect has suddenly dawned upon us, just as an aspect of a Jastrow-figure can (Wittgenstein 1958: 197). So the cognitive function of metaphors is of the same kind as the cognitive function of aspect-seeing.

If correct, then Black's analysis adds support to the cognitive pluralism I advocated in the introduction, the reason being that Black maintains that metaphors have a cognitive function, different from that of literally interpreted sentences. I do not doubt that there is more than grain of truth in Black's theorising, not least his seminal analysis of similarity.

1.3 Criticism of Black

An appealing trait of Black's arguments is that they provide much stimulus for consideration and debate, including a promising starting point for a critical assessment. Accordingly, I shall begin with a short critical note on isomorphism, an issue I shall return to in the next chapter.

a) Isomorphic relations are one-to-one relations. But surely, there is no one-to-one relation between a human and a wolf. Further, if we cannot neatly separate metaphors and their objects because the object of metaphor is partly constituted by them (as Black suggests), then all talk about isomorphism sounds very strange. However, I do not doubt that there are some kind of structural relations between the topic and vehicle of a metaphor, but I do not think it is fortunate to call them 'isomorphic'. Black's use of 'isomorphy' smacks of the scientistic jargon that is much too popular among analytical philosopher, often used to make their theories look scientific.

b) A more thorough discussion of the idea of aspect-seeing is opportune here, bearing in mind the importance of this notion for my project. David Cooper has criticised the idea of metaphoric seeing-as. He asks us to think about the metaphor RICHARD IS A LION. Does understanding it require that I have, say, to close my eyes and try to visualise the king's profile as leonine? Obviously not. But Cooper seems to take seeing-as literally, while in most cases metaphorically seeing-as means 'understanding-as'. We understand Richard *in leonine terms*. Further, as we have seen, seeing-as involves noticing aspects. I contemplate a face and suddenly notice the likeness to another face. I see that the face has not changed; yet I see it differently, without having any new sensory experience. In short, I notice an aspect. So even if we take seeing-as *verbatim*, we do not have to make any effort to visualise the profiles of kings or anything else. But this does not mean that imagination does not play any role. Robert C. Roberts says that one might see an aspect of the face by construing it in relation to another face, as something like an act of imagination (Roberts 2003: 67). My considered guess is that metaphors do a similar job. We notice or create new aspects of humans by construing them metaphorically in lupine terms without having to have a special, additional sensory experience of humans. Compare this to one of Wittgenstein's example, that of seeing a duck-rabbit figure first surrounded by pictures of ducks, then surrounded by pictures of rabbits. Chances are that we would see the figure as a duck in the first case, a rabbit in the second case. But we do this without having a special sensory experience of the duck-rabbit (Wittgenstein 1958: 195). Analogously, understanding humans in lupine terms is like seeing a picture of a human being surrounded by pictures of wolves. But the pictures we are talking about are concepts, that is, the concepts of a human being and that of a wolf, with the former 'surrounded' by the latter.

However, Cooper has got more up his sleeve and asks us to consider negative metaphors, such as AN ARTWORK IS NOT AN EGG. What would it mean to understand an artwork as being a non-egg? Again, Cooper's criticism is none too convincing. Such negative metaphors can hardly be understood as anything but derivatives from 'positive' metaphors, like AN ARTWORK IS AN EGG. In connection to such a metaphor, the artist can be thought of as a bird laying eggs. We could also stress that the artwork comes from the spiritual inside of the artist, in an analogous way as the egg comes from the physical inside of the bird. It seems plausible that one must somehow be able to understand what it means to understand or see an artwork as an egg in order to understand the negative metaphor. It is not inconceivable that tests could be made that would show that we comprehend negative metaphors slower than the positive ones.

Cooper has some examples of positive metaphors, ETERNITY IS A SPIDER IN A RUSSIAN SAUNA and TRUTH IS A WOMAN. But to my mind, these metaphors are completely incomprehensible if one does not understand their complex contexts. Maybe by understanding these contexts we can understand eternity *as* a spider and truth *as* a woman. When saying in his *Beyond Good and Evil* that truth is a woman, Nietzsche seems to be implying that truth resists dogmatic efforts of comprehension, in a similar fashion as most women do not like suitors who court according to formulas (Nietzsche 1976:3). So, truth is seen as a woman in that it is desired but not easily acquired, and definitely not attainable with the aid of formulas. Leaving aside the fact that the metaphor reeks of male chauvinism, it is hardly a proto-typical metaphor. Tolstoy's Russian sauna metaphor is certainly not proto-typical, whatever other merits it might have. But is it really a metaphor and not only gibberish unless there are ways to show that eternity can be understood *as* such a spider? Maybe I am guilty of circular reasoning; maybe I just assume that metaphors involve aspect-seeing. Then again, I might not be guilty of circularity. Maybe proto-typical metaphors are 'seeing-as metaphors', while non-typical ones are not necessarily so. It seems intuitively plausible that a simple, easy to understand, seeing-as metaphor like our wolfish one is proto-typical.

Cooper puts forth a more systematic criticism of the seeing-as idea. Where X really is Y, the force of saying that one sees X as Y is that its being Y dominates and organises our view of X. But it is difficult to see how this can have any application in cases of metaphors where X is not really Y. How can my view of X be dominated and organised by its being Y when I know full well that is not Y? My simple answer to this is that I can perfectly well know that what I see on the screen are just some lines (X); nevertheless, I see the lines as a duck (Y). My view of X is dominated and organised by Y. In fact, Cooper admits that there are metaphors where it makes sense to say that they show us X as being Y. But, even in these cases, it is hard to see that making us seeing X as Y is one of their essential functions (Cooper 1986: 232-236). However, I do not find Cooper's argumentation particularly convincing. In the first place, Cooper does not explain what he means by 'essential functions'. Secondly, I think the preceding discussion shows that there is a host of metaphors, which have *among* their essential functions the showing of X as Y. In the third place, if helping us to notice or create aspects of X by route of understanding them through the characteristics of some Y is not one of the essential functions of typical metaphors, then what is? My conclusion, then, is that Cooper's criticism is both partly insufficiently developed and partly wrong. And I believe that Black was on the right track; metaphors have a seeing-as function, at least in prototypical cases.

As I see it, there is something *holistic* about metaphors. After all, we *connect* concepts with the aid of metaphors. This fact points in the direction of metaphors as being *Gestalts*, as Joseph Glicksohn and Chanita Goodblatt maintain. Metaphors are emergent wholes, which cannot be understood by focusing solely on their constituent parts because they are (as Black said) constituted by an interaction between their primary and secondary subjects. Similarly, Gestalts are constituted by the interaction between their parts (Glicksohn and Goodblatt 1993: 83-97). I find this analysis is inspiring. I think that not only are metaphors themselves emergent wholes, but that they also give us some kind of a *holistic representation* of reality, a theme I shall return to in a later chapter.

c) This does not mean that I categorically accept interactionism. In the first place, I think that Black's critics (Searle, Lakoff, Turner) are right about its being unclear for why we have to understand both the subject and the predicate of a simple metaphoric assertion in the light of each other, and hence differently from the standard use of these expressions (Searle 1993: 93-94 and Lakoff and Turner 1989: 131-132). Do we really have to understand 'zero-sum game' as somehow marriage-like in order to understand the metaphor MARRIAGE IS A

ZERO-SUM GAME?[9] It is hard to see why one has to understand the vehicle in the terms of the topic while it is obviously true that the topic must be seen in the light of the vehicle. Secondly, I wonder what the criteria would be that would allow us to determine that someone had really understood an expression used in a metaphor in virtue of having grasped it in the light of another expression. What do I know when I know that I and others have seen the wolf as somewhat human and that seeing the animal in this way is an integral part of understanding the metaphor MAN IS A WOLF? What kind of criteria do I have for knowing that others or I possess this knowledge? I simply cannot see what kind they would be.

1.4 The Abstractionists

Yet those whom I call *abstractionists* might be able to save the day for interactionism. The abstractionists think that the interaction does not take place between the concrete meaning of the two terms inter-acting but on a more abstract, 'higher' conceptual level. Eileen Cornell Way talks about conceptual '*supertypes*', and Sam Glucksberg about '*superordinate categories*' as the *locus* where inter-action takes place or terminates. But before we examine Way's and Glucksberg's abstractionism, I shall briefly mention Tamar Sovran's version of abstractionism, the 'theory of reconciliation'. There seems to be a semantic tension between topic and vehicle on a concrete semantic level, but on a more abstract level they become 'reconciled'. For instance, the expression 'islands of hope' seems semantically contradictory, but, if we understand it metaphorically, then we *abstract* isolation, plurality, and separateness from the concept of an island and make them into qualities of hope. Since there is nothing absurd about an isolated or separated hope, then topic and vehicle are reconciled, thanks to the process of abstraction (Sovran 1993: 25-48). According to Way, it is not the similarity between wolf and Man that plays the most important role in the old metaphor. The aggressive disposition and competitiveness we find in wolves and humans are different. Rather, we abstract from these different kinds of qualities and find similarity between wolves and humans in a more *abstract* kind of aggressive disposition. This abstraction is a *supertype* in

---

[9] Black uses this example in Black 1993: 29. Neither Searle nor Lakoff analyse it, but I use their approach in dealing with it.

relation to human and lupine aggressive dispositions. This supertype is on a higher level within a hierarchy of concepts, just as the concept of mammals is a supertype, relative to the concepts of humans and wolves. The basic role of metaphors is to show or create abstract relations, which are usually hidden in literal language. In literal language, the details and distinctions between concepts are often more important than these abstract relations (Way 1995: 187). Further, while literal language has the function to express the generally accepted ways of classifying things, metaphors introduce new modes of classification (Way 1991: 22).[10] In fact, Way is not the first theorist to think along these lines. Viewing metaphors as being creative in the dimension of meaning is quite popular.[11] But even if that were true, then we should not forget that not all metaphors have the function to invent new categories; when Romeo metaphorically says, "Juliet is the sun", he certainly is not inventing any new category. And even if all of them had that function, I cannot see why we ought to believe that they monopolise semantic invention. Could not we invent new categories without the aid of metaphors, understood in the abstract-tionist fashion? Were all the categories of zoology invented with the aid of abstractive metaphors? The onus is certainly upon anybody who might think so.

Sam Glucksberg also stresses the creative role of metaphor and provides us with interesting examples of this creativity. He maintains that metaphoric expressions often refer to categories for which we do not have any word. Thus, the name of the purported mass-murderer John Demjanjuk became a metaphoric (not metonymic) expression in Hebrew for a certain kind of killer. Demjanjuk was a proto-typical member of this category that lacked a word for it, and his name was used as a label. Glucksberg thinks that metaphors are means for cate-gorisation. Metaphors are class-including relations and metaphoric propositions are class-including propositions. The metaphoric compar-ison (the simile) "sermons are like sleeping pills" can be paraphrased

---

[10] In Way 1991, she introduced her 'theory of dynamic type hierarchy' (D.T.H.).

[11] Thinkers as different as Nelson Goodman and Paul Ricœur think along these lines (Ricœur 1977: 244). Goodman has put emphasis on this role before Ricœur started to publish works on metaphors. Metaphors, Goodman says, re-describe reality and introduce new natural kinds (Goodman 1976: 68-70). The fact that several thinkers defend this view in vastly different ways can add a quasi-inductive support to it, given that it cannot be somehow refuted.

without problem to the class-inclusive propositions "sermons are sleeping pills". The same does not hold for literal comparisons like "bees are like wasps". It could be true but the same does not hold for "bees are wasps" (Glucksberg 2001: 38-40). Literal comparisons cannot, therefore, be expressed as class-including propositions.

"Cigarettes are time-bombs" is a metaphoric proposition, and, in this proposition, cigarettes have been included in the class (category) of deadly or terrifying things. The category of deadly things is a superordinate category to the category of time bombs (Glucksberg and Keysar 1993: 401-424). (The similarities with Way's theorising are obvious.) Glucksberg notes that a metaphor has a double reference whereby the vehicle both refers to the superordinate category (deadly objects) and the literal referent (time-bombs), which exemplifies the superordinate category (Glucksberg 2001: 46). It is important to note that the vehicle refers to an attributive category that ascribes certain properties to the topic. In HER LETTER WAS A KNIFE, we attribute to the letter some of the properties of a knife, especially those properties it shares with other members of the superordinate category of piercing and dangerous objects. (At the same time the knife is a prototypical example of a piercing and dangerous object; compare the idea of a double reference.) What we are dealing with is an *interactive process*. The topic contributes with dimensions for the attribution of properties, and the vehicle with the properties that can be attributed to the topic. If the topic is a road, then the colour of the road does not usually belong to its dimension for the attribution of properties.

We see the interaction if we compare two metaphors, SOME ROADS ARE SNAKES and SOME LAWYERS ARE SNAKES. It is obvious that the different topics have their own dimensions for a possible attribution of properties. The first topic opens up the possibility of being attributed the properties that snakes have in common with winding objects. The other opens up the possibility to be attributed the properties snakes share with dangerous and devious creatures (Glucksberg 2001: 52-59). If I have understood Glucksberg correctly, then the dimensions of the topic determine which of the properties of the vehicle become salient in the metaphor. The properties of the vehicle then determine which of the dimensions of the topic become salient. Thus we have an interaction between topic and vehicle.

Glucksberg and other abstractionists obviously have some good points; I think it is possible that their abstractive approach can suit a host of metaphors. But the abstractionists do not seem to have any theory of metaphoric meaning, though I do not exclude the possibility that such a theory of meaning can be developed on the basis of their theories. The basic problem with the abstractionists is precisely that their approach is *too* abstract. Why would we need metaphors if metaphors basically have this abstract function? The easiest way to denote an abstract concept is by using a literal expression because they can provide us with direct understanding, while metaphors do so by route of another object. There does not seem to be any reason why we should use this more complex way to grasp something that could be grasped directly with the aid of literal expressions.

Further, the abstractionists, especially Sovran, overestimate the conciliatory side of interaction. If they can be so easily reconciled on an abstract level, why use them at all? Could it be that there is an inherent tension in metaphors so that their contradictions cannot be quite reconciled? The answer could be found in the first version of the theory of interaction, I. A. Richards' version. He maintained that the interaction between tenor (i.e., primary subject) and vehicle is not only a question of interaction between similarities but also between *dissimilarities*. When Hamlet says, "What should fellows as I do crawling between heaven and earth?", then the dissimilarities between Man and bug are not less important than the similarities, the implication being that Man should not be crawling around. Richards says:

> Thus, talk about the identification or fusion that a metaphor effects is nearly always misleading and pernicious. In general, there are very few metaphors in which disparities between tenor and vehicle are not as much operative as the similarities. Some similarity will commonly be the ostensive ground of the shift, but the peculiar modification of the tenor which vehicle brings about is even more the work of their unlikenesses than of their likenesses (Richards 1936: 127).

So, at least in some important cases, the interaction at the abstract level is not only a question of reconciliation but also of a permanent tension. The interaction partly consists in the tension between reconciliation and strife.

My intuition is that metaphors certainly do interact on an abstract level and that interaction is a necessary part of them. Nevertheless, they have a concrete dimension, somewhat like the dimension of the pictorial, which hardly can be explained in words and of which we have a tacit knowledge. I shall show why and how later in this book. I shall also try to show how the inventiveness of metaphors is closely connected with their ability to grasp the intuitive, organic, and tacit – precisely the opposite of the abstractions of the abstractionists.

The basic function of metaphors is to show one object (as described in the topic) in the terms of another object (as described in the vehicle). In order for this to happen, there must be a kind of a *background interaction* between topic and vehicle that takes place on a level of abstraction (supertype-level or level of superordinate categories). So, whereas the abstractionists put the abstractive interaction in the foreground, I regard it as being a necessary background condition for any M to be a metaphor. Thus in MAN IS A WOLF, the background interaction terminates in the abstract conception of aggression, loneliness, and the like (remember that the tension does not disappear). But in the foreground, no interaction takes place and there is no dimension of abstraction, only the diffuse way that the properties of a wolf become the properties of Man. There is a tacit aspect in our understanding of this; we cannot really explain how Man is being seen in the light of wolves any more than we can give a satisfactory description of faces. But we have no problems in grasping the abstractive interaction at the background level. There is, then, a grain of truth in interactionism, but nothing more.

1.5 Conclusion

In this chapter we have discovered that the arguments of the iconoclasts are none too convincing, the cognitive theory of metaphors carries the day. Metaphors have cognitive content and can probably help recreate language. Moreover, it is hard, even impossible to define the concept of metaphor, which in all likelihood is an amoebaean one. We have also found out that if metaphors are paraphrasable at all, then it is only in a rough and tough way; we can make sketches of metaphors, quasi-paraphrases, nothing more.

Also, whilst interactionism has its good sides, interaction nevertheless cannot play the leading role, only the supporting one in the drama of metaphors on the stage of abstractions.

A typical metaphor is constituted by seeing-as when it is structured by a tensive, background interaction on the abstract level. I do not rule out the possibility of metaphors that are not structured by a background interaction or even those that are structured by a non-tensive background interaction. I do not even think metaphors constituted by foreground interaction impossible. But my main objective is to determine the nature of typical metaphors, and, above all, to show that metaphors have cognitive import and are not just fancy ways of talking.

Metaphoric discourse is no masquerade; there is no literal face behind the beautiful mask.

I.2. The magic of metaphoric masques
Ricœur on Metaphors

Paul Ricœur definitely did not regard metaphors as masks, but might have agreed that they are *masques*. For masques are something magical, beautiful, playful and ambiguous and so are metaphors in his thinking. With their magic wand, metaphors create the human world of meaning.

Before we look at Ricœur's theory, I must warn the reader that it is very hard to compare him to the interactionists and other analytical theorists because of his Continental provenance. His agenda is the significance that symbolic structures, such as metaphors, have for our existence, and not any abstract understanding of meaning. Like so many Continental philosopher, he loved synthesising, fusing together different theoretical fragments, adding a touch of his own.

2.1 Poetic of the Will

His theory of metaphors is a part of much larger philosophical endeavour. The theory has its roots in Ricœur's idea of a *poetic of the will*.[1] Ricœur defined it as "a general philosophy of the creative imagination, considered in turn on the level of semantic innovation and practical representation, on the individual level, and on the cultural and social level" (Ricœur 1981a: 39). He seems to stress two aspects of poetic, one being the ordinary meaning, i.e., the study of that which concerns poetry and the poetical, the other the study of making or creating (compare ancient Greek *poiesis*, i.e., creation, fabrication or production).[2]

---

[1] That very expression inspired me to articulate the poetic of emotions, introduced in the third section of this book.

[2] The idea of a 'poetic of the will' made its first appearance in Ricœur's dissertation, *Le volontaire et l'involontaire*. He mentions the importance of the poetic of will for his later reasoning in Ricœur 1986: 237. Several theorists think that this idea has informed Ricœur's entire philosophical project. See for instance Skúlason 2001: 42-43, and Mukengebantu 1990: 209-222.

One must bear in mind that Ricœur started out as a phenomenologist who wanted to investigate the will in a purely phenomenological way; finding out in the process that willing is a kind of thinking (Dornisch 1975: 5). Now, the central idea of phenomenology is that consciousness and all mental acts possess intentionality. Being conscious means being conscious *about* something, willing is willing something; thus consciousness and the will have *intentional* objects. Apprehending consciousness, the will, and diverse mental acts is impossible without analysing their intentional objects. But the French thinker quickly found out that these objects must themselves be meaningful and so, following the hermeneuticians, he maintained that meaningful objects cannot be understood without being interpreted. He thus grafted the branch of hermeneutics onto the trunk of phenomenology and opted for a *hermeneutical phenomenology* (Ricœur 1986: 43-81).

Having intentional objects means both that mental acts, so to speak, transcend the mind and that these objects are something to be interpreted. They only exist in cultural settings, in and through symbolic structures (Ricœur does not use that expression). Thinking about things consists typically in forming sentences in our head, and those sentences are interpretable. Further, some objects of our desires can only be identified in a cultural context; in order to understand a religious mystic's longing to be unified with God, we have to understand his cultural-religious setting. Achieving this understanding requires interpreting symbolic structures, particularly as they appear in such cultural products as religious language and imaginative literature. These products transcend the individual mind.[3] It seems to me that understanding the will means understanding products of the human spirit (poeisis) and that a substantial portion of these products must be understood in terms of ordinary poetics. Thus, we have the poetic of the will.

Ricœur believed that, in order to understand consciousness, we must interpret its meaningful manifestations, i.e., its intentional objects.[4] Thus, like Wittgenstein, he rejected mental philosophy. But

---

[3] The French philosopher did not write exactly like this; this is my reconstruction of his ideas; I 'translate' them into my idiom by, for instance, using my expression 'symbolic structure'.

[4] For his presentation of phenomenological hermeneutics, see Ricœur 1986: 43-81.

Ricœur certainly did not ignore the subjective; he allots it a place in his complex philosophical structure. So he is like me a moderate intersubjectivist and like him I make room for subjectivity. I will later show where these pockets of subjectivity are to be found in emotions, tacit knowledge and elsewhere.

Strangely enough, Ricœur ignored the private-language argument, even though he had been strongly inspired by the Wittgensteinian idea of seeing-as, especially with regard to metaphors and narratives. Yet, Ricœur and Wittgenstein differ significantly in many ways, not least when it comes to the concept of interpretation. Wittgenstein uses the concept much more narrowly than his French colleague. Also, in contrast to Ricœur, he stresses our bodily reactions as an important source for our creation of meaning. I have already shown how in Wittgenstein's view, expressions of sensations have their roots in bodily reactions. I believe both that Ricœur could have enriched his theory of symbolic structures by taking heed of this Wittgensteinian moderately naturalistic approach, and that the Wittgensteinians ought to take heed of Ricœur's less restricted concept of interpretation and his emphasis on cultural analysis. The concept of interpretation and the analysis of symbolic structures are central to my project, as will be seen later in this book.

Even though he was not an existentialist, Ricœur was an *existential* thinker, more concerned with the role of metaphors in human existence than their logical-linguistic nature. He was less concerned with the linguistic meaning of metaphors than with the way they endow our lives with meaning. His theory of metaphors is an integral part of a panoramic vision of the human world in which metaphors, narratives, religious language, imaginative literature, imagination, and even actions form a great chain of meaningful being. This vision has its roots in the poetic of the will.[5] In 1968 the French students on the barricades chanted the slogan "l'imagination au pouvoir!" ("power to the imagination!"). Ricœur could have replied by saying that imagination is already all-powerful. Its products dominate our world; in the realm of words it creates symbols, in the realm of sentences metaphors, and in texts narratives. The process of creation has strong

---

[5] Ricœur did not express his view this way but it is not inconceivable that he might have (Ricœur 1999). See also Venema 2000.

metaphoric traits, a process whereby X is seen as Y. Thus, in mythology, the sun is seen symbolically as a god; the imagination uses the word 'sun' as vehicle for the symbol. It uses a sentences like "truth is light" to express the corresponding metaphor and a whole text to tell the tale of how the sun-god created the rays of truth.[6]

Ricœur was an analogically minded thinker. He tended to have an as-if approach to things, an approach that calls to my mind the German philosopher Hans Vaihinger and his philosophy of the *as-if* (*Philosophie des Als Ob*). He thought that all thinking in the last analysis is analogical. We only know our subjective impressions and see the world as being analogous to them. We see things as if they were objectively given. Causality is really an analogy to our inner, subjective experience of acting. Our world-view consists of useful fictions; atoms are fictions, but it serves the physicist's interest to believe that they are real (Vaihinger 1924: 27-32). Vaihinger's approach is obviously mental-philosophical while Ricœur's view is intersubjectivist and informed by the idea that we can only understand ourselves by taking detours through the land of cultural products. Vaihinger seems to think that merely focusing on the isolated subjects does the trick, a notion that Ricœur would never have accepted. However, he certainly would have accepted Vaihinger's claim that "Denken macht Umwege" ("Thinking takes detours") (Vaihinger 1924:105).[7] Because consciousness is a cultural product that is soaked with language, we have to make a long detour around the signs in order to understand our own consciousness ("…nous prendrons le long détour des signes") (Ricœur 1969a: 253).[8] This reminds me of Charles Baudelaire's famous lines, "L'homme y passe à travers des forêts de symboles" ("Man strays through a forest of symbols").[9] We

---

[6] These examples are my own creation, the products of my imagination.

[7] As far as I know, Ricœur never discussed Vaihinger, but I reckon that we could reconstruct the French philosopher's thinking as an intersubjectivist transformation of Vaihinger's subjectivist philosophy of the as-if. But such a reconstruction could be the theme of another book.

[8] The kinship with the poetic of the will ought to be obvious; Ricœur is really talking about a poetic of the cogito.

[9] The English translation is the work of Florence Louie Friedman (Baudelaire 1962: 25). Anybody, knowledgeable in French, sees that her translation is not 'accurate', missing the central point of Man traveling towards some unspecified goal.

The French original can, for example, be found in this bilingual edition, Baudelaire 1975: 51. The translation there is also not 'accurate'.

travel towards ourselves through this forest and while journeying; we tell stories about who we are, stories replete with metaphors.

In this book I shall position myself in between Wittgensteinian thinking and Ricœurian hermeneutics. There is a *slight* tendency towards an unwarranted objectivism in the Wittgensteinian scheme of things, a tendency that anti-objectivistic hermeneutics can correct.[10] At the same time, there is a tendency towards too lofty speculations in hermeneutics, corrigible by the down-to-earth Wittgensteinians and their praiseworthy use of concrete examples. Perhaps the branch of Wittgensteinianism should be grafted onto the trunk of hermeneutics and *vice versa*.

I have, indeed, grafted one French[11] or Ricœurian branch on my trunk, the one of 'poetic in a wide sense of the word'. This is the reason that I call the last section 'The Poetic of Emotion'. There I discuss the narrative, metaphoric and textual traits of emotions. I want my philosophical poetic to be cautious and fallibilistic; the aim is to see how far the paradigm of the poetic can be articulated, how much poetic moment there are in various realms of human existence that usually are not regarded as belonging to the realm of the poetic.

2.2 Ricœur on Creativity and Imagination

Ricœur's theories about metaphors (or, for that matter, narratives) are incomprehensible unless we familiarise ourselves with his idea of creativity in the realm of language.[12] He agreed with Noam Chomsky that humans are essentially creative in their use of language. If they were not, Chomsky asks, how could we explain the fact that even small children can create and understand sentences they have not heard before? (Chomsky 1968 and Ricœur 1969: 80-97). Ricœur added that metaphors are the best instrument we have for linguistic innovation. New metaphors are 'alive' and make us see things in a fresh, new way. They create new meaning and thus play an important epistemological role. Ricœur seemingly thinks that metaphors create

---

[10] I am inspired by Jürgen Habermas' analysis of Wittgensteinian and hermeneutic thought. But he is discussing the social sciences; I am not (Habermas 1977: 220-285).

[11] The French philosopher Gaston Bachelard wrote a book on *The Poetic of Space* long before Ricœur's time and thus used 'poetic' in a wide sense.

[12] For a compelling analysis of the role of creativity and imagination in Ricœur's thinking, see Richard Kearney 1989: 1-31.

new conceptual systems that enrich our understanding of the world.[13] By getting new ways of seeing things, we learn more about them. Thus Ricœur is a *metaphorist* of a kind, thinking that metaphors play an essential role in our cognition and in our lives in general. (We have already seen that he thinks that the world of meaning we inhabit is created by a sort of metaphoric process.) The same does not hold for dead metaphors, which Ricœur did not regard as being real metaphor. In an expression such as 'the legs of the chair', the expression 'leg' has lost its metaphorical meaning and has acquired a literal one (Ricœur 1977: 230).

Ricœur's general theory of metaphors is pretty eclectic but has a point of departure in Monroe Beardsley's *tensive* theory of metaphor. He distinguished between the subject and the *modifier* of a metaphor. In MAN IS A WOLF, Man is the subject, and wolf the modifier. There is a tension or opposition in metaphors. In MAN IS WOLF, the tension is created by a logical contradiction. 'Man' is normally defined as 'a two-legged, rational, speaking, animal', 'wolf' as 'four-legged, non-rational, predator'. So "Man is a wolf" is a contradictory proposition and hence we have tension. More precisely, there is tension between the central and the marginal meanings of the modifier. The central meaning is the designation of the modifying word; the marginal meaning is its connotations. 'Wolf' designates a certain animal while its connotation can be 'loneliness', 'viciousness', etc. These are the *credence properties* of the word, that is, the properties people associate with the designated object (Beardsley 1962: 293-307).

According to Ricœur there is not only tension within the modifier but also between Richards' tenor and vehicle[14] and Black's focus and frame as well as his primary and secondary subject. They create con-tradictions within the metaphor. There are also tensions between a) the literal and figurative interpretations of an utterance; b) between the differences and identities, which the metaphoric copula creates. To put

---

[13] He was undoubtedly inspired by Nelson Goodman (Goodman 1976: 72-84).

[14] In many ways Ricœur's theorising is closer to Richards' tensive brand of interactionism than to Black's non-tensive version. As we shall see in the main text, Ricœur always emphasised the tension in metaphors, the dialectical interplay between similarities and dissimilarities. (For his treatment of Richards' theories, see Ricœur 1977: 76-83.)

it tersely, Ricœur regards these oppositions as being of dialectical nature and thus having a dialectical solution, a synthesis. The solution is the creation of a new metaphoric meaning and reference (Ricœur 1977: 247). At the same time, he thinks that Beardsley was right when he called metaphors 'miniature poems' (Ricœur 1977: 122 and Beardsley 1981a: 144).[15] But how can metaphors have references if they are poems of sorts? In order to understand this apparently contradictory view, we must know that, according to Ricœur, a metaphor is not only a question of a strange way of using nouns as for instance, in MAN IS A WOLF, where the two nouns are used in a non-standard way. A metaphor is also expressed in a predicative sentence ("Man *is* a wolf") and exists as a part of discourse, i.e., on the level of the use of language. More precisely, discourse is the objective side of the use of language; it is not passing and non-objective like *parole*. Perhaps discourse is related to Gricean utterance types whereby parole is like tokens of utterances. Utterance types are conventionalised expressions; for instance, 'fire!' is a conventionalist expression of warning. However, it can be used in different ways, say, to mislead someone (Grice 1968: 225-242). Even so, in every dis-course, we intend something by that which we say; we have the inten-tion of referring somehow to something by our words (Ricœur 1969: 80-97). The same holds for metaphoric discourse.

I admit that I find this a bit hard to understand (it is difficult enough to comprehend the concept of a discourse). Does this mean that even a crazy joke refers to something? Could it be that the sentence used in telling even an absurd joke must refer to states of affairs in a possible world? Be that as it may, I think that Ricœur is playing a linguistic variation on phenomenological themes when he says that we always intend something with our discourses. One of these themes is that consciousness always has an object, that is, we think about something or wish something; there is no such thing as thinking about absolutely nothing. Likewise, discourse always has an object; there is no such thing as a discourse that is not about anything at all, in Ricœur's view.

---

[15] Beardsley thought, in stark contrast to Ricœur, that metaphors are purely linguistic and have no reference to reality (Beardsley 1962: 293).

Ricœur seems to have thought that the reference is already potentially present in the metaphoric sentence because it is by necessity a predicative sentence. But the reference in question is of a different nature than that of sentences understood or used in a literal fashion (Ricœur 1977: 224). Ricœur calls this kind of reference 'a split reference' (an expression originating from the works of linguist Roman Jakobson). If we understand a sentence in a metaphoric way, then we understand it both in a literal and an imaginative fashion simultaneously. (Ricœur does not use the expression 'imaginative', but it is on the tip of his tongue.) These two interpretations, the literal and the imaginative, each have their way of referring. In the interaction between these two different kinds of references, a split reference is being created that is necessarily connected to a new way of seeing things. The verb 'to be' is used in a non-standard way in a metaphoric discourse. It means 'to be and not to be' (as the way storytellers in Mallorca end their stories by saying, "it was and it was not") (Ricœur 1977: 247-248).[16] Giving concrete examples was not Ricœur's strongest point, so I shall provide some myself. When we say something metaphorically, for instance, "Man is a wolf", we cannot mean it seriously unless we think that the sentence somehow refers to something. At the same time we cannot seriously intend to say something metaphoric with the aid of the sentence unless we recognise that the sentence is strictly speaking not true; we do not believe that is refers to anything real. (It might, of course, be true despite our beliefs; maybe we all are incarnated wolves.) We speak as if it is at the same time both true and untrue that Man is a wolf. The sentence refers both to reality and to some fantastic dimension. Thanks to the split reference, metaphors help us talk about the aspects of our existence that cannot be talked about directly (Ricœur 1984a: 80 and elsewhere). We can only talk about such an aspect by route of another concept; maybe there are aspects of Man that can only be understood by route of the concept of wolf. Presumably, literal sentences are the instruments we use when we are talking directly about facts that are easy to refer to. I do not need metaphors to state that right now, I am writing on my PC, because I can say this directly.

---

[16] He borrowed the reference about the storytellers from Jakobson. For a short overview of Jakobson's influence on Ricœur's theory of metaphor, see Max Statkiewicz (2003): 561.

This analysis suits me, actually, perfectly well. I shall play a variation on this theme in Section III.

Another part of Ricœur's analysis, which suits me well is the one on the relationship between emotions and metaphors. That relationship can only be understood by route of the way the French thinker connects emotions to imagination. He chastises Black for having left the problem of innovation unsolved. I think that Black, like so many analytical philosophers, was a bit afraid of that which smacked of subjectivity, and imagination does. Anyway, Ricœur thinks that theory of imagination is required to plug this hole in Black's thinking. This theory is hermeneutic in character, imagination is not essentially a matter of vision, but is rather linguistic and poetic by nature. As I see it, the reason for Ricœur's view of the imagination is his intersubjectivism; visual images can only be given identity through language, which is essentially intersubjective in the intersubjectivist view. Being linguistic by nature, imagination is a necessary tool for semantic innovation, which brings it in the vicinity of metaphors. Verbal imagination performs the metaphoric task of saying something in the terms of something else. At the same time, imagination needs images, in Richard Kearney's words: "Without any visual aspect the verbal imagination would remain an invisible productivity" (Kearney 1989: 15). The very visual seeing-as is an indispensable complement of creative semantics. I think that in Ricœur's world, semantic innovation without images is blind and empty without verbal imagination.[17]

It is not by chance that I allude to Kant. Ricœur's emphasises that his theory of imagination must adopt Kant's concept of productive imagination as schematising a synthetic operation. But what is schematism in Kant's scheme of things? According to him, the schematism is created by the productive imagination and mediates between sense experience and categorical understanding. It completes the passage of sense experience from an inner, mental image to being raw material for the categories of the understanding. It gives sense-experience a rudimentary unity before it is taken over by the

---

[17] The Wittgensteinians would certainly agree with Ricœur's contention that linguistic imagination is primordial but hardly endorse that the visual imagination plays a necessary, complementary role *vis-à-vis* the linguistic one. As I have said earlier, Ricœur gives more latitude to subjective experiences than Wittgenstein did.

categories of reason. Further, the transcendental schema has moments both of inner images and of thought (Kant 1996: 213-222, B 176-186, A 138-147). This reminds me of Wittgenstein's idea of aspect-seeing as being half-thought, half-sensation. It is no wonder that Ricœur fuses the conception of schematism with that of aspect-seeing in his theory of metaphors and narratives.

Metaphors also synthesise in a similar fashion as the Kantian schematism (compare the role of imagination) (Ricœur 1984a: ix). Seeing in a metaphoric way requires a unification of thought and imagination, just as the transcendental schema has moments of both thought and inner images (Ricœur 1981a: 279). The synthesis of the metaphor consists in fusing together apparently disparate concepts. Disparate concepts such as those of wolf and Man acquire an over-lapping meaning in the metaphor MAN IS A WOLF (Ricœur 1984a: x).

Kant thought that the role of the imagination was to provide the concepts with images. In Ricœur's view, it performs a not entirely different role for verbal metaphors because metaphoric meaning denies the difference between sense and representation; it is situated in between the verbal (the realm of the sense) and the non-verbal (the realm of representation). It is precisely in the non-verbal dimension that the images, produced by the imagination, come into the picture. The verbal part of the metaphoric meaning needs images, just like Kant's concepts. In this fashion, Ricœur crosses the borderline between semantics and psychology; the subject (metaphoric meaning) simply requires such a move. To my mind, this must mean that he thinks that there is an ineliminible subjective moment in metaphoric meaning.

We also need imagination to be able to *see* likenesses, seeing that two phenomena are like each other is not just recording sense-data. Furthermore, imagination is the ability to produce new kinds by assimilation but not above the differences, as in the concept, but in spite of and through these differences. Still further, imagination contributes both to the suspension of ordinary reference and to the projections of new possibilities of re-describing the world, possibi-lities inherent in metaphors. When we say metaphorically that Man is a wolf, we suspend ordinary references, and we certainly need a reasonably vivid imagination to be able to do that.[18] This kind of suspension is also at work in the kind of emotions that are operative in our understanding of metaphors. The emotions in question are poetic, for instance, the fear and pity we feel for the heroes of tragedies. They are not ordinary, 'real' feelings but somehow *metaphoric* feelings (my expression). It feels as if we fear and pity someone. Just as poetic language cancels the first-order reference of descriptive discourse to ordinary objects, poetic feelings cancel the first-order feelings. The last-named feeling ties us to the first-order objects of reference. Such poetic emotions "accompany and complete imagination in its function of *schematization*, of the new predicative congruence." (Ricœur 1978: 154). It is a kind of insight into the like and the unlike and the instantaneous grasping of the new congruence is not only seen but also felt. That it is felt shows that the emoter is included in the meta-phoric process as a knowing subject. He is being absorbed as it were into the process; he feels like what he sees like. He sees what is happening on the stage as if Oedipus has killed his father and married his mother, even though strictly speaking it is not really happening. He feels like he is a part of the tragic process. In my interpretation of Ricœur's thinking, the emoter can learn from this dialectic between distantiation and involvement. The 'as' moment in the poetic emotion (feel as) provides the distance, and the moment of feeling provides the involvement. The distance gives us a somewhat objective, bird's eye view while the involvement endues us with the ability to see the world through the eyes of someone enduring a tragic life.

Just as in the case of his analysis of imagination, Ricœur seems to presume a subjective moment in the metaphoric process; it requires emotional experience but of a peculiar as-if kind. Again, I reconstruct his arguments and put in some of my own examples. As Ricœur's treatment of the relationship between metaphors and emotions remained sketchy, I am not going to discuss it in any details. He is saying that there is by necessity two subjective moments in any (?) metaphoric process, the moments of productive imagination and poetic emotion. I have no quarrel with the first moment but would any old metaphoric process require poetic emotions on the part of the creator or receiver of the metaphor? I find it hard to believe that I

---

[18] I am fully aware that my treatment of his theory of imagination is superficial. But the nature of imagination is not one of the many themes of this book.

cannot create the metaphor PELE WAS THE KASPAROV OF SOCCER unless I had some kind of a poetic emotion. But Ricœur is arguably talking about prototypical metaphoric processes or even those processes that matters most for our existence. Nevertheless, by focusing solely on the poetic aspects of metaphors, he loses sight of the work-a-day metaphoric work, the nitty-gritty of plain metaphors. However, it must be said in all fairness that many analytical philosophers, including Black, tend to go too far in the opposite direction, focusing one-sidedly on non-poetic metaphors, either the ones of ordinary parlance or those of science.

Be that as it may, I find Ricœur's way of opening up a space, however small, for the subjective in the metaphorical process an interesting one, and a possible correction to the objectivism of most analytical theorists. It must be emphasised that he does not reduce emotions to sensations (raw feels) but maintains that there is a cognitive moment in emotions (Ricœur 1978: 154). We will discover in the third section that this view has many adherents, including the present author.

2.3 The Cognitive Function of Metaphors

As I sort of hinted at, Ricœur maintained that the cognitive functions of metaphors and imaginative literature are closely related, perhaps even identical. Apparently, he thought that one of the cognitive functions of imaginative literature is to give insights into our life-world, i.e., the work-a-day world of that which is given such that we never reflect on it (Ricœur 1977b: 149-150).[19] Paradoxically, this insight can be attained because of the way fictional literature suspends both ostensive and descriptive reference. Art (and not only literature) opens our eyes to the given, that which we do not notice in our daily lives, by distancing us from it or alienating it, and, owing to this

---

[19] Husserl says that the imagination plays an important role when we thematise segments of our life-world. We can, for instance, get a grip of such a segment by alienating ourselves, so to speak, from its givenness by imagining an alternative reality. Thus, imagination helps us to see that this segment of our life-world, which before seemed given in an unproblematic fashion but is not so (Husserl 1962: 383.) Certainly imaginative literature (not least fantasy fiction) could aid such thematisations of our life world.

alienation, makes it conspicuous.[20] The suspension and the way art makes certain aspects of the ordinary salient can make us more conscious about our familiar surroundings. Most of the time, the contrast in the visual qualities tend to neutralise one another in our ordinary experience, but paintings can emphasise these contrasts by exaggerating them. In this way, visual art can help us grasp or become conscious about that which is given. Art recreates reality and helps us understand it precisely because of this recreation or transformation. Science and literature have in common an ability to give us a deeper understanding of reality by challenging common sense. (Science says, for instance, that time is relative, common sense that it is absolute). Both science and literature use language in a hypothetical manner, both approach reality by making models of it. This analysis squares very well with my intuitions. Moreover, the idea that art helps us understand reality owing to its recreative powers also fits my idea of co-authorship splendidly.

But Ricœur's strange contention that poetic reference is a function of metaphoric reference does not impress me.[21] I cannot see any arguments for this view in his writings. However, he seems to be under strong influence from the way Jakobson and Beardsley linked metaphors and poetry. So perhaps we should evaluate Ricœur's contention by route of an evaluation of both Jakobson's and Beardsley's theories. Jakobson maintained that metaphors are essential to lyrical poetry, not least because of the role similarity plays in this kind of poetry. Rhyme is, for instance, based upon the similarities of the sound of words (Jakobson 1971: 239-259).

Beardsley opines that explication of metaphors is the model for all explication (presumably of imaginative literature). We have already seen that Beardsley thought that metaphors are poems of sorts, and he writes as though poems are kinds of metaphors. Just as a metaphor is one utterance, even a long poem can be regarded as one utterance and explicated in a similar manner as the metaphoric utterance (Beardsley

---

[20] Ricœur admitted being influenced by a theorist named François Dagognet. We are possibly also hearing echoes from the Russian formalist Victor Shklovsky who said that 'estrangement' is one of art's most powerful devices (Shklovsky 1965: 5-24). The idea of estrangement plays a certain role in a later chapter in this book.

[21] He borrowed the expression 'metaphoric reference' from Douglas Berggren (according to Statkiewicz 2003: 560).

1981: 144). It is perhaps possible that, given both Ricœur's idea of metaphoric reference (refiguration) and the analyses of Beardsley and Jakobson, one can show that poetic reference is a function of the metaphoric one. However, there is a host of poems that resists both Jakobson's and Beardsley's analyses. Goethe's extremely lyrical *Wanderers Nachtlied II* (*The Wayfarer's Nightsong II*) does not, for example, contain any metaphors. And William Carlos Williams' best-known poems are certainly lyrical but are also lacking anything resembling metaphors.[22] Of course, we could interpret them as being metaphors in their own right, meaning that a given poem by Williams could be interpreted as being one metaphor. However, all kinds of texts could be interpreted that way. So I do not see how we are bound to regard poems as macro-metaphors or poetic reference as a kind of a metaphoric reference. Yet, I do not exclude the possibility that a prototypical lyrical poem has a reference of the metaphoric kind.

Ricœur says that metaphors refer to possible worlds, and those worlds are hardly the analytical ones but rather the worlds of our potentials.[23] We need to use our imagination in order to find out what these potentials are. (Notice that, according to Ricœur, metaphors do not only have a cognitive function, but also play an existential role, in part because they help showing us our potential.) A successful meta-phoric reference helps us see Man in a new fashion through the lenses of the metaphor. Thus, the metaphor creates a new reality (or realises a potential?). At the same time, the metaphoric reference consists in referring to this new reality.

According to Ricœur, metaphors, even purely poetic ones, are models that both represent and recreate reality (Ricœur 1977: 244).[24] He says that, "...metaphor is to poetic language what the model is to scientific language" (Ricœur 1977: 240). I want to add that metaphors are often like thought-experiments. We imagine how the world would be if we were wolves of sorts, not necessarily only in a playful

---

[22] Dominick LaCapra has a somewhat similar criticism of Ricœur (LaCapra 1983: 127-128.

[23] Samuel Levin is closer to the analytical idea of possible worlds when he says that in metaphors we create worlds, for instance, a world where clouds are angry (Levin 1993: 121).

[24] In his later writings, Max Black defends a similar idea. Perhaps he was inspired by Ricœur. But the French thinker certainly was influenced by Black's earlier theory that scientific models were metaphors of sorts (Black 1993: 30).

manner, but also as part of a serious effort to understand ourselves a little better.

Ricœur thinks that Black was right in saying that regarding X in a metaphoric fashion means seeing it as if it were Y. Ricœur adds that seeing X metaphorically as Y gives us a kind of stereoscopic vision of the phenomena because of the split reference; we see them simultaneously as similar and dissimilar (Ricœur 1977: 231).[25] To see, to imagine, and to think become one. Ricœur uses Aristotle's example about the cup of Dionysius being the shield of Ares. In order to be able to create, to use, and to understand such a metaphoric expression, we must be able to do two things at the same time. The first is that we must be able to employ the following schema for thought: "A (the cup) is for B (Dionysius) the same as C (the shield) is for D (Ares)". The second is that we must able to bring into play our imagination in order to see how this schema applies to Dionysius and Ares (Ricœur 1972: 93-112 and Aristotle 1965: 61 (Chapter 21)).

Just like Ricœur expands Beardsley's concept of tension, he also expands the Wittgensteinian concept of seeing-as into the concept of *being-as* (être-comme). The objects we refer to in split references both are and are not at the same time and in the same respect (Ricœur 1977: 313). It would be an exaggeration to say that his theory is easy to understand, but it must have as its precondition an epistemic conception of reality or at least some segments of it. Given such a conception, certain phenomena exist in virtue of being conceptualised or perceived in certain ways. Thus, paintings have such an 'epistemic mode of being'; in some sense they are only a bunch of atoms, in another sense they are artworks, depictions, etc. If it is only possible to understand certain objects as both being and not being at the same time and in the same respect, then you might say that their mode of existence is being-as. Perhaps Ricœur would say that a sad painting has such a being-as. From one point of view the painting is just a painting or even just a bunch of atoms; from another point of view, it is a painting, which is metaphorically sad. A sad painting is and is not sad; in some sense the quality of being sad is something projected onto it by minded beings, in another sense this is an objective quality.

---

[25] The French philosopher borrowed the idea of a stereoscopic vision from Douglas Berggren and Dedell Stanford (Ricœur 1979: 152).

Not just any painting is receptive to such a projection; projecting melancholy onto a typical Watteau painting could prove a hard task, for they 'resist' such attempts. Further, we can test whether a painting is sad or only seemingly sad. On closer scrutiny we may discover that the painting's sadness was ironic.[26] If not, we can say that the painting is metaphorically sad, even though it is from another point of view a plain painting or just a collection of atoms.

As reader might have guessed, I am very sympathetic to Ricœur's emphasis on the tensive aspect of metaphors. And his ideas of the split reference and configurative potential of metaphors are very inspiring; the same holds for his emphasis on the role of imagination and subjective experiences in the metaphoric process and his fusion of Kantian and Wittgensteinian perspectives. But we shall see in the next chapter that my alethic theory of metaphoric meaning provides a somewhat more precise answer to the question of the cognitive power of metaphors.

Before concluding this chapter, I have a confession to make: I have been too busy 'translating' the French philosophers' thoughts on metaphors into the language of analytical philosophy. So let us end this subchapter on a more Continental note. Ricœur says that it is not by chance that he called his book on metaphors '*La métaphore vive*', the living metaphor. There is a linguistic imagination that generates and regenerates meaning through the living power of metaphoricity (Kearney 1989: 14). As I see it, he regards metaphors as the living, creative moment of the world of meaning, something that is also woven into the web of the soul. We need living metaphors to understand the life of the mind, not least because that life is constituted by such metaphors. Further, the title of the English translation of his book was not accidental (*The Rule of Metaphor*). The translator, Robert Czerny, says that he chose the title because Ricœur seems to agree with Aristotle's contention that the greatest thing one can be is to be the master of metaphors but one cannot learn from others how to make them, and the implication is thus that there is no rule for making them (Aristotle 1965: 65 (Chapter 22)).[27] Another reason for the title was that the book shows that there are language-

---

[26] I took this example from Nelson Goodman (Goodman 1976: 78-79).
[27] There certainly are no rules for how to apply any possible rules for the making of metaphors; compare Wittgenstein's analysis of rules.

rules that impinge on metaphor and that there are domains of discourse over which metaphors hold sway (Czerny 1977: vii-viii).

To this I want to add: The master of metaphors is the ruler of discourse.

2.4 Conclusion

We have seen that it is hard to compare Ricœur's theory of metaphors to analytical theories, even though he appropriates a lot from these theories. Ricœur's theory must be understood against the backdrop of his poetic of the will, his general theory of symbols, creativity and imagination. His theory of metaphors is tensive and dialectical. To be sure, interaction plays a role in his view of metaphor but rather a supporting one. Despite its faults, his theory helps us understand the cognitive and existential import of metaphors as well as its tensive nature.

I.3. Understanding Metaphors: The Alethetic Theory

This chapter will demonstrate that understanding metaphors requires our knowing their cognitive contents. To do so, I shall introduce what I call my *alethetic theory* of the understanding of metaphors. According to this theory, the precondition for understanding metaphors[1] (*both* linguistic and non-linguistic) is our knowing their truth-like values in a somewhat similar fashion, as we understand certain sentences by knowing their truth-conditions. This means that we have to know the way they represent or could represent given segments of reality in order to understand them. Representation (symbolisation), albeit of a peculiar kind, constitutes their basic cognitive content.

The reader should note that I am only talking about the understanding of metaphors; I shall *not* try to answer the thorny question of whether or not linguistic metaphors have a special, non-literal meaning. Notice also that I focus on the logic of metaphoric understanding and basically ignore the psychological processes of such an understanding. Instead, I am trying to uncover the conditions that must obtain if person **P** can be said to have correctly understood metaphor **M**. I am not discussing the psychological process(es), which made **P** understand **M**.

3.1 Why Alethetic Theory?

I have already explained my concept of alethetic values and the etymological root of the word 'alethetic' in Greek 'aletheia'. But I did not mention that Heidegger used *aletheia* in the sense of 'disclosure' or 'unveiling' (Unverborgenheit). One of the reasons that I call my theory 'alethetic' is that I think that metaphors have a *disclosive*

---

[1] When I talk about 'the understanding of metaphors', I mean, 'the understanding of given metaphors' (MAN IS A WOLF, etc.), not 'the understanding of what kind of phenomena metaphors are'. However, if we discover how we understand given metaphors, we shall probably be pretty near to answering the question of what kind of phenomena they are.

function, as I indeed shall show later in this chapter. But what is disclosure? In Heidegger's thinking, disclosure is a primordial form of truth, a sort of *ur-truth* (this is my neologism, sounding a bit Heideggerian). All our mental acts have intentional objects and before we can find out whether they really exist, our intentionality has to disclose these objects. So before we can find out whether the proposition "unicorns really exist" corresponds to reality, our intentionality must disclose unicorns as intentional objects. The 'same' phenomena can be disclosed in various ways; for the carpenter, the hammer is being disclosed as a tool, but for the physicist, it is a collection of atoms. The carpenter *discloses* the hammer as a practical tool by using it without reflecting over the fact that it is a tool. If he were constantly reflecting on its practicality, then the hammer would cease to be a practical tool; it is only a practical tool if it is used unthinkingly. It is only when the hammer breaks that reflection sets in, and the carpenter perhaps thinks, "what can I do to make this thing function?" (Heidegger 1977: 212-230 (§44)).[2]

It seems to me that Heidegger thought that disclosure operates as absolute presupposetions, i.e., that which makes truth and falsity possible. It does not make sense to ask whether the metre in Paris really is one metre long because it is an absolute presupposition for measurement in the metric system.[3] Analogously, it does not make sense to ask whether disclosure really is true or false (Heidegger 1954).[4] So Heidegger thinks that there is more to knowledge than knowing truth values and I certainly do agree. The idea of disclosure is of great value for my project, not least my conception of metaphors.

---

[2] Heidegger regarded disclosure as a kind interpretation, even the primordial kind. So he uses a very wide concept of interpretation, Wittgenstein a rather narrow one. I try to steer a middle course.

[3] It would not surprise me in the least if Heidegger's notion of disclosure was not somewhere in the back of Foucault's mind when he created the concept of *episteme*, i.e., the idea of there being conceptual grids that determine truth and falsity in some sciences, and even society in general in certain epochs (Foucault 1970). There are also affinities between disclosure and the way paradigms work according to Thomas Kuhn, both because paradigms constitute that which can be true and false in a given science in a given epoch and also because Kuhn underscores the practical, non-reflective aspect of the scientific enterprise (Kuhn 1970).

[4] I confess that what I say about Heideggerian disclosure in this book is an amalgam of that which he says in *Sein und Zeit* (Being and Time) and *Vom Wesen der Wahrheit* (Of the Nature of Truth). Heidegger scholars might not be impressed.

This brings me to the second reason for my calling this theory an alethetic one. I think that metaphors have their own set of alethetic values. In order to understand my theorising on this issue, we must return to my concept of visual symbolic structures (**V.S.S**). Metaphors can be expressed in caricatures and other kinds of **V.S.S.**s. This is indeed one of George Lakoff's points. A caricature can show a person with a green face, a metaphor for an envious individual (Lakoff 1993: 240-241). Goodman makes a similar point, using as an example a caricature in which a politician is depicted as a parrot (Goodman 1976: 84). Such a caricature is obviously understandable, but it does not possess any truth-values. If understanding such metaphoric caricatures does not have to be reduced entirely to the knowing of truth-conditions, then it might indicate that understanding this kind of metaphor requires evaluating other alethetic values than truth.

My analysis of **V.S.S.** can be important for our understanding of linguistic metaphors, especially if Black is right about linguistic metaphors having less in common with descriptive statements than with **V.S.S.**s. (Black certainly does not use this term.) My theory definitely would not get any worse if Black were right about metaphors' transforming their objects.

The reader will recall that I have endorsed this theory and expressed agreement with parts of Black's cognitivism about metaphors. As I implied, we talk as though metaphors represent objects, whether these objects be concrete or abstract, real or figments of our imagination. And, in fact, we have good reasons to speak in this fashion. Consider a variation of Chomsky's infamous sentence **S1** "green ideas sleep furiously" (Chomsky 1968). With most readings, this sentence would be meaningless. It is admittedly somewhat metaphor resistant but nevertheless we can imagine situations where the sentence is used or understood in a metaphoric fashion. Someone utters **S1** and means by **S1** or is interpreted as meaning by **S1**, or both, "the young person (a greenhorn), who is full of strange ideas, is quite lively despite the fact that she is in a rather quiet phase". Given that metaphors cannot be translated adequately into literal language, this will only be a sketch of the metaphor. Nevertheless, on a metaphoric reading of **S1** it is understood as an assertion about a certain state of affairs. The different elements of **S1**, like 'green ideas', stand for objects, which are parts of this state of affair and so on. The metaphor

GREEN IDEAS SLEEP FURIOUSLY obviously has a cognitive content, without which the corresponding sentence would be nonsensical. This example strengthens my conjecture that we understand metaphors by virtue of knowing their cognitive content.

If this example is insufficient, consider such tired old sentences as **S2** "Man is a wolf". Understood literally, **S2** is a false sentence. In order to be understood metaphorically, **S2** must be understood as having some cognitive content, different from the literal one. Reading it metaphorically, we must understand **S2** as giving us some information about man or wolves, or both. If not, **S2** is either a literally false sentence or sheer nonsense. Thus, in order for **M** to count as a metaphor, **M** must have some 'positive' cognitive content.[5] We use metaphors like MAN IS A WOLF because we think that they are somehow cognitively apt or adequate, even though it is strictly speaking untrue that man is a wolf.

Further, a metaphor can be 'invalidated', i.e., shown to be cognitively unsuitable or incorrect. If humans were extremely peaceful and full of brotherly love, MAN IS A WOLF (as it is ordinarily interpreted) would be invalidated. The same holds for other metaphors, for instance, MARRIAGE IS A ZERO-SUM GAME. If there were no agonistic moments in marriage, then this metaphor would not be correct. The fact that metaphors can be invalidated is yet another indicator that metaphors can have a cognitive import. They can be 'verified' by being shown to fit correctly certain phenomena and 'falsified' by being shown to have an incorrect fit.

From this analysis, aided by what was said in the earlier chapters of this section, we can conclude that metaphors have cognitive contents. We have also found some evidence suggesting our having to know the cognitive contents of metaphors in order to understand them.

3.2 T-Correctness

Let us take a look at cognitive content of metaphors. The yardstick of this content cannot be truth or at least not truth alone. (Knowing the truth-values of certain literally interpreted sentences *might* be one of the conditions for understanding metaphors.) As we have seen, the

---

[5] Understood as a literally false sentence, it has a negative cognitive content. A true sentence or a correct map possesses a positive cognitive content.

reasons for this are that a) metaphors are not equivalent to a finite number of propositions, and b) they are somehow related to the **V.S.S.**s. If some **V.S.S.**s have their own alethetic value, then why not metaphors? I propose that we call the alethetic values of metaphors *T-correctness*, i.e., 'transformative correctness'. Briefly, to be T-correct, a symbolic structure must be able to provide a 'twisted' understanding of given phenomena.[6] It is somehow cognitively correct, fitting, adequate, right or apt. In addition, metaphors do not monopolise T-correctness. Their logical neighbours, like models, caricatures (both pictorial and linguistic), many kinds of imaginative literary works (for instance satire), literary interpretations and stylised pictures, can also have this alethetic value. I propose that we call this class of symbolic structures *transformative symbolic structures* (**T.S.S.**). They, so to speak, transform or 'twist' our ordinary picture of reality and thus give to us a deeper or at least different understanding of it. They are both transformative and informative at the same time.

It is probable that some would object to my analysis on the ground that we cannot possibly say that **T.S.S.**s are correct or incorrect because they transform and twist reality and cannot, therefore, represent it. But, in the first place, there are ways of judging (at least given a certain convention) whether a given **T.S.S.** transforms a given segment of reality **R** or creates a completely new object. If there were 'only' a transformation, i.e., the **T.S.S.** somehow representing **R,** then there would be some correspondence between some important aspects of the **T.S.S.** and **R**. If **R** had been "changed utterly" into a completely new object, such a representation would not be possible. There would not be any correspondence between any important aspects of the object and the **T.S.S.** (I rely on common-sense understanding of 'important aspects'.) Secondly, we saw earlier that mathematical models of physical reality twist and transform their objects but not beyond scientific recognition (once again I rely on common-sense understanding of the terms used). It is not likely that mathematical

---

[6] These are the 'non-Lakoffian' moments of my concept of metaphoric understanding.

relations exist in nature. Mathematics and metaphors cause metamorphoses, but these metamorphoses can be cognitively productive.[7]

Let us scrutinise T-correctness further. A **T.S.S.** must have some
kind of a structural, though definitely not isomorphic, relation to the
object it represents. The reason for this is that the concepts of literal
truth and of realistic representation are both logically tied to the concept of isomorphism. Given that we regard a symbolic structure **SS** as
a realistic representation of a segment of reality **R**, then we are
logically committed to the idea that **SS** is isomorphic with **R** in an
important way. If there are important structural features of **R** that **SS**
does not represent, then we must admit that **SS** was not really such a
realistic representation after all. It does not matter whether there is
such a thing as an objective and realistic representation of reality, that
is, one not 'contaminated' by convention and practices.[8] The
important matter is that we must be able to show there is an isomorphic relation between **SS** and **R**, either in a completely convention-
free fashion or in a given convention, whenever we state that some **SS**
is a realistic representation of some **R**. **R** itself could very well be a
product of a convention, a figment of someone's imagination or even
a product of a collective illusion.

This analysis holds both for pictures depicting objects in a realistic
manner and for sentences being literally true about some states of
affairs. If it is literally true that Smith is a human, then we must somehow regard the sentence "Smith is a human" as 'picturing' certain
facts or being isomorphic with them. If it turns out that Smith is really
a computer programme, then we cannot talk about any isomorphic
relation between the sentence and reality. Again, the isomorphic
relation could be completely conventional.

It must be emphasised I am not advocating any picture theory of
language; I am only saying that the concept of the truth of literally
understood sentences is logically tied to the notion of a correspond-

---

[7] I do not think that mathematical symbols are **T.S.S.**s. Mathematics can transform
reality (the **T.S.S.**s cannot but do anything else), but pure mathematics constitutes its
own reality. Therefore, I do not think that mathematical axioms and theorems are T-
correct.
[8] As the reader might guess, I do not think there is any way in which we can transcend
practices and conventions, the latter two being interwoven.

dence between structural features of sentences and their objects, whether or not this correspondence is based on convention.

Metaphorically understood sentences have a different logic. In order to understand the sentence "man is a wolf" in a metaphoric fashion, we must exclude the possibility of a one-to-one correspondence between the structural features of the (metaphorically understood) sentence and its objects. In striking contrast to this, there must be an isomorphic relation between any good map or diagram and their objects. (Remember again my proviso about conventions.) This quality makes maps and diagrams more like literally understood sentences or realistic depictions than metaphors. Therefore, Black's way of likening these **V.S.S.**s to metaphors is not very helpful.

Let us return to T-correctness. The structural, but not isomorphic, relation in question is more like the relation of pictorial caricatures or stylised pictures to their objects than anything else. It is a conceptual necessity that a caricature cannot have an isomorphic relation to its object. A given picture **Ca** must somehow 'twist' or 'distort' the object in order to count as a caricature.[9] We have already seen that metaphors can be expressed in caricatures. I think that it is fairly obvious that even linguistic metaphors are in a non-trivial way like pictorial caricatures of their objects. Likewise a pictorial metaphor is non-trivially like a linguistic caricature. This view is not new; both Stephanie Ross and Saul Worth said so thirty years ago. According to Worth, both metaphors and caricatures bring together disparate elements; metaphors presumably assemble different concepts while caricatures bring together our beliefs about segments of reality and some symbolic elements. In Goodman's example of caricature, the parrot symbolises mindless mimicry and this symbol we bring together with our beliefs about certain politicians. Neither caricatures nor metaphors have truth-values, for neither shows things entirely as they are nor as they are not (Worth 1974: 195-209).[10] In my terminology, they twist

---

[9] Saying this does not commit me to any objectivistic idea of pictorial representation. Twisted or distorted pictures of objects mean in this case simply twisted or distorted according to commonly accepted standards of pictorial representation of objects. As is well known, theorists like Nelson Goodman and Ernst Gombrich maintain that what counts as realistic depiction is relative to convention (Goodman 1976: 34-39 and Gombrich 1977).

[10] Worth's conception of metaphors as fusing disparate element together and showing things both as they are and as they are not owes much to Ricœur.

reality. As hinted at, such twisting can also be found in literature; Jonathan Swift's satires certainly twist ordinary reality in order to make us understand it better. And nineteenth century Icelandic writer Benedikt Gröndal in his satires described emperor Napoleon the third and other dignitaries as well to do Icelandic farmers of his time. The metaphoric moment is easy to see and also the similarity to pictorial caricatures. One could have depicted Napoleon the third as a well to do Icelandic farmer of that time and gotten much of the same effect as Gröndal did with his satire. Keeping to French rulers, the typical caricatures of the late French president Charles de Gaulle are good examples of the pictorial sort. They portray his nose as a grotesque protuberance in order to expose his megalomania. Such caricatures are similar to a linguistic metaphor like MAN IS A WOLF, which makes a virtual caricature of Man in order to highlight some of his features. Notice that in these two cases there are structural similarities between the symbolic structures (the caricature and the metaphor) and their objects. Drawing from our earlier analysis, we must maintain that these similarities could be conventional creations like certain metaphors and pictures. We have seen examples of the way metaphors in a sense create similarities by 'transforming' reality. Pictures can do the same; perhaps certain photographs or paintings of de Gaulle created aspects of the similarities in question. According to Ernst Gombrich, a caricature of the last king of France, Louis-Philippe, depicted as a pear partly constituted the way people perceived him (Gombrich 1977: 291-292). So why should not certain photographs of de Gaulle putting on airs have similarly coloured people's perception of him and thereby to their perception of possible similarities between the 'real' president and the caricatures?

Stephanie Ross can help gain another insight into the depiction of Louis Philippe as a pear. Ross points out that there can be important similarities between caricatures and similes. Following her lead (although Ross did not herself use these specific examples), we are invited to see the King of the French as a pear or Nixon as a bomb, etc. This imagery brings us in the vicinity of metaphors like LOUIS PHILIPPE WAS A PEAR. Both the caricature and the metaphor involve new ways of seeing: neither can be defined successfully and neither turns on resemblance or likeness (compare Gombrich's point about pictures and Black's about metaphors). Ross also emphasises that caricatures and metaphors have their standards of appropriateness

(Ross 1992: 116-117). Once again, she has led us on the right track, but she has not explained what these standards are. Let us, then, examine them more closely. Just like metaphors, caricatures can be cognitively apt or correct, or more precisely T-correct. My feeling is that many of the best caricatures of de Gaulle are at least as enlightening[11] as a host of realistic pictures or literally true sentences about him. The same holds for some metaphors applied to the French leader. A metaphor like FRANCE HAS BECOME A WIDOW, used by French president Georges Pompidou after de Gaulle's death, tells us at least as much about the political stature of de Gaulle as many literally true assertions about him do. Let us consider the following statements about de Gaulle:

"He was a dominating figure in French politics for decades and was respected, even loved by most Frenchmen. He was not just any old politician, but a man who almost single-handedly saved France from chaos and possible military dictatorship in 1958, changing the political institutions of the country radically in the process and becoming almost an elected dictator. This he did after having been the symbol of French resistance during the Second World War."[12]

The above statements certainly comprise true assertions, but my hunch is that Pompidou's metaphor is more enlightening even though the sentence he uttered was literally false. The metaphor captures in a poignant, striking manner the *feeling* of the magnitude of de Gaulle's importance for the French. The poignancy of the metaphor is some-thing that a series of literal assertions simply does not possess, and there is something about dramatic greatness that must be expressed in a poignant, striking manner.

We may also contemplate that if de Gaulle had been an anonymous person without any power whatsoever, then the metaphor would have been incorrect and consequently would have been invalidated. We can invalidate not only metaphors but also other T-correct symbolic structures such as caricatures or satires. Because they do not possess truth-values, we cannot falsify them but 'only' invalidate them. Had de Gaulle been a modest person with no great ambitions on behalf of

---

[11] By 'enlightening' I mean, 'giving a deeper insight' or 'giving a better understand-ing'.
[12] This is not a quotation but something I made up.

France, the caricatures would not have been cognitively apt and would have to be invalidated.

Caricatures are closely related to non-realistic, non-abstract, 'stylised', 'serious' pictures (and they are almost certainly **T.S.S**.s). Ross, in fact, emphasises this relationship. She thinks, probably correctly, that the difference between them and caricatures is basically a difference in the way they are used in social practices. Caricatures tend to be humorous, satirical, and topical, the others not (Ross 1992: 117). When I think about stylised pictures, I am especially thinking about portraits, which are not entirely abstract, but also not realistic, at least given our modern, Western conventions. Think of Alexander Calder's caricature-like drawing of Jean-Paul Sartre that emphasises the intensity of Sartre's eyes and thereby his powerful presence; at the same time, the drawing calls to attention to his frog-like features which are 'stylised' through exaggeration. Another case in point is Otto Dix' expressionistic portrait of the philosopher Max Scheler. Dix uses strong colours and exaggerates Scheler's facial features in order to emphasise his strong passions, both spiritual and carnal. Such portraits, as well as caricatures and suchlike, *show* rather than tell and have thus an alethic function different from those of true propositions. This portrait, just like Calder's portrait, is an excellent example of a T-correct symbolic structure.

Exaggeration obvious plays an important role in these two portraits. We have also seen the importance of exaggeration for many metaphors and perhaps all caricatures (which also brings to mind Ricœur's excellent arguments in favour of the role of exaggeration in arts).[13] We certainly inflate Man's wolfishness in the famous metaphor. It is also often overlooked that such bona fide cognitive devices as scientific models tend to be exaggerations. It is an exaggeration to say, for example, that electricity is a current, but modeling electricity this way has become indispensable. We must also bear in mind that it is easy to construct the metaphor ELECTRICITY IS A CURRENT on basis of the model or the other way round. We also need to remind ourselves that no scientist would ever say that electricity is literally a current.

---

[13] The Indian neuroscientist V.S. Ramachandran emphasises the role of exaggeration or amplification in caricatures and visual art generally. His analysis seems convincing and is obviously related to Ricœur's view of visual art. (Ramachandran 2004: 20-40).

Black thought that scientific models were metaphors or at least a close relative (Black 1962: 219-241 and Black 1993: 30).[14] Certainly such models are **T.S.S**.s. Models twist reality to our advantage, with exaggeration being one of the most useful devices. We might say, tongue in cheek, that scientists make caricatures of reality in order to understand it better.

Not only do we learn from exaggerations in scientific activity, we learn from them in our daily lives. A typical music teacher corrects the pupil by exaggerating his mistakes. Maybe caricatures, metaphors, models, and other **T.S.S**.s make certain features of reality salient by magnifying them through exaggeration. In sum, exaggeration can provide us with a salutary twisted understanding that enhances our grasp of our world.

3.3 Metaphoric disclosure

Another important tool for metaphoric cognition is disclosure. But my conception of disclosure is at least as Wittgensteinian as it is Heideggerian, the inspiration coming from Wittgenstein's analysis of saying and showing.

It is true yet trivial that caricatures, stylised portraits, and pictorial metaphors show rather than tell. But what about linguistic metaphors? I think that they have an ineliminable aspect of showing, i.e., that they tend to be better at showing than telling. In order to argue that this is the case, we shall turn to the theories of British philosopher Frank Palmer. He contrasts showing with telling in a Wittgensteinian way. The latter is a simple description of states of affairs like "I am not feeling very well; my wife has left me". The former does much more. Poems worth their salt do not only contain the poet's descriptions of his or her state of mind but rather show it with the aid of images, metaphors, rhythm, etc. (Palmer 1992: 190). Palmer only discusses metaphors in passing, but his analysis is helpful for the understanding of metaphors. Using a fresh linguistic metaphor is not just telling how things are but rather showing them in a broad sense of the word. I think that 'disclosing' is a better word than 'showing' since we are talking about symbolic structures (metaphors) that need not be visual,

---

[14] In his earlier article he expressed some qualms about models being metaphors, but not in the later one.

though they can be. The metaphor, FEYERABEND IS THE NIETZSCHE OF THE PHILOSOPHY OF SCIENCE, certainly cannot be visual, unless it is a metaphor for their appearances. Not only would it be almost impossible to make a picture of their thought, it is also difficult to see how one can have mental image of them. This shows that there are metaphors that neither express nor evoke mental images by necessity. It is not even certain that such expression and evocation matter at all to the creation and understanding of metaphors, even visual and linguistic, but concrete ones. Maybe whatever mental images that are evoked by metaphors are incidental to their meaning and function.[15] But perhaps, mental images can be a part of the connotations, awakened by visual metaphors. Be that as it may, when I am talking about structural similarities between visual images and metaphors, I am not talking about mental images.

Let us look closer at our abstract metaphor about the two philosophers. On the face of it, their thinking and writing do not seem very similar. Feyerabend's writing is light-hearted and Austrian, like a Viennese waltz; Nietzsche on the other hand writes in a dramatic, Teutonic fashion with the style of a *Heldentenor* from a Wagnerian opera (note my use of similes and metaphors).[16] They also tended to write about different issues. In contrast to Nietzsche, Feyerabend did not discuss religion much; unlike Feyerabend, Nietzsche did not write much about the philosophy of science. But a closer look shows that there was an anarchistic streak in both thinkers and both loved to provocate. In a spirit similar to Nietzsche's audacious and challenging notion of truth being a woman, Feyerabend daringly said that we need a dream world in order to understand the real one (Feyerabend 1975: 32). Furthermore, although their writing styles were different, neither of them followed the sober style usual of scholarly works. Their particular styles are integral to their philosophical projects: Feyerabend's jocularity emphasises his rather blithe take on science; Nietzsche's thunderous rhythm underscores his philosophising with the hammer.

---

[15] I am definitely not the first theorist to doubt that mental images are central to metaphors. Black thought of metaphors as purely linguistic, implying that mental images were not of great importance for them (Black 1962).

[16] Try to read Feyerabend's *Against Meth*od while reading Nietzsche's *Zarathustra*. Then you will see my point, or, rather, my point will be disclosed!

The metaphor can show or disclose (or partly create) aspects of the relationship between the thoughts of these two thinkers. The metaphor can be disclosive in the sense of being an eye-opener, helping us to understand the hidden relations between them. But a point-by-point comparison between them is not necessarily enlightening. Their philosophical and stylistic differences, not to mention their belonging to different periods with different intellectual horizons, make for serious obstacles for such a comparison. This is where metaphors come into the picture (would one need metaphors to compare Hempel and Popper?). There seems to be something holistic about metaphors that defy point-by-point comparisons. (Compare the idea of metaphors as Gestalts.) It certainly does not seem to make sense to say that we can determine the alethetic value of the metaphor solely by a point-by-point comparison of Nietzsche's and Feyerabend's philosophies. (In a point-by-point comparison, we treat the sentences as literal assertions, which tell rather than show or disclose).

Most importantly, we should not be able to understand this metaphor unless we know under what conditions it would be T-correct, that is, those conditions in which there are non-trivial structural similarities between the philosophies of Nietzsche and Feyerabend. But these are not normal similarities, at least given our conventional view of similarities; rather, these are the 'twisted' similarities between the caricature and its objects. We have seen that the **T.S.S.**s can be enlightening on account of their transformative abilities. The cognitive import of these T-correct structures is their ability to show or disclose reality. 'Disclosure' means that they give us new, holistic perspectives on phenomena. We see (understand) them in new light and see hitherto hidden connections between them. Indeed, David Cooper entertains the possibility that metaphors can be part of disclosing processes by showing us new perspectives on things. But, in contrast to me, he uses 'disclosure' strictly in the Heideggerian sense, seemingly regarding metaphors as absolute presuppositions (Cooper 1986: 251-257). That, of course, is no capital crime. Cooper's ideas are well worth contemplating, and we shall see in a later chapter that both his and Heidegger's theories can be fused with mine.

In my view, seeing-as (understanding-as) is a sort of a disclosure. When we suddenly see a cloud as a clock, we see connections between elements of the clouds that were hidden before. Seeing-as means twisting the things we see; we twist clouds into clocks. Seeing-as with the aid of metaphors gives us a twisted understanding. We understand the idea of man twisted into the shape of the idea of wolves. In the case of the Feyerabend-metaphor, we understand the thinking of Feyerabend in the light of the thoughts of Nietzsche. Or we 'see' Feyerabend as Nietzsche: the light-footed Austrian has been twisted into the dithyrambic German. Thanks to this we have gained fresh insight into their respective ideas. The reason is that disclosure enlightens rather than informs, since it does not necessarily convey any new factual information. It provides us with a synthetic, comprehensive view rather than an analytical and factual one.

I have intimated earlier that disclosure is a type of showing; seeing-as or understanding-as are useful, even essential, tools of disclosing, making it a kind of semi-interpretation. Even the disclosive power of William Carlos Williams' austere, non-metaphoric poems is partly due to a moment of seeing-as. These poems help us to see ordinary things in a new light, *as* being connected in sublime ways. We understand them afresh but in a twisted manner. Furthermore, we cannot get any twisted understanding without disclosure, even though there can be disclosure without twisted understanding. Disclosing a curve as having the same structure as the development of the fever of a patient does definitely not count as twisted understanding. One of the reasons for this is that there is no moment of seeing-as involved. And even though there is a moment of seeing-as involved in the disclosing of a hammer as a tool by simply using it without reflection, calling it a 'twisted understanding' seems strange. The reason is in the first place that such a way of viewing the hammer is as primordial as any understanding can get and therefore hardly twisted. Secondly, there is a moment of reflection involved in understanding something in a twisted way and that moment is absent in the case of the hammer. When seeing politicians as parrots or the objects of the workaday world as sublimely interconnected we are aware that "it ain't necessarily so".

Be that as it may, the upshot of what I have been saying about these issues is the following: no **T.S.S.** without T-correctness; no understanding of T-correctness that is not twisted understanding; and no twisted understanding without disclosure.

Given our discussion, I think it is fairly obvious that knowing the conditions of a metaphor's T-correctness must be a necessary condition for the understanding of its meaning. Further, metaphors can lead to indirect understanding in the Lakoffian sense, i.e., in the sense of showing one thing in the terms of another (Lakoff and Johnson 1980: 5). In contrast, such **T.S.S.** as stylised pictures can give us twisted understanding but not by necessity an indirect understanding because they do not necessarily show us one thing in the terms of another. Certainly the portraits of Scheler and Sartre do not show us anything in terms of anything other. Nevertheless they give us twisted understanding. Thus, we have discerned between metaphors and at least some other types of **T.S.S.**s.

As a result of my analysis in this chapter, I state the following: *I understand a given metaphor iff a) I know under what conditions the metaphor would be T-correct, and b) I know the kind of indirect understanding it would give.*

Let us call this statement **S**. I do not exclude the possibility that we also have to know the truth-conditions of certain literally interpreted sentences in order to understand a given metaphor. Sketches of metaphoric content in the form of attempted quasi-paraphrases in literal language come to my mind. If this were the case, I should have to remove the *iff*-clause. Nevertheless, obtaining conditions a) and b) remains essential for such an understanding.

Metaphors cannot be said to exist unless they can be understood; they owe their existence in part to the way they are understood. (A word that cannot be understood is obviously not a word, and the way it is understood is part of its mode of being.) So **S** is a part of my explication, even a definition of the concept of a metaphor. I add to this my conclusion from the first chapter that for M to be a metaphor, there must be at least two *necessary* conditions: a) that there is tensive background interaction between the topic and the vehicle on a level of abstraction; and b) that one object is being shown in the terms of another object. To a) and b), we must add more necessary conditions that concern contexts. Understanding metaphors can be reconstructed as the application of rules like "M counts only as T-correct *iff* conditions C2 obtain for M" or "IU counts as indirect understanding given by M *iff* conditions C2 obtain for IU". Since there is no rule for the application of rule, the context decides and shapes the application.

So what we have here is necessary condition c), that metaphoric understanding is always contextual.[17]

Now, what of the difficulties of finding an essential definition of the concept of metaphors? The answer is that **S** is not a definition, and even if **S** were true of all and only metaphors, metaphors still have all kinds of important aspects that **S** does not even mention, for instance, the aspects discussed in the last two chapters.

It is time to introduce the notion of a metaphoric structure. I stipulate that the following is a *sufficiency* condition for X having a metaphoric structure: X has a metaphoric structure if being seen or understood in the terms of something else is one of the preconditions for X's identity. Consider a visual caricature of a politician depicted as a parrot, implying that the politician mindlessly repeats what his or her masters, whoever they may be, say (call it 'a politician-cum-parrot caricature'). This drawing only counts as a caricature of this kind if and only if it is interpreted such that the parrot is understood as some-thing else, namely a certain politician. The drawing gets its identity as a politician-cum-parrot caricature owing to our projecting a meta-phoric structure onto it. If not, it could be regarded as simply a drawing of a strange creature with a parrot's body and a person's head. The draughtswoman could have seen the creature in a dream. But then the draughtswoman did not put any metaphoric structure in the drawing, and, at least from her point of view, it has no identity as a politician-cum-parrot caricature. Objects such as caricatures are, however, partly constituted by interpretation. We can thus interpret (and at the same time give an identity to) the drawing as a politician-cum-parrot caricature, even though the draughtswoman did not intend it so. The same would of course hold for a caricature, expressed in words, for instance in a satire. And the same thing holds for meta-phors, just like caricature they are partly constituted by interpretation.

It must be added that the more metaphoric structures there are and the more importance they have in our world, the higher degree of metaphoricity there is. If our acting, being and knowing have meta-phoric structures, then there is a high degree of metaphoricity in our world. Further, if a given field of human endeavour is replete by

---

[17] Contexts in their turn are parts of practices, but I am not going to elaborate upon that. Suffices it to say that my thoughts on those issues are rather Wittgensteinian.

necessity with metaphors, even though there are not any metaphoric structures in the field, then the field has a high degree of meta-phoricity. This degree cannot of course be measured, only estimated with the aid of informed judgment.

3.4 Conclusion

This chapter has aimed to demonstrate both that there is a host of alethic values and that metaphors have their own set, meaning that they have cognitive functions. Metaphors share a host of features with caricatures and other **T.S.S.**s, among others some cognitive features. Metaphors disclose or show rather than tell. Furthermore, they give both indirect and twisted understanding. Most importantly, metaphors obtain certain conditions of correctness (T-correctness), the knowing of which enables us to understand them. Lastly, I have introduced my definition of a metaphoric structure, a notion of great importance for my project. The same holds for the notion of metaphoricity.

If the reader had any lingering doubts about metaphors as being more than masks, I hope my alethic theory has helped in assuaging these doubts.

I.4. Metaphorism, Iconodulism, and Ana-logic
Transcendental Metaphors and Analogical Reasoning

There are two interrelated themes in this chapter *and* the next. The first is the question of whether there is an *ana-logic*, i.e., a special way of reasoning with the aid of metaphors, similes, comparisons, and analogies. The second is the question of metaphorism and iconodulism, i.e., the twin ideas that metaphors rule over the human realm, including its language. More precisely, I discuss the contention(s) that our thinking, knowledge, and lives are soaked with metaphors and/or that metaphoric expressions are the primordial linguistic expressions, while literal expressions are derivates. In my terminology, the question is whether or not language, (human) reality, and knowledge have metaphoric structures. If all of them have such structures, then there is a very high degree of metaphoricity in our world.

There are two kinds of iconodulism, which are more or less compatible: a) the view that metaphors are primordial to literal language, and b) the view that language in its entirety is metaphoric and that there is no such thing as literal language. Metaphorism has two basic aspects: a) an *ontological* one that holds that the world, or at least the human world, is essentially metaphoric, it has a metaphoric structure, and b) an *epistemological* one that asserts that metaphors, perhaps having a transcendental status, constitute our cognition, providing it with a metaphoric structure. We have already discovered that Ricœur was metaphorist of sorts.

A comprehensive metaphorist thinks that there is a high degree of metaphoricity in our world. I shall examine the comprehensive, extreme (even transcendental) metaphorism and iconodulism of Friedrich Nietzsche and the somewhat less extreme metaphorism and iconodulism of Hans Blumenberg, Jacques Derrida, and Mary Hesse. We shall see that Hesse has contributed to what I have called 'ana-logic'.

4.1 Transcendental Metaphors

Transcendental metaphorism is the belief that metaphors constitute our experience or the world of meaning, or both, in similar fashion as Kantian forms or even in the way Husserlian transcendental ego does. Can one be a comprehensive metaphorist without being a transcendental metaphorist? Yes, I believe so. You can think, for example, that it is an empirical fact that metaphors permeate the world of meaning and thus be a metaphorist without thinking in transcendental terms. You could be a transcendental metaphorist without being a comprehensive one if you believe both that metaphors only constitute the basic structures of the world of meaning in a transcendental fashion and that the aspects of this world that escape these basic structures are not so important. But it helps to be a comprehensive metaphorist if you are a transcendental one.

Friedrich Nietzsche was a transcendental metaphorist, at least when he wrote his famous article on metaphors, "Von Wahrheit und Lüge in Aussermoralischen Sinn" ("On Truth and Lying in an Extra-Moral Sense").[1] In this article, he obviously subscribed to the a) and b) of metaphorism and for that matter the a) and b) of iconodulism. According to him, our concepts have their roots in metaphors; in the last analysis, they are of a metaphoric nature (translated into my vocabulary, they have a metaphoric structure). But how can this be? Nietzsche's answer is that if we analyse the creation of concepts, we shall discover their metaphoric nature. 1) The first step of this creation is that impulses in our nervous system become transformed into images in our brains. 2) The images are then transformed into sounds, that is, words. 3) The words, which originally had a close contact with images and were more or less metaphoric, are transformed into concepts. Nietzsche likens the transformations to the jumping from one sphere to another while he hints at his own description of being necessarily metaphoric. This process can only be described in a metaphoric fashion, as indeed any description of a process.

---

[1] When talking about Nietzsche's ideas, I am simply referring to this article, which was written in his early period when he had a strongly aesthetic view of the world. In his second period, he renounced this aesthetic view and heralded science and philosophy as the ultimate achievements of the human spirit. I doubt that he was a metaphorist during that period. However, he returned to an aesthetic view in his third and last period. For the problem of determining the different periods in Nietzsche's thinking, see Carlsson (2005): 27-32.

A word becomes a concept when it no longer expresses the unique experience that created its meaning. In order to create concepts we must treat things that are actually different as being one of a kind. No two leaves are exactly the same; nevertheless we subsume all leaves under the abstract concept of a leaf. A concept is a visual sign or a metaphor, which tries to purge itself of its own images. It is like a coin with its images worn-down; it has lost much: a coin without images depreciates. And a concept does not have any value to speak of; it is a metaphor that has lost its sensual power. But even in a faded concept there always remains a metaphoric residue.

Both metaphors and concepts reinterpret reality, but the former does so explicitly while the latter hides its reinterpretation. Nobody believes that the metaphor MAN IS WOLF is literally true; the metaphor does not hide its reinterpretation of Man as being somehow wolfish. Since there is no such thing as a non-interpreted reality, metaphors are closer to truth (if there is such a thing) than concepts. Whereas a metaphor is dynamic and fluid, a movable feast, a concept is rigid and immobile, an immured vapidity. Concepts are frozen metaphors that try to freeze and control reality. Metaphors, on the other hand, strive to undermine the stiffness and rigidity of concepts. If reality has any substance, it is Heraclitian, ever-changing. Since metaphors continually change and open ever-new perspectives, they are in some sense better cognitive tools than concepts because they share structural similarities with this world in which *panta rhei*.

Dutch philosopher Jos de Mul maintains that Nietzsche implicitly gives the metaphor a sort of transcendental status. By virtue of a metaphoric instinct, human beings create a world full of meaning. The metaphor is the mother of metaphysics. Metaphors mould our experience and provide the conditions for its possibility. It is really not clear in de Mul's texts whether the transcendental moment in question is of a Kantian kind, even though he talks about Nietzsche's metaphorism as Kantianism without a transcendental subject".[2] In the Kantian way of thinking, the transcendental dimension is constant, eternally unchanging, and in Nietzsche's view, metaphors continuously change and recreate reality all the time. At the same time, it is

---

[2] As de Mul acknowledges, this expression originates in Ricœur's works, but the French philosopher was not talking about Nietzsche (De Mul 1999: 54).

misleading to say that metaphors form experience; instead, experience and metaphors are interwoven.[3] Our inner images, our metaphors, are without given origins, neither a product of any transcendental ego nor copies of anything given, but rather copies of other copies without originals, in other words *simulacra* (De Mul 1984: 273-284). The metaphors are mirrors that mirror each other. And this has consequences for our conception of truth. Nietzsche famously said:

> "Was ist also Wahrheit? Ein bewegliches Heer von Metaphern, Metonymien, Anthropomorphismen, kurz eine Summe von menschlichen Relationen, die, poetisch und rhetorisch gesteigert, übertragen, geschmückt wurden und die nach langem Gebrauch einem Volke fest, kanonisch und verbindlich dünken..." (Nietzsche 1966: 314)

> (What is truth then? A moving army of metaphors, metonyms, anthropomorphicisms, in brief, the sum of human relations which, in a poetic or rhetorical manner, are elevated, transferred, and romanticized, and which appear to a people, after long usage, as canonic and binding...")[4]

This quotation displays Nietzsche's dazzling and provocative style, which makes criticising him a difficult task. Does he really mean what he says? Well, not meaning what he says is in keeping with what he is saying! If he is true to what he says, then we must take the bulk of what he says as being metaphoric. He is also telling us that what we ordinarily call 'truth' is rather some kind of fiction, though frequently a useful one, a tool in our struggle for survival. But let us assume that he means what he says *verbatim*. In that case, it would be tempting to say that he is simply incoherent because he talks as though he knows the purported unknowable reality or non-reality. J. P. Stern points out that by calling truth 'an army of metaphors', Nietzsche is implying that there is a non-metaphoric world. Stern argues that his reflection, which aims to transcend the distinctions between truth and falsity, actually presupposes this distinction (Stern 1978: 74). In Nietzsche's defence it should be said that he does say that even if the opposition between the particular and universal is anthropomorphic, we cannot exclude the possibility of its coming from the very fabric of reality.

---

[3] In an email to me, dated 28th of April 2008, professor Sigríður Þorgeirsdóttir pointed out that it is more fruitful to liken the purported Nietzschean transcendental function of metaphors to the phenomenologists' conceptions of the transcendental, which is woven into the empirical and not hovering above it. For an introduction to Husserl's concept of the transcendental, see Kockelmans 1967: 183-193.
[4] Quoted after de Mul 1999: 48, seemingly translated by him.

By implication, even if we humans are conned by concepts into thinking that they mirror reality and even if it is not given unto us to know reality, there might nevertheless be an objective, *metaphoric* Ding-an-sich.

David Cooper criticises Nietzsche in a similar fashion as Stern but focuses on his metaphorist view of language. Cooper says that this view is not coherent. If it were the case that humans have forgotten that their language was once metaphoric, then there must have been a time when they were aware of its metaphoric nature. But then they must have been able to discriminate between the metaphoric and the literal and would have not, therefore, spoken only metaphorically (Cooper 1986: 262). I do not find this criticism very convincing. We cannot exclude the possibility that a swift Gestalt switch had occurred at which point people all of a sudden stopped speaking solely metaphorically while at the same time starting to discriminate between literal and metaphoric meaning, forgetting in the process that they had ever spoken in this primordial metaphoric way.

So Nietzsche's epistemological and linguistic, even ontological, metaphorism is more plausible (or less implausible) than Stern and Cooper think. But being plausible is not the same as being true. The basic problem with Nietzsche's ideas is that he implicitly shares the distrust of metaphors with iconoclasts and other non-cognitivists. Because truth is metaphoric, then there is really not any such thing as truth, at least not any non-perspectival truth.[5] But, as we have seen, metaphors can have a cognitive function in a pretty straightforward, non-perspectival way. Further, he wrongly thinks that metaphors are expressions of mental images; compare my earlier criticism of that view, ironically using a metaphor involving his own not so visual theories as an example. This view of his shows that he was a mental philosopher, believing that language and concepts are built upon a foundation of mental images.

Nietzsche is not the sole thinker to give metaphors a sort of transcendental status. The American pragmatist Stephen Pepper gave metaphors something akin to a transcendental value in connection

---

[5] As is well-known, Nietzsche has often been called 'perspectivist', i.e., a thinker who believes that there is no such thing as universal truth, only different perspectives on the world, each true in its own way. For instance, Carlsson 2005: 28.

with philosophical thinking. Philosophy has its basis in *root metaphors* or basic analogies. These metaphors in turn form the basis of *world hypotheses* (Pepper 1942: 96). These hypotheses are based on common-sense approaches. A thinker has some common-sense domain as a starting point, and he tries to understand other domains with reference to the first one (Pepper 1942: 91). Thus the metaphor, THE WORLD IS A MACHINE, has its roots in commonsensical ideas about machines. There are but four possible world hypotheses: a) *formism*, "the world is formed by a craftsman" (Platonism is an example, things are formed on basis of the ideas as though they were the plans of a craftsman); b) *Mechanism* ("the world is a machine": Naturalism is obviously of this kind); c) *Contextualism* ("all phenolmena and events are unique and must be understood in the light of a given context": Pragmatism is contextualism); a) *Organicism* ("everything is grows and dies like plants": Objective idealism exemplifies organicism) (Pepper 1942: 141).

This idea has been quite influential, and we shall later look at how it inspires Hayden White. He is not the only theorist who has looked to Pepper; American philosopher Earle MacCormac, who discusses '*basic* metaphors', wants to extend Pepper's theory and use it to gain new insights into science, theology, and so on (MacCormac 1985: 47-48). This project might turn out to be useful. All the same, Pepper uses the expression 'metaphor' somewhat nebulously. He does not discriminate between metaphor and analogy and, in fact, seems to treat the root metaphors as fictions. Just like Nietzsche, he might be committing what I call 'the *fictional fallacy*,' automatically assuming that metaphors belong to a realm of fiction and pure fantasy. But we have already discovered that they do not have to be of a fictional kind.

Another variation on the metaphor-is-transcendental theme was played by German philosopher Hans Blumenberg. He called his thinking *metaphorology* (Blumenberg 1996). A core concept of metaphorology is '*absolute* metaphors'. A metaphor is absolute if and only if it cannot be dissolved in concepts, and it must also have a content that gives direction for modes of relating to the world. Such a metaphor structures the world and represents the totality of reality, which cannot be experienced and of which we cannot ever get a full view. In addition, an absolute metaphor regulates thinking in a given epoch. TRUTH IS LIGHT is an example of an absolute metaphor. I want to point out that we use this (dead?) metaphor without thinking in our work-a-day lives; we talk about seeing this or that in a clear manner, or this or that throws light on the issue, etc. Let us consider the machine metaphor, so dear to Pepper. It has laid the foundation for innumerable theories, among them that the universe is a gigantic clock or that the brain is a computer. Blumenberg submits the '*metaphorics of the background*', i.e., the implicit use of metaphors. The machine metaphors certainly are often implicit ones in our day and age of technological progress.

There is indeed no great difference between absolute metaphors and myths, Blumenberg says.[6] Not only are metaphors related to myths, they are also close relatives of metaphysics, for metaphysics is often metaphorics, understood in a literal fashion. Even though we cannot grasp the world as a totality by means of theoretical propositions, we can try to find images that can represent the totality of the world. We are talking about an intuitive, image-oriented way of thinking, which becomes useful when logic falls short. Such metaphoric thinking cannot find true-blue truths; the truth of metaphors is a truth in the making. But this does not diminish the value of metaphoric thinking because our thought is not only regulated by language: images have an even stronger hold on our thinking.

Many of our abstract concepts have roots in metaphors. This feature we can see in the German expression *Wahrscheinlichkeit* (probability, 'semblance of truth'). It was originally a metaphor; people thought that probability was like a more or less illusory image of truth. But by and by this metaphor became an abstract concept.

Blumenberg also sees metaphors in a historical perspective; metaphorology is also part of the history of concepts (*Begriffsgeschichte*). As an example of his historical approach, we can mention his analysis

---

[6] It is worthwhile to compare Blumenberg's intimation that absolute metaphors are myths of a kind with Ricœur's contention (to be discussed later) that there are strong affinities between myths and metaphors. The absolute metaphors also have a similar function as Heidegger's disclosure. The affinities between Blumenberg's absolute metaphors and Pepper's root metaphors, on the one hand, and Kuhn's paradigms and Foucault's epistemes, on the other, ought to be clear. Kuhn and Foucault share with Blumenberg the conviction that concepts and patterns of thought can only be understood historically (Foucault 1970 and Kuhn 1970). For all we know, Kuhn and Foucault might have been inspired by Blumenberg and Pepper.

of the absolute metaphor of the 'naked truth'. That metaphor originally had a real political significance. Rebels believed aristocrats and clergymen were hiding their spiritual emptiness and lies behind colourful clothing. Stripped of these clothes, these elites' had their emptiness exposed. The role of metaphorology is both to find out where we can expect to find absolute metaphors and to try to find criteria for their identification.

An obvious weakness in Blumenberg's theory is his tendency to equate metaphors with images. Also, the strengths and weaknesses of Continental philosophy in Blumenberg's reasoning are pronounced. His work suffers from the lack of clear definitions and a love of obfuscation; nevertheless, his work also undoubtedly demonstrates both the ability to synthesise (to think holistically) and a valuable historical bent that helps us recognise that concepts ebb and flow in the course of time and thus we cannot neatly separate them from their history. And, of course, we must not forget that works of Continental philosophy often must be read as wholes, not as simple sums of arguments.

This might be the correct manner of reading Derrida's works. Some readers are, no doubt, eagerly waiting a discussion of this hotly debated Frenchman, knowing that his work on metaphors owes a huge debt to Nietzsche. In fact, Derrida is surprisingly moderate in his studies on metaphors. As the reader recalls, Nietzsche likened the concept to a coin that has lost its original picture and has become something apparently abstract, gold or silver in general. To this Derrida adds that the concept has gained something.[7] He plays with the double meaning of the French term *usure*, meaning both 'erosion' and 'usury' (Derrida 1974: 6-7). Derrida writes as though there is a dialectical relationship between concepts and metaphors whereby they supplement each other. And we cannot draw a sharp dividing line between them; metaphors can also be called 'concepts'.[8]

Metaphysics is saturated with metaphors; its core concepts are metaphoric, for instance 'theory', 'foundation', and 'concept'. For these metaphors, there are no meta-metaphors. Any attempt to expli-

---

[7] He said quite correctly that Ricœur has misunderstood him and has missed that he thinks that the concept also gains in its development from a pure metaphor (Derrida 1978: 1-44 and Ricœur 1977: 285).

[8] For discussion of the relationship between metaphors and concepts in Derrida, see Lawlor 1992: 11-27.

cate them leads to an infinite regress because they can only be explicated by other metaphors (Derrida 1974: 23). Further, the metaphor is in its turn metaphysical by nature: "... (a) metaphor remains in its essential features a classical element of philosophy, a metaphysical concept" (Derrida 1974: 18).[9] Regional discourses or individual sciences, for instance, provide philosophy with metaphors; mathematics is the exception because it is beyond the sensible and only the sensible can be metaphoric (Derrida 1974: 26). It seems that Derrida believed that any possible metaphor must contain in them a moment of sensible images.

However imbued our metaphysical tradition is with more or less illegitimate metaphors, our need to speak metaphorically about Being is not only a product of this tradition. We really have no possibilities of talking about it directly. We have no choice but to talk about Being in a quasi-metaphoric way (Derrida 1978: 11-44). Here we see a similarity to both Ricœur's contention that we must use metaphors when speaking about things of which we only have an indirect knowledge and to Blumenberg's line of thinking.

But whatever Derrida might have thought about metaphors and metaphysics, he certainly was no believer in the first thesis of metaphorism. In his view, there cannot be any one moment that decides the essence of language or anything else for that matter. From this repudiation, it follows that there cannot be one crucial metaphoric moment that decides meaning. Further, he was a staunch anti-essentialist and cannot, therefore, have believed that language had a metaphoric essence, unless he was contradicting himself. What is more, he thought that meaning cannot be determined and this necessarily implies that it is impossible to determine it as being metaphoric.[10] So Derrida cannot be called 'a full-fledged iconodulist or metaphorist', in stark contrast to Nietzsche.[11] Unlike Derrida, Nietzsche's ideas of metaphors are definitely not dialectical: there is no such thing as a

---

[9] Derrida later said that he had only been quoting Heidegger and had never thought himself that metaphors were essentially metaphysical. But it is hard to interpret his article on the white mythology in that way (Derrida 1978: 11-44).

[10] I will make a *pons asinorum* to his sceptical view of language in a later footnote.

[11] David Novitz seems to have thought that, since Derrida denied that there is a given literal meaning, he must have thought that language is essentially metaphoric. Novitz might have overlooked the fact that "language is essentially metaphoric" does not follow from "language has no given, literal essence" (Novitz 1985: 105).

dialectical relationship between concepts and metaphors. Additionally, Derrida implies that metaphors are a source of knowledge while Nietzsche considers them as creators of illusions.

Ricœur almost certainly goes too far in making Derrida an extreme sceptic concerning the possibility of a rational, philosophical language. He maintains that Derrida ignores the potential of metaphors to express propositions because he believes that a metaphor is only question of words, not of sentences ((Ricœur 1977: 293).[12] Be that as it may, there is no transcendental metaphor in Derrida's thinking. He is really a somewhat moderate metaphorist, just like his critic Ricœur. What is really challenging in his theory of metaphors is his contention that we can only explicate metaphors with the aid of other metaphors, which is tantamount to saying that they cannot be paraphrased in a literal manner. One of the reasons for this is that our philosophical language is by necessity saturated with metaphors. Even the expression 'explication' itself is metaphoric (Derrida 1974: 54). The weakness with Derrida's arguments is that he does not show that 'explication' is really being used metaphorically. It is tempting to say that it is dead metaphor, a homonym that has no metaphoric function any more, though it has roots in an old metaphor. Ricœur criticises Derrida in a similar fashion. In fact, he says that the so-called metaphors that supposedly constitute philosophical and metaphorological concepts are dead ones and dead 'metaphors' are not metaphors at all (Ricœur 1977: 285-293). Nevertheless, Derrida might have a point. We seem to use several metaphors when we talk about metaphors, and not necessarily dead ones. I do not think we can exclude the possibility that we have no option but to use metaphors to if we want to discuss the nature of metaphors. Even the word 'metaphor' has its roots in a metaphor: *metapherein* in ancient Greek means, 'to transfer'. That metaphor certainly is dead nowadays and has hardly any metaphoric function anymore. But what about such metaphoric expressions as 'living metaphors' and 'dead metaphors'? Have they lost all their metaphoric juice? My feeling is that they have not, that they are sort of 'living dead', metaphoric zombies. And even if they had lost their metaphoric powers, a host of other metaphoric expressions we use for

---

[12] Derrida protested against this interpretation but without any real arguments (Derrida 1978: 11-44). A very difficult discussion of their debate can be found in Lawlor 1992: 11-50.

metaphors or aspects of them are very much alive. Think about all the metaphors that Black uses in his analysis of metaphors, for instance FOCUS and FRAME. It certainly is ironic that Donald Davidson, the arch-foe of iconodulism, expresses himself in a metaphoric manner when discussing metaphors: "Metaphor is the dreamwork of language…" (Davidson 1984: 245). Or what about Max Müller's metaphoric contention that metaphors are the sickness of language? (According to Beer 1996: 159). No wonder that Paul de Man came to the conclusion that even those philosophers who are staunch foes of metaphors are bound to use metaphors when showing the poverty of metaphors (De Man 1979: 11-28). Nevertheless, Ricœur has an interesting proposal concerning how we can get out of this apparent *aporia.* He says that the philosophical discourse can liberate itself from a metaphoric literal discourse and at the same time utilise the metaphoric on the premises of rationality. Such a discourse can analyse metaphors without getting into an infinite metaphoric regress (Ricœur 1977: 293). This must mean that the metaphors of philosophy must be explicable with concepts that are not entirely metaphoric.

A problem remains, nonetheless. Ricœur does not really argue in favour of this contention, however attractive it seems. Let us see whether Earle MacCormac fares any better. He says that every view of metaphors is bound to be rooted in *basic metaphors,* for instance, METAPHORS ARE ANALOGIES. This is a kind of metaphor upon which several scholars base their research (compare Pepper's root metaphors). Despite of this, we can evade the regress. In the first place, MacCormac writes, we should regard our statements about metaphors as statements on a meta-level while allocating concrete metaphors to the object-level. This approach means that we can still discern between literal and metaphoric use of language on the object-level, even if our statements on the meta-level are permeated with metaphors. We can then say meaningful things about object-level metaphors without landing into the maelstrom of infinite regress. But MacCormac believes this distinction falls short because it does not explain the status of the metaphors on the meta-level. If our understanding is intuitive and if that is sufficient, then it might be the case that we only need intuitions in order to understand metaphors in general. But then both the meta-level itself and research on it are superfluous. The solution is that research on metaphors is not only a matter of logical analysis but also a matter of looking into the empirical side of metaphors. The empirical part of the research programme escapes the regress (MacCormac 1985: 19).

The weakness of MacCormac's analysis is that he does not put forth any real arguments in favour of his contention that a theory of metaphors requires a basis in basic metaphors. Are we unavoidably bound to interpret "metaphors are analogies" metaphorically in order to do metaphoric research? But what if metaphors are simply analogies in some prosaic, straightforward manner? MacCormac unfortunately does not discuss this possibility.

The lesson learned in this subchapter is that it is hard to see why we should believe in comprehensive or transcendental metaphorism, or both. One reason is that we have seen the weaknesses of the more or less transcendental speculations of Nietzsche, Pepper, and Blumenberg. More importantly, it is difficult to find knockdown arguments in favour of the idea that experiences are constituted by metaphors. It seems plausible that experiences contribute to the creation of metaphors and are shaped by metaphors in their turn, as Nietzsche indeed acknowledges. But then the difficulty of defending any Kantian transcendental metaphorism mounts because it is hard, or even impossible, to discriminate between the contributions of metaphors and experience. It is no less difficult to discriminate between the influence of metaphors on experience, on the one hand, and the influence of non-metaphoric theories and tacit expectations, on the other. We are really grappling with a complex web of experiences, metaphors, expectations, theories, and so on. If this holistic view of mine were true, then it would be very hard to defend any Kantian version of a transcendental metaphorism; it only makes sense if we can neatly separate the constitutive contribution of metaphors to our experiences from other factors. Of course, this does not hold for a possible Husserlian transcendental metaphorism. But all kinds of obstacles would meet anybody who would want to defend this kind of transcendental metaphorism. Suffices it to mention the fact that the Husserlian idea of a transcendental ego has been criticised severely by among others his own students (for instance Heidegger 1977). Developing a Husserlian transcendental metaphorism could be a strenuous task.

4.2 The Iconodulism of Mary Hesse

Like Nietzsche (and apparently in contrast to Derrida), British Wittgensteininan Mary Hesse is a follower of the iconodulist theory of meaning. She defends the basic thesis of iconodulism and calls it 'the thesis of the primacy of metaphors' (thesis **M**): "Metaphor is a fundamental form of language and prior (historically and logically) to the literal" (Hesse 1993: 54). She uses the family-resemblance analysis of Wittgenstein as means for justifying **M**. According to this analysis, linguistic expressions have no essential meaning; they are only linked to each other by diverse relations of resemblance and difference. This web of relations of meaning can be called 'a network'. Therefore, Hesse propounds her 'network theory of meaning'. Expressions have no given meaning, for meaning consists in the use of an expression in a way that differs slightly from earlier employments and thus all meaning is displacement. We thus never descend into the same river of meaning twice. This process means that any new use of an expression is displaced or shifted in relation to earlier employments.[13] The implication is that all shifts of meaning resemble metaphoric displacements of meaning and that this kind of change is happening all the time, albeit on a tiny scale. But I do not find this argument convincing. First, even though such shifts of meaning were to happen all the time, this purported fact does not vindicate thesis **M**. Remember that everything in the universe resembles anything else in some respect; these shifts might resemble metaphoric shifts without really being metaphoric. Further, do they not also resemble metonymic displacements? The creation of metonyms consists precisely in displacements. 'Ibsen' displaces 'Ibsen's works' in the sentence "have you read Ibsen?", 'Ibsen' being understood as a metonym for his works. It is possible that language is basically metonymic, not meta-

---

[13] There are striking resemblances between this view of language and the structuralist and post-structuralist view, must notably Derrida's. He thought that language was a network of meaning that was in principle infinite. The meaning of every single word is dependent upon the meaning of every other word in this vast network, a change in the meaning of any single word meant that the meaning of each other word changed, however slightly. Here his idea of différance comes into the picture. The latin expression 'differere' means both 'difference' and 'to postpone'. Any attempt at grasping the true meaning of a word is an attempt to understand the difference between its meaning and the meaning of all the other words in the network. But since their number is infinite, a full grasp of the difference is always postponed, always eludes our grasp (Derrida 1991a 59-79 and 80-111).

phoric. Thirdly, I do not understand why the shifts of meaning need to be figurative ones. Let us assume that I use the expression 'child' today slightly differently than yesterday. This usage does not have to mean anything but that the extension of 'child' as I use the word today has changed from yesterday's use. We cannot exclude the possibility that most shifts of meaning are of this kind. Fourthly, I do not see why we must assume that such shifts of meaning happen all the time. To be sure, it is an empirical fact that languages change, but maybe the change tends to be sudden and radical. In fact, Hesse does not provide us with any empirical evidence for her theory about the constant shift of meaning. Finally, her theory is certainly not logically true. We can without any problem envisage a language with a vocabulary that never changes.

Hesse thinks that big chunks of Black's theory of interaction suit her theory of networks quite well. Nevertheless, she is critical of some of Black's claims. In Hesse's view, he makes two main mistakes. In the first place, he retains the division between literal and figurative meaning; secondly, he shies away from justifying a special metaphoric meaning by invoking resemblances because he thinks that doing so would make easy the paraphrasing of metaphoric meaning through series of analogies, and the peculiar metaphoric meaning would then evaporate. However, according to the theory of networks, resemblances and differences are irreducible primary relations, which are logically primordial to predicates. It is certainly not only relations of resemblance and difference that form the network. The network also contains synonymy, contrasts, structural analogies, paraphrases, metonyms, synecdoches, ostentive definitions, etc. (Hesse 1988b: 324). The relations of resemblance and difference are, however, of the greatest importance, and they show themselves, that is, they cannot be expressed in words. The reason for this ineffability is that they are the preconditions for linguistic meaning and, therefore, preconditions for propositions.

This analysis is very engaging, but I have certain qualms about it. It seems to me more convincing to say that language and the relations of resemblance and difference are mutually dependent. Without the relations, there is no language, and without language, no resemblance and difference. It is hard to see how you can know that there is such a thing as resemblance and difference if they cannot be recorded by some symbolising device, language or some functional equivalent. Just postulating the existence of differences and resemblances *an-sich* is not very helpful. To ask what comes first, on the one hand, language and other symbolising systems, and, on the other, the relations, is like asking, "What came first, the chicken or the egg?"

What place does Hesse allot what we usually call the 'literal use of language'? The answer is that the literal is a borderline case that suits scientific and workaday language well. When we use language scientifically or in an everyday manner, we objectify as it were the world and linguistic meaning. We simply assume that the expressions we use have permanent meaning in order to facilitate our ability to predict either events in ordinary lives or scientific experiences (Hesse 1988a: 1-16).

According to Hesse, science is suffused with metaphors; theoretical explanations are metaphoric re-descriptions of the domain of explananda (Hesse 1966: 157-159). I am not going into the details of her argument but only concentrate on one aspect, her contention that real argumentation is more like analogical logic than propositional logic. The latter is based on clear symbolisation and a finite enumeration of premises, which makes the deduction clear and simple. But in real arguments we modify and extend the meaning of concepts all the time with the aid of parallels, models, and metaphors. The rational steps from premise to conclusion are as rule non-demonstrative; the steps are taken with the aid of inductive, hypothetic, and analogical reasoning. The reason is that the bulk of our concepts, not least the scientific ones, are family concepts. They do not fit deductive reasoning well, owing to their tendency to change meaning in the light of evidence, perceptual prejudices, and criteria for good theories (Hesse 1988b: 317-340).

Now, mathematics is indispensable to natural and even social science. But the creation and definition of mathematical structures take place within the confinements of pure mathematics. Using them to describe nature can only be performed analogically because there can only be analogies between nature and mathematical structures. Analogy thus governs our attempts at understanding nature.

This argument is compelling and inspiring. Indeed, I think there might be an analogical moment in formal logic. For instance, the material implication (*iff*) in logic can be viewed as an analogy to such ordinary language expressions as 'if and only if'. The material implication 'feeds off' these ordinary language expressions. Or, it is born of them and can only be understood in the light of them. If this supposition is correct, then other basic categories of formal logic are also analogical by nature, being only meaningful if they are regarded as analogous to certain ordinary-language expressions. But let the reader be advised that this is only a contribution to possibilology, not a new theory about the nature of logic.

Just like Derrida, Mary Hesse maintains that we can only paraphrase a metaphoric expression with another metaphoric expression; attempts to paraphrase metaphors lead to an infinite regress. This statement is tantamount to saying that metaphors cannot be paraphrased. Further, it has the implication that there is no such thing as an escape from the metaphoric horizon; metaphors rule the world of meaning and cognition, i.e., our human world. If Hesse is right, then her argument could be an opening for a transcendental view of metaphors, or at least a very radical metaphorism and iconodulism. But let us look at her argumentation. If one tries to paraphrase a metaphoric expression like 'a sharp wind' with 'a wind that cuts like a knife', then 'wind' can only be understood in a metaphoric fashion. If we try to paraphrase 'a loving God' with 'a God who loves like a father', then we still use 'father' and 'loves' in a metaphoric way. But Hesse does not really explain why this leads to infinite regress. Is there no chance to translate 'knife', 'love', and 'father' into literal idiom? Nevertheless, Hesse might be right even if her argumentation could be better. Let us see why she thinks that metaphors become impoverished in paraphrase. In the English version of the Bible, it is written of Jesus' resurrection that he "...ascended into heaven". Hesse asks us to think about a pedantic paraphrasing in modern psychological fashion: "and after 40 days the disciples' vivid sensations of the presence of the dead Christ were eclipsed, leaving his words and works as an inspiration". She points out that this paraphrasing is not theoretically neutral. It implies a materialistic, positivistic ontology that is no more theoretically neutral than the ontology of the Bible (Hesse 1988a: 4).

As I have hinted at, I do not think that thesis **M** is true; I think that what I call 'thesis **N**' is closer to truth. **N** is the thesis that there is no clear-cut separation between literal language and figurative language. The concept of literal meaning is just as problematic as the one of figurative meaning. We can garner some support for **N** in the works of American psychologist Ray Gibbs. He points out that most philosophers of language simply presuppose without argument that there is such a thing as literal meaning, that it can be described and analysed in a simple manner, and that it is the foundation of meaning. But a closer look shows that there is no consensus for the understanding of literal meaning. Sometimes people use 'literal' as the antithesis of 'figurative', sometimes meaning 'prosaic, oriented towards facts' or 'serious use of language'. Despite this, most theorists think it is simple to find out what the literal meaning of a word is. But this is not as easy as it seems. Many words have a vague, diffuse meaning. New and unexpected uses of words also create problems. What if someone all of sudden creates the verb 'to pizza', meaning, 'to eat pizza'? How do we determine the literal meaning of the word? Surely not by consulting a dictionary or studying the ordinary way the word is used (Gibbs 1994: 24-79). The kinship between Gibbs' analysis and Kittay's analysis is readily apparent: both forcefully and convincingly argue against any clear-cut separation between the literal and the non-literal.

To Gibbs' theorising I want to add that there was a moment when every word was new and there were no accepted ways of using it and no entries for them in whatever dictionaries people possessed. By implication, there have been moments in the history of every word when its literal meaning was not fully determinable. The meanings of every word (at least verbs and nouns, hardly connectives and suchlike) can, for all we know, have been metaphoric at the moment of its birth. This would mean that words are at this moment vehicles for showing one concept in the light of another concept.

At first glance it seems obvious that if there is such a thing as non-literal language, then there must be literal language, which is primordial, just like the expression 'imperfect' would be meaningless without the expression 'perfect'. Likewise, the expression 'non-literal meaning' would be meaningless without the expression 'literal meaning'. From this it presumably follows that iconodulism of the variety b) must be wrong; there must be such a thing as literal meaning. But David Cooper points out quite correctly that this is just like saying that because there is something that is natural, then there must be something that is supernatural (Cooper 1986: 264).

Now, given thesis **N** and Gibbs' analysis (which is in accordance with **N**), then we cannot determine the truth-value of the iconodulist view that metaphors are primordial to literal language. It is impossible to draw a sharp line between literal and non-literal ways of using language and probably impossible to find out which is the primordial one and this means that Derrida was on the right track. Perhaps there is a necessary dialectic between the two so that they cannot exist without each other and so that the line between them is blurred, and, at the same time, there must be tension between them.

Further, if we cannot show that metaphoric language is primordial or even 'the only game in town', then it weakens our possibility of vindicating comprehensive (ontological) or transcendental (epistemological) metaphorism, or both. If **M** had been true, then it would have given support to these kinds of metaphorism, given that language shapes cognition by necessity and given some epistemic view of ontology. But **M** is not true. Of course, we do not have to believe that language shapes our cognition and world-view, and we can even claim that metaphors are not essentially linguistic. So maybe we can vindicate comprehensive or transcendental metaphorisms, or both, without the aid of **M**. But then the onus is on the purported followers of this view. There is any number of interesting ideas about the nature of cognition and the fabric of the world that do not overlap with comprehensive or transcendental metaphorism. As it stands, metaphorism, whether comprehensive or transcendental, is an inspiring but far too speculative hypothesis (compare my criticism of Nietzsche). So why believe in comprehensive or transcendental metaphorism? That is the task of those who adhere to this view.

4.3 Conclusion

My Solomonic judgement to the dispute between the iconodulists and the iconoclasts is that their debate is much ado about not very much. Perhaps we should be 'mysterians' about language, that is, sceptics about our possibility of understanding the nature of language. Maybe we are too close to language to understand its nature. Maybe 'meaning' is a primitive concept, not further analysable. The lack of agreement among philosophers of meaning could point in that direction.

I shall address again the issue of analogical reasoning, metaphorism, and iconodulism in the next chapter. For the time being it suffices to say that I find Hesse's conception of analogical reasoning quite compelling while rejecting her thesis M about metaphoric language being the primordial form of language. Instead, I introduced my thesis N about there not being any clear-cut separation between literal and non-literal ways of using language. I derived some inspiration from Ray Gibbs when formulating this thesis.

MacCormac's, Blumenberg's, and Pepper's ideas are invigorating and challenging but I have my qualms about transcendental metaphorism. Both Nietzsche and Derrida can, of course, provide us with tremendous inspiration, as long as we understand that they were provocateurs, thinkers who wanted to rouse us from our dogmatic slumbers. Be that as it may, there is undoubtly a fair degree of metaphoricity in our world.

I.5. Generative Metaphorics
The Cognitive Semantics of the Lakoff School

At the end of last chapter, I discussed briefly the theories of American psychologist Raymond Gibbs. He is a follower of the so-called cognitive semantics of George Lakoff. According to this theory, metaphors are conceptual, not linguistic, entities. They permeate our knowledge and our world, including the world of linguistic meaning. In my terminology, the cognitive semanticists believe that metaphoric structures abound and consequently, there is a high degree of meta-phoricity in our world. They are thus metaphorists, albeit somewhat more moderate than Nietzsche. I have already endorsed what we can take as their definition of metaphor: "The essence of metaphor is understanding and experiencing one kind of thing in terms of another" (Lakoff and Johnson 1980: 5). Actually, Lakoff and his team maintain that they are not really defining the concept of metaphor; what I refer to as 'their definition' is what they call 'an empirical statement', form-ing an essential part of an empirical theory. Experience, they say, shows that we understand different linguistic expressions as a result of a single conceptual metaphor. On the basis of the conceptual metaphor LIFE IS A DAY, we understand poetic metaphors like "Do not go gently into that good night" and "But when our brief light goes out there is one perpetual night to be slept through". If these metaphors were nothing but linguistic expressions, we should not be able to see any connections between these two linguistic expressions. But we certainly do (Lakoff and Turner 1989: 137). Metaphors can manifest themselves both in a linguistic and non-linguistic way. A caricature can show an envious person having a green face; the same metaphor can be expressed linguistically in the sentence, "he is green with envy". Further, we can express metaphors in rituals. An example of a ritual-metaphor is the custom in certain countries of carrying a newborn baby to the highest floor of the house, expressing the wish that the child will do well (metaphorically move upwards) in life (Lakoff 1993: 240-241). This means that metaphors cannot be defined in a syntactic way. Thus a simile can express a metaphor. Metaphors have nothing to do with figurative meaning; literally intended sentences can be metaphoric as long as the sentence shows us one concept in the light of another. I can mean literally that "he won the debate", but at the same time say something metaphorically because I show a debate in the light of a concept that is derived from the conceptual domains of war or sport.

5.1 A Generative Theory of Metaphors

I think that this theory could be called 'the generative theory of metaphor'. Different linguistic expressions, pictures, rituals, and so on can be called 'parts of the surface structure', which are generated by the conceptual metaphors that belong to the deep structure. The conceptual metaphors are often expressed in poetry, for poetic metaphors develop and extend our work-a-day metaphors in a creative manner. "Death is a dream" is a poetic development of the conventional metaphor DEATH IS SLEEP (Lakoff and Turner 1989: 71).

One of the most central ideas of the Lakoffian School is the idea that metaphors have their basis in human experience. Again and again we observe sick people being able to rise again after a prolonged period of lying down, and this can be a sign that they are getting well. (Most of us have, of course, had the experience of being too sick to sit or stand in an upright position.) Because of this common observation, we have created a host of metaphors that equate 'up' with 'good' and 'down' with 'bad' (Lakoff and Johnson 1980: 15). This statement brings us to the three different kinds of conceptual metaphors and their relations to the world of experience. In the first place, we have the so-called *ontological* metaphors. They have their basis in our dealings with physical objects. Thanks to them, we experience non-physical objects (actions, ideas, and feelings) as physical objects of sorts and thus they are made easier to conceptualise. Secondly, the Lakoffians talk about the metaphors of *orientations* that are grounded in our spatial orientation, i.e., the fact that we differentiate between up and down, forwards and backwards, centre and periphery, surface and depth, and so on. This spatial orientation is intimately connected to the human body, as in the 'up' and 'down' metaphors. The third kind of conceptual metaphors is *structural*. They structure concepts in the terms of other concepts (Lakoff and Johnson 1980: 14-21 and 25-32). The Lakoffians call the conceptual field to be understood 'the *target* domain', the field in which the target domain is understood is called '*source* domain'. In the metaphor LIFE IS A JOURNEY, life is the target domain, journey the source domain. We understand our lives in the terms of journeys.

Metaphors are the products of a semantic process called *mapping*, i.e., sets of conceptual correspondences (Lakoff 1993: 207). When we map, we activate structures in the *image-schema* of the source domain, an image-schema being a recurrent pattern in our mundane, corporeal experiences. They are formable and flexible patterns in our sensori-motoric processes. We bring them to our experience in the shape of expectation of order at the same time as they can be modified in light of new experiences. Examples of image-schemas can be 'balance', 'object', 'figure-background' or 'source-path-goal'. We are, in all pro-bability, genetically programmed to have these image-structures; it seems plausible that we must be able to objectify segments of the flux of experience (sense objects), to keep our balance, and to experience figures on backgrounds in order to survive. The image-structures are internal to our bodies, which could, therefore, be the *loci* of pre-linguistic meaning.

In light of this we can return to the problem of how we activate the structures in the image structure for source domains. The structures correspond to the structures in the target domain. In other words, we apply structural aspects of one set of concepts to another set. Look at the metaphor RELATIONSHIPS ARE MEANS OF TRANSPORTA-TION. It is only in virtue of a mapping that it makes sense to use metaphoric expressions like WE HAVE DERAILED for OUR LOVE HAS SHIPWRECKED. We activate the structural analogies between derailing and the crisis of a love affair. In this connection, Lakoff proposes his *Invariance Principle*, the principle that metaphoric mapping preserves *cognitive topology* (the image-schema structure) of the source domain in a way consistent with the inherent structure of the target domain. This principle is in its turn governed by the principle of the dominance of the target domain. It is the structure of that domain that activates the structure in the source domain and limits automatically that which can be mapped (Lakoff 1993: 215-216).

Having introduced the basic terminology of the Lakoff School, I shall now discuss their brand of metaphorism. Our language and our diverse activities are soaked with metaphors. In my terminology, this means that language and our basic activities have metaphoric structures and that metaphors are co-authors of our reality. The reason for this rule of metaphors is that conceptual schemas structure language and action and these schemas are to a great extent of a metaphoric nature (Lakoff and Johnson 1980: 3). These conceptual schemas project both metaphoric and non-metaphoric conceptions onto our experience. Aided by such schemas, we project our conception of bounded objects on fogs and mountains, which are not really bounded objects at all. Sentences like "the fog is in front of the mountain" are meaningful in light of the conceptual schema that makes us see fogs and mountains as things. Notice that we are using a metaphor of orientation when saying that the fog is in front of the mountain. The source domain is our way of orientating in the world. In reality (whatever that may be), there is no such thing as in front of or behind something. This metaphor is actually relative to culture; the African Hausa tribe would have said that the fog is *behind* the mountain (Lakoff and Johnson 1980: 42). Something similar holds for a host of metaphors and conceptual schemas. All the same, there are universal conceptual schemas and metaphors, rooted in our common bodily structure.

But why do metaphors permeate our conceptual schemas? One of the most important reasons is the purported fact that metaphors can make our experiences meaningful and coherent. We can structure a great range of individual experiences with the aid of conceptual metaphors like LOVE IS A JOURNEY (Lakoff and Johnson 1980: 139). Another reason is that a host of our most important concepts are either very abstract or have unclear demarcations; it is easier for us to handle them by understanding them in light of more concrete and better defined concepts. Time is a very abstract concept, and we can understand some of its dimensions with the aid of conceptual metaphors such as TIME IS MONEY. Emotional concepts are usually difficult to define. There is no clear-cut separation between being in love with someone and being just fond of that someone. But we get a better grip of certain aspects of love by calling it metaphorically 'a journey' (Lakoff and Johnson 1980: 85 and 115). Something similar holds for concepts like those of Self and mind; they are constructed by metaphors. They are intangible phenomena and can only be understood in the light of other, more tangible phenomena. We understand Self and mind only indirectly, through the lenses of other concepts (Lakoff and

Johnson 1999: 235-289). The distant kinship with Ricœur should be obvious.

Conceptual metaphors structure the way we think and experience things, more than a little like Kant's forms. Take a look at the metaphor ARGUMENTATION IS WAR. This conceptual metaphor generates several expressions like "your arguments cannot be defended", or "she attacked the weak points in his arguments". Owing to the popularity of the metaphor, we tend to see argumentation as war and we act accordingly (Lakoff and Johnson 1980: 4-5). Conceptual metaphors not only form our language and modes of action but also our values. If we speak metaphorically about the war against inflation, we start to regard inflation as an enemy (Lakoff and Johnson 1980: 22). Conceptual metaphors are not isolated but form systems of linguistic expressions, values, and ways of acting; they are 'metaphors we live by'.

One of the most important ways conceptual metaphors structure our world-views is the way they highlight some aspects of reality while downplaying or hiding others. If we regard argumentation as war, then we tend to focus on its conflictual aspect and ignore its collaborative aspect, i.e., the fact that argumentation can be a part of cooperative search for truth (Lakoff and Johnson 1980: 10).

Despite of the great power of the metaphor, one must bear in mind that the metaphoric structuring is always only partial, never total. If we were to regard time only as money, then the expression 'time' would be synonymous with 'money'; but then we are talking about the same concept expressed in different ways, not a concept that is structured by another concept (Lakoff and Johnson 1980: 13). It is owing to the fact that a host of our concept is non-metaphoric that certain conceptual metaphors can aid our understanding of the world. Our spatial concepts are to a great extent non-metaphoric. We live for the bulk of our lives in an upright position, making it natural for us to slice the world into up and down. And because of the structure of our body, it is likewise normal for us to divide objects into those that are in front of something and those that are at the back of something. Further, our bodies are bounded and well-defined wholes. We have a tendency, therefore, to regard other phenomena, be it fog or love, to be likewise bounded. In this fashion, our body is our main source for concepts. Concepts are mainly bodily created; non-metaphoric concepts make the basis for conceptual metaphors, as we have indeed already seen (Lakoff and Johnson 1980: 56-58). The Lakoffians cannot, then, be called 'radical or comprehensive metaphorists'. But metaphorists they are: their metaphorism is semantic, epistemological, and ontological with a transcendental twist.

Lately, Lakoff and his associates have taken a *neuronal turn*, maintaining that metaphors are firmly rooted in neuronal processes. Metaphorical conceptualisation involves some of the sensorimotor processes that are activated in perceptual and motor experiences. Further, primary metaphors come into being when two brain areas are activated at the same time again and again. After some time, both paths of activation meet and form a single circuit linking both areas together. Thus, the metaphor AFFECTION IS WARMTH arose because we experienced physical warmth when hugged and affecttionate people often hug others. The brain areas for warmth and perception of affection are activated together (for instance Johnson 2007: 155-175).

That the use of metaphor is rooted in neuronal activity and is often subconscious does not make it a-rational or irrational. There is kind of *imaginative rationality*, which tends to appear in the shape of *metaphoric reasoning*. In such reasoning, deducing from conceptual metaphors is of essential import. This process is rational because it is criticisable and its conclusions can be defended with aid of arguments. It is imaginative because imagination plays an essential role when we, for instance, learn to see things in a different way because of a new metaphor. The metaphoric way of reasoning cannot be easily formalised. One basis for this resistance to formalisation is that metaphoric reasoning is not first and foremost about concluding in a logical manner from a given set of premises; it is rather about finding ways to make our experienced reality *meaningful*. (Compare the Lakoffian idea of metaphors as tools for making our experiences coherent.) Another reason is the fact that metaphoric implications are not compelling in the same way as deductive implications. Let us look at the metaphor LIFE IS BUSINESS. It implies that our fellow human beings and we are competitors or partners, that human relations are really contractual relations, and that life is a competition. In their turn, these implications can have their own implications; for instance, the implication that human relations are contractual relations can also imply that we must keep our word. But all these implications appear to follow for some but not all who believe in the metaphor. At the same time, it would not make any sense to say that none of these implications is compelling for a rational person who believes in it. Metaphoric reasoning is not an abstract process but a part of experiences that are structured, consciously or not, by the metaphors by which we reason. We can never grasp the 'lived' metaphor entirely with the aid of rules or formulas; nothing can replace the spontaneous, metaphor-based experience.

The different experiences and backgrounds of individuals and cultures create a certain individual and cultural variation in metaphoric reasoning. Nevertheless, it does not really make sense to say that such reasoning is purely subjective or relative. You cannot both believe firmly in the metaphor LIFE IS BUSINESS and at the same time reject all its implications. This holds universally and is not a matter of subjective taste.

The basic structure of metaphoric reasoning is twofold. In the first place it consists of drawing new implications from a given experiential metaphor, and, in the second, in moving from an earlier metaphor to one that changes our understanding and experience. This process is not an irrational convention because experiential metaphors are not incommensurable. We can compare such metaphors rationally because they tend to have a common implication. Our business metaphor has an implication or two in common with LIFE IS SPORT; both imply that people are competitors. I might have led my life in accordance with the business metaphor and believed in its implication that success makes one happy. But I find out that I have not become any happier despite the success. This experience gives me reason to doubt the correctness of the metaphor. At the same time, I can compare it with the sport metaphor, which has some of the same implications. But maybe I find out that the success, implied by the sports metaphor, is of a different nature than the one of the business metaphor. Through a complex process of trial and error I start to live in accordance with the sport metaphor because, say, the communal feeling of sports makes me happier than my older business-like manners. The same or related implications build bridges between the metaphors. Due to this, our change of metaphors we live by does not have to be irrational conversions. We must also remember that conceptual metaphors are not arbitrary, but are constrained by objective realities, and the same holds for the implications of the metaphors (Johnson 1983: 371-389).

I find their idea of metaphoric reasoning quite inspiring, and I think that it can be combined with the aforementioned insights of Hesse, i.e., the idea that there is a sort of analogical reasoning that plays an ineliminable role for our thinking. Both have contributed significantly to ana-logic.

5.2 Four Kinds of Criticism against Generative Metaphorics

Writing about the critical debate on the Lakoffian School would require a book of its own. So let me just focus on three different criticisms before turning to my own. First, (a) we have the internal criticism of the blending theory, which shares the basic outlook of the Lakoffians; secondly, (b) there are the attempts at empirical falsification of the Lakoffian theories by an associate of Sam Glucksberg; thirdly, (c) we have also the contention that the Lakoffian theories are not empirically testable; fourthly, (d) I raise my own criticism that these theories are *scientistic* and overly objectivistic.

a) A former collaborator of Lakoff's, Mark Turner, joined forces with French linguist Gilles Fauconnier in order develop 'the theory of *conceptual blending*' or 'the theory of *conceptual integration*'. Conceptual integration or blending is a general cognitive operation on a par with analogy, recursion, mental modelling, conceptual categorisation, and framing. It serves a variety of cognitive purposes. In blending, a structure from input mental spaces is projected onto a separate, 'blended' mental space.[1] According to blending theory, we cannot simply describe metaphors as projections from the source domain to the target domain like the Lakoffians do. We have to postulate the existence of mediating instances, more precisely, a *blended* space and a *generic* space. This blended space contains an intermingling of elements from the target and source domains. At the same time, the blend acquires emergent qualities, qualities that are found in neither the target nor the source domains but are being

---

[1] A short and accessible introduction to the blending theory can be found in Fauconnier and Turner 1998: 133-187. Their *magnum opus* is their book from 2002, *The Way We Think*.

created in the blend. The generic space connects the target and source domains by virtue of having some abstract qualities in common with these domains. Later, Fauconnier and Turner almost ceased talking about target and source domains and started to use the terms 'input 1 and 2', the blend being the 'output'. Whatever the terminology, a metaphor becomes a four-way affair instead of a two-way affair between target and source (For instance Fauconnier 1997). We are dealing with four mental spaces: two input spaces, a blended space, and a generic space. But what are mental spaces? Fauconnier and Turner answer as follows: "…small conceptual packets constructed as we think and talk, for purposes of local understanding and action" (Fauconnier and Turner 2002: 40). If you climbed Mount Rainier in 2001, then you can store your memories about the event in a mental space that includes you, Mount Rainier, the year 2001, and your climbing the mountain. The *raison d'être* of mental spaces is to juggle representations that are incompatible in the real world. This mental juggling gives rise to metaphors and counterfactual reasoning among others (Fauconnier and Turner 2002: 30). Let us take a look at a metaphor that also contains counterfactual reasoning, IF CLINTON WERE THE TITANIC, THE ICEBERG WOULD SINK. In this metaphor, there is a blended space in which Clinton is the Titanic and the scandal is the iceberg. Further, we have a generic space that has a structure taken to apply to both inputs: one entity that is involved in an activity and is motivated by some purpose encounters another entity that poses an extreme threat to that activity (being entities is one of the abstract qualities the input spaces have in common). In the generic space, the outcome of that encounter is not specified; the outcome is to be found in the blended space. In that space, Clinton overcomes the obstacle, because in this space Titanic is unsinkable. In this way, the blend gets emergent qualities, including the unsinkability of the Titanic. If we had projected the inferences from source to target, then Clinton would have lost the presidency, because the source domain, the Titanic, is sinkable. The target domain does not help either, because in that domain Clinton just barely survives. In the blend, however, Clinton triumphs overwhelmingly by defeating an extreme danger, thus showing his great political skill (Fauconnier and Turner 2000: 133-145). In Fauconnier's and Turner's view, the inadequacies of Lakoffian model reveal themselves because it cannot explain metaphors of this kind. It seems to me that they have a point, not least because their generic space performs the same or similar functions as my background interaction at the abstract level. There is nothing similar in the Lakoffian book, making its theory of metaphors somewhat too simple.

b) Let us now turn to the purported falsification of the Lakoffian theories. Ray Gibbs has made some empirical inquiries into our understanding of metaphors. Not surprisingly, he maintains that his studies corroborate Lakoff's and Johnson's theory that idioms have a systematic basis in conceptual metaphors (Gibbs 1993: 265-318). But Sam Glucksberg's associate, Matthew McClone, has a different view. According to the Lakoffian view, our intuitions concerning idioms ought to mirror directly the way their meaning is represented in our semantic memory. But such an introspective approach can be misleading. Take the expression 'spitting image'. It is tempting to understand it as having roots in our view of corporal fluids (spit). However, etymology shows something very different. 'Spitting image' is a contraction of 'spirit' and 'image' (McClone 2001: 97).[2] Furthermore, McClone says that Boaz Keysar's research points in the direction of people understanding stock expressions such as "the argument was shot down" without any use of such conceptual metaphors as ARGUMENTATION IS WAR (McClone 2001: 104). But McClone does not seem to know that the Lakoffians have never said that we must activate the conceptual metaphors directly when we use metaphors. Gibbs says in fact that we can understand the conventional meaning of idiomatic metaphoric phrases without evaluating the metaphoric knowledge that forms the necessary background of these phrases (Gibbs 1994: 19).

Be that as it may, McClone insists that his own research shows that the Lakoffians are wrong. He asked his 'guinea pigs' to interpret the sentence "our marriage is a roller-coaster ride". If the Lakoffians were right, then the guinea pigs would only be able to understand the sentence in the light of the conceptual metaphor LOVE IS A JOURNEY. But only a few did so. Instead, they associated 'roller-coaster ride' with exciting or dangerous events. (This interpretation is

---

[2] This theory is not universally accepted. The *Oxford English Dictionary* does not recognise this explanation and, among others, professor Larry Horn of the department of linguistics, Yale University, is said to think that this etymology is wrong (cf. Michael Quinion's webpage at http://www.worldwidewords.org/qa/qa-spi1.htm).

in accordance with Glucksberg's theory). To make matters worse, a Lakoffian interpretation of 'roller-coaster ride' can lead to absurdities, McClone says. Think about a sentence like "my recent trip to L.A. was a roller-coaster ride". If we interpret 'roller-coaster ride' as 'journey', then 'the trip' in the sentence is a 'journey'. But it is clear that the sentence "my recent trip was a journey" is a tautology (McClone 2001: 106). Another experiment that McClone conducted suggests, according to him, Lakoff's being wrong and Glucksberg's being right. He asked a group of people to comment on the sentence "Dr. Moreland's lecture was a three-course meal for thought". Only a handful associated this sentence with the purported conceptual metaphor IDEAS ARE FOOD. They actually focused on great quantity or great quality. When asked to create a metaphor with a similar meaning as the aforementioned one, only a few created 'food-metaphors'. Most of them made metaphors with vehicles that belonged to the same attributive category as a three-course meal (and this of course fits Glucksberg's view admirably!). They created, for instance, metaphors like DR. MORELAND'S LECTURE WAS A GOLDMINE OF INFORMATION. They thought that metaphors of this kind were more like the original metaphor than such metaphors as DR. MORELAND'S LECTURE WAS A STEAK FOR THE INTELLECT (McClone 2001: 99).

I cannot be the judge of the quality of McClone's research. But Dan Chiappe, who is definitely no Lakoffian, thinks he can. He says that McClone's selection of examples is too one-sided (Chiappe 2003: 55-61). If that is the case, then McClone might be concentrating on examples that confirm his and Glucksberg's position while ignoring others. However, I should not know. But I am sure that McClone makes some excellent points in his analytical criticism of the Lakoffians. He criticises their contention that metaphors transcend their linguistic manifestations and influence conceptual structures. Now, this Lakoffian contention is solely based on these linguistic manifestations. So how do they, for instance, know that one thinks about theories in light of concepts of buildings, because one often uses expressions, associated with buildings, when one talks about theories? Why does one use such expressions when one talks about theories? The answer is that one thinks about theories in light of concepts of buildings. This is obviously circular, McClone says, and I think he is right (McClone 2002: 95).

c) Irish-Canadian psychologist John M. Kennedy and his associates take on the Lakoffian claim that their theory is empirical. According to Kennedy and John Vervaeke, the Lakoffians do not employ good empirical strategies for research, and that they have a thin empirical basis for the theory. To make matters worse, their theory is not falsifiable. No metaphoric expression can falsify the claim that expressions like 'argumentation is war' are based on an implicit metaphor. Kennedy and Vervaeke add, "Instead, expressions that are evidence against one implicit metaphor can be taken simply as evidence for some other implicit metaphor, such as 'ARGUMENT IS A BUILDING' that can be buttressed" (Kennedy and Vervaeke 1996: 275). The existence of expressions that cannot be subordinated to an implicit metaphor, for instance, 'arguments have premises', can simply be taken as an indicator that we have some non-metaphoric concepts concerning argumentation. (Remember that the Lakoffians are not comprehensive metaphorists.) Even worse, the theory operates with an override clause, which makes it even more difficult to falsify. If an extension of an implicit metaphor fails, then the clause can explain it away. One can maintain that the target domain of the metaphor in question has features that are now and then resistant to the implicit metaphor. So if the extension of the metaphor fails, then it can be a sign of this resistance; if it succeeds, then it is a confirmation of the theory. However, Mark Johnson pointed out in an email (12 June 2002) to me that he and Lakoff have retracted the clause. So much better for them, but I have not found this retraction anywhere in their published writings.

Kennedy and Vervaeke have got more up their sleeve. They give some interesting examples about the difficulties involved in trying to determine the level of generality in the Lakoffian model. One of the examples is ARGUMENTATION IS WAR. We can say that war involves movements in space and that we can describe arguments as sequences of actions. Further, actions can take place in space and in actual fact; there are many examples in English of the description of arguments in spatial terms: "he bypassed my arguments", "he vaulted my conclusion", and so on. On the basis of this observation, one might be tempted to think that ARGUMENTATION IS WAR is derived from ARGUMENTATION IS MOVEMENT IN SPACE. Further, Kennedy and Vervaeke point out that there is a host of expressions about argumentation in the English language that is connected to the

game of bridge. Should we conclude that there is an implicit conceptual metaphor ARGUMENTATION IS BRIDGE? Does this perhaps show that both the bridge and the war metaphor are derived from
a more general metaphor, namely ARGUMENTATION IS COMPE-
TITION? The conclusion must be that determining the level of
generality is difficult, which further undercuts the testability of the
theory.

We do not only use expressions from bridge when we talk about
arguments; we also use expressions derived from cooking. Think
about such expressions as "he cooked up some arguments" or "his
ideas are half-baked". Maybe the conclusion is that processes, which
happen in a given sequence, be it the waging of war, cooking food or
argumentation, can be used to map each other. But then, Kennedy and
Vervaeke note, no process is more fundamental or more general than
the other. If they are correct, then the alleged metaphoric deep structures are nothing but *ad hoc* constructions.

Kennedy and Vervaeke think that there is a moment of arbitrariness in the Lakoffian theory. Think about the following sentences:
"He is a solid citizen", "he is dense", "Don't talk to him, he is heavy",
"he is so thick", "he is many-faceted", "he is so durable", "he is so
hard". Do these examples show that there is an underlying conceptual
metaphor like PEOPLE ARE STONES? This sounds counter-intuitive, but this is the way Lakoff and his cohorts argue when trying to
show that a host of expressions have their basis in certain conceptual
metaphors. Furthermore, Kennedy and Vervaeke maintain that we can
regard expressions like "he undermined my beliefs" as a manifestation
of either the war metaphor or the metaphor of arguments as movements in space. The problem is that we have no criteria for discriminating between those expressions that are manifestations of many
underlying conceptual metaphors and those that are manifestations of
only one such metaphor. Yet again, we see the arbitrariness of the
theory.

Kennedy and Vervaeke now try to remedy this unsatisfactory state
of affairs with the aid of a method for the testing of expressions in
order to find out whether or not the expressions are being used metaphorically. They call the method 'multiple-meaning account':

> If a term (e.g. *attack*) is synonymous with another set of terms (e.g. *assault*),
> and if the term (*attack*) is also synonymous with another set of terms (e.g.

criticize), and yet if the two sets are not themselves synonymous (e.g., *assault* is not synonymous with *criticize*), then the term attack has two independent meanings (Kennedy and Vervaeke 1996: 280).

They point out that 'attack' and 'assault' can be said to be synonymous in the expressions "we attacked the castle" and "we assaulted the castle". But when we use them in connection with arguments, we see a completely different picture. In the proposition "he attacked my arguments", 'attack' simply means, 'criticise forcefully', but 'assault' in "he assaulted my arguments" means 'criticise in an angry way'. 'Attack' in the context of argumentation is then synonymous with 'criticise'. This distinction points in the direction of 'attack' having in this context a non-military, abstract meaning.

This criticism is forceful and thought provoking. The method of multiple-meaning account should be useful for anybody working seriously with metaphors. However, Kennedy and his associates might be rather too severe with the Lakoffians. It might be the case that their theory is not testable at the moment but that does not mean that it cannot be made testable in the future. The history of science is full of examples of non-testable theories that were later made testable and even did well in those tests. The ugly duckling became a beautiful swan. Nowadays, there is great controversy in physics over the string theory, which is not really testable, but has enormous explanatory power. If it becomes testable and if tests confirm it, then physics will in all probability be able to unify quantum mechanics and the theory of relativity (for instance Hawking 1988: 168-173). In any case, the Lakoffians should be given more chances to develop their programme before it is thrown onto the dust-heap of quasi-science.[3] Maybe the neuronal turn will save it from that fate. Actually, Kennedy and Vervaeke seem to share my view (Kennedy and Vervaeke 1996: 275).

d) I think that the reason for the scientistic pretensions of the Lakoffians (and the blending theorists) is the excessive commotion surrounding cognitive science. Not too many years ago, there was great enthusiasm for behaviourism. It was supposed to be an objective, hard-nosed science, well supported by countless experiments and

---

[3] The influence on me from Imre Lakatos theory of budding scientific research programs that should be allowed to develop is obvious (Lakatos 1970: 91-196). Maybe Lakatos saves Lakoff!

observations. But where is it now? And where will cognitive science be tomorrow? On the same dust-heap as behaviourism? The Lakoffians would do their theory a world of good if they dropped their scientific pretensions. These pretensions have led to a dogmatic belief in the idea that our dealings with material bodies are the source of metaphors. But it would not surprise me the least bit if a substantial part of our primary metaphors and myths were derived from our subjective experience and our social interaction. Are our subjective experiences and our social interaction any less important for our survival than our observations of things? It is not by chance that we call the world-view of primitive people 'animistic'; they view material objects as being saturated with some kind of subjectivity. The wind is regarded as a sentient, supernatural being that decides to blow when it thinks fit. Thus in the Old Norse mythology, Kári is the god of the wind, and in some sense he is the wind itself. And like in most mythologies, the whole world is seen in analogy with society; it is created because of strife among supernatural beings and is perpetuated because of the balance of power between groups of such beings (on old Norse mythology, see Cotterell 2002: 114-131). If one wants to find out what kind of metaphors are central in human existence, then it seems a good idea to study the metaphors of 'primitive' cultures. Chances are that they are similar to the original metaphors, created by our remote ancestors. It would not surprise me at all if those hypothetical metaphors were derived not only from experiences connected to the body and moving objects but also from subjective and social experiences. Lakoff and Johnson ought to consider this. Like most cognitive scientists, the Lakoffians ignore the private-language argument;[4] on the communal interpretation of it, meaning can only exist in social space. This interpretation opens up the possibility for metaphoric meaning not only existing solely in social space but also being the product of social interaction. Certainly, Johnson stresses that meaning is intersubjective, but he apparently thinks that this is a contingent empirical fact, not something that essential belongs to the concept of meaning as Wittgenstein thought. (Johnson 2007:

---

[4] Wittgensteinian critics of cognitive science point out that it tacitly assumes a Cartesian view of the world, a separation between object and subject where the subject exists in splendid isolation from other subjects. In the light of the private-language argument, this cognitivist approach is not very fruitful. See for instance Glock 1996: 310.

147-152). He does not see that such Wittgensteinian insights undercut any attempt to situate metaphoric meaning in neuronal processes and bodily activities. The neuronal model has further problems: Metaphors possess aboutness that cannot be reduced to neuronal and bodily activities. MARRIAGE IS A ZERO-SUM GAME is *about* marriages and even zero-sum games. Purported facts about them constrain the meaning of the metaphor. But marriages and zero-sum games are not in our heads. To make matters worse, trying to locate metaphors in our neuronal processes is like trying to understand music by analysing the physical structure of the airwaves that 'carry' music.

Johnson admits that neuroscience is in the early stages of its development and that therefore many scholars have been reluctant to draw any conclusions about meaning from this nascent science. Perhaps the Lakoffians should have joined this group of cautious scholars. But then again, bold conjectures can further science.

There is no lack of bold conjectures in cognitive science, for example the theory that the mind consists of relatively isolated modules. Its followers would hardly accept the Lakoffian claim that sensorimotor modules do the job of conceptual ones. Whether Johnson is right about the theory of modularity having empirical difficulties I would not say (Johnson 2007: 156).

There is nothing particularly scientific about claiming that meta-phors are neuronal; as it stands this theory seems rather speculative. The same holds for the theory that metaphors originate in the way we observe things and bodies. I do not doubt that some very important metaphors have this origin, but I see no reason to think that sub-jectivity and social interaction cannot be the cradles for some of the metaphors we live by. I am also critical of the Lakoffian claim that our practices are the ramifications of our metaphors and not vice versa. My hunch is that there is a dialectical relationship between the two; our practices are shaped by metaphors that are in their turn shaped by them.

The Lakoffians would benefit greatly if they stopped regarding their theorising as a pure nomological science and start viewing it more as a mixture of philosophical analysis and humanistic reflections with an empirical twist. As for the analytic part, we have seen that I use their purported empirical statement about metaphors as an excellent analysis of the concept of metaphors. Further, they could learn a thing or two from Wittgenstein, not least the way he builds bridges between the body and society, on the one hand, by regarding meaning as essentially intersubjective, and, on the other, by viewing a large chunk of it as having its ultimate roots in bodily reactions (compare the analysis of pain mentioned in the introduction).

I think, moreover, that learning some bridge-building techniques from Wittgenstein would have done Paul Ricœur a world of good. Ricœur focused too much on culture and society in his analysis of metaphors, narratives, and other symbolic structures. The body is almost absent. But his focus on the importance of culturally created metaphors could be a welcome corrective to the somatic focus of the Lakoffians.

5.3 Conclusion

The Lakoffians deserve credit for having drawn attention to the body as an important source of metaphors. They and other metaphorists have shown that metaphors play necessary semantic, epistemological, and ontological roles. There is a greater deal of metaphoric structure in our world than meets the eye, a high degree of metaphoricity. But this does not mean that I always agree with their explanations of how these structures come about or how they function.

Lakoff and his associates have also shown the limitations of comprehensive metaphorism, by showing that many conceptual metaphors are functions of non-metaphoric concepts. At the same time they have contributed to ana-logic, in a similar but distinct manner as Mary Hesse. Further, just like Ricœur, they have argued forcefully in favour of metaphors providing indirect understanding of phenomena we find hard to comprehend. They argue in very different way from the French thinker, and since both put forth plausible arguments and I cannot find any good counterarguments, I regard the theory as plausible, in light of my principle of quasi-induction. But Ricœur certainly cannot be accused of unwarranted scientism and one-sided focus on the body, in contrast to the Lakoffians. Their theory of generative metaphorics can be criticised for having rather weak empirical foundations.

But this does not change the fact that a moderate metaphorism is a respectable position. We shall later see that certain important phenolmena have a metaphoric structure.

I.6. The Heresy of Paraphrase Revisited
Can Poems be Paraphrased?

We have already discovered that there are strong arguments in favour of metaphors *not* being *paraphrasable*. We have also seen that it is not unusual to regard metaphors and poems as being closely related. Therefore, it should come as no surprise that I want to consider whether or not poems can be paraphrased. I hope to kill two birds with one stone. The first one is to show that poems and metaphors are typically not paraphrasable; the second is to anticipate a later chapter in which I try to show that poetry can disclose our tacit knowledge of emotions.

I shall begin with a short account of the contention that poems are not paraphrasable by one of the principal figures of New Criticism, Cleanth Brooks. I then turn to Stanley Cavell's and Joel Weinsheimer's criticisms of Brooks, and in turn I shall criticise them. I continue with a brief discussion of the concept of interpretation. Next, after defining the concept of a paraphrase, I shall try my hand at paraphrasing a couple of poems in the light of that definition. A thought-experiment follows with the intention of showing that, even though there might be paraphrasable poems and metaphors, poetry and metaphors would be useless if it was not the rule that they are not paraphrasable. The last part of this chapter presents an argument in favour of my thesis that this resistance to paraphrasability is due to our understanding of poetry being tacit.

6.1 The Problems of Paraphrase

The idea of the non-paraphrasability of poetry was one of the central tenets of the New Criticism. That this school of criticism does not exist any more is perhaps one of the explanations for the fact that the thesis of the heresy of paraphrase has not been discussed much in recent years. But it is well worth probing into and decidedly needs rejuvenation. My aim is to show that there is more than a grain of truth in the thesis that *prototypical* examples of poetry cannot be rephrased in any satisfactory manner. Further, I shall try to explain the non-paraphrasability of poems through my contention that our knowledge of them is typically tacit.

It is said that a lady once asked the darling of the New Critics, T. S. Eliot, what he meant by the line "lady, three white leopards sat under a juniper tree". He replied, "I meant 'lady, three white leopards sat under a juniper tree'". The implication is, of course, that the line is not paraphrasable. One of Eliot's greatest admirers, the New Critic Cleanth Brooks, coined the phrase 'the *heresy* of paraphrase'. Another New Critic and poet, Archibald MacLeish, said, "A poem should not mean but be" (MacLeish 1964: 1069). Obviously, poems cannot be retold if they only are, but do not mean. They can, however, be meaningful and at the same time impossible to rephrase satisfactorily. It seems intuitively plausible that a poem is typically an ambiguous text. All aspects of a poem are inseparable: its rhythm, style, sounds, images, emotional flavour, along with its intellectual aspects and the denotations and connotations of its words - even its graphical presentation. The whole is bigger than the sum of its parts; a poem is a holistic phenomenon. If this is the case, then form and content cannot be separated in any clear-cut manner, and so abstracting the content (the message) from the poem is a risky and none-too-rewarding business. Further, rhythm often plays a major role for the meaning of a poem and rhythm can hardly be mirrored by propositions. Add to this the importance of metaphors in a host of poems and the difficulties (even impossibilities) of paraphrasing metaphors and the thesis of heresy seems quite plausible. It does not get any less plausible if we consider the following: we can often improve upon everyday utterances and academic texts by clarifying them. Indeed, we can clarify texts by rephrasing them. In contrast, it does not make any sense to say that we improve upon a poem by clarifying it, either by paraphrasing it or otherwise. It is actually an open question whether we can make changes to a poem without having created a new one.

I think it is high time to take a look at Cleanth Brooks' theory of heresy. He denied neither that poems could be paraphrased up to a point nor that such a paraphrase can be useful in some contexts. (The reader will recall my idea of sketches of metaphors and Kittay's theory of the exposition of metaphors.) What Brooks did deny is that a paraphrase can replace a poem or capture its essence. Moreover, attempts at a complete paraphrase of poems need metaphors in order to capture their meaning, but these metaphors in their turn stand in need of a paraphrase. Certainly, many poems contain propositions, which are easily rephrased, but we must not mistake them for the inner core of these poems. Such propositions are justified in the context of the poem as a whole, not in connection with a general paraphrase. Thus, a proposition like John Keats' "Beauty is Truth, Truth is Beauty" gets its precise meaning and significance from its relation to the total context of the poem (Brooks 1968: 157-176). He was criticising Yvor Winters' contention that any poem worth its salt must be paraphrasable. He admitted that a paraphrase was not equivalent to a poem, i.e., that a poem was more than its paraphrasable content. Winters said that every line of good poetry communicates a certain quality of feeling as well as a paraphrasable content (Winters (1959): 30-74). I am, however, not going to discuss Winters, the reason being that he did not have any systematic theory about the relation between poetry and paraphrasing.

Stanley Cavell treated Brooks a bit heavy-handedly, but his arguments nevertheless reveal some weaknesses in Brooks' theory of heresy (Cavell 1969: 74-82). When Brooks holds that any paraphrase can only be an approximation, he is denying the ordinary contrast between what is approximate and exact in an illegitimate fashion. An arrow pointing approximately north points exactly somewhere. Believing that we cannot paraphrase poems is like believing that pointing to an object would actually require one touching it. One then realises that this would make life very inconvenient, and we must reconcile ourselves to the commonsensical idea that we can only approximately point to objects. To Cavell Brooks resembles the kind of philosopher who imposes a demand for absoluteness upon a concept and then finds that our use of this concept does not meet this demand, at which point the philosopher then proposes that we accommodate this discrepancy as nearly as possible. Cavell's point is that there is usually nothing wrong with ordinary language, but there is something wrong with demands of absoluteness. And Brooks is really demanding an absurd absoluteness for the meaning of poetry. (This is how I understand Cavell's ironic way of writing.) Brooks does not understand that if we set such phrases as 'giving the meaning' or 'saying exactly what something means' into ordinary contexts in which they are used, we shall discover that we need not worry that we have not done these things exactly. We simply have been playing the language game in a correct fashion, each of them having their own standards for correctness. Demanding absolute paraphrasability is like demanding that bridge be played by the rules of chess. Brooks is theorising when he should be non-theoretically attentive to the work-ings of ordinary language. His way of arguing is an example of when language is idling.[1] (Again, I reconstruct Cavell's idiosyncratic way of expressing himself.)

According to Cavell, there are cases when it makes to say that we cannot paraphrase poetry, cases when we know what the poems mean but cannot say it. This is typical of symbolist, surrealist or imagist poetry and suchlike, exemplified by Hart Crane's line, "The mind is brushed by sparrow wings", or from Wallace Stevens, "a calm darkens among water-lights". Cavell most eloquently states: "One may be able to say nothing except that a feeling has been voiced by a kindred spirit and that if someone does not get it, he is not in one's world, or not of one's flesh. The lines may, that is, be left as touchstones of intimacy" (Cavell 1969: 81).

A proper discussion of Cavell's criticism of Brooks would demand a critical treatment of the whole idea of ordinary-language philosophy, but that would require writing another book. We may note that even Cavell admitted that there are unparaphrasable poems. We shall later see that I need not vindicate any further my version of the heresy; it suffices to show that prototypical poems are not paraphrasable.

We encounter a different kind of criticism in Joel C. Weins-heimer's article, "The Heresy of Metaphrase".[2] According to him, a paraphrase does not describe what the poem is about; it *is* what it is about. As such, a paraphrase does not consist of statements about the possible message of the poem or about what truth it gives. Rather, the paraphrase is what the poem is: it does not make any statement about the kind of poem it is. But if I said that a given poem is composed of five stanzas written by John Donne and is metaphoric, then I am

---

[1] Cavell is alluding to Wittgenstein's famous contention that certain confusions arise when language is like an engine idling, not doing its work (Wittgenstein 1958: 51 (§132).

[2] I only take on some aspects of Weinsheimer's rich article, and I do not even touch his compelling notion of 'metaphrase', i.e., a meta-statement about a poem that is not logically tied to it.

making assertions about the poem. Further, paraphrase is not outside the poem, but it is instead the outside of the poem in a similar fashion as the shell is not a turtle but is its outside. We can remove the shell but what is left is not the turtle. The same holds for the paraphrase. We can remove it but what is left is not the poem. Weinsheimer thus concludes that paraphrase is another name for ineliminable aspects of the poem's meaning.

In my view, it could very well be true that the paraphrase can capture some essential aspect of the poem, but that does not exclude the possibility that it can never capture other equally essential aspects. After all, removing the turtle from the shell means that the shell is no longer a part of the turtle. And the shell is only one of the many vital parts of the turtle. In similar fashion, paraphrase might capture some vital parts of the poem, but not all and not even its heart. The heart of the turtle is not in its shell.

Weinsheimer says in no uncertain words, "Brooks defines poetry negatively as unparaphrasable and positively as paradoxical" (Weinsheimer 1982: 312). He adds that there is no necessary connection between these two definitions. Paradoxes can be paraphrased with the utmost ease. But a few pages later, Weinsheimer admits that Brooks probably did not think that all poems were paradoxical (Weinsheimer 1982: 325). This admission flatly contradicts his earlier statement about Brooks' purported definition. To make matters worse, Weinsheimer suddenly appears to presume that Brooks thought that being paradoxical is a precondition for a poem's not being paraphrasable (Weinsheimer 1982: 320). I for one do not believe that Brooks thought so. I think that he used the term 'paradox' in a very wide, metaphoric sense that covers absurdities, ambiguities, ironies, diverse kinds of contradictions, etc. Further, we shall see below that a poem can be beyond the reaches of paraphrase even though it does not contain anything resembling a paradox. No less important is my thesis that only prototypical poems are thus non-paraphrasable.

Now, do I have to accept Brooks' objectivistic view of poems as being self-contained and not shaped, even created, by interpretation in order to vindicate the thesis of heresy? Definitely not. I certainly do not think poems are solely the products of interpretations; if they were, then they would not have any essence and there would be nothing to paraphrase. But I subscribe to the idea that they are partly shaped by interpretations and cannot be anything else. (Compare what I said earlier about metaphors being partly constituted by interpretation.) If this is the case, then the correct interpretation of their essence would be impossible, and, by implication, they would not be paraphrasable. I agree with David Best's contention that the concept of interpretation has as its precondition an agreement about what is being interpreted. In order to be able to disagree about how a given object should be interpreted, people must first conceptualise the object in the same way. Different interpretations of a novel imply agreement that the phenomenon interpreted is a novel. Another precondition for such interpretations is an agreement, at least to some extent, about what happens in it. *Mutatis mutandis*, the same holds for the interpretations of any given poem. To be sure, sometimes two or more interpretations of an artwork are equally good. It can be compared to the fact that seeing the duck-rabbit figure on one occasion as a rabbit, another as a duck are equally valid ways of seeing it. But there are constraints on the way it is viewed; you cannot see the figure as a clock. Something similar holds for our interpretations of other artworks; we can interpret *King Lear* in various but equally good ways, but not as a comedy. The same, of course, holds for any given poem (Best 1985: 19-25 and elsewhere).

The Norwegian philosopher Ole Martin Skilleås points out that if all interpretations were equally valid, then we could understand any given interpretation of any given literary work to be an equally good interpretation of any other literary work. We could, for instance, understand any given interpretation of The *Waste Land* as an interpretation of Lord Byron's *Childe Harolde*. (Skilleås 1995: 222).[3] That seems pretty absurd. We have, then, no reason to believe that literary interpretations are entirely subjective or that literary works are solely created by interpretation, even though we also have no reason to believe that literary works can exist in splendid isolation, untainted by interpretation.

In my terminology, the reader certainly is the co-author of any literary work, bringing to it his or her perspectives, evaluations and concepts. Some of these are in their turn cultural products, making

---

[3] He uses other examples.

culture yet another co-author.[4] Trivially, an interpretation without preconceptions is impossible; the reader cannot perform any interpretation unless he or she master concepts like that of a novel, text and literature and interpret the work in light of them.[5] Such conceptual mastery is of course also required in natural sciences. But interpreting a literary text is also dependent upon the position of the reader in time. I cannot interpret a certain literary work as the first novel ever or a parody of another work unless I am in certain position in time. From another position in time these works might look quite different (a physicist does not seem to have such problems). It is important to note that our position in time is not only a liability; it can also be an asset. Being contemporary with the author (or being the author himself) can give us an insider view of the work, while there also are benefits of hindsight.[6]

I will return to this temporal aspect of interpretation later. Now I just want to add that the amount of disagreement about the correctness of literary interpretations points in the direction of interpretations being partly shaped by subjective factors and cultural relativity. My educated guess is that literary interpretation provides twisted understanding. The subjective factors, cultural relativity and temporal perspectives provide the twisting while thinkers like Best have shown us that interpretation can give us genuine understanding.

The upshot of this is that the alethetic values, which are the yardsticks of literary interpretation, are different from those of propositional truth. There is no co-authorship involved in a proposition like, "this is a table", uttered in standard conditions. And since the correct literary interpretation does not exist, we can only talk of adequate literary interpretations, not true ones. Due to the twisted understanding involved, a literary interpretation is either T-correct or T-incorrect. So the alethetic values of interpretation are adequacy and T-correctness, not propositional truth.

---

[4] On the communal interpretation of the private language argument, this must be the case, the given being forms of lives, i.e., cultures.
[5] In Heidegger's parlance, the reader must disclose the text as something, for instance a poem or a novel.
[6] I do not hide the influence from Gadamer and Ricœur (Gadamer 1990 and Ricœur 1986).

Let us return to Best and Skilleås. The upshot of their analyses is
that we must assume that poems have a minimal core not created by
interpretation. (I stress the expression 'minimal core', for no poem
consists solely of its core and everything outside the core is shaped or
created by interpretation.) Paradoxically, the reader can only become a
co-author by granting the work certain independence, treating *as if* the
text had a completely independent core even though it, strictly
speaking, does not. Having to approach the text in the as-if mode in
order to understand it means that the reader must employ ana-logic. If
he did not treat the text as an independent object, it would not make
sense to say that there is any number of equally good interpretations of
the *same* text. However counterfactual the existence of this core might
be and however difficult it may be to isolate it from the reader's
interpretations and intentions of the writer, the core is what I have in
mind when talking about the qualities of poems in this chapter. One of
the qualities in question is the quality of wholes being than the sum of
its parts. I am not saying that all wholes possess this quality, only that
poems do or at least proto-typical ones do; their whole is bigger than
the sum of their parts. This view gains support from the fact that there
can be more than one equally valid interpretation of any given poem.
The whole would not be greater than its parts if the meaning of the
poem were fully determined by the sum of the meaning of its parts.
The fact that the meaning of the poem is thus underdetermined by the
meaning of its parts makes the plurality of valid interpretations
possible and shows, at the same time, that the whole of the poem is
greater than the sum of its parts. This wholeness does not mean that
the poem is a harmonious unity. There is nothing wrong with looking
for hidden disharmonies, trying to unmask a purported poetic whole as
actually being less than its parts or focusing on some hidden parts of
it. Such inquiries seem to be part and parcel of the deconstruction of
poems, an endeavour that undoubtedly has its redeeming qualities.[7]

The fact that the poem as a whole is bigger than the sum of its part
is one of the reasons for the difficulties involved in paraphrasing it.
Our determining exactly what the whole is can prove a Herculean
task, since knowing the exact meaning of the parts does not help, and,

---

[7] On deconstruction see Culler 1983. On a deconstructivist view of Brooks, see Culler
1983: 201-205.

therefore, paraphrasing is a strenuous activity. I shall return to the relationship between the parts and the whole below.

6.2 Defining Concepts, Analysing Examples

Brooks was on the right track, and I want to use the remainder of this chapter to give his thesis a more solid foundation. I shall begin by putting forth a stipulative definition of the concept of a non-para-phrasable text on the grounds of his analysis: "A text is non-paraphrasable if and only if a paraphrase can neither replace the text nor capture its essential meaning". Such an essential meaning can be conveyed in a summary of the text. Admittedly, the notion of essential meaning is not exactly clear; I must rely on the reader's intuitive understanding of what the essential meaning of a text is (the same goes for notoriously unclear notions like those of 'poetry' or 'every-day understanding'). Let it suffice to give the following example. In the lyrics of the Beatles' song *She loves you,* the core (essential) meaning seems to be that A is telling B that B wrongly thinks that his girlfriend does not love him any more, but that is not right, etc.

By 'paraphrase of a poem' I mean, 'a prosaic (non-poetic) re-wording or summary of a poem'. As for the concept of 'paraphrase', it is useful to refer to a couple of definitions from dictionaries. One of them states that paraphrase is "rewording of a text, giving the meaning another form" (*The New Bantam English Dictionary* 1979: 655). Another defines the verb 'to paraphrase' as "to explain or translate with latitude" (*Concise English Dictionary*, 1990:293). The latter defi-nition obviously indicates that there is a certain connection between the concept of a paraphrase, on the one hand, and the concepts of explanation (in the sense of explication) and translation, on the other. This seems plausible because when we translate a text we try to say the same thing in other words, which is tantamount to an attempt to paraphrase it. (We might even say conversely that a paraphrase is a kind of translation.) And when we explicate a text we try to make it easier to understand by using a different set of words to say the same thing but in a clearer manner. Sometimes an explication is closer to a summary that in its turn tries to give the essential meaning of a text or an utterance.

On the basis of the discussion above, I define 'paraphrase' as 'the rewording or the summary of a text, giving the meaning another form, in some cases clarifying the text and capturing its essential meaning'. I stipulate that a paraphrase must be able a) to replace the original text or b) to capture its essential meaning, or both a) and b). Paraphrases of the first kind I call *reworders,* they are roughly the same as Gutten-plan's re-statements, which is all there is to paraphrasing in his book. The second I simply call *summaries*; they are attempts to capture the essential meaning of the poem. Metaphoric sketches are kinds of summaries; summaries of poems can be sketches in a similar fashion. Now, a summary of a poem is an interpretation of a poem that in some cases is based on that which I call a 'depth interpretation' (if not, I call it 'a straight summary'). Such an interpretation tries to unveil hidden essences of meaning in texts and, in the case of poetry, can usually be expressed in a few poignant sentences. I call summaries based upon depth interpretations *probers* because they try to probe into poems and other texts, plumb their depths. In order to qualify as a prober, P must translate the text with the aid of 'the translation manual' for a certain depth interpretation. If the interpretation were, for instance, of the deconstructivist kind, the manual would include some deconstructive rules (or anti-rules). They would be close relatives to metaphoric sketches, given that no poem can ever be paraphrased in a satisfactory manner, that every prober is just a sort of hinting at what the real essence of a given poem is. My educated guess is that this is the case but I will concentrate on the question whether or not prototypical poems can be paraphrased in both my senses of the word.

Now, is rewording a poem really an option? If we reword it, are not we just making another poem? The answer is that according to modern conventions, we certainly would be doing so. But they are not necessarily the only game in town. And all conventions can be stretched, because there is no meta-rule, so would we break the modern convention if we reworded a poem a tiny bit, for instance by shifting the order of words here and there? So reworders are controversial, but the same cannot be said of summaries. Since it is not controversial that a summary of a poem can count as a paraphrase, I shall mainly focus on summaries; I shall not discuss probers much because they are borderline cases of paraphrases, being so close to interpretative analysis. So straight summaries of poems is my main target in this chapter.

As for the word 'meaning', I use it in this chapter as 'sense plus connotations (and suchlike)[8] of words, utterances, and texts', but not as 'reference'. In short, I am talking about the meaning we grasp by understanding and I set completely to the side the question of whether or not we can ultimately reduce this kind of meaning to the truth-condition of sentences. This type of meaning can be both the utterer's meaning and the textual meaning.[9]

In contrast to the question of the truth-conditions, I shall briefly discuss possible answers to the question of whether it holds for all utterances, texts, and suchlike that they are somehow not fully paraphrasable. Let us look at some arguments against the thesis that no utterance can ever be paraphrased. To begin with, it seems intuitively strange to maintain that commonplace utterances like "John and Mary went home" are not really paraphrasable or that they are as difficult to paraphrase as poems by T. S. Eliot. Secondly, there are cases when the ability to rephrase utterances is a necessary condition for understanding them.[10] If someone is asked whether he has understood a presidential candidate's speech and he responds by reiterating it *verbatim*, we can congratulate him on his good memory, but we still lack evidence for his understanding. That evidence we can only get if he can rephrase it. Thirdly, I think that the possibility of paraphrasability is built into the very concept of a linguistic expression of an empirical theory. Can we test the theory if we cannot paraphrase it, for instance, if we think that its original formulation is not clear enough for testing? Some paraphrasability does indeed seem possible, which, of course, does not prove that there are fully paraphrasable utterances. Consider again the case of John and Mary. In more male-chauvinist times than ours, rewording "John and Mary went home" as "Mary and John went home" would perhaps not quite have captured the original. The reason is that there could have been a convention saying that a man's name must be mentioned first because males are more important than females. If that were the case, "Mary and John went

---

[8] 'Suchlike' can be the intonation of utterances, the rhythm or the graphic form of texts.

[9] In order to avoid misunderstanding, we should *not* take 'textual meaning' to be 'sentential meaning'. 'Textual meaning' is simply the sense of the text, with all its connotations, which we try to grasp without worrying about the author's intentions.

[10] I use 'rephrase' and 'paraphrase' synonymously. The same holds for 'paraphrasability' and 'rephrasability'.

home" would have had important connotations, different from the original. It goes without saying that had the sentence appeared in a poem, the reworder would have changed its meaning radically, given the importance of connotations in poetry. So even if rewording a poem was not simply creating a new poem or destroying it, it would be an extremely difficult undertaking, in probability doomed to failure.

I shall now illustrate the thesis of heresy with an example. Consider the following lines from Ezra Pound's *Canto I*, which incidentally consists to a large extent of a translation of Homer's *Odyssey*, aside from its last lines where all of a sudden a modern voice starts to speak. Here is an excerpt from the poem:

> And then went down to the ship,
>
> Set keel to breakers, forth on the godly sea, and
>
> We set up mast and sail on that swart ship,
>
> Bore sheep aboard her and our bodies also
>
> Heavy with weeping, and winds from sternward
>
> Bore us out onward with bellying canvas,
>
> Circe's this craft, the trim-coifed goddess.
>
> Then sat we amidships, wind jamming the tiller,
>
> Thus with stretched sail, we went over sea till day's end.
>
> Sun to his slumber, shadows o'er all the ocean,
>
> Came we then to the bounds of deepest water,
>
> To the Kimmerian lands, and peopled cities
>
> Covered with close-webbed mist, unpierced ever
>
> With the glitter of sun-rays
>
> Nor with stars stretched, nor looking back from heaven
>
> Swartest night stretched over wretched men there.
>
> The ocean flowing backward, came we then to the place
>
> Aforesaid by Circe (Pound 1975: 3-5)

While rephrasing these lines, and for that matter the whole poem, is not easy, it does not seem impossible. In light of what I said earlier, I shall ignore pure rewording and probing, the latter would probably also require making probers of the *Cantos* as a whole or even also the

Odyssey. Consequently, I shall concentrate on making a straight summary: "We went down to the ships, plunged them into the sea, and sailed on the ocean, which is of godly provenance. We carried our black sheep (here to be understood literally) aboard as we boarded the vessel, while we were in tears. The wind was blowing our way, so the ship sailed rather quickly. This was due to the magical powers of Circe, who is a goddess."[11] And so on and so forth.

Let us assume that we show this paraphrase to a stranger, who knows neither Pound's poem nor Homer's epic and ask him what kind of a text this is. Is it a paraphrase of a novel, everyday discourse in a pre-modern civilisation, a fairy-tale, a modern poem or an epic? Would it not require quite a leap of imagination on his part to determine that this is actually from the two last categories? Contrast this to a paraphrase of a scientific paper or book. In most cases, we would have no problem identifying the nature of the object of the paraphrase. One could hardly mistake a paraphrase of Einstein's book on the theory of relativity for a paraphrase of a novel or a book about politics. Rephrasing a scientific text is, then, probably more rewarding than paraphrasing a poem, a fact that ought to count in favour of the thesis of heresy. The attempted paraphrase of *Canto I* also counts in favour of the thesis. The paraphrase seems like an empty shell, far removed from the complex organicity of Pound's poem. It cannot capture the particular rhythm of the poem that suggests among other things the movements of the ship. Further, Pound's use of Homer creates a set of associations, which are hardly paraphrasable in any fruitful manner. And just the very *Verfremdungseffekt* (the effect of estrangement) of taking this part of Homer and wedding it to a completely different type of discourse, as Pound does at the end of the poem, cannot be easily captured by a paraphrase. We can, therefore, subsume Pound's poem under my definition of a non-paraphrasable text. (Note that the poem is unparaphrasable despite the fact that it does not contain any paradoxes, or at least not in my interpretation.)

---

[11] It must be said in all fairness that using a more archaic language in the attempted paraphrase would have probably made it more like the poem itself.

6.3 Visiting Possible Worlds

I do not doubt that there are cases where we could paraphrase poems in a similar fashion as non-poetic texts. Take a look at the following example, a well-known poem by William Carlos Williams:

This is Just to Say

I have eaten
the plums
that were in
the icebox

and which
you were probably
saving
for breakfast

Forgive me
they were delicious
so sweet
and so cold (Williams 1985: 70)

We can try to summarise the poem in the following (straight) fashion: "I ate the plums, which were in the icebox. In all probability you kept them in order to eat them at breakfast. I am sorry, the plums were tasty, and they were very sweet and cold". This straight summary seems to be a sufficient replacement (but it would be an even better replacement if we made its rhythm conform to that of the poem). Therefore, this is an adequate summary, given my stipulation. Admittedly, the task at hand is a bit more difficult if we want to make a prober out of it. We could base it on a depth interpretation of the poem as conveying the message that we human beings are easily led into temptation, but in most cases that is something we have to live with it. C'est la vie!

The obvious problem is that the number of possible depth interpretations is infinite and, *mutatis mutandis,* the same holds for the number of probers. But who says that there is no such thing as the correct depth interpretation? (The fact that I for one do not think it is the case does not prove that it is futile to search for the correct interpretation.) And who says that such depth interpretations are always useful? Brooks certainly would have contested their usefulness. In our case the result of such a contesting is something Brooks would have disapproved; namely, that if a poem can only be summarised, not given any fruitful depth interpretations, then it is paraphrasable for all intents and purposes. So if there is such a thing as paraphrasable text, Williams' poem is, unless its soft rhythm plays a decisive role for its meaning.

Now, does this mean that the thesis of heresy is wrong? No, not at all. In the first place, by just looking at a straight summary of the poem, we should not have the slightest clue that it was a summary of a poem, unless told so. The same would hold for a possible reworder or a prober. Think of a reworder where I replaced "have eaten" with "ate" or "probably" with "in all probability" and changed the make up the lines such that the poem would lose its form of poetry, look like prose (in that case it could be mistaken for a written message with apologies). The aforementioned prober would not have to be a paraphrase; it could be a part of an essay on the human condition. So it seems that a paraphrase of this poem has certain features in common with paraphrases of more 'poetic' poems, such as Pound's *Canto 1*. Secondly, and much more importantly, Williams' poem cannot be a prototypical example of a poem for the simple reason that it is a kind of poem that is parasitic upon non-paraphrasable ones. Poems like Williams' get their identity from challenging high modernistic poetry or even poetry as such. It is almost as if the American poet is teasing us by implicitly saying, "Look, I have presented this text in a poetic form, therefore it is a poem, since poetry has no essential nature. Whatever is presented as a poem is a poem".[12] The identity of such a poem consists of among other things their balancing between being poems and anti-poems; the aesthetic device used is the *Verfremdungseffekt*, the shock of having something unpoetic presented as poetry.

Imagine a possible world **P.W.1** where we only have what we in our world call 'paraphrasable poems'. Let us call them **p.p.**s for the sake of convenience; let us assume that Williams' poem really is paraphrasable and that it is a prototypical example of a paraphrasable poem. Is it certain that this possible world would need the notion of

---

[12] Anyone knowledgeable about William Carlos Williams knows that he himself would never have said such a thing. But the point is that someone who writes such a poem could have said it without sounding inconsequential. The author of the *Idylls of the King* (Alfred, Lord Tennyson) could not have.

poetry in order to classify the **p.p.**s in meaningful and useful way? No, because the difference between prose and what we call 'poetry' would be so unclear that the inhabitants of **P.W.1** would have no use for the notion of poetry.

The arch-**p.p.**, Williams' poem, might be called 'a parody of 'real' poem' in our world. In **P.W.1** it would not make sense to call it a 'parody'. In a similar fashion, it does not make sense to ask whether there would be parodies of the *Mona Lisa* in a possible world where the painting does not exist. A painting that in our eyes would look exactly like the *Mona Lisa* but with a moustache would not be a parody in the possible world in question.

Let us look at another possible world. We might imagine a possible world **P.W.2** where art has always been like the avant-garde art of the twentieth century. In **P.W.2**, a person called Marcel Duchamp could display a urinal at an art exhibition, sign it 'R. Mutt', and call it *Fountain,* but it would still not be the same artwork (or anti-artwork) as in the actual world. For Duchamp's *Fountain* is whatever it is by virtue of being an implicit attack on prevalent notions of art. Those notions would be quite different in **P.W.2**. In an analogous manner, Williams' text (poem?) would not have any shocking effect in **P.W.1**, in a glaring contrast to the effect it could have had in our world some decades ago. Even if **P.W.1** actually employed the concept of a poem, Williams' text would not count as an anti-poem, since it has not broken with any tradition. Add to this the fact that a host of people in our world would flatly deny that Williams' text is a poem but rather see it as a piece of everyday discourse, undeservedly called a poem. So whatever virtues this poem might possess, being a prototypical poem is not one of them. This means that if my earlier description of the typical features of poems is correct and if Williams' poem is a typical example of a **p.p.**, then we can conclude by saying that non-paraphrasable poems are prototypical and the paraphrasable ones are parasitic upon them.[13] So for all we know, the poems that Cavell admitted were not paraphrasable should be counted as prototypical. If that is the case, then Cavell's assault on the thesis of heresy fails.

---

[13] I take my chance at maintaining that this (and everything else I say in this chapter) holds for poetry in general in our empirical world, not just poetry in our epoch and culture.

Something similar holds for metaphors. There might very well be subclasses of metaphors that could be paraphrased even though others could not be. But even if there could be perfectly paraphrasable metaphors, they could not be typical metaphors. Now, if it holds for all metaphors that they are paraphrasable, then there would an extremely thin line between non-metaphoric symbolic structures and the metaphoric ones. In fact, linguistic metaphors would be nothing but literal linguistic units, masquerading as something else. Something similar would hold for non-linguistic metaphors. But we have discovered in this book that metaphors (at least prototypical ones) perform all kinds of tasks, not least cognitive ones, in a different manner than non-metaphoric symbolic structures. This could not be the case if prototypical metaphors were translatable into literal language or its non-verbal analogues. Further, I doubt that the use of metaphors would have survived at all if all of them were paraphrasable (compare what I have said about poetry). What would have been the use of metaphors had all of them been thus paraphrasable? But then again metaphors might 'force' themselves upon us by being somehow the backbone of our being, Lakoffian or Nietzschean style. If that were the case, then they would still be of use for us, regardless of whether they were paraphrasable. Now, let us assume that there was a high degree of metaphoricity in our world, thanks to our concepts being largely metaphorically structured but at the same time linguistic metaphors were easily paraphrasable. Surely, the importance of linguistic metaphors for us would be undercut by their very paraphrasability.

6.4 Tacit Knowledge and Paraphrasing

I think that the deeper explanation for the non-rephrasability of typical poems and metaphors is that our understanding of them is basically *tacit*. If we possess propositional knowledge of a given **X**, then we can describe **X** adequately by putting forth a series of true propositions about its nature. However, if we cannot rephrase a certain poem or metaphor, then we cannot describe it adequately with the aid of propositions (or indeed anything else). Therefore, our understanding of it cannot be entirely propositional.

But what more precisely is tacit knowledge? It is a kind of knowledge that we cannot adequately express in propositions. It is a sort of implicit or intuitive knowledge. Among the prototypical examples of such knowledge are our diverse types of know-how. A cyclist and a swimmer have know-how, which enables them to cycle and swim without necessarily being able to explain their know-how with the aid of propositions. We certainly cannot learn to cycle or swim by acquiring propositional knowledge; we acquire the skills in question primarily by trial and error. If we were to try to cycle or swim consciously and in the process apply propositional knowledge to the task at hand, we should risk losing our control and crash or drown (Polanyi 1958: 49-50).

It was the Anglo-Hungarian polymath, Michael Polanyi, who coined the expression 'tacit knowledge'. He was inspired by *Gestalt* psychology in his analysis of tacit knowledge. The *Gestalt* theorists maintained that we could recognise a physiognomy (in our case a face) as a whole without being able to identify its parts. Polanyi then famously said, "we know more than we can tell" (Polanyi 1966: 6). Our knowledge of a physiognomy, for instance a face, is tacit. The reason is that we know a physiognomy as a whole without being able to identify its different parts (Polanyi 1966: 4). I can know the faces of friends and relatives with a somnambulistic certainty without being able to describe them in such a way that my hearers or readers can individuate a given face without having ever seen it.

Wittgenstein never used the expression 'tacit knowledge' but had it on the tip of his tongue:

> §78. Compare *knowing* and *saying*:
> > how many feet high Mont Blanc is-
> > how the word 'game' is used-
> > how a clarinet sounds-
> If you are surprised that one can know something and not be able to say it, you are perhaps thinking of a case like the first. Certainly not of one like the third (Wittgenstein 1958: 36 (§78)).

These remarks have been a tremendous inspiration for Norwegian Wittgensteinian Kjell S. Johannessen. He thinks that besides know-how, there is a brand of tacit knowledge that he calls 'knowledge by familiarity'. (I shall use the abbreviation KF for the remainder of this book.) The knowledge of the way a clarinet sounds can be an example of such knowledge. Johannessen maintains that KF is 'intransitive'; i.e., it is a type of knowledge that cannot be entirely transferred to other means of expression. Further, the knowledge in question is closely connected to experiences of certain kinds, for instance, music or *Gestalten* (Johannessen 1994: 217-250). It is obvious that knowing how a clarinet sounds is not know-how, in contrast to the ability to play the instrument. Knowing the sound of a clarinet is possessing tacit knowledge *about* a phenomenon. Actually, not only is our knowledge of the sounds of instruments of this kind but our knowledge of artworks generally is as well. We can be very familiar with a painting or a symphony without being able to describe them in words. Furthermore, not only perception of Gestalten, but perception and sensation in general have tacit sides. There are limits to how much of our perceptions and sensations we can describe in words due to their subjective and personal side (Johannessen 2006: 229-242). Johannessen seems to think that our sensory knowledge has an ineliminable moment of KF. We have no problem knowing the colour of things but describing colours to a colour-blind or completely blind person is so to speak impossible. The same kind of problem encounters anybody who tries to describe sounds to a deaf individual.

In some ways KF is closer to propositional knowledge than to know-how, even though it certainly is *not* knowledge by acquaintance, i.e., direct empirical knowledge. Just like propositional knowledge, KF is *know-that*, not the ability to perform tasks. Further, we can only acquire KF by personal acquisition, and so KF must be personal knowledge (Johannessen 1981: 108-126). The personal nature of this kind of knowledge means that it has an ineliminable subjective moment (Johannessen 2006: 229-242). Unfortunately, Johannessen has not yet elaborated the nature and scope of this subjective moment, but postulating its existence certainly goes against the grain of more objectivistic interpretations of Wittgenstein's private-language argument. (Johannessen is not discussing that argument in this context.)

He says, surprisingly, that linguistic devices, such as metaphors and analogies, play a certain role in hinting at our KF. Johannessen does not use the expression 'hinting at KF', but I think it is fairly obvious that it does not make sense to say we can explicate tacit knowledge in a satisfactory manner: we can only hint at it. In fact, Wittgenstein himself says that in describing a musical passage, we only hint at it (Wittgenstein 1958: 183). When I talk about 'the articulation of KF', by 'articulation' I mean something in the direction of 'hinting at KF' or 'making a sketch of KF'. The tools for the articulation are metaphors, analogies, similes, other poetical devices, meaningful gestures, etc. Using them for the purposes of articulation means communicating in an indirect fashion. The similarities to Ricœur and Lakoff are obvious. These three different thinkers find a common ground in stressing the necessity of using indirect (more or less metaphoric) approaches to the ineffable. They arrive at similar conclusions from very different premises, arguing forcefully for their case. Since I cannot find any good counterarguments, I conclude in a quasi-inductive way that they are right.

Regardless of quasi-induction, saying that language plays a role in the articulation surely sounds like a contradiction in terms. Admittedly, Johannessen is bit unclear on this issue. It is not clear whether he thinks that the linguistic devices *must* play role in the articulation of all forms of KF. Is their use perhaps optional? Are there any forms of KF in which language has no role to play whatsoever? I think it suffices to say that there are cases of KF where language plays an important, perhaps necessary, part in the articulation, and that there might be cases where language is of no use. My hunch is that language plays an important role, say, in the articulation of our knowledge of faces, in our ways of walking, and, as we later shall see, in our tacit knowledge of emotions. It does not make sense to say that person P knows John's way of walking or his face unless there is a way of putting forth assertions like "P knows John's way of walking" or "I, P, know that this here is John's face". Only with the aid of such linguistic means as assertions can we discern between knowledge about faces or ways of walking and pure reactions to them. That Fido barks happily whenever he sees John does not mean that he knows that this is John's face (*mutatis mutandis* the same holds for the dog's reaction to John's way of walking). Seeing the face (or the person walking) triggers some reaction in Fido, but he hardly possesses the concepts of a face and a person. He cannot be said to subsume, therefore, that to which he reacts to, under the concept of a face. (It is fairly obvious that we cannot assert anything unless we master some concepts. As far as we know, Fido never asserts anything.) Thus, he does not really know John's face, and even if he does possess such knowledge, it would not be prototypical knowledge of a face. Prototypical knowledge of faces and suchlike would be knowledge possessed by a minded being, endowed with linguistic competency and a mastery of concepts. (Whether the knowledge, which this being possesses, has a pre-conceptual foundation is altogether another matter). One of the reasons for this requirement is that the concept of knowledge was created to account for knowledge that such a being possesses. The onus is upon anybody who thinks that non-minded beings possess conceptual knowledge, at least of the abstract kind.

The upshot of this is that some kind of language, a symbolic system that provides the means for the creation of assertions, is of essential importance for the constitution and understanding of at least certain kinds of KF.[14] This fact could point in the direction of language having a role to play in the articulation of this type of KF. However, *literally* meant or understood assertions, or both, have an essential role to play in informing us about the fact *that* John has a face and thus determine it as a certain object of which one can have KF. In contrast, literal assertions are not of any greater help when it comes to giving information about *how* his face is, which is the proper domain of KF. Assertions of this type are not very successful in describing John's face or for that matter his manner of walking. Try to make people recognise a face they have never seen on the basis of descriptions alone and you are almost certainly bound to fail (that is, unless the face has some strange individual mark like a huge wart). Try to make people visualise correctly an unknown face solely on the basis of descriptions, and your attempt is doomed. Such descriptions alone cannot help us to identify John's face or way of walking, even though they can be a part of the articulation of our KF of the face and way of walking. I can probably describe *types* of faces and manners of walking with the aid of literal assertions, but I can hardly individuate a face or way of walking in that fashion. Here, meaningful gestures can come in handy; pointing at John can do wonders in identifying him. Similes and metaphors improve the situation. I can say, for instance, "he walks like an old cow" and thus use a simile.[15] And when describing his face I can say metaphorically "he has a beaver's face".

---

[14] As in the rest of the book, I use 'language' in a pretty wide sense of the word, meaning 'the totality of symbolic systems and their meaningful application'. Thus, meaningful gestures are parts of language.

[15] I follow Andrew Ortony in regarding similes as being non-literal. A literal comparison would be "John is like his sister; they have both red hair and green eyes" (Ortony 1993: 342-356). Notice that in the literal comparison no conceptual boundaries are being transgressed, in contrast to similes where two conceptual domains are being compared.

There are cases where such metaphors and similes are apt and cases where they are not. It would usually not be apt to call a toothless person's face 'a beaver's face'; a round face with two very prominent front teeth would be a hot candidate for the 'beaver-face' moniker. So we can at least make sketches of our tacit knowledge of faces with the aid of such metaphors. What metaphoric sketches should I need to make in order to articulate my propositional knowledge that $2 + 2 = 4$? Assertions like "two and two equals four" do the job nicely. Further, if I describe my pencil as being literally white and seven centimetres long, what is left out in this literal description, which would require hinting with the aid of metaphors and meaningful gestures? The answer to both questions is 'nothing'.

We also need analogies and metaphors when hinting at sensory knowledge. The closest we come to describe colours successfully (not to the blind though) is by analogy; telling a person who cannot perceive green that it is a colour somewhat like blue and brown. And perhaps we can describe music to someone who has never heard it or cannot perceive it by likening it to the sound of birds or the wind, using perhaps metaphors like INSTRUMENTS ARE HUMAN MADE BIRDS or A SINGER IS A HUMAN BIRD. Gestures and the use of examples are likewise of paramount importance. I can point at samples of different hues of red and add that this and things like that count as red objects.

So there are cases where the articulation of KF seems to require figurative language, propositional knowledge usually does not stand in such a need. There is an obvious kinship here with Ricœur's, or even Lakoff's, idea of the role of metaphors in expressing that which cannot be expressed directly.

There is one aspect of the articulation of KF I have not mentioned. As the good Wittgensteinian he is, Johannessen stresses the role of examples in such an articulation. To give yet another example of my own making, I cannot explain what baroque music is solely in words, even though I instantly hear that certain musical pieces belong to that genre. But I can give examples of baroque music, say, some pieces of Italian baroque, on the one hand, and some pieces of German baroque on the other. Additionally, it would be advisable to give examples of borderline cases and even examples of rococo and renaissance music as an instructive contrast. I want that interpreting literary works also involves comparison between examples. To interpret a given poem as baroque poem requires knowing a host of examples both of baroque poetry and other kinds of poems. A person who lived in the middle of the baroque epoch was in no position to compare a poem written at the same time with later poems of the baroque kind, let alone the much later romantic poetry. Interpreting a baroque poem in the light of romantic poetry was not an option this person had; his temporal perspectives created and limited his horizon of possible interpretations. Our horizon is limited in a similar way; thus our temporal perspectives shape our literary interpretations decisively; time twists our interpretations.

We shall later discover the importance of concrete examples for the knowledge of emotions; actually we shall see how Johannessen's analysis of KF can be used in the analysis of the articulation of emotions.

I think that there is a large grain of truth in this analysis. It seems to me that our knowledge about faces and at least some kinds of poetry is KF. It is tacit knowledge, it is know-that, and definitely not know-how. I shall utilise this analysis for my own 'anti-heretical' purposes. As I suggested, my view is that our understanding of a non-rephrasable poem is essentially some kind of tacit know-that.

We have also discovered in an earlier chapter that Glicksohn and Goodblatt have compelling arguments in favour of metaphors being Gestalten. In my view, the same holds for poems (at least typical ones). Just like a Gestalt, a poem is a whole bigger than the sum of its parts. It is even better to say that it is a family of Gestalten. There are different, equally valid, ways of interpreting poems, just like there are different ways of aspect-seeing a Jastrow-figure. Such aspect-seeing can show us bizarre, non-harmonious images, and, in analogous fashion, a valid interpretation of a poem does not need to show a poem as a harmonious whole. Just as the lines of the Jastrow-figure constrain possible aspect-seeing, there are constrains upon interpretations of poetry; there is a way in which a poem is a thing. There must, therefore, be family resemblances between the Gestalten, i.e., the interpretations.

Compare poems with faces, the latter being *bona fide* Gestalten. Both are vehicles for expression, albeit in a different ways. Both require interpretation and semi-interpretation, the latter being of great importance due to the Gestalt nature of both. But the semi-interpretative part is of a greater importance in the understanding of faces, due to the fact that a face is not much more than a Gestalt, a poem has all kinds of non-Gestalt meaningful dimensions such as propositional content. The way to uncover that content is usually interpretation proper.

As for the way we use semi-interpretation when dealing with faces, we see for instance certain kinds of faces as sad or glad. But inter-pretation proper is also of importance for the understanding of faces. We ask questions like "is the smile genuine?" In an analogous fashion we wonder whether to take a given poem as sincere or ironic. It holds for both poems and facial expressions that their meaning can take on lives of their own, severed from the intention of the poet or the 'owner' of the face. The case of the poem as having a meaning dif-ferent from the intended one ought to be well known. Less well studied is the fact that people can have facial expressions whose meaning eludes them. Thus, many Norwegians have an expression of innocence without knowing it. They seem unconsciously to make their faces baby-like, being constantly wide-eyed, and sort of into making their faces round, possibly subconsciously emphasising that they are harmless like babies. Further, a given person can constantly have a fearful or nervous expression without realising it. These nervous ex-pressions can be barely perceptible twitches that are at first glance something marginal but upon a closer look reveal something important about the person.

To be sure interpreting such indexical signs is in many ways different from interpretation of symbols. I would not call any attempt to understand indexical signs 'interpretation', only cases when under-standing such signs is a key to uncover meaning. Thus, drawing the conclusion that there is a fire burning because one sees smoke is making an ordinary empirical hypothesis, not interpreting. Drawing the conclusion from such tell-tell signs as blushing that a person feels embarrassed is trying to uncover meaning and therefore an inter-pretation of sorts. Such an indexical interpretation is somewhere in between interpretation and semi-interpretation; sharing the inferential aspect with the former; the sensory aspect with the latter.

The aforementioned marginal twitches can be likened to the seemingly marginal aspects of poems and other texts that the deconstructionists love to focus on. Deconstructing a poem might be similar to our focusing on an unusual expression in a given face, one quite different from its ordinary expression, perhaps revealing something genuine about the person behind the face. Deconstruction could also be analogous to the focusing on a half-hidden aspect of the face and seeing it in the light of it. It could even be likened to what happens when we imagine a part of a given face in isolation and not as a part of any Gestalt. Nevertheless, the fact remains that any face is bigger than the sum of its parts. The same holds for poems, however fruitful it might be to deconstruct them (for a deconstructionist view of poetry, see Derrida 1991: 222-237).

I am not saying that grasping a poem or a metaphor is an exact structural analogue to the perception of a face. (I am certainly not ignoring the dangers of the analogical fallacy.) Rather, we cannot grasp a poem or a complex metaphor unless we are able to identify their different parts, because perceiving a face is so swift that we do not have the time to identify its different part consciously. But it might be the case that we perceive the parts subconsciously. More importantly, understanding a poem is like studying a face and its expressions over some time and in various circumstances; a face has many aspects and really knowing it requires studying it in this extensive manner. The face is the sum of all these aspects. Still, the face goes on being a Gestalt. The same holds for poems and our understanding of them. Interpreting a poem is like interpreting various expressions of a face over some time in order to determine the character of a person behind the face (compare the way I interpret the facial expressions of a typical Norwegian). Of course, we do not do not determine the character of persons on the basis of facial expressions alone. But nor do we interpret a poem on the basis of its words alone. Our cultural background and that of the poem and the poet co-determine the interpretation just like our understanding of the various actions of a person and not the facial expressions alone co-determine our understanding of that person.

Now, if the knowledge of faces is tacit (more precisely a KF) by virtue of our perceiving them as being bigger than the sum of their parts, it is tempting to think that the same holds for poems and metaphors (at least prototypical ones). Our understanding of typical poems and metaphors is closely related to knowledge by familiarity, or, more precisely, understanding by familiarity. The understanding of symbolic structures (including poems) is in many ways different from knowledge, for instance, the knowledge that this face is Jimmy's face or that Mont Blanc is in France. Understanding is the product of inter-pretation or semi-interpretation, or both, and therefore 'borrows' the alethetic values of interpretation. This means that propositional truth is not the sole alethetic value of understanding. With regard to know-ledge, truth is its dominating alethetic value. Knowledge is not neces-sarily based on interpretation and semi-interpretation and does not therefore have to 'borrow' their alethetic values. Thus I use Johannessen's expression 'understanding by familiarity' (he actually seems to prefer 'intransitive understanding') rather than 'knowledge by familiarity' (Johannessen 1994: 217-250).

A paraphrase in the sense of a summary or a metaphoric sketch is an attempt to reduce the understanding of poetry and metaphors to knowledge claims, to the alethetic value of truth. A straight summary seems to be a kind of description of a poem's main content and pos-sibly also its basic formal features. Such a description would consist of a series of propositions that have truth as their alethetic values. A poem, which cannot be rephrased, cannot be adequately described. The difficulties in paraphrasing poetry and metaphors show that such a reduction is impossible, at least in typical cases. At the same time, Brooks has correctly shown that a paraphrase can have some worth in helping us to understand a poem. In a similar fashion, a face or the sound of a clarinet cannot be adequately described, but descriptions can help identify them: "John has a round face", "the clarinet sounds like the song of certain birds", etc. Both the paraphrases and the descriptions are put forth in propositions and are in Brooks' terminology *pointers*; they point towards the truth (Brooks 1968: 196-197).

But as I said earlier, if there is a kernel of truth in the idea of para-phrase, it is that they are sketches, and the sketches do not possess truth-values, even though they can point in the direction of truth. They possess the alethetic value of validity. Just like we can have different equivalent sketches of metaphors, we can sketch poems in equally valid manner. Making a summary is sketching a poem. Sketching a poem in its turn is hinting at or articulating our KF of it and that endeavour often requires analogies and metaphors. (If our knowledge of metaphors is also KF, then it could explain why it often seems impossible to paraphrase them in a non-metaphoric manner.) For instance, a metaphoric expression like CANTOS I IS A ROUGH TRIP ON THE SEA can be a part of fruitful prober of the poem.

Earlier, I stipulated for the sake of argument that a prober could capture the essence of a poem. My analysis has, however, shown the emptiness of such view if it is not taken just as a stipulation. A sketch cannot, then, capture whatever essence the poem possesses, but there are sketches that are invalid. Sketching Williams' poem along the lines of its being about someone who just ate an ice-cream soda is such an invalid sketch.

Well, I certainly hope that my theories point in that very direction. Actually, my theory about the tacit nature of our understanding of poetry gives my analysis the virtue of testability. There must be some ways of finding out empirically whether or not our understanding of non-paraphrasable poems is tacit. If it were to turn out that it is not the case, that fact would weaken my defence of the non-paraphrasability of typical poems. And if there were serious logical flaws in my possible-world examples, then it would be hard to see how I can uphold my defence. So whatever lack of merit my arguments might have, I am not moving in vicious circles. Nobody can accuse me of simply deciding by fiat that poems are typically not paraphrasable.

6.5 Conclusion

I have tried to defend the thesis of paraphrase in this chapter. I have countered Cavell's and Weinsheimer's critic of the thesis while criticising theorists like Brooks for naive objectivism concerning poetry. Poems are partly constituted by interpretations and interpretations can only be T-correct, not true or false. Being partly dependent upon interpretation means that poems are not thing-like objects, as Brooks seems to have thought. But such objectivism is not a necessarily condition for the validity of the heresy-thesis. Further, I analysed the concept of paraphrase anew, maintaining that there are two main types of paraphrases, reworders and summaries. In their turn, there are two kinds of summaries, 'straight' ones and probers, the latter being based on depth interpretations. Then I used a possible world thought experiment to show that prototypical poems are not paraphrasable (the same holds for prototypical metaphors). A prosaic text can be improved with the aid of a paraphrase, but a typical poem only destroyed. The deeper explanation for the non-rephrasability of poetry and metaphors is that our understanding of them is basically tacit, or, more precisely, knowledge by familiarity. One of the reasons for this is that poems are Gestalten. We have thus strengthened the foundations of Brooks' original thesis. At the same time, we have discovered the importance of KF and the way that metaphors, analogies and other devices of ana-logic can help us articulate that knowledge, for instance when we articulate our knowledge of a poem in a prober.

Only the anti-heretic can undertake the logical mystery tour of poetic interpretation. The heretics will be left behind in the grey land of paraphrases and empty phrases.

I.7. Notes on Ana-logic and Summary of Section I

7.1 The Notes

Ana-logic is definitely not formal logic; it is closer to informal logic. In some ways it is more a method or an approach than logic in the classical sense of the word. This we can see from the way we have to use an *as-if approach* to many things. As I said in the last chapter, we simply cannot understand a text unless we regard it *as if* it were independent of interpretations, even though strictly speaking it is not, even though it really is a function of interpretations. We cannot even confer upon T an identity as an individual text unless we think in such an as-if manner. T cannot be understood as a text unless it is seen as an independent object. In the next part of this book, we shall discover that Paul Ricœur thought that as-if thinking were dominant in the world of narratives, even our mental world.

My hunch is that the concept of ana-logic is an amoebaean concept, so I do not make any attempt at enumerating possible necessary and sufficient condition. So I use ana-logic in order to explicate the concept of ana-logic! The following (a-j) are its basic features and functions, the list is hardly exhaustive:

a) Ana-logic does not break with the foundations of ordinary logic, as can be seen from the acceptance of the principle of contradiction. However, since this principle is totally abstract, it can only be used as an analogue to the kind of concrete reasoning that takes place in the domain of ana-logic (the influence of Hesse on this argument ought to be clear). So in some sense, ana-logic is the true home of the principle of contradiction, not formal logic.

Further, I have agreed with Wittgenstein that there is no rule for the employment of rules, and the same holds by implication for the rule we call 'the principle of contradiction'. We cannot use that rule in any mechanical manner. The lack of meta-rule means that our practices and co-determine the use of the principle of contradiction, compare the Wittgensteinian analysis that I endorsed earlier.

b) One of the reasons that ana-logic does not break with the principle of contradiction is that it has to use deduction of sorts and it is hard to see how one can perform deduction while breaking with the principle. Ana-logic uses deduction because it has to demonstrate the relevancy and usefulness of the analogies, similes, and metaphors it uses (compare Lakoff's and Johnson's various examples of the implications of metaphors). Once again the deduction in question is analogous to abstract deduction. As we have seen, Hesse has ably demonstrated that the actual use of deduction in science and everyday life is of an ana-logical nature.

c) Yet, in contrast to *formal* deductive logic and in common with rhetoric, ana-logic must employ examples. When using examples we invoke the similarities between the examples and objects in the field under scrutiny, hoping that our examples possess the kind of similarities that are relevant to the point we are making. The analogical moment is of course the focusing on similarities. Using examples (and other tools of ana-logic) is evidently of great importance when we are discussing purported amoebaean concepts. If the concept of metaphor were that kind of concept, finding prototypical examples is mandatory and they must have the relevant kind of similarities with each other and all thinkable candidates for 'metaphorhood'.

One of the many reasons that we need examples when reasoning in an ana-logical way is the fact that there is no such thing as an inductive proof for the fruitfulness of metaphors; it can only be shown with the aid of examples. At the same time, ana-logic is necessary when we perform complex induction. We do not need it when we see several figures of exactly the same kind on a paper; we inductively conclude that all the figures are of the same kind. But in more complex cases, ana-logic is needed for discovering important similarities between different objects. Let us say we are trying to determine inductively whether all high-functioning autistics have an impaired understanding of literature. We must then find out whether subjects A, B, C are, despite their differences, sufficiently similar in the relevant aspects to be counted as high-functioning autistics. We also have to find out in a similar fashion if their responses to different texts really count as not understanding literature in the relevant way. Further, something similar applies to the process of determining what texts do count as being literary, due to the fact that the concept of the literary is an amoebaean one. The same holds of course for the use of any amoebaean concept.

d) In stark contrast to formal deductive logic, ana-logic is usually based upon *enthymemes*. Aristotle famously analysed enthymemes and examples in his *Rhetoric*.[1] Ana-logic might even be called 'rhetorical logic', and Aristotle certainly was the founding father of ana-logic. But note that it is not necessary the business of ana-logic (or poetics for that matter) to show us how to be persuasive. Ana-logic leaves the business of persuasion to rhetoric.

e) Ana-logic operates in a *horizontal* manner, in contrast to the *vertical* ways of deductive logic, i.e., the way the deductive logicians start reasoning as if from above, going down from premises to conclusion and taking ideas asunder in order to analyse them. Operating horizontally means that it *connects* (*synthesises*) phenomena, for instance, with the aid of metaphors. (We connect the concepts of Man and wolf in MAN IS A WOLF).

f) Aristotle maintained in his *Prior Analytics* (69a) that there was a peculiar way of thinking about examples or particular cases that differed from both induction and deduction. When reasoning about particular cases, we reason from part to part without recourse to a whole, i.e., a universal concept. Johannessen points out that this requires analogical reflection because in dealing with such particular cases some judgement is needed to determine whether there are sufficient similarities between the concepts in order to justify subsuming them under the same concept. He adds that this leads us to Kant's reflective judgement (Johannessen 2006: 229-242).

Reflective judgement is closely connected to the employment of ana-logic. When we reason horizontally, i.e., analogically, then the objects of thoughts are concrete and unique and cannot without further ado be subsumed under general rules. We grope for the correct concept and pass informed judgment about which concepts are fitting. We judge the objects under scrutiny on the basis of their similarities and dissimilarities, are they similar enough in the relevant respect to be

---

[1] He did so in Book II, Chapter 20 (1393b and 1394a) and Chapter 22 (1396a, 1396b, 1397a)).

subsumed under this or that concept? So reasoning horizontally means passing informed judgements.[2]

When we think *vertically*, we use the Kantian determinant judgement; i.e. we subsume different objects under one given rule. And since concepts are rules, then we have to employ our faculty of judgement whenever we use concepts. (For Kant's concept of judgement, see Kant 1963:33-36).

g) In horizontal reasoning, *aspect* seeing (semi-interpretation) plays an essential role. That which David Best calls 'interpretative reasoning' can be of paramount importance and his idea of such reasoning is closely related to ana-logic. But he should have called it 'semi-interpretative reasoning'.

h) Connecting and synthesising means seeing or creating new connections; therefore, we must use our imagination when connecting and synthesising (compare Lakoff's and Johnson's conception of 'imaginative rationality').

i) Thinking in terms of as-if is one important way of thinking in an ana-logical manner, compare the examples given at the beginning of this chapter.

j) It has been said that the logic of analogy requires that we use a well-known domain to throw light on a less well known one. In physics, Rutherford famously used the well-known solar system to throw light upon the so to speak unknown atomic structure (Carroll 1988: 49). This probably holds as a general rule. The problem is, however, that it is often hard to determine whether we know more about domain A than B. We can know more facts about domain A while knowing more about the general laws governing the 'behaviour' of the objects in domain B. There is no such thing as measuring knowledge; do we for instance know more about movies than about our minds and our dreams? Maybe we know less about movies and more about

---

[2] Abduction or inference to the best explanation is in many wise like the employment of reflective judgement. We grope for the best explanation without the aid of a given rule and need to use our imagination for all its worth (Peirce 1992: 186-199). Perhaps, abduction belongs to the realm of ana-logic, which would vastly enhance its importance, due to the fact that abduction in contrast to deduction and induction can provide us with genuinely new knowledge. But for the time being the possible analogical nature of abduction belongs to possibilology.

dreams than we think or possibly it is the other way round. Maybe this uncertainty means that we should be extremely cautious when it comes to employing analogies. Maybe it means that we should be open to the possibility that, sometimes, using analogies from a less well-known area to get a grip on a better-known area (if they can be compared) could be preferable heuristically than doing it the other way round.

Now let us look at possible pitfalls involved in ana-logical reasoning and some possible objections to its fruitfulness. One pitfall of ana-logical thinking is that which I call 'the analogical fallacy'. We commit this fallacy when we conclude that some resemblance between A and B means that they belong to the same class or that there is a causal relation between them. Because the Mayan and the Egyptian pyramids have the same shape, some have been led to think that the Mayans had learned the noble art of pyramid building from the Egyptians. But we have no evidence of any contact between them. Besides, with pre-modern technology, this shape was the only possible one for the building of structures of this size. And of course, we must not forget the often-mentioned fact that everything is similar or dissimilar to everything else in one or other respect. It might be noted that because of the dangers of such fallacies, modern biologists are sceptical of using similarities between species as a foundation for their classification (Sterelny 2001: 104).

But does not this just show that the idea ana-logic itself is a fallacy? Was not Davidson right when he said that statements about similarities are trivially true because everything is similar or dissimilar to everything else? If every statement about similarity is true in virtue of everything being similar to everything else, then a statement about similarity can never be false. This means that these kinds of statements are tautologies. But tautologies cannot contain any new information, and, by implication, statements about similarities cannot either, the critics say. This would mean that ana-logical reasoning is pretty empty. But Andrew Ortony has put forth some excellent criticisms against this contention. He points out that the proposition "similarities are tautological" cannot be true both because it seems intuitively absurd and because there are statements about similarities that have given us new information. The claim that the atom has a structure similar to the solar system is one that was certainly was informative. Tautologies, however, cannot provide any new information. (Ortony 1993: 347). I see no reason to doubt that analogies can provide us with genuine information; therefore ana-logic is definitely not any tautological sham.

Furthermore, I maintain that ana-logic is indispensable for our reasoning and of least as great importance as deductive logic, being in some respects logically prior to it. We have already seen that thinking in terms of as-if is of outmost importance for us. Induction and abduction certainly are of no less importance for our understanding of the world and ana-logic plays a part in both. No less important is the fact that the lack of rules for the following of rules makes us dependent upon ana-logic, the reason being that every employment of any given rule requires an evaluation of whether the ever new circumstances in which the rule is employed is sufficiently like previous circumstances in the relevant aspect to justify an employment of the rule. To identify that employment as sufficiently like previous employments in the relevant aspect to count as an employment of the rule (Johannessen 2006: 229-242). Given that concepts are (at least) partly constituted by rules, then any use of any kind of concepts requires the utilisation of ana-logic. And even if rules weigh less in the constitution of amoebaean concepts, ana-logic is of no less and even greater importance in their employment, the reason being that we must rely on comparison with several different *examples* of previous ways of using the concept. Only such a comparison can help us to find out whether our employment of it is sufficiently like earlier employments in the relevant way to count as a successful use of the concept.

I am not saying anything new or original when I say that concepts constitute our world to a large extent and that abstract thinking means using concepts.[3] Without ana-logic no use of concepts, by implication, ana-logic is in a way a primordial form of thinking, making the employment of concepts possible and therefore plays an ineliminable role in constituting our world. This means that any kind of deductive reasoning would be dependent upon ana-logical reasoning because deductive reasoning concerns the relationship between concepts and mastering concepts requires an ana-logical approach. At the same

---

[3] This does not exclude the possibility that even abstract thinking has non-conceptual, tacit sides. Neither does it exclude the possibility that there might be non-abstract, non-conceptual thinking.

time, ana-logic is dependent upon deduction of sorts; therefore there is interdependence between them. Neither is logical prior in relation to each other, both are equally primordial forms of thinking.

Remember that Johannessen correctly says that sensations and perception have tacit component and can only be hinted at with the aid of analogies, gestures, examples and metaphors, in other words in an ana-logical fashion. Given the enormous importance of sensations and perception in our acquisition of knowledge, then ana-logic is a major player in the world of cognition, being also the co-ruler (even co-author) of the world of concepts (of course there is mutual influence between concepts and percepts).

To understand the world, we must be masters of ana-logic, for as the great Stagirate tells us, to be a master of metaphors is to possess the greatest talent of all (Aristotle 1965: 65 (Chapter 22). Indeed, the master is *metaphorically competent* to a great degree. Being able to create new, original metaphors on a regular basis makes a person extremely metaphorically competent, and the ability to discriminate between metaphors and non-metaphors is a minimal requirement for possessing metaphoric competence. Those, whom Samuel Guttenplan calls 'metaphor blind'[4], among them those who take everything literally, are those who do not have any metaphoric competence. They cannot employ ana-logic. In contrast, it is the hallmark of a metaphorically competent person that he or she can employ this logic.

Ricœur says that narratives humanise time (Ricœur 1984a: 52). In my view, ana-logic humanises logic, takes it down from the airy heights of empty abstractions into the chaotic, organic human world.

7. 2 The Summary

In Section I, I have discussed the nature of metaphors, the question of whether they have a particular meaning or are only masks for literal meaning. I have also discussed their scope, the question whether our world and language are under the sway of metaphors.

I started with a short introduction to different views of metaphors. I criticised the iconoclastic view of metaphors while endorsing the cognitivist views and the idea that metaphors are constituted by aspect

---

[4] Guttenplan 2005: 24

seeing. At the same time, I expressed my qualms about Black's interactionism while placing metaphoric interaction where I think it belongs, in the abstract dimension, having a tensive nature.

In the second chapter, I focus on Paul Ricœur's eclectic and existential theory of metaphors. I showed how his theory is connected to the idea of the poetic of a will and associated ideas of the role of imagination in human life. I critically evaluated his theory about the cognitive function of metaphors while lauding his defense of a tensive theory of metaphors.

In the third chapter I stated that it is the cognitive function of metaphors that gives us a basis for understanding them. We understand a metaphor **M** if and only if we know what kind of conditions must be obtained if **M** can be said to be correct. Correctness or rightness of metaphors is a special alethetic value. Metaphors can be cognitively apt or correct in a similar fashion as caricatures can be, they are T-correct and give us twisted understanding. They have a disclosive function. At the end of this chapter, I put forth definitions of 'metaphoricity' and 'metaphoric structure'.

In the fourth chapter, I discussed the theories of the metaphorists, who think that our lives and worldviews are soaked by metaphors, or, have a high degree of metaphoricity. These theorists tend to be what I call *iconodulists*: they think that language is essentially metaphoric. They even talk as though metaphors have a transcendental status, an inspiring theory but also a much too speculative one. I discussed the theories of such metaphorists and iconodulists as Nietzsche, Blumenberg, Derrida, and Mary Hesse, and I claimed that there is more than a grain of truth in Hesse's view of analogical reasoning. I also agreed with the iconodulist theory that literal language is not the foundation of language. But I expressed my uneasiness about the ability of metaphors to provide such a foundation. I also doubted that we can draw a sharp line between the literal and the non-literal.

In the fifth the chapter I discussed the cognitive semantics of the Lakoff School. I criticised the Lakoffians both for their pretentious scientism and for being too iconodulistic and metaphoristic. I also questioned whether their theories are testable. I found, however, their theory of metaphoric reason very inspiring. By wedding it to Hesse's analogical reasoning and some ideas of my own, we get 'ana-logic'.

Such logic is a necessary supplement to formal deductive logic. At the same time it forms one of the backbones of narra-logic and the ENAL.

In the sixth chapter, I stated that metaphors are not really para-phrasable and that poems can also be hard to paraphrase. I tried to rejuvenate the old thesis about the 'heresy of paraphrase' by analysing a couple of well-known poems and by performing thought-experi-ments of the 'possible-world' kind. They show that paradigmatic examples of poems are not paraphrasable. A prosaic text can be im-proved with the aid of a paraphrase, but a typical poem cannot. The deeper explanation for the non-rephrasability of poetry is that our understanding of it is basically tacit.

II. THE RULE OF NARRATIVES

II.1. The Story and The Narrative
Introducing Some Notions of Narratology

In this short introductory chapter I discuss briefly the concept of a narrative and my notions of storied structure and narrative structure, the study of which belongs to narratology. These concepts will play an important role in this book, since I shall attempt to show that several phenomena have such structure. My discussion of narrative and story, not least their relationship between each other, is basically a prelude to the definitions of concepts of these structures.

1.1 Narratives and Stories

Roland Barthes famously said that narratives are

> ...able to be carried by language, spoken or written, fixed or moving images, fixed or moving images, gestures and the ordered mixtures of all these substances; narrative is present in myth, legend, fable, tale, novella, epic, history, tragedy, drama, comedy, mime, painting...stained glass window, cinema, comics, news item, conversation (Barthes 1977: 79).

This is quite correct. It would be foolish to think that narratives have to be verbal representations of stories. Surely, a silent movie, a ballet, a pantomime or a comic strip without words can 'tell' a story. The reason that I put 'tell' between quotation marks is that these non-verbal narratives *show* or represent stories. In non-verbal media, stories are not told in a non-metaphoric sense of the word. I shall, therefore, use in this book the expression 'narrating a story' in the sense of 'representing a story by description or by showing'; I shall use 'telling a story' only when I am talking about stories narrated in words.

Students of narrative very wisely discriminate between story and narrative.[1] Story is *what* is being recounted, independent of the medium used. Narrative is the *way* the story is told; the same story can be told by the means of words, cinematic images, etc. In the terminology of the structuralists, the narrative (or discourse) is the signifier, the story the signified (Genette 1980: 27). Actually, Paisley Livingston maintains that the French concept of discourse is too wide and with unclear edges. He wants to replace it with that of 'utterance' in a broad sense of the word, and replace the concept of a story with that of an utterance-content, likewise in a broad sense. An utterance, then, designates "…any act or performance (or product thereof) expressive of thought or belief, where expression requires that the action be performed in order to indicate some attitude…A motorist's intentional flashing of the turn signal is…an utterance…" (Livingston 2001: 276).

A story is something potentially narrated; a narrative is an actualisation of that potentiality. Some theorists who are influenced by cognitive science maintain that we can fairly easily separate story and narrative. Whereas a story is a mental image, a cognitive construct, a narrative is embodied in some material medium (words, moving images, etc) (Ryan 2005: 347). Others think that a story is something abstracted from a narrative (for a discussion, see Shen 2005: 567). According to this view, the narrative is the form, the story the content. I am not going to take sides on this issue, but it would not surprise me the least if the second approach were more fruitful for analysing fictional works and the first for everyday stories. Marie-Laure Ryan defends the first view with an example of a person who creates a mental image, a story, of events she experiences on her way home, a story she might or might not tell her family. This implies, of course, that there is a clear-cut separation between mental images and language, in a broad sense of that word, including systems of imagined,

---

[1] I strongly believe in the fruitfulness of this separation, but some of the theorists discussed in this book do not discriminate between narratives and stories. When discussing their theories, I follow their use of terminology while criticising them for not discriminating between these two concepts.

It must be added that there are scholars who discriminate between narratives and stories but in completely different ways from me. Thus, some sociolinguists reserve the term 'narrative' for the general class, 'story' for the prototypical form. Others say that story is one kind of narrative and that there are other kinds of narratives, including habitual or hypothetical narratives (Riessman 2008: 6).

visual symbols. Now, Wittgenstein's private-language argument goes against the grain of such a clear-cut separation. Given my critical adherence to that argument, I seriously doubt that such a separation is possible.

I want to focus for a while on some differences between narratives and stories: the former is something told; the latter is not. A narrative can (some say must) involve an explicit or implicit narrator and a likewise explicit or implicit narratee.[2] It goes almost without saying that the concept of a narrator is logically linked to that of a narrative, but not to that of a story. The second difference has to do with time: a story has *erzählte Zeit* (recounted time), a narrative *Erzählzeit* (time of narrating). It can take a cinematic narrative two minutes to tell the story of five years in a person's life. For written narratives, the *Erzählzeit* is usually measured in space, more precisely, the lines devoted to time sequences in a book. Thus, a history textbook might use 20 lines to tell the story of the Thirty Years' War.[3] The third has to do with the nature of sequences: both narratives and stories have beginnings, middles, and endings, forming a whole. But a narrative can start by telling the end of the story or the middle, or even next to the end, like the film *Citizen Kane*. Someone (I think Jean-Luc Godard) said that a narrative must contain beginning-middle-end but not necessarily in that order. Thus, there is freedom involved in a narrative, constrains in a story.

But what do we mean when we say that the *same* story can be told in various ways? What are the criteria of sameness? Does the movie *Pride and Prejudice* tell *exactly* the same story as the novel? Obviously not. The movie, for instance, does not show Wikham's flirting and Lizzie Bennet's discovery that she is not really in love with him. The BBC TV-series from 1995 was certainly more faithful to the story than movie, but it was not exact, nor was it supposed to be. Nevertheless, we cannot exclude the possibility of the two media, the one of the written word, the other of the moving images, being

---

[2] A narratee is an implicit or explicit receiver of a narrative. This concept was created by Gerald Prince (Prince 1982: 16-26).

[3] The concept of these two different types of time was originally introduced by the German literary theorist Günther Müller and taken up again by Gérard Genette who actually refers to *Erzählzeit* as 'pseudo-time' (Genette 1980:34).

incommensurable almost in a Kuhnian sense.[4] That would make the two media virtual paradigms and the same set of facts (in our case the facts are stories) being interpreted quite differently within them, at the same time as the facts (the stories) are functions of paradigms. Perhaps every single narrative is its own paradigm, in which case one could not say that several narratives can 'tell' exactly the same story. This would hold equally for fictional and non-fictional stories and narratives.

If narrative and story relate to each other as form and content, respectively, it seems plausible that they constrain each other in various ways. This means that not only do *narratives-paradigms* constrain stories but also the other way round. It is hard to see how you can write a long novel telling the story of A who went to the bakery and then returned home. And if you do, your novel could not contain many descriptions of actions, but rather detailed descriptions of what A saw and experienced on the way, the way A looks, etc. Thus this story constrains the narrative, making a description that contains many actions impossible. The same holds for countless stories and narratives, even every conceivable one.

1.2 Definitions

As I hinted at, I do not have any great ambitions to analyse the concepts of story and narrative; it is more than a little tempting to regard these concepts as amoebaean ones. Actually, Donald Polkinghorne thinks that the concept of story is a prototypical one (he does not discriminate between narratives and stories). Such a prototypical story identifies a protagonist and a predicament. Then it describes attempts to solve the predicament, and after that, the outcomes of such attempts, including the reactions of the protagonist to the situation. Finally, it must show the causal relationship among each of the elements of the story (Polkinghorne 1988: 112). However, Polkinghorne does not give examples of a prototypical stories and how they relate to less prototypical specimens. But surely, any attempt at showing that the concepts of story and of narrative are prototypical would require the giving examples and analysing them. My basic

---

[4] Kuhn famously maintained that scientific paradigms were incommensurable (Kuhn 1970: 227-240). I say "almost in a Kuhnian sense" because the comparison might be farfetched.

ambition, however, is not to solve once and for all the problem of the nature of the concepts involved; my ambition is much more practical one, that of putting forth a *stipulative* definition of a *storied structure* and a *narrative structure*. But the following I think is true and would have to be a part of any acceptable definition of 'a story': besides being a potential utterance-content of narratives, a story is narratable, i.e., has a *schematic representation* of a sequence of events, real or fictional, involving agents and the objects of their actions. This means that stories are like sketches, waiting for the narrator to use them as basis for something analogous to paintings. This also means that even non-fictional, true stories are not only found but also at least partly made. In many cases, especially when we are dealing with inanimate objects not created by humans, stories are made in the way that a sentient being takes a slice out of space-time, sees certain processes as interconnected events, sees one point in time as the starting point of these events, another point of time as the climax of the process, and yet another point as the end. At the same time, the sentient being sees those points of time as parts of a continuum; the time sequence of the story constitutes a whole, something akin to a Bergsonian *durée*.

Indeed, we could compare stories to Chomskyan deep structures and narratives to surface structures. Each narrative articulates the deep structure in its own manner, but is constrained by the deep structure. (I shall return to the Chomskyan metaphor in a later setting.)

Furthermore, we could compare stories and narratives *in general* (both those about the human and the non-human world) with important moments of Kantian epistemology: stories are like the intuitions, and narratives are like the categories. We shall see later in this section that both have interrelated cognitive functions. Those of stories consist in organising reality and conferring on it significance at a primitive level like the intuitions, while narratives finish the job of making reality understandable.

The agents and objects that appear in stories and narratives may or may not be human, may or may not be animated, and may or may not be abstract entities. Thus, one can tell the story in which the agent is the Hegelian *Weltgeist* or a story in which the object is Norway under occupation by Germany. One can also tell a story in which the agent is a smart fox, outfoxing a stupid hedgehog. Further, one can tell the story of stones that fall from a cliff that create a big hole in the sand below. And one certainly can tell the story of the wrath of Achilles and its consequences for such objects as King Agamemnon or the hero Hector. (Notice my use of analogies in my attempt to grasp the nature of stories and narratives and their relationship to each other.)

I briefly mentioned that stories are constituted or created. Does this mean that I think that all stories and narratives are fictional? Not at all, for I agree with Peter Lamarque and Stein Haugom Olsen who point out that the concepts of narratives and of fictions are distinct. Narrative *per se* is nothing but a formal feature of texts without any referential or ontological implications. "John was happy and then John was unhappy" has a narrative form, while "John was happy" has none. But nothing follows from the facts that one of these sentences has a narrative form and the other not about whether these sentences have truth-values or not (Lamarque and Olsen 1994: 224-226). I think this is largely true. Lamarque and Olsen borrowed their particular idea of a narrative form from Gerald Prince's definition of narrative. 'Narrative', according to Prince, "is the representation of at least two real or fictive events or situations in a time sequence, neither of which presupposes or entails each other" (Prince 1982: 4). This helps us to rule out propositions like "electrons are constituents of atoms" or "Mary is tall and Peter is small" since these propositions do no not describe any event at all. Further, it is useful for discriminating between a narrative and a simple description of an event (Prince 1987: 58). Still further, it helps us draw a line between a narrative and a logical inference: "All men are mortal, and Socrates is a man; therefore Socrates is a mortal". There is no time sequence here, and the last sentence is entailed by the first two sentences.

I do not, however, agree with Prince's definition of a narrative. In my scheme of things, narrative representation is a special one; it is an utterance in a broad sense. The schematic representations of a story are not utterances. Further, something is lacking in Prince's definition, namely the way the two situations or events relate to each other. They must somehow constitute a whole, a unity. The story often provides such a unity by establishing a causal connection between the events and situations. If there are no causal connections between them, then we have only a chronicle of non-related events, not a real story, no unity. Actually, E. M. Forster connected causality to plots, and he discerned between story and plot. The story has to do with chronology of the events, the plot their causality. "The king died and then the queen died" is a story, "the king died and then the queen died of grief" is a plot (Prince 1987: 72). Well, I think that the first example is fairly obviously an example of a chronicle, not a story. Further, I do not think that causality alone can create a plot.[5] In the first place, there can be many causal relations represented in a narrative that have nothing to do with either the main flow of the narrative or, by implication, the plot. Consider a sentence in a hypothetical novel like "he tip-toed in order not to wake her". If this causal description has no further consequences for the storyline, then it does not have anything to do with the plot. It is what Barthes calls 'a catalyst' (Barthes 1977: 94). A plot is like a melody or a theme in a musical work, which can be quite complex. It is that which we try to express in synopses of stories. In some ways, plots are the form of stories; a story, which only exists as a mental representation, would nevertheless have a plot as kind of skeleton. Furthermore, in stories where the actors are minded or sentient beings, even imaginary ones, their reasons for acting must be taken into account. And such reasons are, at least from one point of view, logical preconditions for actions, not only causes.[6] The explication of these reasons must be one of the task of most narratives, since the bulk of all narratives are about minded beings. It would not surprise me at all if a prototypical narrative were a narrative about such beings. Be that as it may, a plot of some sorts must govern the telling (description or showing) of events in a narrative. We could say that the plot is a feature of the story, represented by the narrative. But we could perhaps say like Peter Brooks that plot is a feature of both (Brooks 1996: 255). Actually, it does not matter to my project whether or not Brooks is right. Of far greater importance is the fact that Louis Mink and Paul Ricœur think that the plot unifies the story or the narrative, or both, because of aspect-seeing. (I shall discuss this in the next two chapters.) This squares pretty well with what I have said earlier about minded beings *seeing* points of space-time *as* this or that.

---

[5] The concept of plot is a hotly debated one. I basically, but not entirely, rely on an intuitive understanding of it. I shall return to it in the next chapter. For a short overview over different theories about plot, see Dannenberg 2005: 435-439.

6 I am invoking a moderate version of the logical-connection argument (L.C.A.), according to which motives for actions are logically connected to acts. The motives are, therefore, not causes. See for instance von Wright 1971: 83-131.

I also want to mention, almost *en passante*, that a plot is in some ways a paraphrase of a story. But while paraphrases typically distort metaphors and poems, the paraphrase involved in the plot is a necessary part of the story. This shows that caution is called for when we try to find the common ground of metaphors and narratives, as we shall indeed try later in this section. It must be emphasised that I am not saying that we can paraphrase every possible story in an adequate fashion; paraphrases of great novels are nothing but skeletons of the real thing.

Anyway, we can safely say that N is a narrative if it is a full-fledged, non-schematic 'told' (in the wide sense) representation of events, which form a whole, in part owing to causal connections between the events in the story, which N relates and N is told by an explicit or implicit narrator to a likewise explicit or implicit narratee.

Note that I am only stating sufficiency conditions for narratives; there might be a host of narratives which cannot be subsumed under this definition. Note also that Lamarque and Olsen's analysis is still valid in light of this definition. "John was happy but then became unhappy *because* his parrot died" is a narrative according to my definition. It is easy to see that it could just so happen that it is true or untrue. The same holds for the non-narrative sentences embedded in the narrative, "John was happy" and "John's parrot died". The narrative form is incidental to the question of truth or untruth.

This brings me to the concept of a storied structure and my stipulative definition of it, to be used in the remainder of this book: *X has a storied structure iff it a) essentially unfolds in time and has a given beginning, middle, and end; b) this unfolding forms a unified whole.*

We cannot subsume chronicles under this concept even though they unfold essentially in time; their unfolding lacks unity. The height of mountains, the relativity of time, human-made timetables, lists of objects, definitions, mathematical and logical proofs (the results, not the processes!) certainly cannot be subsumed under the definition; none of these 'objects' unfold in time. Further, X has a maximum degree of what I call *narrativicity*[7] if and only if its tellability is a

---

[7] 'Narrativicity' should not be confused with 'narrativity', which is the quality of being a narrative. Prince maintains that there are degrees of narrativity. Some novels, for instance, have more narrativity than others (Prince 1982: 145).

precondition for its existence. Emotions, thoughts and human lives have a high degree of narrativicity; that is, they conform to the definition and their tellability is a precondition for their existence. As we have seen, mathematical proofs have zero degree of narrativicity. This means that narrativicity concerns the role of narratives and stories for X; if X is entirely constituted by narratives or stories, or both, then it has more narrativicity than if it were not constituted by narratives or stories, or both, but nevertheless were soaked with narratives or stories (being by necessity imbued with narratives and stories means also having a high degree of narrativicity, even though X did neither possessed a storied nor narrative structure).

This brings me to my conception of a narrative structure: *X has a narrative structure iff a) it has a storied structure; b) it belongs essentially to it that it be narrated; c) it has an actual or potential, explicit or implicit narrator and a narratee; and d) it contains implicit or explicit agents or characters of some sort (they do not have to be living agents; they can be abstractions or whatever).*

A narrative, be it fictional or historical, very obviously has a narrative structure because a) is met obviously; b) is likewise met because N would not be a narrative unless it was narrated; c) is satisfied because a narrative must be narrated by someone to an actual or potential narratee; and d) is fulfilled because a narrative describes changes and it must, therefore, contain explicit or implicit agents. Even a narrative of the ice-age can refer to climatic changes or glaciers as agents of change. They are, therefore, characters of sorts.

Now, if X has a narrative structure, then it has more narrativicity than Y, which only has a storied structure. The reason is that X has also a storied structure. A fictional narrative has more narrativicity than a historical one even though both have narrative structures. The reason is that the object of a fictional narrative entirely depends upon its storied and narrative structures; a true historical narrative has, however, objects that are partly structured by non-narrative and non-storied means. (The height of a mountain can be decisive for the nature of a historical occurrence, but, as I said earlier, this property of the mountain has no storied structure.)

If a person believes that everything has a storied or even narrative structure, so to speak, then that person is a *narrativist*. A narrativist thinks that narratives and stories permeate our lives, constitute our experiences, our actions, and ultimately our Selves. I shall discuss the theories of various narrativists and their critiques in this section as well as the third and fourth one; the reader will discover that I am a cautious, moderate narrativist. I shall also use 'narrativity' in a somewhat different way when I 'measure' the importance of narratives or stories, or both, in certain fields of human endeavour. If narratives or stories, or both, play an important and essential role in sociology but only a minor one in economics, then sociology has *ceteris paribus* a higher degree of narrativity than economics. If central moments of human existence such as the Self had a storied and a narrative structure, then our existence has a high degree of narrativity. But again there is no formula for the 'measurement' of narrativity anymore than that of metaphoricity. We must use informed judgment to estimate the 'amount' of both.

We will discover that a host of phenomena have a storied structure and that structure is given in a pretty objective way. But our epistemic access to these structures is through narratives that shape and mould our picture of them. There can be no such thing as the correct narrative of such a structure.

1.3 Conclusion

I have introduced here the notion of a narrative, some themes of narrativist philosophy, and my definitions of storied structure and narrative structure. We saw that if narratives are the form and stories are the content, then narratives are utterances, and stories their utterance-content. At the same time, there are important analogies between them.

II.2. Historical Narratives
Their Nature and the Nature of Narrative Explanations

In this chapter I shall discuss some theorists of historical narratives, most notably Louis O. Mink, Arthur Danto, W. B. Gallie, Jerome Bruner, and Donald Polkinghorne. I am going to take on such issues of narrative theory as the nature of historical narratives and narratives in general, their explanatory roles, and the question of their rationality. The questions I shall be asking are questions like "are narratives explanatory and if so, is there a peculiar narrative way of explaining?" If the answer is "yes", does it mean that narratives belong to the realm of reason or are they somehow subjective, products of our flights of fancy and nothing more? Even though my main focus is on historical narratives, I shall not discuss much the problems of the historical sciences. Rather, I am focusing on the nature of non-fictional narratives, historical narratives being the form of non-fictional narratives that has been most thoroughly studied.

Whenever the protagonist of Jaroslav Hasek's famous novel *The Good Soldier Svejk* attempted to explain something, he invariably did so by telling a tale. He had good reasons for doing so. Both Mink and Danto have put forth some convincing arguments in favour of narratives being essentially explanatory devices of a particular kind. To be sure, they concentrate on historical narratives, but much of what they say has significance for fictional narratives as well. It is also relevant for my idea of *narra-logic*, the narrative analogue to ana-logic.

2.1 Danto

Danto's theories about narratives focus on the main idea that narratives are means for explanation. This we can see in our workaday world. When we need an explanation for singular events, then the most common and the most satisfactory answer has the form of a narrative. I ask you "why did not he come to the meeting?" and you explain by telling a story of how he got ran over by a car on his way to the meeting. Danto says, "A story is an account, I shall say an

explanation, of how the change from beginning to end took place..."
(Danto 1985: 234). In this connection, Danto says that a narrative both
explains and describes at the same time. As a support for this contention, he asks us to consider the following example of a narrative:

> The car was driving East behind a truck; the truck veered left; the driver of the
> car thought the truck was making a left turn, and proceeded to pass on the right;
> but the truck then sharply veered to the right, for it had gone left to make a
> difficult turn into an intersection which the driver of the car had not seen and so
> there was a collision (Danto 1985: 202).

It would be absurd to claim that this story only describes what
happened and does not at the same time explain it. The explanation for
the collision is found in the middle of the story, when the driver of the
car misunderstood the actions of the truck driver and acted
accordingly. This holds for all stories: the middle provides the cause
that explains the event in question. Indeed, any causal explanation,
even in the natural sciences, has the form of a narrative (Danto 1985:
237).

Providing causal explanations is not enough; a narrative must be
relevant for the intention of the storyteller. One of the reasons for this
is that "...any narrative is a structure imposed upon events, grouping
some of them together with others, and ruling some out as lacking
relevance" (Danto 1985: 132). The relevance in question depends
upon the intentions and interests of the narrator. For Marx, the story of
the class struggle in France is theoretically relevant for his theory of
history as one of class struggle. For Edward Gibbon it is morally
relevant to tell the story of the decadent Byzantine rulers in order to
show the contrast to the more enlightened monarchs of his own time
(Danto 1985: 133).

According to Danto, relevance is a necessary moment in a
narrative. The reason is that a description does not automatically
become a narrative just because it describes events in a time sequence
while explaining them at the same time. Consider the following
example: *E:* Naram-Sin built the temple in Sippar as a result of pressure from the priests, then the Thirty Years' War started because of
the mutual hatred between the Catholics and the protestants, then
Arthur Danto woke up at seven o'clock in order to reach a lecture
(Danto 1985: 117). It goes against the grain of common sense to call
this 'a narrative'; the events do not form a unity and it is precisely the

job of narratives to unify events. The unifying job is done both by the explanatory power of the narrative and its relevance to given projects. Furthermore, Danto says that an implicit reference to a stable, continuous object is an important precondition for a narrative's unification. *E* does not contain any reference to a stable object, and only such objects can be said to be changeable, which is fundamental because the role of narratives is to describe change (Danto 1985: 235).

At the same time, Danto points out that the beginning and the end of a narrative are not causally connected but form the contours of a temporal whole. We can say that they are connected as part and whole, and that the connection is obviously conceptual, not causal. It is obviously built into the concept of temporal whole that it must have a beginning and an end.

He defines 'narrative unity' in the following fashion:

.... if N is a narrative, then N lacks unity unless (A) N is about the subject, (B) N adequately explains the change in that subject which is covered by explanandum, and (C) N contains only so much information as is required by (B) and no more (Danto 1985: 251).

Danto's most original contribution to the analysis of historical narratives is perhaps his idea of *narrative sentences* (Danto 1985: 143-183 and 342-365). The following would be a narrative sentence, according to Danto: (NS1) "The Thirty Years' War started in 1618". Those who experienced the start of the war could not have known that they were experiencing the start of the Thirty Years' War, unless they could have foreseen the future, which Danto thinks is logically impossible. Descriptions in sentences of this kind have as part of their truth-conditions events that take place after the events to which the sentences primarily refer. In our case, the event primarily referred to is obviously the start of the war in 1618; the end of the war is a later event that is a part of the truth-conditions for the sentence. The events described in a narrative sentence can always be put in new narrative contexts. NS1 was a perfectly meaningful sentence in 1649 but not NS2: "in 1618 there started a war, which postponed German unification for over 250 years". NS2 is a narrative sentence, which puts the events of 1618 in a new narrative context.

Danto says that the structure of the narrative entails the openness of the future. If the future were determined once and for all, then events would not influence future states. If this were the case, historical narratives would have no work to do because their job is to establish causal links between events. Indeed, if the future were determined, events in the past and future would be independent of each other, and so narrative redescriptions of a given event in the light of later events would be impossible. The narrative redescription, given in NS2, would become meaningless because there would not be any connections between the Thirty Years' War and the later development in Germany (Danto 1985: 353).

Besides not discriminating between narratives and stories, one of the problems with Danto's analysis of narratives is that he does not put forth a non-ambiguous definition of the concept of a narrative. Certainly, a satisfactory *definiens* would give prominence for narrative sentences and the explanatory role of narratives. Instead, Danto hints that turning points, crises, and climaxes are important parts of the structure of narratives (Danto 1985: 354). It remains unclear, then, whether he thinks that they are necessary conditions for narratives. What is clear is that Danto discriminates between 'atomic' and 'molecular narratives'. An atomic narrative comprises only a beginning, a middle, and an end; a molecular narrative is a combination of atomic narratives (Danto 1985: 250-255).

We can sum up Danto's theory of historical narratives in the following manner:

1. The narrative describes how one or more permanent objects changes and provides causal explanations.
2. The narrative describes and explains at the same time.
3. A narrative contains narrative sentences, and they play a decisive role in it.
4. The events are described in a temporal sequence.
5. The course of time makes new redescriptions possible or even mandatory.
6. It must hang together, partly causally, partly logically.
7. It requires the openness of the future.
8. a) The narrative has a temporal beginning and end; b) it often contains climaxes, crises, and turning points.
9. It is either atomic or molecular.

Danto shows us that historical narratives have their own logic, in part owing to the peculiar nature of the narrative sentences. He is also right about narratives being explanatory, but he focuses too one-sidedly on causal explanations; we shall discover later that narratives also explain in a non-causal fashion.

Even though Danto only speaks about historical narratives, his model can be helpful for the understanding of fictional narratives. Such narratives explain the 'events' of the fictional world and use narrative sentences of sorts, whereby the later events, which provide parts of their truth-conditions, are events appearing later in fictional time.

But the fact that Danto ignores fictional narratives might be the explanation for his ignoring the concept of a plot. (He might though have been close to operating with that concept when he said that climaxes and so on were often a part of a narrative.) Maybe he somehow thought that plot only exists in the realm of fiction, not history. That is consistent with the hidden positivistic tendency of his analysis; both his description of full-fledged narratives as being mechanical combinations of atomic narratives and his attempt to find the logical form of narratives reveal this inclination. A consideration of his atomic narratives tells us that his calling them 'narratives' or 'stories' is not in accordance with ordinary parlance. Am I really telling a story when I say, "I opened the door and then I went inside"? It is definitely not a prototypical narrative. A prototypical narrative would be longer and would have a plot of sorts: "I came home late that evening, walked up the steps, opened the door, and then went inside. And, believe or not, all my friends were standing there, shouting 'surprise!'" There is obviously a plot in this story but not in the sense of the aforementioned atomic 'narrative'. They can, however, be called 'proto-stories' because they have some of the moments of stories, for instance, the linking of events in time. They are certainly among the raw materials we use when we recount a narrative. But I simply cannot see how a plot can be created just by combining atomic narratives or stories into molecular ones. I could combine my little example of an atomic narrative with countless others of a similar kind without creating anything resembling a narrative with a plot. What matters is the *manner* in which the narrative is constructed out of smaller units (atomic narratives or whatever). The selection of units is decisive. In fact, Donald Polkinghorne quite correctly says that Danto focuses on narrative sentences rather than narrative discourse, and the result is that he treats history as though it were a chronicle, a series of specific connections but lacking a unified theme (Polkinghorne 1988: 50). Polkinghorne's point is undoubtedly similar to mine.

There are still further problems with the idea that narratives comprise the combination of narrative sentences. Narratives do in fact often contain a host of non-narrative sentences, some of which are often essential to the narrative. Consider Tolstoy's way of opening *Anna Karenina* with a statement about the difference between happy and unhappy families. Everybody knowledgeable about the novel knows that this statement plays a crucial role. The same holds for Ivan Karamzov's claim that if God is dead, then everything is permitted. This claim is a very important part of Dostoyevsky's narrative of the *Karamazov Brothers*. In historical narratives all kinds of non-narrative sentences can be decisive. One cannot, for instance, tell the tale of the destruction of Pompeii unless one informs the receiver of the location of that town. Moreover, Danto ignores non-linguistic narratives, like ballets or comics without words. Further, non-linguistic representtations often play a major role in a narrative, such as the role of maps in historical narratives.

Despite the fact that Danto seems to believe that narratives are theories of a kind, he appears to think that they do not form or influence facts in any way, which is all the more strange in the light of his stress upon the decisive role of theory in the realm of arts (Danto 1964: 571-584). Does he really think that artworks are theory-dependent while historical facts are not? Regardless of his analysis of art, if narratives are theories of kind, then it is plausible that they co-determine historical facts, just like scientific theories co-determine facts.

2.2 Mink, Gallie, Bruner, Polkinghorne

Maybe we can find an antidote to Danto's crypto-positivism in Mink's work. According to him, the very idea of a narrative form has some conceptual presuppositions that shape the subject of narratives.[1] The most important is the beginning-middle-end structure of narratives. The experiences of our lives do not by any necessity have the form of narrative, but when we tell the tales of these experiences, this narrative structure shapes them. Some events are called 'beginnings', others 'ends', and so on. But do not these events exist in an objective fashion, independent of whatever narrative structure we might impose upon them? No, says Mink, the concept of an event is pretty unclear. Was, for instance, the Renaissance an event? We may speak of a war as an event but a war comprises battles and battles of engagements of units and engagement by units of actions by individuals and so on. Secondly, we cannot refer to events as such but only events under a description, so there can be more than one description of the same event which are all true but refer to different aspects of the event or describe it at different levels of generality. But cannot the *same event* be said to be described by two narratives, one truer to the facts than the other? No, Mink says, there is no such thing as 'the same event' completely independent of descriptions. Historical events are abstractions from narratives.

In the natural sciences, one of the major functions of theory is to provide scientists with stipulations what counts as a unit-event and what descriptions of events are acceptable. But if the same were applied to historians, historical narratives would simply become superfluous for the understanding of events. Stipulations like those in natural sciences would rule out redescriptions of events and without such redescriptions, no narratives (Mink 1991: 219-220).

Now, could we not decide the truth-values of historical narratives simply by matching the different, referring statements in it with reality? No, responds Mink. Historical narratives are more than just a logical conjunction of past-referring statements, in stark contrast to chronicles. The only ordering relation in a chronicle is 'and then'. Narratives, however, contain indefinitely many ordering relations and indefinitely many ways of combining them. It is such a combination

---

[1] Mink also says that particular narratives express their own conceptual presuppositions and that they are, in fact, our most useful evidence for understanding conceptual presuppositions that are quite different from ours. It is through the plots of Greek tragedies that we can best understand the Greek idea of Fate, he says (Mink 1991: 215).

that creates the coherence of narratives or lack of it. Historical narratives claim truth, not only for each of its individual statements taken distributively, but also for the complex form of the narrative itself. Only by virtue of such a form can there be a story of triumph or tragedy, of plans miscarried or successful adventures.

Actually, narrative form cannot be said, only shown, and therefore it is meaningless to test its truth-value in any ordinary, empirical way. We can neither summarise nor restate a narrative as an inventory of conclusions or findings. Therefore, if anyone asks for reasons for accepting or rejecting them, the answer would not simply be a recital of a piece of evidence, as is usual when we try to find support for a generalisation. It would rather be the repetition of the way in which the narrative has ordered the evidence.

The cognitive function of narrative form is not only to relate a succession of events but also to embody an ensemble of the inter-relationships of many different kinds as a single whole. So while we can decide empirically what are the facts or the relations between them, we cannot resolve disputes about the possible combinations of relations. And just as evidence does not dictate which story is to be constructed, so it does not bear on the preference of one story to another. With regard to the narrative treatment of an ensemble of interrelationships, we credit the imagination, the sensibility or the insight of the individual historian. Narrative form in history, as in fiction, is an artifice; it is the product of individual imagination (Mink 1991: 217-218).

According to Mink, narrative is primarily a cognitive instrument, rivalled only by theory and by metaphor as one of the irreducible ways of making the flux of experience comprehensible. Narrative is particularly important as a rival to theoretical explanations. Theory makes possible the explanation of an occurrence only by describing it in such a way that the description relates logically to a systematic set of generalisations or laws. One can understand the operation of a spring-powered watch only in so far as one understands the principles of mechanics. This requires describing the mechanism of the watch in the terms and only in the terms appropriate for these principles. One could not understand the operations of a watch and fail to understand the operation of a millwheel or vice versa. But a particular watch also has a history. It is produced in one place, shipped to another, bought by someone, admired by another, and cursed by the third party. At each moment of its career, it is or may be a part of a connected series of events, which intersects its own history. At each such moment it will be subject to a particular description that is appropriate only *because* of that intersection. From the standpoint of theoretical understanding, the type of appropriate description is given, and it is not problematic. But the particular history of the watch escapes theoretical understanding simply because envisioning that history requires the attribution of indefinitely many descriptions of it, which are either relevant or irrelevant to the sequence that intersects its career. Mink says that this is what the narrative form uniquely represents, and why we require it as an irreducible form. On the one hand, there are all the occurrences in the world in their concrete particularity. On the other hand, there is an ideally theoretical understanding of those occurrences that would treat each as nothing but a replicable instance of a systematically interconnected set of generalisations. But between these extremes, the narrative is the form in which we make comprehensible the many successive interrelationships that are comprised by a career (Mink 2001: 213-214). The upshot of this is that while nomological sciences generalise, narratives 'singularise'.

It is worthwhile to consider whether Mink is going a bit too far in his constructivism. If there is no way to confirm or disconfirm narratives in an empirical manner, how is one to tell the difference between, say, a factual history and counterfactual one? I can write a plausible counterfactual story about how Germany and the world would have developed if right-wing nationalist Hugenberg had become chancellor instead of Hitler. Nevertheless, this story is not a candidate for being a historical narrative due to empirical reasons.

We are well aware that historical accounts are regularly criticised for containing inaccurate or even blatantly wrong statements. However, Mink's theorising renders such criticisms worthless, on par with voodoo or rain dancing. And I should rather believe in the importance of such criticisms than in Mink's exciting but perhaps too speculative theories. I also find a bit odd his insistence that the narrative form is analogous to Wittgenstein's logical form. Logical form is something that is essential shared between a symbolic structure and that which it successfully symbolises (Wittgenstein 1922: 81 (§4.124 and elsewhere). But is it not Mink's point that narrative form does not necessarily share a structure with what the narrative symbolises, that the structure is imposed upon its object? Mink appears to think that these two forms are of the same kind and therefore not sayable. But they are not of the same kind, so they are either sayable, and if not, then unsayable of some other reasons than Mink's own. However, it would not surprise me at all if there were a grain of truth in Mink's theorising, that narrative form is something that must be disclosed and is not entirely expressible in propositions that can tested empirically. This means that knowing narrative form requires not only evaluating truth-claims of propositions but also the alethetic values of disclosure. Surely, the whole of narrative is bigger than its parts; it is more than just a sum of empirically testable propositions. And surely it shapes its object, possibly twisting it in the process, bringing twisted understanding into the play.

But are empirical, non-narrative theories all that different from narratives? In the first place, our observations through which we test these theories are theory-laden and thus shaped by theory. Secondly, a theory stating a natural law has an infinite number of testable implications, and so the theory can hardly be understood as just being the sum of its empirical implications (see for instance Popper 1959). Nevertheless, by testing these implications in a scientific manner, we can hope to be able to decide the fate of the theory rationally. This of course on the condition that science is not simply a social construct or some kind of an illusion. Or even on the condition that theories are not absolutely depended upon something akin to conceptual schemes (for instance paradigms) and therefore only evaluable within the confinement of the scheme. If that is not the case and given that narrative form is not unsayable, then we ought to be able to evaluate narratives in a rational fashion. Whatever limits there are to the rationality of science they are more or less the same as whatever limitation the rationality of narratives might have. Now, I see disclosure as a perfectly rational operation so if narrative form is something to be disclosed and nomological theories are not, then it does not mean that narratives are any less rational than such theories. The rational moment of disclosure is its ability to enlighten us; we shall learn more about this ability later. We will focus on Mink for a while; he seems to underestimate the rational potential of historical narratives of several reasons. In the first place, he is wrong about the unsayable being beyond reason; disclosure surely is not. Secondly, he underestimates the role of the empirical in historical narratives. Thirdly, while being right about narratives being a particular form of explanation, he does not see that such explanations belong to the realm of reason. Narratives explain *post festum*; there is an asymmetry between explanation and prediction in historical narratives. Such narratives do not make predictions because they are bound to regard the future as open. Any recurrence in a narrative of covering laws is incidental. So even if they can utilise covering laws, their basic role is to 'singularise' rather than to generalise. They help us make sense of the past by making past events cohere. We have rational ways of choosing between historical accounts, at least relative to some paradigm or something of that sort. Some accounts are productive for historical research, some are not. Some are plainly wrong, like the one about Adam and Eve, if it is considered as a plain historical narrative (but it is not necessarily wrong if regarded as a metaphoric fable about the human predicament or as a moral thought-experiment). A narrative about early civilisations that does not contradict established scientific evidence about the origin of Man is *ceteris paribus* better than a creationistic narrative. So the truth-values of certain propositions *constrain* narratives, even though narratives themselves might not possess truth-conditions. Chances are that they possess another set of alethetic values, for instance T-correctness. Further, Mink ignores the crucial difference between narratives and stories. We will later see that storied structures abound and that they have certain objectivity while narratives have a stronger moment of subjectivity and constructivity, somewhat Minkian style. At the same time, narratives are essential for the articulation and understanding of the storied structures; more about that in a later chapter.

Actually, Jerome Bruner maintains that stories cannot be true but can possess *verisimilitude* or lifelikeness. There are two essentially different modes of thought, the *narrative* and the *paradigmatic*, i.e., the logico-scientific mode. When operating on the paradigmatic level, we try to convince people of the truth of our propositions with the aid of arguments; when on the narrative level, we try to make stories life-like. The word 'then' functions in tellingly different ways on these levels. There is a gap between the 'then' in the logical proposition "if x, then y" and "The king died and then the queen died" (Bruner 1986: 11-13). But is there really a gap between the narrative and the logico-scientific mode? Bruner does not seem to be aware of the explanatory power of narratives; he seems to think that the paradigmatic thought monopolises causal explanations and for that matter truth and other alethetic values. Further, he all but ignores the possibility of logico-scientific thought being replete with narratives in such a manner that paradigmatic thought does not play any significant role in it.[2] There might be no such thing as pure paradigmatic thought, and the concept of it could very well be a lofty abstraction from real arguments. However, my hunch is that the discrimination between the two can be fruitful if corrected in the way already suggested. To be sure, they are ideal types, in any narrative research worth its salt, there is a moment of the paradigmatic and in logico-scientific thought of the best kind, there are narrative elements. But both are instruments for rational inquiries, paradigmatic thought has truth as its main alethetic value while in narrative inquiries such alethetic values as T-correctness and Bruner's verisimilitude take the centre stage. I will discuss the problem of narratives and alethetic values in the next two chapters, now I will turn my gaze to Donald Polkinghorne's somewhat Ricœurian way of elaborating this differentiation between paradigmatic and narrative discourses. He says that both convey factual information by their sentences, but they impose additional kinds of information in the form of the coherence they impose upon their sentences. The kind of coherence imposed by narrative discourse differs radically from that of paradigmatic discourse, not least because the plot creates the kind of coherence in question, and there is no such thing as plot in paradigmatic discourses. Historical narratives have two referents, the first to the events that make up the story, the second to the plot. When a receiver of a historical narrative recognises the type of story being told, understands that it is an epic, tragedy, etc., then the receiver has comprehended the secondary referent. Notice that the same events can be organised in a protocol or chronicle and thus by a paradigmatic discourse. But then the sentences about the events are organised differently, in a way not at all resembling a plot. Meaning held in second-order referent is a result of a particular kind of plot, and it is used to draw first-order events together. The logic of coherence of the second-order referent is different from formal logic. This logic of plot is used in narrative to make events cohere into meaningful wholes. The kind of truths narrative history is concerned with is of a different

---

[2] For such a view of scientific thought, see for instance Harré 1990: 81-101.

order than the kind generated by the formal logic of scientific discourse. The test of truth of historical narrative is its capacity to yield a plot from a set of first-order real events. The test in question is one of coherence rather than of correspondence. Further, historical narratives take the types of plots we find in literature and myths and try to find out whether they pass the test of endowing real events with meaning. When it all comes down to dust, historical narratives are a test of a culture's capacity to fictionalise, to endow real events with the kinds of patterns of meaning that its stories form from imagined events. In this fashion, historical narratives transform a culture's collection of past events (first-order referents) by shaping them into a second-order pattern of meaning. The truth of second-order referents is established by the principles of coherence that a particular culture follows. Analogously, in formal science, reference to the accuracy of the first-order observation only partly determines the truth of a research report. Determining the truth requires in addition a second-order logical coherence among the statements. This brings to mind Polkinghorne's view that paradigmatic thinking has its own ways of creating coherence (Polkinghorne 1988: 60-63). Overall, I find Polkinghorne's analysis very compelling, with the notable exception of the expression 'second-order referent'. He regards paradigmatic discourse as organising facts in a way similar to narrative discourse. But if the latter has a second-order referent, are we not compelled to say that the former also has a second-order referent, namely the category of theory or the category of a chronicle or a protocol? Where we end up seems strange and counter-intuitive to me, for the implication is that a theory refers to the category of theory. I have, however, no problem with the idea that there is way in which a discourse organises its referents in a manner that partly decides their cognitive import. A chronicle of the facts of the holocaust surely has a different cognitive import than a narrative of the holocaust recounting a terrible tragedy. In the narrative, the facts about the events are seen as parts of a whole, but in the chronicle they are isolated, without rhyme or reason.

Just like Bruner and Polkinghorne, W. B. Gallie also wanted to draw a sharp dividing line between narratives and argumentation. Argumentation uses completely different processes than narratives. The conclusion of an argument is compelling, and following the argument correctly gives us the ability to predict its deductive conclusion. This is not the case when we follow a story: its ending cannot be deduced or predicted. Because the story holds surprises and coincidences, we must follow it through to the end. We cannot predict the ending with absolute certainty and confidently skip over half the story. However, even if the story does not have predictability, its conclusion must have a sense of *acceptability* or rightness, which means that it must be somehow plausible. When we look back from the end of the story, we accept that the end follows from the events that have led to it. Understanding a story means understanding its internal coherence, the way the story unifies the various chance events and various responses to them. The story must make sense. The central moment of a story is its *followability*, not its predictability. To follow a story means to understand the successive actions, thoughts, and feelings of the characters and to be *pulled* forward by this development, almost as though against our will. Our interest is pulled forward by the presumption that the result of the story is one of a few specifiable kinds: either the hero will win or lose, rescued by his own cunning or by someone else, etc. In the last analysis our sympathies or antipathies with the characters and our fellow men are that which determine followability. Our sympathies with the hero 'demands' that the story ends in a particular way, say, in his escape from prison. But even if our ability to follow a story is thus rooted in our emotional life, it is also an intellectual capacity. There are people who excel in following and even creating stories while others do not, even though the latter might include those who excel in abstract, systematic studies. The paradigmatic mode of thinking is their thing, not the narrative one (Gallie 1968: 22-50 and Gallie 2001: 40-51).

I reckon that Ricœur is right about Gallie's filling a lacuna in Danto's thinking. Danto focuses too one-sidedly on the nature of narrative sentences, while Gallie understands the necessity of viewing the narrative texts as a whole (Ricœur 1984a: 149). I want to add that Gallie, in contrast to Danto, sees the necessity of focusing on the pragmatics of narrative. One consequence among others is that we must take account of the receivers of the story, that is, the readers or the listeners and their emotional make-up. At the same time, just like Danto, Gallie quite correctly stresses the explanatory role of narratives, which are ideally self-explanatory (Gallie 1968: 23). If we know the 'what' of a story, we usually know its 'why'; we can explain Oedipus' way to kingship by recounting his story.

2.3 Conclusion

As we have seen, I think Danto and Mink are on the whole right about stories having explanatory power, that they are particular modes of explanations. Danto's analysis of narrative sentences is quite convincing. We have also discovered that while Danto neglects the constitutive and shaping power of narratives, Mink overestimates them. He underestimates the rational potential of narratives. But he certainly is correct about the configurative role of narratives. At the same time, Gallie rightly shows that followability is a central feature of narratives. While Bruner underestimates the explanatory power of narratives, he also argues forcefully in favour of a fruitful separation of paradigmatic and narrative reasoning. Polkinghorne draws from Bruner's ideas and the ideas of other theorists to productive effect.

Notice that none of these theorists differentiate between narratives and stories. Being blind to the existence of storied structure, they tend to overestimate the moment of constructivity and subjectivity in the world of narratives/stories (Danto is of course an exception, over-estimating the moment of objectivity in narratives). They are right about there being large moments of constructivity and subjectivity in narratives but they do not see the objectivity of storied structures.

Narratives certainly have a cognitive role to play; they have an explanatory function. We may say, therefore, that there is nothing wrong with Svejk's propensity to explain by recounting.

II.3. Fictional and Non-Fictional Narratives
On White's Tropology, the Concept of Literature and Related Issues

This chapter as well as the next one considers the relationship between fictional and non-fictional narratives. I shall take as a point of departure Hayden White's 'deconstruction' of that difference and give a brief overview over his theories, especially the ones concerning the relationship between narratives and metaphors. I shall then turn to various responses to his theorising. I shall begin with Noël Carroll's criticism of White and follow with Peter Lamarque and Stein Haugom Olsen's criticism. In the course of that discussion, I shall put forth my own critique of White and his critics and as part of that endeavour introduce my own view of fiction, non-fiction, and the concept of literature.

3.1 White's Narrative Tropology

One of the basic themes of this book is the relationship between narratives and metaphors. An implication of White's theories about history is that there is an essential interaction between narratives and metaphors in the field of history. In the first place, historical narratives are in a way metaphors and their truth is metaphoric. Such narratives not only describe historical events but also suggest a similarity between these events and those story-types we use to endow the events of our lives with meaning. Black correctly says that metaphors have analogical implications and something similar seems to hold for historical narratives in White's view. These narratives are complexes of symbols that direct the reader towards the structural icons of those events in his or her literary traditions. When a historian describes a given concourse of events as a tragedy, he or she is really alluding to fictional tragedies, in the same way as metaphors create a host of allusions (White 1978: 88). At the same time, this similarity with fictive narratives does not make historical narratives fantasies or lies. Fiction is meant to correspond to the general outlines of some field of human existence, which is no less real than the reality to which historians refer (White

1978: 122). This is to my mind an interesting point. Kafka's story *Die Verwandlung* (*Metamorphosis*) is in a way a pure fantasy but can be said to correspond to a slice of that field of human existence we call 'relationship between members of a family' or even the human condition in general. Secondly, historical narratives have as a precondition that the field they represent has been constituted or formed by figuration in which metaphors figure prominently. This process of pre-figuration is *precritical* and *precognitive*. It constitutes the concepts that a historian needs in order both to identify the objects of this domain and to characterise the kinds of relationships that they can sustain with each other (White 1973: 30-31). But to understand this, we must become familiar with the general outlines of White's theory of historical narratives. In his view, stories are made, not found; events are given a narrative structure by the suppression or subordination of certain facts and the highlighting of others (the kinship with Mink is obvious). This making of stories is done by using the techniques of emplotment for novels: characterisation, motific repetition, variations of both tone and points of view, and alternative descriptions (White 1978: 84). Both historians and authors of fiction have to use the same poetic techniques for fusing together events in a comprehensive totality, which is capable of serving as an object of representtation, even though the former presumably write about real events and the latter about imaginary ones (White 1978: 125).

As I hinted at, White thinks that historical narratives are mainly like fictional ones. This does not mean that he believes that historical facts do not exist. They do exist and can be embedded in narratives in countless different ways, none of which is inherently truer than the other (White 1978: 121). Thus, in one narrative the death of a king can be the end of an era, in another the dramatic turning point when the fortunes of his subjects turn for the better, and in yet another it is the beginning of some new historical process. Historical narratives require emplotment, just like fictional narratives. And emplotment is the way by which a sequence of events fashioned into a story is gradually revealed to be a story of a particular kind, say, a tragedy. At the same time, the historians also explain events with the aid of emplotment. An explanation of an event would be different if it were understood as part of a tragedy than if it were a part of a comedy (White 1973: 7). In a tragedy, a certain event might be the consequence of a tragic misunderstanding. At the same time, what is tragic from one point of view is comic from another. Our subjective values play a decisive role. But this does not mean that there are no limits to emplotment. For instance, John F. Kennedy's life can hardly be emplotted as a comedy (White 1978: 84). As for the Holocaust, it would not be acceptable to emplot it as a comedy if it were presented as a literal representation and the comic moment as inherent in the facts (White 2001: 377).

But why does the historian need to emplot his discourse? The answer is that in order to understand something new, we must somehow familiarise it. One way of doing it is to subsume it under a well-known causal law, something that the historian finds hard to do because of the lack of fruitful nomological explanations in history. Instead, the historian familiarises historical events by given them a shape we know, namely the shape of fictional stories (White 1978: 84-88). This holds especially for traumatic events that are hard to comprehend. Who can really understand the terrible suffering of the victims of the holocaust, the anguish of six million people? But put into the familiar fictional form of tragedy it might become somewhat easier to understand. This I find very convincing, it certainly adds support to the idea that metaphors help us understand the ineffable. It is easier for us to understand the holocaust if we regard it metaphorically as a tragedy.

White opines that the problem is both that history has no generally accepted technical terminology and that there is no agreement upon what its specific subject matter is. Therefore, it does not have any other instrument for rendering the strange into the familiar except for the techniques of figurative language (White 1978: 94). Deep down, we can only know the actual by contrasting it with or likening it to the imaginable, i.e., the fictional (White 1978: 98).

There are four basic modes of emplotment for a historical narrative: tragedy, comedy, romance, and satire. These four kinds of emplotment correspond to four modes of argument and to four modes of ideological implication, as can be seen in the following scheme (White 1973: 29).[1]

Mode of emplotment	Mode of argumentation	Mode of ideological implication
Romantic	**Formist**	**Anarchist**
Tragic	**Mechanist**	**Radical**
Comic	**Organicist**	**Conservative**
Satirical	**Contextualist**	**Liberal**

In a romance, the hero triumphs over an evil after a great ordeal. In comedy, there is hope for the temporary triumph of Man over world, but in tragedy, despite the tragic fall of the hero, there is a moral lesson to be learned, and the spectators gain in consciousness. They certainly have no hopes of doing so when exposed to satire, because in satire Man is ultimately a captive of the world rather than its master (White 1973: 8-9). Formism is idiographic, classificatory, and descriptive. One explains by classifying and describing. Mechanistic explanations are quite straightforwardly causal and typically in the form of deductive-nomological theories. And as one might guess, an organicist world-hypothesis depicts particulars in a historical field as parts of synthetic processes. From this point of view, individual entities aggregate into wholes that are greater than the sum of parts. They are then explained in a teleological fashion. Finally, contextualists explain events by setting them within their wider contexts of occurrences. I am not going to discuss the ideological implications in any detail; I

---

[1] White acknowledges his debt to other thinkers for the content of this scheme. Thus, the modes of emplotment are borrowed from Northrop Frye, the modes of argument from Stephen Pepper, and the modes of ideological implications from Karl Mannheim. Note that White, in contrast to Pepper, does not seem to have a metaphorist view of the whole world, only the world of history or the studies not (yet?) elevated to the status of science. He seems to presume that the natural sciences are not based upon prefiguration (White 1973: xi).

shall only mention that radicals cannot really accept formism because this approach tends to regard the objects of its classification as given, not as parts of a whole and there is no possibility of any deeper explanation. More important to our discussion is White's contention that there are no extra-ideological grounds on which to arbitrate among the conflicting conceptions of the historical process and of historical knowledge appealed to by different ideologies. We cannot really claim that one of the conceptions of historical knowledge, favoured by a given ideology, is more realistic than another because ideologists disagree over what constitutes an adequate criterion of realism. Nor can we claim that one conception of historical knowledge is more scientific than another without prejudging the problem of what a specifically historical or social science ought to be (White 1973: 26). If I have understood White correctly, then ideologies are a necessary component of any historical narrative, and the very existence of this component is one of the factors that make objectivity an unattainable ideal for historians.

According to White, the aforementioned constitution of the field of historical investigation is actually a pre-figuration in which the field is structured by one of the four tropes: metaphor, metonymy, synecdoche, and irony. If we prefigure a field of objects though metaphor, we see the similarities between the phenomena. (White seems to use 'metaphor' quite broadly, encompassing both analogy and simile.) If we look at the world through the lenses of metonyms, we tend to divide the objects into two halves, one of which is the essence or the cause of the other, just like when we use metonyms like 'fifty sails' for ships. We imply that the sails are the essential part of the ship. So no wonder that a field prefigured by metonyms easily yields to mechanistic explanations. A synecdoche, as White uses that term, is organically integrative, unlike the reductive metonymy (ships are reduced to sails). Usually, synecdoche involves the whole representing the part or the other way round. But White says that a synecdoche integrates two parts within a whole that is qualitatively different from the sum of its parts. An example could be HE IS ALL HEART whereby 'heart' is understood figuratively as not designating a part of the body but a quality of personality. It almost goes without saying that this integrative trope corresponds to organicism. Metaphor is representational just like formism. In a metaphor like MY LOVE IS A ROSE, 'rose' represents the beloved. In irony, it is the other way round: one negates on the figurative level what is being affirmed on the literal level. White regards oxymoron and catachresis as being types of irony. The connections to satire should be obvious.

In White's view, these four *master tropes* (Kenneth Burke's expression) also correspond to the Piagetian schema of cognitive development. The early, sensori-motor stage of human development corresponds roughly to a metaphoric way of seeing things; the next representational stage has affinities with metonymy; the operational stage with synecdoche; and finally the logical with irony (White 1978: 12).[2] The last connection is pretty obvious; it is hard to be ironic unless one has a way of coolly analysing an object. Also important to White is Piaget's contention that the shifts between the different stages are like Gestalt-switches (paradigm-shifts in Kuhnian termino-logy) (White 1978: 6). *Mutatis mutandis*, the same holds for shift between tropes. Such shifts mean a re-structuring of the perceptual fields so that perception under the auspices of one trope cannot be compared to the perception under the auspices of another.[3] There is no neutral way of assessing the claims of each way of perceiving the world; they are 'incommensurable', to use Kuhn's catchword yet again. Since the tropes structure the field of historical narratives, they are by implication incommensurable. (These are to my mind the consequences of White's theorising.) This further strengthens White's view that there is no such thing as a true narrative. In the last analysis we can only choose between historical narratives on aesthetic (the attractiveness of emplotments) or moral (ideological) grounds (White 1973: xii). However, there is a thing or two we can learn about histori-cal occurrences, thanks to narratives. Our understanding of them increases to the degree that we are successful in determining how far they conform to the strategies of sense-making that we find in literary art (White 1978: 92). We experience the fictionalisation of history as

---

[2] White does not only find affinities between his tropology and Piaget's theories, but also Freud's theory of dreams, Marx's theories, etc.

3 At the same time, White hints at there being some sort of development involved, in a similar fashion as Piaget's cognitive development. This idea of development derives from Giambattista Vico, who maintained that in the earliest stages of its history, mankind thought metaphorically, and then moved on to metonymic and synecdochic stages. Ironic mode is the last and 'highest' of the tropological modes. The idea of the four master tropes is of Vicoian provenance even though it has older roots (Vico 1984).

an explanation in a similar fashion as we regard great fiction as something that illuminates our world (White 1978: 99).

The trouble is that the closest thing that I have come to finding any argument in favour of the idea of prefiguration is in his attempt to show the analogies between his tropes and Piaget's idea of cognitive development, or for that matter Freud's theory of dreams or Marx's theories. White says that the 'fact' that there are analogies between the tropology and the thinking of these three thinkers vindicates his theory (White 1978: 19). But, in the first place, we cannot take as given that the tropes correspond to Piaget's stages (or Freud's analysis of dreams) in any meaningful way, and, secondly, Piaget's own theories (as well as Freud's and Marx's) have been criticised so severely that merely invoking his name does not prove anything (on the criticisms of Piaget, see for instance Giddens 1982: 335) And of course invoking names is not a justifiable way of confirming theory. To be sure, this does not mean that the tropology cannot be given a more solid foundation. Maybe White is onto something when he says that logic is also under the sway of tropology. Inspired by Hegel, White says that syllogism displays signs of troping:

> The move from major premise (All men are mortal) to the *choice* of datum to serve as the minor (Socrates is a man) is itself a tropological move, a 'swerve' from the universal to the particular which logic cannot preside over since it is logic itself that is being served by this move (All men are mortal) to the choice of datum to serve as the minor (S is a man) is itself a tropological move, a swerve from the universal to the particular which logic cannot preside over since it is logic itself that is being served by this move. (White 1978: 3)

White says that if this is true of classical syllogism, then it must be even truer of those pseudo-syllogisms and chains of such syllogisms that make up historical narratives and other products of humanistic science. But as far as I know, White has not developed the idea of syl-logistic troping any further.[4] I do not exclude the possibility that such an idea could be a welcome addition to ana-logic. Until that happens and until White finds better arguments than his *ad hominem* argu-

---

[4] Would not the alleged fact of the troping of logic undercut White's claim that natural science is basically beyond troping? After all, natural science is dependent upon logic. Actually, he sometimes seems to think that troping plays a role in natural science, for instance, by claiming that metonymy is the favoured trope of science. He seemingly portrays Darwin as having done much troping (White 1978: 131). But perhaps troping does not play any role at all in physics.

ments involving Piaget and Freud, I do not see why I should accept his idea of tropology. To make matters worse, White overindulges in ana-logic, committing the analogical fallacy by dealing in dubious, far-fetched analogies. I do not feel compelled to think that there is any interesting analogy between Piaget's sensori-motor stage and the use of metaphors. The behaviour of infants without language does not seem to have anything to do with the employment of a symbolic, often linguistic, category such as the metaphor. Nor do I find it necessary to postulate a link between romances, not even in White's broad sense of that word, and metaphors, let alone formism and anarchism. Having said this I want to laud White for his inspiring analysis of the relationship between historical narratives and metaphors. I think he is right about us having to use the techniques of fictional stories in order to familiarise historical events that are hard, even impossible, to understand. Thus fiction can have a similar function as metaphors often have, making the ineffable understandable.

3.2 Carroll's Criticism

Noël Carroll challenges White's idea that historical narratives are not true in any ordinary sense of the word but only metaphorically true (Carroll 2001: 246-265). As Carroll interprets White, this means that a narrative can be true in the same sense as it can in a way be true that our last meeting was a farce. Carroll accuses White of crypto-positivism because he assumes that there is no historical truth because historical narratives cannot mirror the past as it really was. This assumption does not prove, however, that historical narratives do not possess ordinary truth-conditions. This is precisely Carroll's point. He points out that home movies are made, but they can nonetheless pro-vide accurate information about real lives. So even if historical narra-tives are invented, that does not preclude their capacity to provide accurate representation. In fact, narratives can provide accurate infor-mation of the past through the kind of features they track. Those features include the ingredients of the courses of events, and they in their turn include, among others, background conditions, causes and effects as well as practical deliberations and ensuing actions. White seems to think that there is a disjunction in that either there is one real story or a multiplicity of fictional stories. But this is not so, Carroll says. Take for instance the appointment of Sandra Day O'Connor to the American Supreme Court. This event can figure in a host of a course of events, some in the history of the Day-O'Connor family, others in narratives concerning the social advancement of women in the US. But this does not indicate, let alone prove, that all these stories are fictional. Events can also have different significance in different courses of events. The appointment of Antonin Scalia to the Supreme Court has another significance with regard to the debate on abortion than to the history of Italian-Americans. But the significance in this example is cashed in causally; it is not a poetic creation. (Remember that White seems to treat all creation of meaning in history as a matter of emplotment.) The kind of meaning that an event has in a narrative is a question of its significance with respect to subsequent events, most often as causation or practical reasoning. This kind of significance is hardly arbitrary and definitely not imposed by the form. According to White, the form (in our case the narrative one) creates the content, i.e., the historical truth or reality (White 1987: x). Furthermore, White seems to think that, because historical narratives involve selection, suppression, and so on, they cannot accurately mirror reality and are, therefore, fictional. But this is a residue of old-fashioned empiricism, which reveals White as a closet empiricist. To make matters worse, a reconstruction of a course of events does not become a distortion or a fiction just because it involves selection. We cannot, like White seems to do, argue from the infeasibility of absolute stories (i.e., mirroring reality as it is) to the fictitiousness of all historical narratives. That events figure in different stories presents no obstacle to their being non-fictional. What makes them different stories is that the interests of discrete events are relative to the questions that historians ask of the evidence. It is precisely this relativity that rules out the possibility of absolute stories, but it certainly does not make historical narratives fictional. Rather, it makes the accuracy of historical narratives assessable in relation to what questions are being asked about a relevant course of events. Still further, that we may have to revise our narratives in light of subsequent events does not show that these narratives are fictions, only that there are more stories to be told. Moreover, White is wrong about stories only being invented and never found. Consider the fact that we often plan at least parts of our lives first by telling or visualising stories to ourselves and then trying to enact them. Such stories can play a role in the actual actions of historical agents and thus have causal efficiency in historical events (Carroll 2001: 251). This I think is quite correct. The consequence is that there are situations in which a historian can and must represent such actual stories in historical narratives. (In the last chapter of this section, I shall bolster this contention.)

White conflates the use of imagination with fiction. He is seemingly oblivious of how our imagination plays a central role in our understanding of the world without reducing our comprehension to figments of our imagination. Could I grasp the thing I am seeing right now as computer unless I can imagine that it has sides, which I cannot see? Evidently not, but this does not make the sides I cannot see unreal or fictional. Further, White seems to think that a true interpretation of historical facts must be an absolute interpretation. Such an interpretation would have to be the final word on the subject, and since there are no such interpretations, then literal truth in this field is impossible. But, in contrast to what White seems to think, the truth of one literary interpretation does not make impossible another interpretation being true as well, as long as they do not contradict each other. One can maintain that Orwell's *1984* is about Stalinism and at the same time accept the truth of another interpretation that holds the book to be about totalitarianism.

White appears to presuppose that truth is the only epistemological value relevant to the assessment of historical narratives. Either they are literally true or metaphorically so. But we must also evaluate a historical account with regard to other alethetic values, for instance, various standards of objectivity. A narrative about the outbreak of the American Revolution that fails to recount the debate over taxation could very well contain only true sentences and still be inadequate. This shows that selections in historical narratives are also subject to objective standards, even though these standards are not reducible to truth. They are, however, related to truth. This holds for a standard (an alethetic value) like comprehensiveness. The aforementioned narrative about the American Revolution is simply lacking in comprehensiveness, which one intuitively feels diminishes its degree of truth (this comment on intuition is my addition). It is hard to see why we need an alethetic value like metaphorical truth, Carroll says (need I add that he does not use the expression 'alethetic value'?). Furthermore, White is guilty of committing the fictional fallacy; he thinks that if X does not mirror reality, then X is a fiction. My expression 'fictional fallacy' captures Carroll's point nicely even though he does not use it.

Carroll has some excellent points. First, he is right about some stories being found rather than made. Secondly, he is right about causation and practical deliberations playing a role in the making of the significance of historical narratives. Thirdly, he is right about our being able to represent historical chains of causations in a fairly objecttive manner. Nevertheless, there are three weaknesses in Carroll's arguments, the first concerning the nature of events, the second the definition of historical narrative and of emplotment, and the third metaphorical truth. In the first place, Carroll himself seems to be guilty of a similar empiricist fallacy that he correctly accuses White of committing. He presumes that events are concrete objects, somewhat like things. But, as Mink pointed out, E is only an event under a description; the description gives the event an identity. In one description, E is an eruption of a volcano; in the other it is a series of processes in molecules and atoms. In one description, E is a murder; in another it is an act of self-defence. A given narrative N can describe a given E differently from the one given in N1 or in a non-narrative representation. These descriptions need not conflict and can be equally true, given different perspectives. Thus, one narrative can give the Battle of Stalingrad the identity of 'the turning point of the second world war', and another one the identity of 'the end of old Stalingrad'. There is a way, then, in which narratives decisively shape their objects.

Secondly, Carroll gives the impression of thinking that if N describes causal chains and represents events in a chronological order; it suffices for N to qualify as a narrative. But chronicles also describe causal chains and represent events in a chronological order. As White points out, a chronicle "…does not so much conclude as simply terminate; typically it lacks closure, the summing up of the 'meaning' of the chain of events…" (White 1978: 16). To become a real historical narrative, N must also be emplotted. And being emplotted means having a literary component, the implication being that historical narratives have such a component, in contrast to what Carroll seems to think. Thus, we have the best of both worlds in good historical narratives: causal chains that make them rationally assessable and a literary dimension due to its necessary emplotment.

Thirdly, if Carroll thinks that metaphorical aptness or even metaphorical truth is spurious, then he is dead wrong. We have already seen that metaphors can represent reality in their own fashion. We may add that Nelson Goodman has quite correctly pointed out that it can be more difficult to prove that a person is literally schizoid or paranoid than that he is metaphorically a Don Juan or a Don Quixote (Goodman 1978: 177). So it is not necessarily easier to determine the cognitive value of a literal statement than a metaphoric one.

White, committing the fictional fallacy yet again, apparently regards all metaphors as being simply figments of our imagination, with no relations to reality. They are not necessarily so. From this it follows that if historical narratives are somehow metaphorically apt or not, rather than true or untrue, then it does not follow that their cognitive claims are not rationally assessable. Indeed, these cognitive claims are assessable *because* of metaphors.

3.3 Lamarque and Olsen on Fiction and Non-Fiction

Peter Lamarque and Stein Haugom Olsen disagree vehemently with White and other post-modernist theorists. One of White's faults is that he assimilates the notion of historical truth with the problematic notion of literary or imaginative truth, they say. But not much is gained from trying to explain historical truth through the even more problematic concept of literary truth. Secondly, White sometimes talks like there are, on the one hand, historical facts to be interpreted, and, on the other, that the facts are the products of interpretation. Thirdly, he confuses the objective sense of the term 'history' with history in the descriptive sense. (Thus, what has actually happened in England in the course of time is English history in the objective sense, while a historian's account of it is history in the descriptive sense). Events figure in a story for White, thus he forgets that, in historical accounts, the descriptions of events figure in stories, not the events themselves. (I guess that this means that the events are subsumable under the concepts of history in the objective sense, while descriptions make up history in the account sense.) However, in fiction, events are created by being described; i.e., they are invented. Fictional events are constructed and definitely not reconstructed. In contrast, an historical account often reconstructs events. If past events were constructed, they would cease to be past events and simply become fictional events. Lamarque and Olsen admit that history in this descriptive sense involves the use of literary techniques, but this does not mean that historical accounts thereby become literary works. Nor does it follow that we can identify literature with history. The fact that historical accounts necessarily make use of literary stylistics cannot be a basis for concluding anything about the cognitive value of such accounts. Now, past events are only events under a description and our interests and purposes determine what kind of description we choose. But this fact does not affect the difference in logic between the types of discourses constituting, on the one hand, the practice of history and, on the other hand, the practice of imaginative literature (Lamarque and Olsen 1994: 304-310).

This point can hardly be understood unless one knows the significance of practices in the thought of Lamarque and Olsen. Practices determine what counts as a literary fictional narrative or as non-fictional narrative. The concepts of narrative, literature, and fiction are logically separated. The concept of a narrative is defined by some formal feature. It has an essential temporal dimensions; it imposes a structure (for instance, a plot) on events by connecting them as well as recording them, and even defining them (e.g., the Hundred Years' War). It also involves a narrator and it is told from some perspective. It is indifferent to subject matter, discursive ends, truth, and reference. In contrast to the term 'literature', 'narrative' is not an evaluative term (Lamarque 1990: 131-132 and Lamarque and Olsen 1994: 226-227). A narrative is a literary one if and only if it conforms to the standards of the literary institution. This institution is a rule-governed practice (Lamarque and Olsen 1994: 256). The intentions of an utterer and the response of an audience (their practices) make a work literary, not the semantic nature of sentences. It becomes a literary work if and only if the members of the literary institution take a literary stance towards it. Taking such a stance means among others that the work is being evaluated aesthetically. This means that any given narrative, including historical ones, can be read as a literary one, provided that the reader takes the appropriate literary stance towards it (Lamarque and Olsen 1994: 435).

Now, if the semantic nature of sentences, contained in a work, is irrelevant to its status as a literary work, the question of whether the work refers to reality is irrelevant to the understanding and evaluation of it. *Anna Karenina* would not cease to be a literary fictional narrative even though by chance every single sentence in the novel happened to be true (they do not use this example) (Lamarque and Olsen 1994: 1). To my mind, this implies that these narratives would still be literary works of art even though no literary fictional narrative contained any sentences having truth-value. In order to count as a literary fiction, a fiction must be a make-believe fiction, which involves some kind of distantiation, some kind of willing suspension of disbelief. Not every fiction, moreover, counts as a literary one; daydreams can be totally fictional but that does not make them literary works.

Though Lamarque and Olsen raise some good points against White, I am quite critical of their approach to fictional narratives and the concept of literary works. Their utterer-response model implies that we can call a mathematical treatise 'a literary work' if an audience takes a literary stance towards it. If I am right about this, would not Lamarque and Olsen's theory then simply empty the concept of a literary work of art of any content? We could, then, subsume anything under the concept in question. We could even imagine a situation were the literary institution decides against regarding novels as literary works and accepts only mathematical treatises as being such works. In light of this, it is impossible, to ignore completely the internal properties of a text when we decide whether or not to subsume it under the heading of a literary work. Consider the following: We are about to decide whether to take a literary stance towards three books. One of them consists of a list of names, the second one of narrative sentences about real events, written sparsely, in a bureaucratic manner, the third is a narrative about an imagined world. Would not the last one be the hottest candidate for becoming an object for such a stance, perhaps the only serious contender? This means that semantic features and internal properties put some constrains upon which books we can confer the identity of a literary work. To be sure, these constrains do not determine such a conferring. Forty years ago, a Swedish poet published a volume of poetry consisting only of numbers and the letter J. Nevertheless, critics accepted it as a literary work of art. But it is tempting to say that they should not have done so; whatever qualities that the book might have possessed, being a proto-typical literary work is not one of them.

Further, the conception of a literary institution is also problematic. In the first place, it does not seem fruitful to liken this alleged institution to pecuniary practices, as Olsen and Lamarque do. They believe that adopting the practice of using money means to ascribe monetary value, and, likewise, adopting the practice of literature means to ascribe literary value (Lamarque and Olsen 1994: 442). But I want to point out that even an anarchist enemy of pecuniary institutions accepts the value of money in practice, but there is no such universal acceptance of literary value. The latter fact speaks against the existence of a literary institution.

Secondly, it is hard to see how this conception can yield anything but a circular definition of the concept of literary work. In fact, Lamarque himself hinted at Olsen's definition of this concept in a review of one of Olsen's books, written before they started their collaboration (Lamarque 1979: 468-471). Lamarque seems to have forgotten his qualms about this definition. In the late 1980s, a young Norwegian student named Ole Martin Skilleås developed this criticism in his own way in a brilliant MA thesis. According to Skilleås, the definition is circular for the following reasons: 1) It defines 'literary qualities' as 'the qualities of literary works which are identified in the literary response'; 2) 'the literary response (appreciation)' is defined as 'the response adopted to literary works by the members of the literary institution'; 3) the literary institution is distinguished by other institutions by the fact that it employs the literary response to literary works. The defining criteria for both the literary attitude and the literary institution depend on each other, thus producing circular definitions. Furthermore, the idea of a literary institution has problems in explaining how literary works and the institution originated. If the rules of the institution of literature were a precondition for the existence and appreciation of literary aesthetic qualities, then the genesis of the literary institution becomes problematic. There must have been an initial literary work, and if the institution existed prior to the work, then it must have been in Platonic form. But, if a literary work existed before the institution, then it would be a mystery how it could have been evaluated (Skilleås 1988).

I tend to agree with Skilleås' criticism. He did not mention, however, that the founding father of the idea of the aesthetic institution, George Dickie, admitted that his definition of 'the aesthetic institution' could not be anything but circular. He defined 'the artworld' as 'that which confers the status of being work of art upon objects'. At the same time, he defined 'a work of art' as 'objects that have had the status of a work of art conferred upon it by the artworld'. The circularity is obvious, and we can ask if the concept of a literary institution can evade this problem. (Just replace terms 'artworld' with 'literary institution' and 'work of art' with 'literary work' and try to find a non-circular definition!) Dickie maintained that he had defined the term 'artworld' so richly that his circle was not vicious but instead productive. Further, one should not focus too one-sidedly on definitions but also on empirical descriptions of the institutional activity. The concept of language is an institutional one but just defining it *in abstracto* does not help us much. Dickie believes that we need a rich description of linguistic practices, and the same holds for the practices of art (Dickie 1974 and Dickie 1995: 213-223). Perhaps he was right, and perhaps the same could be done for the concept of the literary institution. (Skilleås should have mentioned this possibility.) However, given that empirical descriptions play an essential role in the understanding of this institution, we can ask questions like "how great a percentage of readers, professors, critics and so on must agree upon L being a literary work in order for L to deserve that status?", "How can one determine who are the members of the institution?", "Where exactly is the border between acts that are part of the institutional practices and those that are not?" I cannot for the life of me see how these distinctions can be drawn, and they need to be drawn clearly because we are discussing an essential definition.

Think also about the possibility of the institution suddenly deciding that only historical narratives and biographies count as literary works of art (compare my earlier example). My intuition tells me that this means that the acts of the purported institutions cannot have the conferring power that Lamarque and Olsen think they have. The semantic and formal nature of works must count in the defining of the concept of a literary work of art, including a literary narrative. How else can one explain the fact that there must have been something akin to a literary work before the institution came about (if it ever did)? If it makes sense to talk about this institution, then it must have picked some texts as being literary in its moments of birth.

Still further, the concept of 'literary stance' has all kinds of problems of its own. It seems to imply a purely aesthetic attitude towards texts. Taking such an attitude means focusing solely on the features of the text that can produce aesthetic delight or its opposite, while ignoring its moral, political, and cognitive value. But this rarefied aestheticism is very problematic, especially in the light of Carroll's criticism of those whom he calls 'the autonomists'. They think that we can only read literature *qua* works of art if we concentrate on literary works' aesthetic aspects and ignore their moral dimensions. (They think that literature is autonomous in the sense of not depending upon morality, politics, etc.) But even if it were true that we must focus solely on aesthetic features in order to appreciate literature as art, who says we have to appropriate literary works as works of arts? And can we really understand strongly moralistic literary works in a purely aesthetic fashion? Can one ignore the political and moral aspects of George Orwell's novel *1984* and at the same time understand the book? Carroll would certainly say "no"; he maintains that there are certain works, like *Uncle Tom's Cabin* and *Catch-22,* which demand moral assessment. Further, he has pointed out that nobody has come up with a compelling characterisation of what is uniquely artistic, i.e., not 'infected' by morality and politics. In most cases we have to deploy various kinds of reasoning, including moral reasoning, in order to understand literary works. Understanding narratives requires moral knowledge; emotions play an important role in the understanding of narratives, and emotions are imbued with moral concepts. Indignation for injustice is obviously a moral emotion and only by understanding that emotion can we understand a book like *Uncle Tom's Cabin* (Carroll 1998: 126-160).

I want to add that there is no such thing as make-believing a moral vision; grasping such a vision just does not involve anything resembling a willing suspension of disbelief. I make-believe Raskolnikov's murder of the old lady but hardly the moral vision of the novel. Thus, given that understanding this vision is an essential part of understanding the novel, then make-believing is not all there is to understanding novels.

This does not mean that there is one given, correct interpretation of this vision of the novel or literary works in general. And even if there were no such thing as *the* correct interpretation of a literary work, only a multitude of more or less subjective interpretations, it would not make any difference. It would be the case that one could legitimately interpret a literary work without solely make-believing it. There could be interpretations that portray the works as conveyors of empirical or metaphysical truth. Interpreting them in these ways is not a matter of make-believe. In some cases, it would be a matter of firm beliefs that the essential core of a given literary work was this or that empirical or metaphysical truth.

Now, determining the genre or style of a literary work is in many (perhaps all) cases an important part of understanding it. Determining the Harry Potter books as belonging to the genre of realistic novels is hardly conducive for understanding them. To be sure, what counts as being realistic is partly a matter of literary conventions and not entirely of our epistemological beliefs. (Lamarque and Olsen seem to deny that such beliefs have anything to do with this issue, for instance, Lamarque 1990: 137.) Nevertheless, it flies in the face of common sense to say that epistemological beliefs have nothing to say when we subsume the Harry Potter novels under the concept of fantasy and Amos Oz's autobiographical novel *Panther in the Basement* under the concept of realism.

So Lamarque and Olsen throw the baby out with bathwater when they try to eliminate the semantic and epistemological dimensions of the concept of a literary work (and by implication that of literary narrative). Further, their attempt at defining the concepts of literary artwork and literary narrative in an essential manner fails. I am confident that these concepts are amoebaean concepts. Are, for instance, the Icelandic sagas works of fact or fiction? Further, there is a thin line between literary narratives, on the one hand, and religious and philosophical narratives written in a poetic manner, on the other. An example of that kind of religious text can be *The Gospel According to Saint John*; Nietzsche's *Zarathustra* will do as an example of poetic-philosophic work.

The aforementioned example of a text containing only narrative sentences describing a world of fantasy might contain some of the features of a literary narrative but not all because very few texts do. Actually, I think it is more helpful to talk about *indicators of literariness.*[5] The more weight they have in a narrative, the better reason we have for calling it a 'literary narrative'. The first indicator is *fictionality*; a totally fictional narrative has maximum degree of fictionality. The second indicator is *poeticality*, i.e., the presence of poetic devices, for instance, poetic metaphors, similes, analogy, rhyme or alliteration. An alliterative, rhymed narrative, rich in poetic metaphors, contains a high degree of poeticality. Further, a strong presence of poetic metaphors, similes, and analogies means that the text has a high degree of *tropologicality*. The fourth device is *stylicity*, i.e., the presence of stylistic devices, for instance, bizarre language, usually used to create a feeling of estrangement. (This list of indicators is hardly exhaustive.) The more weight these indicators have in a narrative **N**, the more literariness **N** possesses and the better reason we have to call **N** a 'literary narrative'. (There are obviously rules inherent in these four indicators, rules for what points in the direction of L being a literary work, and, of course, there are no rules for applying them.) So obviously, the concept of a literary narrative is an amoebaean one, we cannot find both necessary and sufficient conditions for its application.

But narratives do not exist *an sich*; they have to be understood and interpreted by the reader or listener (They are co-authors of the narrative.) This understanding or interpretation takes place in the context of various practices, which I conceive in a Wittgensteinian fashion as having unclear boundaries, unlike Lamarque and Olsen's neatly defined literary institution. And the practices as I see them are not created by constitutive rules, unlike the purported literary institution; rather, the practices are primordial in relation to the rules; thus I follow Wittgenstein's dictum that there is no rule for how to apply rules, since the practices determine the application. (The practices, of course, determine the application of my four indicators.)[6] In some practices, a make-believe stance suffices to make a text to be understood as a literary work; in other cases, some kind of moral stance is required as well; in yet other case some epistemological stance, and so on. But there is hardly any formula for what kinds of stances are

---

[5] The influence from Morris Weitz's conception of art as an open concept and Nelson Goodman's theory of the symptoms of the aesthetic ought to be obvious (Weitz 1956: 27-35 and Goodman 1978: 57-70).
[6] I am indebted to Kjell S. Johannessen's Wittgensteinian notion of aesthetic practices (Johannessen 1994: 217-250).

required, besides the make-believe one. If it makes sense to talk about something akin to the 'literary stance', it would be in the plural, a family of literary stances with no clear boundaries to other kinds of stances, including moral and political ones. The upshot is that a literary narrative has semantic, epistemological, pragmatic, and even moral dimensions. It does not exist outside of a family of practices.

I have similar intuitions concerning the concept of non-fictional narratives; I seriously doubt that it can be given an essential definition. I am convinced that it also is an amoebaean concept. Pre-modern historical works are in many ways very different from modern ones. Pre-modern historians like Greece's Thucydides or Iceland's Snorri Sturluson put words in the mouths of historical figures, words that they think these figures probably must have said in given circumstances. [7] To be sure, these are fictional words but are certainly no flights of fancy. Modern historians do not use this technique, using it would not be conductive to them getting tenure.

Looking at ancient biographies, we have similar problems. Plutarch's biographies are very different from modern ones. And where do we place the autobiography of Michel Leiris, which contains both fictional and essayistic moments? What about Augustine's *Confessions* and its fascinating mixture of autobiography and theological and philosophical speculations?

Be that as it may, the borderline between non-fictional and fictional narratives is not given once and for all, even though there are probably proto-typical narratives of both kinds. There is a porous line between the two kinds of narratives, making possible many kinds of interaction between non-fictional and fictional narratives. We shall see in the next chapter that Ricœur thinks that such an interaction is essential to these kinds of narratives.

3.4 Conclusion

We have seen that Hayden White argues that there are fictional moments in historical narratives but also that he tends to overestimate their roles. But his analysis of the relationship between such narratives

---

[7] Thucydides' *The Peloponnesian War* is well-known; Snorri Sturluson's *Heimskringla* or *Sagas of the Norse Kings* are not very well-known outside of the Nordic countries. The book is thought to have been written between 1220 and 1230.

and metaphors is very stimulating. Carroll makes some excellent points in his criticism of White but is in many ways a closet positivist, wrongly thinking that metaphors have no cognitive value. Lamarque and Olsen overestimate the difference between fictional and historical narratives. They are also mistaken in thinking that we can define the concepts of these kinds of narratives in an essential manner. A more fruitful approach is to talk about the 'indicators of literariness' that can be found in varying degrees in both fictional and non-fictional works.

Historical and other non-fictional narratives can refer to real events, however indirectly or metaphorically. (I shall elaborate this statement in the next chapter). Add to this the fact that narratives are explanatory, thus making them rationally assessable. At the same time, they have a literary moment owing to their being configured and emplotted. Therefore, our sensibility, or our aesthetic sense, plays a major role in evaluating non-fictional narratives. After all, Clio, the Muse of history, is the daughter of Beauty and Truth.

II.4. Narratives as 'Factions'
Ricœur on Facts, Fictions and Stories

This chapter continues the discussion of the relationship between fictional and non-fictional narratives, focusing this time on Ricœur's theories. My treatment of his theories of metaphor shows that he is a syncretist who critically appropriates the thoughts of different thinkers in order to create a new and original synthesis. He does the same in his theorising about narratives; Danto, Mink, Gallie, and White are among the thinkers whose thoughts he has appropriated. But we must remember that he is an existential, not an analytical, thinker. Donald Polkinghorne points out that his basic interest is not whether narratives can yield objective knowledge but rather what role they play in human existence (Polkinghorne 1988: 66).

As I see it, Ricœur spoke like narratives were to a certain degree *factions*,[1] i.e., mixtures of factual narratives and fictions (docudramas!). At the same time, he thought that historical and fictional narratives cannot be reduced to one another; they have an irreducible moment of independence.

4.1 Ricœur's Theory of Narratives

An understanding of Ricœur's general theory of narratives is requisite before a consideration of these ideas. To begin with, his theory is grounded in an effort to rejuvenate Aristotle's implicit theory of narratives.[2] Just like Aristotle, Ricœur maintains that the basic function of narratives and plots is to represent actions (Ricœur 1984a: xi). He uses the word 'action' in a very broad sense: comprising not only the behaviour of the protagonists, but also their moral transformation, growth, and education. Further, he includes purely internal changes, affecting the temporal course of sensations and emotions (Ricœur

---

[1] He neither used this term nor any of its cognates and he certainly never employed the expression 'docudrama'.

[2] His theory is implicit in his analysis of the tragedy. A tragedy represents (imitates) actions (Aristotle 1965: 39 (Chapter 6).

1985: 10). However, we may have already encountered a couple of minor problems. The first is that Ricœur's definition of action is perhaps too wide. The second is that we can doubt that the conceptual necessity of narratives being about actions. There are stories about natural events. Then again it could be said that a prototypical story is about human action and that stories about natural events are possibly derivatives of such stories. We may note the strong tendency to anthropomorphise natural agents in narratives about nature. Maybe there is no way to recount any event unless one treats the agents of change as actual or virtual actors, i.e., sort of minded beings. We must also keep in mind that Ricœur is no analytical philosopher looking for necessary and sufficient conditions for the employment of concepts. He wants to understand actual stories that matter to human beings.

Secondly, he uses the word 'narrative' in the same sense as the Aristotelian *muthos*, i.e. 'the organization of events'. (However, it would perhaps have been better to call this aspect of muthos 'plot'). The third Aristotelian aspect is discriminating between narrative in the broad sense, defined as the *what* of mimetic activity, from the narrative in the narrow sense of the Aristotelian *diegesis* (the narration), which Ricœur calls 'a diegetic composition' (Ricœur 1984a: 36). The first sense is roughly what I have called 'story'; the second has traits of both narration (the act of telling) and narrative. The French philosopher puts a great emphasis upon the role of plot and emplotment in narratives. He defines plot on a *formal* level as "...an integrating dynamism that draws a unified and complete story from a variety of incidents, in other words, that transforms this variety into a unified and complete story" (Ricœur 1985: 8). Another, simpler definition of plot is the following: "...the intelligible whole that governs the succession of events in any story" (Ricœur 1981b: 176). It is the plot that turns events into a story.[3] Most importantly, plots have almost a transcendental function in Ricœur's scheme of things. 'Scheme' is here the appropriate word because it is precisely a brand of Kantian schematism at work in the plots, just like in the metaphors. The plot actually performs a synthesis of sorts. It fuses together intentions, causal

---

[3] Ricœur, in contrast to White, does not seem to think that making a story of a given kind is the main work of emplotment. Configuration, then, does not seem to play any prominent role in White's system of thought. Ricœur somewhat hints at the fact that his conception of emplotment differs from that of White's (Ricœur 1984 a: 163.

relations, and chance occurrences in unified sequences of acts. If I understand the French philosopher correctly, he thinks that the plot creates a unified pattern in a chaotic series of events, tying them together, just like the metaphor fuses together phenomena that apparently do not have much in common. The point of the plot (its theme, idea, thought) must be connected to an intuition (*Anschauung*) of circumstances, characters, episodes and so on, analogously to the way Kantian schematism unifies the abstract (thought) and the concrete (images) (Ricœur 1984a: 68). This of course fits my conception of co-authorship admirably.

Now, the French structuralists who invented narratology were not impressed by such concepts as plot, which they thought were subjective and unscientific. All there is to narratological studies is laying bare the deep structures and showing how narratives are generated by these structures. An example of this kind of analysis is Algirdas Greimas' theory of narratives, which owes a lot to Vladimir Propp's seminal analysis of Russian folktales. The deep structure of narratives, at least of folk tales and myths, consists of certain functions or roles, or, more precisely, certain spheres of action, which Greimas calls 'actants'. There are altogether six, and they form three pairs. The first pair is subject and object; in the myth of the Holy Grail the knight Ghalahad is the subject, the Holy Grail is the object. The second pair is sender and receiver; God is the sender of the grail, mankind its receiver. The third pair is the one of helper and adversary; the helper is the sum of the good people and the divine forces that help Galahad, the adversary the sum of the evil forces, which try to obstruct his quest. Several actors can form one actant and the same actor can be several actants. Someone who starts as a friend of the hero (helper) but then eventually lets him down (adversary) is an instance of the latter. On the basis of these formal structures an infinite number of narratives can be generated (Greimas 1983: 197-213).

However inspiring these formal analyses may be, Ricœur thinks that there is something lacking. These formal structures can only come alive or generate narratives if they are aided by a narrative pre-understanding, which stems from our everyday practices that are themselves imbued with narratives. Inspired by Gallie, Ricœur says that one aspect of this pre-understanding is our ability to follow a story. There is a pre-rational, narrative pre-understanding that has a logical primacy in relation to semiotic rationality, which such structuralists as Greimas explicate in their analysis. The relationship between narrative pre-understanding and semiotic pre-understanding is like the one between the pre-rational Kantian schematism and the rational Kantian categorical understanding. The schematism in question is not all together of Kantian provenance since it is not entirely atemporal. It is partly created by the sedimentation of practice with a specific history. This sedimentation gives this kind of schematism a unique historical style, which Ricœur calls *traditionality*. This traditionality instructs narrative understanding, which is decisively shaped by familiarity with literary works and by plot-types handed down by tradition (the hermeneutic nature of this argument should be obvious). This shaping of the narrative understanding by tradition is just as essential to narratives as are the formal deep structures (Ricœur 1985: 14).

Secondly, if a narrative is essentially a mimesis of action and has roots in everyday narrative understanding, then the logic of possible narrative units is only the logic of action. (A part of this logic is presumably that actions are not based on causes but also reasons.) Only by being filtered through the schematism of traditionality, which shapes actions and our understanding of them, can the semiotic logic become the logic of narratives. In other words, actions only become recountable through the schematism of traditionality. The plot has the function of transforming the logic of possible acts into the logic of probable narratives (Ricœur 1985: 43). Ricœur is, in fact, under influence from Claude Bremond who said that patterns of human behaviour are the narrator's material out of which he creates characters, "...the semiology of narrative draws its very existence from its roots in anthropology" (Bremond 1996: 75). I think that these two French thinkers were moving in the right direction. It is easy to see how difficult it would be to understand (or create) a normal narrative if one does not understand the actions that are being described. Can one, for instance, understand the Icelandic sagas unless one knows what an action of revenge is, especially the kind of revenge that was taken as normal in the Icelandic society of the Middle Ages? Those who created these stories could certainly not have done so without familiarity with this particular type of action. Knowing Greimas actantial model alone would not have been of any help.

Thirdly, the transcendental power of the plot enables it to breathe life into the dead formal structures. The plot originates in the act of telling and, therefore, in the pragmatics of language, while the formal structures belong to its semantics (Ricœur 1985: 44). But no semantic analysis can eliminate the pragmatic side. As I see it, it can only make sense to talk of the transcendental role of plot if the plot is situated in the readers' minds (especially their imagination), or in what we can call their 'faculty of narrative understanding'. Looking for the plots in the narratives themselves would be futile, according to such a tran-scendental view. This means that we cannot simply eliminate plots from narratives if we take Ricœur's transcendental brand of reader-response theory seriously. To his theorising, I want to add that perhaps plot is like the Minkian narrative form, something that cannot be said, only shown. The difficulties involved in pinning the plot down and its apparent ineliminability point in that direction.

Dialectical as ever, Ricœur maintains that there is interdependence between the semiotic level and the level of actual praxis. The semiotic contribution is a network of interdefined terms and the like, while the semantics of actions (which concerns the actual praxis) explains the significance of action as well the specific structure of statements that refer to action. Such semantics is actually presupposed in the logic of narrative sentences, for they refer, after all, to actions (Ricœur 1985: 57-58).

However, none of this is comprehensible unless we know Ricœur's theory of mimesis. A narrative is constituted by a *threefold mimesis* (imitation, representation), i.e., three ways of representing reality. No narrative is possible without some pre-understanding of the world of action, since stories have actions as their main topic. If the plot is a representation of actions, then, as I said earlier, we must have a sort of understanding of actions in order to be able to create and comprehend a plot. Further, we cannot understand actions unless we see them as structured in time in a way similar to stories. We fuse temporal units in our actions together as we do when creating a story. This is the first level of mimesis, mimesis (1), the level of the *prefiguration* of the narrative, compare White's theorising (Ricœur 1984a: 54-59). Ricœur seems to think that a narrative is not possible without the narrative moments in our understanding of action. This understanding pre-figures our understanding of a story proper.

Mimesis (2) is the level of the explicit narrative, the level of the creative act that organises disparate actions into a unity with the aid of the *emplotment* (*mise en intrigue*). It does not just organise actions, but also different kinds of events, characters in the story, and so on. Ricœur thus calls mimesis (2) *configuration*. He maintains that the emplotment is related to the unification of understanding and intuition in Kant's reflective judgement (Kant 1963: 33-36). Analogously, emplotment configures the 'thought' (idea) of the narrative and the intuitive presentation of the characters by fusing them together (Ricœur 1984a: 68). Actually, Ricœur, the great synthesiser, borrowed this idea from Louis Mink (Mink 1987: 35-41).

Mimesis (3) is the level where the narrative recreates reality (or 'refigures' in Ricœur's terminology); above all that part of reality we call 'our lives'. Put simply, we can say that mimesis (3) is the effect the story has on people and the effect people have on stories, i.e., the way they interpret them in light of their own background and situation. This level of *refiguration* is where the text plays a role in the reader's life. Our understanding of the text cannot be separated from the ways it changes us.[4] Here, text and reader meet in the act of reading (Ricœur 1984a: 70-71). Mythic tales, for instance, refigure the world of those who know and believe in them; myths are really all-embracing metaphors.

According to Kathleen Blamey, one of Ricœur's points is that narratives can make us see our lives *as* tragedies, comedies, and so on. Blamey says further that humans actually do understand and refigure the events of their lives as though they were events in narratives (Blamey 1995: 579). Some people do not need novels to understand their lives as tragedies or comedies (or both).

I am not going to elaborate upon Ricœur's complex theories about the relationship between narratives and the Self. Let it suffice to say that narratives, in his view, play an important role in the creation and sustention of our identities, even though our lives are not, strictly speaking, narratives. The Self is not given, it is not a thing. It is

---

[4] The affinities with Gadamer's hermeneutics ought to be clear. According to Gadamer, the text changes us by giving us new insights or changing our point of view, or both. A genuine understanding of a text requires applying it to one's own life. At the same time, we change the text by interpreting it in our own fashion (Gadamer 1990: 312-317 and elsewhere).

something dynamic and created and must be appropriated in communication with others and with the aid of stories. Narratives can help make our lives meaningful, and it seems that Ricœur thinks that this meaningfulness is an essential part of the self (Ricœur 1992: 148). He says very eloquently: "Life is an activity and passion in search of a narrative" (Ricœur 1991a: 29).

Now, this search would be in vain without the three mimeseis. The ideas of mimesis and of the essential role of the plot seem to me significant; they square quite well with my intuitions about co-authorship; in historical narratives, historical facts and their emplotment work together as co-authors.

I agree with Ricœur's contentions that plots are ineliminable and that narratives (and stories) are constituted by aspect-seeing. Nevertheless, these theories are not without their weaknesses. I am not quite sure whether we need a sort of quasi-transcendental argument (i.e., the one of schematism) in order to show that plots are necessary conditions of narratives and stories. It might be more effective to 'translate' Ricœur's ideas into a naturalistic idiom and to say instead that we humans are beings who just happen to be wired to understand this or that as being structured by a plot. But the idea that plots cannot be eliminated from stories and narratives remains intact. Trying to eliminate them in favour of some 'real' deep structure is like trying to reduce melodies to mere physical processes. We shall later see that something similar holds for emotions.

The notion of the three mimeseis contains some unclarities. Does Ricœur think that the threefold mimesis is a *conditio sine qua non* for narratives? Put differently, is N a narrative if and only if N somehow involve the threefold mimesis? Or is such N a prototypical narrative with a host of narratives not involving some or even all of the threesome? And how can we ascertain that a refiguration has taken place? Do we have to use empirical or logical means for ascertaining this, or perhaps transcendental arguments, or even some kind of phenolmenological approach?

As far as I know, the French philosopher does not give any clear-cut answer to these questions. I do not think, however, that he was looking for a definition of the concept of a narrative, in keeping with him not being an analytical philosopher. I think he rather wanted to highlight important aspects of narratives, which are crucial in human existence. In my terminology, refiguration (if actual or possible) is a special kind of twisted understanding, since refiguration changes the object while at the same time increases our understanding of it. The fact that I think that there is such a thing as twisted understanding increases my confidence in the plausibility of the idea of refiguration, not least the part of it, which concerns the way our interpretations shape narratives. I am bit less sure about whether narratives really can change people. My intuition is that narratives can change people, but the problem remains that I have not found any good answers to the question of how to ascertain that a concrete refiguration of person has taken place. There is, however, some empirical evidence for the contention that readers of literary fiction can become a bit like the characters they read about by empathising with them (Oatley 2008: 42-43).

Ricœur certainly wanted to highlight the complex interplay between historical and fictional narratives. First, fiction so to speak imitates history by pretending to describe real events (Ricœur 1984b: 450). Secondly, just like historical narratives, fictional narratives have a certain kind of reference (Ricœur 1984a: 80). Fictions and other literary texts refer to possible worlds, worlds that have an existential significance for us because they are inhabitable for us (Ricœur 1977: 227). As noted earlier, Ricœur seemingly uses the expression 'possible world' in the sense of 'the world of our potentials' and the term 'world' in a phenomenological manner, meaning 'the totality of everything that is meaningful, irrespective of whether or not the meaningful phenomena in question have a material mode of existing'.[5] Thus, a mathematical symbol or Peter Pan belongs to the world (or a world) because they are both meaningful objects. They are intentional objects and can, therefore, be referred to. The French thinker does not actually say this directly, but maintains that, for him, a world is the totality of all references, which is opened up by any sort of a descriptive or poetical text (Ricœur 1984b: 80). In some cases, he appears to use the term 'world' in the sense of 'world-view'. When he talks about the

---

[5] Maybe it is wrong of me to use this Husserl-sounding definition. After all, it is Heidegger who is at the back of Ricœur's mind when he is talking about the world in connection with fiction and works of art generally. Heidegger talks about the worlds constituted by eminent artworks as being *loci* of strife between the world and the earth, i.e., the non-meaningful, the material, the obscure (Heidegger 1950).

world of the Greeks, he emphasises that he is not thinking of their concrete situation, but instead the part of their existence that could survive that situation, not in the least owing to written texts (Ricœur 1972: 93-112).

Be that as it may, in my terminology, these possible worlds provide the yardstick for the T-correctness of the refiguration. Again, I have reservations about the possibilities of refiguration of people – but only reservations.

4.2 Fiction and History

After this discussion of Ricœur's ideas on narratives, it is time to return to the relationship between historical and fictional narratives. There is congruency between them for several reasons. One is that both are preceded by the use of narrative in ordinary life. Most of our information comes from hearsay. Narrating is a part of symbolic mediation of action relatable to pre-understanding of the narrative field (mimesis 1). Both fictional and historical narrations are imitations of narrative as it is already practised in the transactions of ordinary discourse. Another is that both fields are measured by the same standard, emplotment. Thirdly, both fields are subordinated to narrative understanding (Ricœur 1985: 156-157). Fourthly, both have as an ultimate referent the human experience of time or the structures of *temporality* (Ricœur 1984a: 82).

The historical narrative does indeed have fictional moments because historians cannot describe historical reality in a completely objective manner; after all, they cannot make direct observations. They have to describe these events on the basis of indirect evidence, partly in an analogical fashion, and analogies and metaphors are among the most important tools of imaginative literature. There are more aspects of the historian's task that necessitate an analogical approach. One of them relates to the two seemingly contradictory tasks that the historian must perform at the same time. He must, on the one hand, immerse himself (*sich einfühlen*) in the past, and see things from the subjective point of view of past persons; on the other hand, he obviously approaches the past as a stranger. The analogical approach can build a bridge between these seemingly incongruous undertakings (Ricœur 1988: 223-225). Now, if this is true, then the historian is bound to employ ana-logic, and thus he provides us with yet another bridge between ana-logic and narra-logic (Ricœur does not use these terms).

This aspect of historical writing means that the historian is bound to create aspects of historical reality much like writers of imaginative literature do. Ricœur thinks that Hayden White has a point when he says that narratives of historical events have literary aspects. White forgets, however, that historical narratives can refer to reality (Ricœur 1984a: 161-168). White actually interprets Ricœur as saying that historical narratives are true allegories, allegories of temporality, i.e., of our experience of temporality and the drama of human existence unfolding essentially in time. This reading of Ricœur is due to the aforementioned fact that, even though historical narratives have a first-order reference to facts, they also have a second-order reference to temporality (White 1986: 140-159). Fictions also have such a reference even though their first-order reference might either be non-existent or be a reference to the world of a fictional work.

Ricœur in his turn chastised White for having read him somewhat too tropologically and almost doing away with the distinctions that Ricœur himself has drawn between fiction and history (Ricœur 1986: 185). Maybe White somehow projected himself into Ricœur.

For some strange reason, neither White nor Ricœur have discussed counter-factual fictional stories. However, the French thinker is aware of the importance of counter-factual scenarios in historical research. He agrees with the thesis that such scenarios are a necessary part of any serious attempt at causal explanation of historical events. He also emphasises that the construction of such counter-factual scenarios requires the active use of the imagination in *emplotting* stories (Ricœur 1984a: 182-192).

But why must there be a counter-factual component in causal explanations in history? We can use an example created by the Norwegian historian Øystein Sørensen: the causal explanation "Hitler's actions and personality were the basic causes of the Nazi takeover in 1933". One of the counter-factual facets of this hypothesis would be "If Hitler had died in 1932, then there would have been no Nazi takeover of Germany". We have no way of experimentally controlling either causal explanations of historical events or their counter-factual 'Other', since we are talking about unique (*einmalig*) situations. But we can, and indeed must, perform thought-experiments in order to evaluate causal explanations. In order to evaluate the importance of Hitler in the Nazi takeover, the historian must perform a thought-experiment, resulting in a counter-factual hypothesis like ""if Hitler had died in 1932, then the Nazi movement would have lost its momentum and faded into obscurity". In order to have any serious scientific value, such a hypothesis must be based on a thorough knowledge of the situation in Germany, human psychology, etc. Hypotheses of this kind have varying degrees of plausibility. The hypothesis about Hitler's early death seems rather plausible, while the hypothesis that the Chinese would have invaded if Hitler had died in 1932 is wildly implausible. These judgements mean that there are rational ways of evaluating the cognitive value of such thought-experiments. Nevertheless, there remains a fictional moment in them. And, Sørensen says, there is a thin line between scientific-historical thought-experiment and counter-factual fictions like novels about what would have happened had Hitler won the war (Sørensen 2004).

I want to add that it is a matter of conceptual necessity for a counter-factual or alternative-world novel or film to take some heed of the facts. A novel describing how the world would have developed had Hitler won the war must keep most facts about the world constant if it is to count as a counter-factual or alternative world story. If not, the novel is more correctly classified as a work of pure imaginative fiction. So the counter-factual fictional story and the counter-factual historical hypothesis are yet more meeting-places of history and fiction. What is more, the making of counter-factual stories is an essential part of human life, helping us to understand the course of our own lives in a manner similar to the historian who increases his knowledge of history by the use of such stories. We also use counter-factual scenarios as part of our practical reasoning about which paths to take in our lives, ranging from decisions about where to buy fruit to weighty existential decisions about what kind of persons we ought to be. Thus, our lives are led at the crossroads of facts and fiction; we are the heroes of our own docudrama!

Let us now return to Ricœur. The fourth meeting place between historical and fictional narratives is what Ricœur, following

Heidegger, calls 'temporality' (*Zeitlichkeit*).[6] The forms of narrative in question have in common an ability to help us come to terms with our temporality, i.e., that we live in time, which we experience as a unity of past, present, and future. The reason for this ability is that temporality is the structure of existence that reaches language in narrativity, and narrativity is the language structure, which has temporality as its ultimate referent.[7] This means that narratives are in the last analysis about the human experience of time (Ricœur 1984a: 77-80). But our experience of time is bound to be paradoxical because of its *aporetic* structure. One aporia is the one Augustine pointed out: time seems to be something objective and at the same it does not really seem to exist. The past is gone and, therefore, unreal; the future has not arrived and, therefore, is not; the present is not here to stay. So it seems that time is an illusion, something subjective. But how come then that we cannot command time to stop or reverse its order, flow into the past? Its unstoppability seemingly makes it something objective. So time is subjective and objective at the same time and in the same respect.

Ricœur says that owing to this and other aporias, we can only use the more or less paradoxical language of literature to convey temporal experience (Ricœur 1984a: 6-7).[8] We can only refer indirectly to temporality and can only use a metaphoric language when doing so. Even a straightforward historical narrative has a figurative side. It refers in a literal fashion to historical events, but it has a secondary, figurative reference to what Heidegger called 'historicality' (*Geschichtlichkeit*), a certain structure of temporality (Ricœur 1984a: 57-58, 61-62, 77-82).

Narratives, both historical and fictional, *humanise* time; time becomes human in the sense of being articulated in a narrative fashion, and a story gets its full meaning when it has become a condition for being in time (Ricœur 1984a: 52). The historical narrative builds a

---

[6] For the German philosopher's theorising about these issues, see Heidegger 1977: 231-437 (§45-83).

[7] This does not hold for just any simple narrative, say, one about me going to the shop, buying food, and returning home. Such narratives are more like chronicles and concern our existence within time, our mechanistic, unthinking everyday life.

[8] Strangely enough, Ricœur does not discuss theories about time in modern physics. However, he might have received some support from those physicists who admit that we do not really know what time is and, for all we know, could be unreal. See for instance Davies 2006: 6-11.

bridge between objective, cosmic time (the time which can be measured) and the subjective, phenomenal time (the time that can be felt or experienced). The historical narrative does this bridging primarily by referring to dates in the story. It uses the time of the calendar, which itself is a bridge between the cosmic and the subjective time. The reason is that it itself is partly a function of objective facts concerning the movements of the celestial bodies and partly a function of culture. It is clearly a cultural fact that our calendar time has the birth of Jesus as a focal point.

Let us take another look at Ricœur's thesis about historical and fictional narratives having a second-order reference to temporality and consider it critically. In my view, the thesis is far-fetched. In the first place, 'temporality' is nebulous concept and the concepts of historical and fictional narratives are not much easier to determine either. Because of these ambiguities, many disparate things can be called 'a given historical or fictional narrative's second-order reference to temporality'. Secondly, it is not clear why we need to assume that historical and fictional narratives have such a reference. Is it impossible to understand such narratives without taking their reference into account? How does one determine this reference? Well, it might be that I am imposing an analytical philosophical mode upon Ricœur's arguments. We can hardly evaluate them unless we do so as a part of his whole endeavour. The same holds of course for his theory of refiguration.

Let us address ourselves again to the bridge-building activity of historical narratives. The second aspect of this activity is the way such narratives refer to the succession of generations. The time of generations is a bridge between the two types of time. In a way, it is objectively determined by biological facts, but in another, there is a contingent, subjective moment in the determination of what a generation is. How are we to draw the exact line between the generation of the Sixties and other generations? Should only those who were born between 1938 and 1950 count? And would it make sense to talk about the generation of the Sixties among Indians who live isolated in the Amazon? These facts would make any historical narratives about the generation of the Sixties partly subjective, while objective facts about this generation would constrain any flights of fancy in a fictional work about the flower-power people.

The third way in which historical narratives tie cosmic and subjective time together is how historians use documents and monuments. They are traces of the past, traces that have a split nature. They are, on the one hand, physical objects, but, on the other, they are something meaningful and consequently also subjective phenomena (Ricœur 1988: 215-219).

Not only historical narratives, but also fictional ones can help us to come to terms with temporality by becoming *laboratories* of sorts for fictive time. (This holds only for certain works of fiction, like Proust's *À la recherche du temps perdu* (*Remembrance of Things Past*) and Mann's *Der Zauberberg* (*The Magic Mountain*).) Ricœur speculates that fiction tries to transcend the divide between cosmic and fictional time by creating imaginary variations over the gap between the two.

Fiction is understandably closer to experienced time than cosmological time. One of its roles is to help us deal with the *non-linear* aspects of our experienced time. Obviously, a fictional tale is not bound to represent the chain of action linearly but can jump between past, present, and future at its own pleasure. The tale can be told backwards or it can be told forwards but with several flashbacks. And this is really how we think about events. We are not bound to think about them in a linear fashion. Fiction, then, is realistic in the sense of representing our normal way of thinking about events. Simultaneously, it can show how experienced time can be inscribed into the physical, and, because of this inscription, it opens up the possibilities for authentic human action. It is a bit tricky to act outside of the physical word. The author must try to create the impression that the fictive events take place in cosmological time. The method fiction uses for transcending the boundaries between cosmic and experienced time is to create imaginary variations of the cosmic re-inscription, which takes place in history. Put otherwise, imaginary variations thematise the gap between these two kinds of time. Virginia Woolf's novel *Mrs. Dalloway* is an example of such a work of fiction. An important part of this novel is the descriptions of the streams of consciousness of the different characters. Obviously, such a description must contain representations of how the characters experience time subjectively. At the same, the experienced time is inscribed into cosmological time by the sound of the Big Ben, which appears again and again in the novel as a reminder of cosmological time (Ricœur 1985: 101-112).

Ricœur's complex and fascinating analysis of narrativity and temporality need not concern us too much here. Of greater importance to us is his idea of the interplay between fictional and historical narratives. They meet in four places: 1) fiction must imitate history; 2) just like historical narratives, fictional ones have a kind of reference; 3) there is a fictional moment in history; 4) both humanise time, help us to come to terms with our temporality, which they ultimately refer to, however indirectly.

These are interesting contention. But his theory of fictional reference is perhaps a little unclear. What exactly does it mean to say that fiction opens up a possible world that is inhabitable? What do I know when I know that a narrative ultimately refers to the structures of temporality or historicality? And why should not an autobiography or even other types of biographies show us our potential? As Norwegian philosopher Ole Martin Skilleås points out, modern biographies, particularly autobiographies, tend to be told from a subjective point of view along with other fiction-like qualities and might, therefore, be as important to our lives as novels (Skilleås 2006: 259-276). Indeed, I have read the autobiography of a great poet that has shown me that I have some of his potential. I could see my own life through his description of his life, more precisely his subjective confession.

Of course, I might have been deluding myself; perhaps I do not possess any of the great poet's qualities. And it is possible that Ricœur was labouring under some illusion when he treated the concepts of fictional and historical narratives as though they are essentially determinable. But what if that were not the case? Maybe prototypical fictional narratives contain historical moments and prototypical historical ones fictional moments, but there could be a host of both kinds of narratives without any such moments.

As for historical narratives, Ricœur seems oblivious of the fact that natural scientists usually cannot observe the objects of their studies directly. It is plainly impossible to observe a black hole. Does this mean that there is a fictive moment in physics? Of course, the answer might be "yes", but that does not help Ricœur in delimiting the work of historians from that of other scholars. It seems to be his goal to draw a line between them, as can be seen from his emphasises upon the non-repeatability of history. But he ignores the fact that astronomers also deal with non-repeatable events. Despite of this, there is no essential difference between astronomy and physics. So the non-repeatability of events studied by scientists does not seem to have the importance in categorising science Ricœur and other hermeneuticians give it. Secondly, he forgets that there have been historians who have written the history of events they themselves were involved in, for instance, Winston Churchill's history of the Second World War. So this kind of historian can for all intents and purposes be said to have experienced directly some of the events they were describing.

4.3 Conclusion

We can learn much from Ricœur. There is enough truth in his idea of the necessity of analogical approach to history to regard it as a welcome addition to my ana-logic and my idea of there being an analogical moment in the narra-logic. There is no narra-logic without ana-logic. Moreover, he is right about the central role of emplotment in narratives and that narratives are constituted by aspect-seeing. Further, the idea of the threefold mimesis is inspiring, above all for my conceptions of co-authorship, twisted understanding, and T-correctness. While seeing no reason to doubt that the readers refigures the narratives he read by interpreting them in the light of his cultural background and situation, I am not sure if there is a way to know whether the narrative refigure him. If it were possible, then it would be a way of thinking and behaving in an ana-logical fashion. Refiguration demands thinking of oneself as someone else metaphorically or as being analogous to that someone and acting accordingly.

Ricœur obviously has a point when he says that there is no gulf between fictional and historical narratives; using my terminology both are in some ways 'factions'. Instead of a gulf, there is a dialectical relationship between them. Further, his analysis of temporality and narrativity is fascinating, even though it is somewhat too speculative for my taste.

Implicit in his thinking is the idea that not only historical but also fictional narratives can inhabit the realm of reason. As we have seen, his attempt to show this connection to reason was not been entirely successful. But there might be another road, one not far from

Ricœur's, to the same goal. Your humble servant will try to localise that road later in this book.

The problems with the French thinker's theories are basically his unclear, Continental way of expressing himself and the likewise Continental lack of examples and definitions. Thus, it is not quite clear whether or not he thinks we can define in an essentialist manner the concepts such as those of fictional and non-fictional narratives. We must still keep in mind, however, that Continental texts can often only be understood as forming a whole, and judging them in parts can be misleading. An ideal evaluation of Ricœur's thinking involves evaluating it as a totality, not evaluating his diverse theories in isolation from each other.

II.5. The Story and The Metaphor:
The N-M

On the Relationship between Narratives and Metaphors

I believe there are symbolic structures that contain elements from both metaphors and narratives. Let us call them *N-Ms*. Such N-Ms can be stories that are at the same time metaphors or stories that have constitutive metaphoric moments. We shall name both of them *metaphoric stories*. We also have *storied metaphors*, metaphors that are constituted by explicit or implicit narratives.

The explanation for the existence of such hybrids is the fact that metaphors and narratives have some important common features. This we can learn from two vastly different thinkers, Paul Ricœur and Mark Turner.[1] Actually, they have had the idea of N-Ms on the tips of their tongues. In order to develop my theory, I shall draw a great deal of inspiration from them.

While Ricœur has his roots in Continental philosophy, the literary theorist Mark Turner has his in cognitive science. On the face of it, no two theorists could be more different. Nevertheless, I think that these thinkers have come to similar conclusions from vastly different premises.[2] They both conclude that metaphors and narratives have certain fundamental features in common, with Ricœur's premises being of phenomenological and hermeneutic provenance, and Turner's of cognitive science. The second thing Ricœur and Turner have in common

---

[1] I could perhaps have added Hayden White to this equation. But it is unclear to me whether he thinks that narratives have constitutive metaphoric moments.

[2] Max Statkiewicz would certainly not agree. He regards Ricœur as a healthy antidote to the purported sterile formalism of both the Lakoffians and the blending theorists (Statkiewicz 2003: 546-552). Unfortunately, Statkiewicz does not really elaborate this point. Moreover, he is not being entirely fair to the Lakoffians and the blending theorists by forgetting their non-formalistic stress on the body and non-formal metaphoric reasoning. He also ignores the possibility that one could use a Ricœurian kind of theorising to breathe hermeneutic life into the sterile, formal side of these theories, in a way similar to Ricœur's successful breathing of life into the desiccated, formal narratological theories of the structuralists.

is that they are both *narrativists,* even though Ricœur is a compa-
ratively moderate one to Turner. The third thing they share is a
staunch belief in the importance of imagination and creativity for our
cognition and creation or grasping of meaning.[3] Ricœur has said in no
uncertain words that the problem of creativity has always been the
single most important theme of his reflections.[4] Turner (and Fauconnier) also focuses on creativity, maintaining that imagination uses conceptual blending (integration) to create our human world, including
mathematics, counterfactual reasoning, visual representation, scientific discovery, and grammar. Even actions and designs are products of
blending (Fauconnier and Turner 2008).[5] Remember that blending is a
metaphor-like operation (compare what I said about Ricœur and
imagination).

In this chapter, then, I shall both discuss the relationship between
these theorists and use their theories as starting points for my own
theory of the N-Ms.

5.1 Ricœur on The Common Ground of Stories and Metaphors

In my reading of Ricœur, he considers metaphors and narratives as
having at least five interconnected characteristics in common (1-5),
besides having at least three 'meeting places' (i-iii):

1) Metaphors and narratives are products of Kantian schematism;
we have already seen that both perform synthesis.

2) Both metaphors and narratives show things as if they were
something else, X as if were Y: "To see as... is the common soul of
metaphors and narratives" ("le voir comme... est l'âme commun à la
métaphore et au récit") (Ricœur 1984b: 448). We see Man as if he
were a wolf in the famous metaphor. (As I said in the last chapter,
seeing-as means performing a synthesis of sorts).

As suggested, metaphors and narratives are lenses through which
we see things. We see things as something else through the lenses of a

---

[3] For instance Turner 2007: 213-236. He is definitely not the only admirer of cognitive science who stresses the importance of creativity and imagination. See for
instance Johnson 2007.
[4] Ricœur said so in an interview with Le Monde on 7 February 1986 (Quoted after
Kearney 1989: 24).
[5] On design and behaviour, see Fauconnier 1997: 171-172.

story, just as we can see the Jastrow-figure as a duck, given a certain perspective. (Another narrative can presumably give a rabbit-per-spective on the 'same' thing.) That a fictional narrative can offer the lenses of aspect-seeing should be clear. To use an example of my own making, Louis-Ferdinand Céline's novel *Voyage au bout de la nuit* (*Journey to the End of the Night*) shows us the world as if it were a deep abyss where irony is a must for survival. It is less obvious that historical narratives show us X as if were Y. But think of the fol-lowing: a historical narrative can show the Peace of Westphalia in 1648 *as if* it were the starting point in the creation of the modern system of states. (This example is also mine.) Notice the ana-logic involved in both narratives. Interestingly enough, Ricœur mentioned *en passante* the possibility of calling 'refiguration' the 'metaphori-sation of the reader's life', broadly using 'metaphorisation' (Ricœur 1995: 257). The point seems to be that the reader starts seeing her life as being X because of the inspiration from a story. A woman in love perhaps starts viewing herself as if she were Anna Karenina meta-phorically. As Arthur Danto points out, to see oneself as Anna is in a way to be her. The woman in question has learned something about herself by seeing herself as Tolstoy's heroine (Danto 1981: 173).[6] In my terminology, the woman uses ana-logic and narra-logic to under-stand and recreate herself at the same time and by the same means. The woman's use and understanding of the story of Anna Karenina and her metaphorisation of her own life form, so to speak, a dialectical unity. She certainly refigures her life.

3) Metaphors and/or narratives create new meaning in at least three different senses of the word 'meaning': a) in a *linguistic* sense; b) in making objects and events *understandable*; 3) in an *existential* sense of making life meaningful. a) Metaphors create a new linguistic meaning by creating a new overlapping meaning for two apparently disparate concepts. MAN IS A WOLF creates an overlapping meaning for 'Man' and 'wolf'. Ricœur seems not to think, however, that narra-tive creates new linguistic meaning. b) Both metaphors and narratives help us make sense almost *verbatim*; i.e., they make things under-standable by creating new sense. Both help us make sense of things by showing us something unknown in the light of something well known. Narratives help making sense of apparently disparate events by

---

[6] There are striking similarities between Danto's analysis and Ricœur's theorising.

showing creatively their causal and logical connections (in a way creating the connections in the process). c) Ricœur apparently thinks that the twosome also create meaning in the existential sense, helping us to see life or some of its aspects as meaningful in the sense of being worthwhile. Narrative myths and other religious or even political narratives can help people find a purpose in life. Metaphors confer this kind of meaning upon the passive side of life, the narrative, active side:

> And whereas metaphoric re-description reigns in the field of sensory, emotional, aesthetic, and axiological values, which makes the world a habitable world, the mimetic function of plots takes place by preference in the field of action and of its temporal values (Ricœur 1984a: xi).

The field of plot comprises not only the action but also the pain that is its result or the pain that spurs the action. Pain is something passive and belongs, therefore, to the realm of metaphor and poetry (particularly elegy). These two belong to the same realm because poetic texts refer in the same way as metaphors; both are creative imitations (Ricœur 1984a: 80). (Ricœur appears to view poems as macrometaphors.) I do not see, however, why we *must* believe that narratives have something to do with activity, while metaphors and poetry deal with passivity. (Again, I emphasise that this may not have been Ricœur's point.) There are stories in which nothing happens, so to speak. Consider Alain Robbe-Grillet's novel *La jalousie* (*The Jealousy*). It is a story of sorts but not much happens. Further, it is easy to create new, fresh metaphors for activities and actions, which are performed very swiftly, for instance, HE RAN WITH THE SPEED OF A JUMBO JET. With regard to poetry, Ricœur must be thinking about lyrical poetry. (As we have seen, he also has elegies in mind.) True, there is a tendency in lyrical poetry to represent the passive, for instance, moods or moody experiences. We can think about Japanese haikus or Goethe's *Wanderers Nachtlied II* (*Wayfarer's Nightsong II*). But what about Rainer Maria Rilke's *Der Panther* (*The Panther*)? It is a lyrical poem but one full of speed and drama with beautiful descriptions of the panther's relentless wandering in his cage. However, there is no lack of pain being expressed in this beautiful poem! Again, it might be possible to show that the concept of a lyrical poem is a prototypical concept and that prototypical lyrical poems represent the passive. Secondly, it does not seem to be especially helpful to say, as Ricœur does, that metaphors create meaning on the level of sentences, narratives on the level of texts. There are at least two reasons for this criticism. The first one is that there are non-linguistic metaphors, which can hardly create meaning on the level of sentences. The second reason is the fact that there are long and complex texts that can be regarded as being metaphors in their own right. Thus, we can interpret the content of Hemingway's novella *The Old Man and the Sea* as a metaphor for the eternal struggle between man and nature. So, if metaphors create meaning, then they can do so on the level of texts. One could say, of course, that texts are only long sentences, but Ricœur apparently does not believe that this is the case, or else his distinction between the level of sentences and that of text would be impossible to draw.

4) Narrative refiguration and metaphoric reference are two sides of the same coin. They have in common the aforementioned split reference, the quality of being true in one sense, untrue in another; that is, they form their objects and at the same time say something important about them. An anecdote or a joke about a person, for example, can be untrue strictly speaking but nevertheless often say something essential about that person (this my own elaboration).

Ricœur's later writings expressed misgivings about his earlier use of words like 'reference' in his works on metaphors because the term is too tightly tied to the logic of propositions. In these later writings, he preferred to talk about both a narrative and a metaphoric refiguretion of reality, i.e., their ability to recreate their object while saying something important about them, owing to the recreation (Ricœur 1984b: 436-437). (Notice that refiguration means seeing-as.) I think that this was a wise move, above all because the idea of a split reference seems a bit far-fetched. One of the weaknesses of the split reference idea is the fact that Ricœur just assumes without any arguments that metaphors are essentially linguistic and that they are expressed in predicative sentences. But, as we remember, there are strong arguments in favour of metaphors being pictorial, behavioural or even mental. Needless to say, such metaphors do not refer, even if pictorial metaphors possibly can denote. Further, one can express linguistic metaphors without using predicative sentences, for instance LET THE DEAD BURY THEIR DEAD. Of course, this does not exclude the possibility of the predicative sentence being the prototypical expression of metaphors, that metaphors are essentially linguistic, and

that so-called 'pictorial' or 'behavioural' metaphors are only derivates. But even if this were not the case, it is easy to see that a pictorial or behavioural metaphor can be refigurating. Surely, we can see
things in a new light thanks to a metaphoric painting (or non-metaphoric paintings for that matter).

5) The narrative discourse is an *extended* metaphor that shows the
world of acting and suffering as being configured (Venema 2000:
105). The narrative plot has moments of metaphoricity, not least
because it describes a less known human reality in light of the
relationship with a fictitious but better known reality; compare
White's theorising (Ricœur 1977: 244). But I cannot see why we must
regard the narrative discourse as an extended metaphor, at least if it is
the configuration alone that makes it metaphoric. I am also unable to
see that it holds for all narrative plots that they describe less well-
known phenomena in light of better known ones (if this indeed is the
French philosopher's point). What less known phenomena are shown
in the light of better known ones in the banal plots of dime novels?

Now to the meeting places. I have discussed two of them in earlier
chapters, the place where myths meet metaphors and historical narratives meet allegories. More precisely, I have already discussed
Ricœur's idea of mythic tales being metaphoric and his contention that
the idea that historical narratives are true allegories. That leaves only
parables. They, most notably the religious ones, are another meeting
place and very obviously N-Ms due their being allegories or at least
having allegoric moments. It is not unusual to define 'allegory' as 'an
extended metaphor' like the *Merriam-Webster Online Dictionary*
does. Given this definition, an allegoric story is a story, which is an
extended metaphor. When creating a typical allegoric story, someone
describes the muses as dancing together, intending this description to
be understood as a metaphor for unity of the different arts. It is very
hard to see how the story can be understood as an allegory unless it is
interpreted in this or a similar way.[7] We cannot give a story the
identity of an allegory unless it is understood in a metaphoric fashion.
An allegory is a story with a metaphoric structure and so are parables.
Ricœur says that a parable is a conjunction of narrative form and

---

[7] But then again we do not have to read it as an allegory; maybe we can just read it as
an instruction of how to dance!

metaphoric process that refers to something other than what is told, says. It has the mimetic power to re-describe human existence, because its ultimate referents are limit-experiences such as joy, death, and suffering. Presumably, they are experiences that border on being beyond our comprehension and at the same time show us the limits of ordinary existence. These experiences require limit-expression in the guise of parables and proverbs; they cannot be adequately expressed in prosaic, literal discourse.

The literary genre of narrative provides the parable with distance, autonomy, and form, while the metaphoric process opens the discourse towards the outside, both infinity of life and interpretation. A parabolic message proceeds from the tension between the circumscribing narrative form and the metaphoric process that transgresses the narrative boundaries (Ricœur 1975: 29-148).

However, owing to my lack of theological knowledge, I shall not elaborate upon the issue of religious parables any further.

In 5) we saw that Ricœur implicitly takes narratives to be metaphoric stories. But as we have seen from my criticism of the arguments in 5) and i), I do not find his implicit arguments convincing. As for 3) and 4), I find his arguments thought-provoking, but I prefer to suspend judgement on them. I just want to mention that Polkinghorne has a convincing way of showing (in a more than a bit Ricœurian manner) that narratives create meaning: "Narrative meaning is created by noting that something is a part of some whole and that something is the *cause* of something else" (Polkinghorne 1988: 6).

Be that as it may, I am, by and large, in agreement with Ricœur's 1) and 2). And I want to distil the following from them: Among the necessary conditions for M being a metaphor and N being a narrative is that a) M and N synthesise; b) M and N show us X as if it were Y.

Obviously, a) and b) are closely connected. To Ricœur's arguments I adjoin the following: All kinds of things are constituted by aspect-seeing, including the visual image of a duck or a rabbit we see in a duck-rabbit figure. All kinds of things are constituted by synthesis; any old theory somehow synthesises its object, at least if the theory is abstract enough and has enough scope. But metaphors, narratives, emotions (Selves maybe too) do not only perform synthesis; they are in addition constituted by seeing-as. I doubt that the same holds for ordinary theories.

Despite my misgivings about some aspects of Ricœur's attempt to link metaphors and narratives, I think that he was heading in the right direction, partly because his theorising fits with my ideas of co-authorship and of the kinship between ana-logic and narrative reasoning (the last idea owes much to Ricœur), and partly because he sees the kinship between metaphors and narratives, even though he might overestimate the closeness of that kinship, especially in the field of meaning-creation.

I want to add *en passante* that Ricœur is much more of metaphorist than a narrativist. Narratives are dependent on metaphors but not necessarily *vice versa*. Further, the imagination creates our world with the aid of metaphor-like processes; narratives are a product of that process. To be sure, narratives are powerful, but they are like mighty vassals of Emperor Metaphor.

5.2 Turner: Spatial Stories and Parables.

Perhaps Mark Turner can help us build even more bridges between metaphors and narratives. We remember that he is one of the founding fathers of the so-called 'blending theory'. As suggested in my earlier introduction of this theory, the blend need not be metaphoric. Non-metaphoric blends can have more than two input spaces. Indeed, the theory of blending is designed not only to explain metaphors but also our linguistic and mental activities in general. It can explain, for instance, how we see other people as beings endowed with con-sciousness. We *unconsciously* create a blend of ourselves and other people (most of our blending activity is unconscious) (Fauconnier and Turner 2002: 44). In this blend we automatically make others con-scious beings by projecting our own consciousness to them (Turner 2004: 90-115). Narratives can also be blends. According to Turner, blended stories play a role in structuring our thoughts. *Narrative imaging* (i.e., a story) is really the fundamental instrument of thought and is crucial for our planning, explaining, predicting or looking into the future. Narrative imaging is to large extent performed with the aid of what Turner calls *parables*, a word that he uses very differently than Ricœur. Turner uses this term specifically to denote narratives, which are projected onto other narratives (Turner 1996: 4-7). The ability to project one story onto another is a literary capacity indispensable to human cognition in general.[8] Therefore, it is no wonder that our world is replete with parables. Proverbs furnish us with fascinating examples. They present a condensed implicit story to be interpreted through projection; think about "while the cat is away, the mice will play". We could, for instance, project this story onto a story about infidelity. The proverb functions as a source-story while the story of the infidelity is the target-story.[9] We can even see our lives in a story about a voyage, even without conscious reflection. We create parables by and large spontaneously, without conscious reflection (Turner 1996: 5). Our mind is literary; it is permeated with stories and metaphors. We construct small stories all the time, mostly without thinking, just as we do not usually reflect over our use of our eyes. We see something most of the time without thinking about it, and the same holds for our narrative activities. Indeed, we organise our experiences in narratives. They originate from small, simple, spatial stories, like a story about the wind that blows clouds through the sky or a child that throws a stone (Turner 1996: 12-13). These spatial stories would not be possible without image-schemas. It is easy to see how we activate the schema SOURCE-PATH-GOAL in spatial stories. We see a thing fall from a table (source), through the air (path), landing on the floor (goal). Then we project this story onto our own life. We experience our mind as a source for wishes and actions. We do things in order to achieve what we wish to achieve. The means we use to reach the target (to fulfil the wish) we tend to regard as the path towards the goal. This actually an example of my own making, but Turner uses one from world literature. The story of Odysseus is structured by the image-schema SOURCE-WAY-TARGET. The source is Troy, the path is the voyage on the Mediterranean ocean, the goal is Ithaca (Turner 1996: 27). This literary story has its roots in a spatial story of the thing-falls-from-table kind. Turner does not exclude the possibility that the same holds for all non-spatial stories but admits that for now we cannot be certain (Turner 1996: 51).

The ability to construct small spatial stories is universal. We are naturally wired to organise the world as stories. To slice the world into

---

[8] According to Turner, C. S. Lewis is the originator of this idea of parables and their cognitive role (Turner 1995).
[9] On the concepts of target- and source-stories, see Turner 1996: 49.

discrete objects means putting the slices in small spatial stories because our identification of objects is dependent upon the typical stories in which they appear. (Turner thus confers a somewhat transcendental status upon spatial stories without saying so explicitly.) A stone is an object that, for instance, appears in a spatial story about stone throwing. Usually, we sort of duck when we see someone take a stone in order to throw it. We experience ourselves as being situated in the beginning of a small spatial story, imagining the rest, and reacting in accordance with this. Here we see an example of narrative imaging. We imagine that the stone is being thrown in our direction because of the fact that we spontaneously situate that event in a spatial story. We can also see that stories must have had an adaptive function. Those of our ancestors who were apt at creating stories about the throwing of stones were more likely to escape such ordeals. As suggested, narrative imagining is our primary way of predicting events, since we predict by situating objects in stories. The same thing happens when we plan something. The adaptive advantage that attends the abilities to predict and plan ought to be obvious.

Narrative imaging is our basic instrument for explanation. We hear drops of water dripping mysteriously from the ceiling. We try to imagine with the aid of spatial story how this puzzling situation could have come about. The story is an attempt to explain the event (Turner 1996: 15-20). From this we can see that Turner is a staunch narrativist, believing that our world is replete with storied structure, an expression he certainly does not use.

I have hitherto been discussing only simple stories in which one projects from a source-domain to a target-domain. But true-blue 'blended stories' (my expression) are more complex. They do not even have to involve source- and target-domains. Turner uses an example from a report about the ship *Great America II* that tried to beat the speed record in 1993, set by the ship *Northern Light* in 1853, sailing the same route as the older ship had sailed. One report of the event created a blended space where these two ships were actually taking part in a competition. Notice that neither in the input space of the older nor in that of the newer ship is there any competition. The blend created new qualities, which did not exist in the input spaces. Notice also that neither of the inputs were the target or source for the other one, but we can nevertheless see both in this way because of this blend. We can, for instance, say the *Northern Light* is falling behind, and that only makes sense if we are thinking within the blend (Turner 1996: 67-69). The fact that the input rooms are neither source- nor target-domains means that this story is no metaphor (Turner 1996: 72-73). This example shows that not all parables are N-Ms, even though some are.

To get a better hold of the relationship between metaphors and parables, we have to know Turner's concept of an *emblem*. An emblem is a parable that has a given story as a starting point and projects a generating story that covers other stories that belong to the *same* conceptual domain. Turner uses the story about the conflict between Sharazad and her father, the vizier, from *1001 Nights* (*The Arabian Nights*) as an example. From this story we project an abstract, generating story about conflicts between parents and their offspring. This generating story fits many others. But if we are dealing with a generating story that fits a story in another conceptual domain, we should be dealing with an N-M. (Turner certainly does not use that expression.) After all, the job of a metaphor is to create connections between conceptual domains; MAN IS A WOLF connects the conceptual domains of humans with that of wolves. Emblems cannot, therefore, be N-Ms; they connect stories in the same conceptual domain.

In *1001 Nights*, there is a story about two kings who both have unfaithful wives. They travel around in order to find out whether they are the only ones who have been treated so badly by their wives. Then, they meet a beautiful girl who is the prisoner of an evil spirit. She has sex with the kings to take revenge upon her keeper. The kings conclude that if a mighty spirit can be taken for a ride in this manner, then their misfortune is not so hard to bear after all. They understand the story emblematically: women are always shrewd and unfaithful. From this story they project a *generic* story: women fool men with the use of cunning. This story can then be projected onto several stories, for instance, the stories of the kings and their wives. But from the point of view of the evil spirit, the story can be understood metaphorically. He mistreated the girl very badly indeed by kidnapping her on her wedding night and by locking her into a tiny box. She takes revenge upon him by cheating on him whenever possible. This story can be projected metaphorically onto stories of marriage in general or at least royal marriages. Kidnapping a girl on her wedding night can be a metaphor for what kings do on their wedding nights, or at least for the king who was in the habit of executing his wives on that particular night (Turner 1996: 21).

Turner has a more or less implicit idea of narrative identity; he thinks that the parables took part in the creation of the concept of a soul. We all know the spatial story in which an actor moves an object. We then project this story onto another story in which the actor has become the soul; the object is the actor's body (the soul moves the body) (Turner 1996: 21). Taking into account of how important the concept of a soul is in the human world, we should see through this example the importance of the parable. The example also shows how non-spatial stories about events in a human soul have their roots in spatial stories.

Turner also says that stories and the relationship between them are our best cognitive instruments for the creation of a biography. A mental room that concerns a person's life seems like a part of her biography. In order to understand who she is, we frequently use our imagination to scrutinise mental spaces, which show her as a child, an adult, and so on. By 'moving' between these spaces, the generic room can become very abstract, even as abstract as the idea of 'animated creature'. But in the blend, her personality is being 'created'; we see her as a particular individual with a given identity, which unifies her at all stages of her life. (This is how I interpret Turner.) The blend can show us how the seemingly incoherent aspects on an individual's life can turn out to be coherent; she can be both a giver and a receiver and so on (Turner 1996: 136). It seems to me that Turner has an implicit theory about our Selves (or personalities or individual identities) being complex constructions of parables. Given his way of thinking, the Self does not exist *an sich* but is somehow constructed, just as objects and events are (Lakoff and Johnson certainly think that the Self is constructed). Perhaps this construction of the Self happens in the same way as the biography is constructed. Our Selves come into being thanks to the parables created by us and our fellow men about our Selves in the past, present, and future. The blend then integrates the parables. If this is how Turner thinks, then he is pretty close to being a full-fledged narrativist, thinking that the Self has a storied structure.

Just like Ricœur, Turner is on the right path. But I do have some critical remarks. First, Turner does not define the concept of a narrative, and so it is rather hard to say what he means when he is talking about narratives. A phenomenologist might be excused for not defining his concepts but hardly a cognitive scientist. Secondly, just like the Lakoffians, he puts too much emphasis on our experiences with objects and focuses too one-sidedly on our bodies. Why should not our subjectivity and social interaction be the foundation for at least some of whatever primordial stories we live by? The communal interpretation of the private-language argument opens up the possibility of social interaction as being the wellspring of such ur-stories, if there indeed are such stories. (The perceptive reader hears an echo of my criticism of the Lakoffians.) Not only does the argument open up this possibility, we can also draw from it the conclusion that even stories originating in our physical existence must exist intersubjectively and perhaps necessarily shaped by social interaction. Well, it should not surprise me at all if there are *ur*-stories we live by, some originating in our experiences of our bodies and other objects, others in subjectivity and social interaction (all existing in a social manner). The latter kind of ur-stories would be abstract, schematic story structures, resembling Greimas' model of actants, having as their source the way we experience others as helpers or adversaries or the way we experience something as (subjectively) desirable. Our brains then somehow store aspects of these experiences, creating a skeletal or abstract pattern out of them that function as a deep structure, which can be activated in various ways given the circumstances. This is admittedly a speculative hypothesis, but it could provide a fillip for empirical research.

Thirdly, Turner's theory that certain simple stories create the foundation for, so to speak, all our cognitive activity seems far-fetched. In fact, it seems he has admitted that his theory is rather speculative (according to a review of Turner 1996, Caldwell 1997). But it can be useful regardless of whether or not it explains our cognitive activities. We do not need to believe in such a theory in order to understand that we often project simple narrative structures onto other structures as we transcend conceptual borders. We experience again and again how such simple structures from folk tales and the like are projected onto novels, movies or just everyday talk around the water cooler. The story of Rambo is projected onto the story of a tough-minded businessman who overcomes all obstacles, even if everything seems hopelessly futile for a while. Such a story is metaphoric because it connects the conceptual domain of warriors with that of business people while it is seen in the light of another story, in this case, Rambo. Turner's theory of parables, then, is sound as a *narratological* theory but not necessarily as a cognitive one. The same holds for the concept of spatial stories; we certainly tell such stories, but how important they are for our thinking and our world-view I should not say.

As in the subchapter about Ricœur, I want to use some of Turner's insights for my own purposes. Accordingly, I shall reconstruct Turner's theory about stories and their relationship to metaphors in the following fashion: Turner discriminates implicitly between what I call *source-goal parables* and *blended parables*. The latter can be divided into three subclasses: I) *Ordinary* blended parables (for instance, the story about the ships); II) Emblems; III) *Metaphoric parables*. The source-goal parables have metaphoric traits; some of them can be full-fledged metaphoric stories. But emblems definitely have no such metaphoric traits, and ordinary blended stories do not require them. However, there are blended stories that are N-M-s, and the same holds for metaphoric parables. Remember that not everything Turner calls a 'parable' is a real story, for instance, his 'spatial stories'.

So there are three kinds of 'Turnerian' N-Ms: a) some goal-source parables (e.g., the story of Odysseus); b) some ordinary blended stories (e.g., the story of the businessman *cum* Rambo); c) metaphoric parables (e.g., the story from *The Arabian Nights*, told from the genie's point of view).

5.3 More on N-Ms

We have seen that stories can be metaphors, but can metaphors be stories? Can they with other words have a storied structure? Giambattista Vico maintained that certain metaphors are like small fables. He had in mind metaphors that were the product of animate qualities being projected into inanimate things (THE WIND BREATHES) (Vico 1984: 129). It is not clear, however, why he thought that such metaphors were kinds of fables. Regardless of his theories, I want redeem my implicit promise of showing that there are storied metaphors, i.e., metaphors constituted by implicit stories. There are still pictures (paintings, sculptures, and photographs) that we can only understand if we regard them as frozen outtakes from stories. We have to put them in a narrative context in order to understand them. Think of a still picture of a scared person; we can only understand such a picture if we put it into the context of a story in which something frightful happened to the person just before the moment of the picture. We simply cannot understand P as being scared unless we know that something scary happened to P, if not in reality, then at least in P's imagination. We can understand the frightening incident as the beginning of story, the scared expression the middle, and an antici- pated event its end. An alternative understanding could be that the beginning is the state of P before the scary incident, the incident the middle, and P being scared as shown in the picture the end. The one interpretation is as good as the other. What matters is that we cannot give the picture an identity of a picture of a scared person unless we regard it as belonging to a narrative context. Thus, the picture has a storied structure.

Similarly, there are metaphors that only function as frozen out- takes from narratives. Think about THE CLOUDS ARE ANGRY (an example that would fit Vico admirably!). We cannot understand any object O as being angry unless we postulate that something has hap- pened, which made O angry. And we can hardly understand O being angry unless we anticipate some kind of a ventilation or dissipation of the anger. We only understand O's anger if we place it in a narrative context. The beginning can be either O before the provocation or the provocation itself; the middle would be either the provocation or O's angry reaction to it; the end is either O's angry state or the ventilation of the anger or its dissipation. This means that we cannot understand THE CLOUDS ARE ANGRY unless we regard the metaphor as an out-take from a narrative. It is easy to see that we have a plot of sorts and characters, i.e., the anger and possibly the shadowy figures provo- cating them. This means that the metaphor possesses a storied struc- ture.

This metaphor is thus constituted by a narrative and is therefore a storied metaphor and by implication a N-M. One does not have to possess great imagination to see that this metaphor belongs to large class of N-Ms. This class must be an underclass in the class of storied metaphors.

Before concluding this chapter, let us look at two possible rejoinders to the idea of N-Ms. The first one is that the only thing that I have shown is that every story can be interpreted as an allegory, in case of which my point would be pretty trivial. But in order to understand my rebuttal to this, one must remember that an allegoric tale is an extended metaphor. In an allegoric story there is an iso-morphic relation between the elements of a story and its message. Thus, the pilgrim in Bunyan's *The Pilgrim's Progress* represents the Christian person; his quest is the life of such a person, there is a one-to-one relationship between the symbols and that which they repre-sent. If not, the story would not be an allegory. But as I showed in an earlier chapter, the relations between the topic and vehicle in a typical metaphor are not isomorphic. In fact they tend to be complex and diffuse, open to endless interpretations. Even in a simple metaphor like MAN IS A WOLF, it is not given how the relationship between the topic and the vehicle should be understood. Should we stress that both men and wolves are flock animals or aggressive or creatures that care for their offspring? Or should we focus on some different aspect of the relationship between topic and vehicle? Given this there are ways of interpreting stories as extended metaphors without inter-preting them as allegories. Take Hemingway's *The Old Man and the Sea*. We can interpret it as being multi-metaphoric; it is at the same time as a metaphor for an old man's battling with diminishing sexual potency, a writer's battle with writer's block and a metaphor for life. In the last one, we interpret the story in the light of the metaphor LIFE IS A JOURNEY and the old man journeys on the ocean. At the same, this multi-metaphoric interpretation can emphasise that the story has an infinite of other potential metaphoric implications.

I am not even certain whether or not myths can be understood as being allegories, even if they undoubtly have allegoric moments, think of the myth of Persephone as being from one point of view an allegory about the life and death of crops. However, primitive man certainly did not believe in the myth solely as an allegory, it had some kind of a literal reality to him. And modern man can take myths and interpret them in his own way because of the complexity of the relationship between the symbols of myth and their purported objects. Think about Camus' use of the Sisyphus myth. In contrast, it is extremely hard to 'recycle' allegories because any change in the relationship between its symbol and its object can put the isomorphism in jeopardy and thus deprive the story of its allegoric character.

The second possible objection to my theory of N-Ms is the following one: My point is quite trivial since every symbolic structure can be interpreted or intended to be a metaphor. But we have already seen in an earlier chapter that it is not clear whether all symbolic structures can be thus used. Further, I think that some stories strongly resist metaphoric interpretation (compare the fact that certain expressions and sentences are rather resistant to such an interpretation). My intuition is that the line between those stories that leave ample room for such interpretations and those that leave little or none is blurred, just like the line between expressions that lend themselves easily to metaphoric interpretation and those that do not.

Let us assume that someone tells the following story "I was walking home, and lo and behold! I met Mary whom I have not seen for ages. We chatted a bit, and then we said goodbye, and I went home". Does this story really contain an invitation to metaphoric interpretation? I do not think so; such simple, everyday stories do not leave much room for such construals. Of course, with enough imagination, one could probably find some way of interpreting this story metaphorically. But what would be the point? Interpretations, stories and metaphors are woven into forms of life where they typically have some purposes and abstracting the purposes away would distort our picture of them. The onus is on those who believe that there is a fruitful way of interpreting the aforementioned story metaphorically.

So we can conclude that it is non-trivially true that there are N-Ms. Further we can conclude that there are at least five types of them: a) some goal-source parables; b) some ordinary blended stories; c) metaphoric parables; d) metaphoric stories; and e) storied metaphors.

5.4 Conclusion

Ricœur and Turner have been most helpful in our attempt to build bridges between metaphors and narratives. Ricœur's approach is 'cultural' (analyses of myths and the like), and Turner's 'materialistic' (spatial stories). They complement each other. From vastly different premises, these two thinkers indeed arrive at similar conclusion: "there are bridges between metaphors and narratives". If we compare them to experimental scientists, Ricœur's 'testing methods' are 'cultural' while Turner's are 'materialistic'. My 'testing method' is a bit of both, and we all come to a similar outcome! At the same time, I do not see any compelling counter-arguments against the existence of N-Ms. These facts speak in favour of there being N-Ms (given my rule of quasi-induction), although that certainly does not conclusively prove their existence.

There is more between the metaphor and the narrative than philosophy could have dreamt of. Certainly, they have common offsprings.

II.6. Don Quixote and Narrativism
The Scope of Stories and Narratives in Human Existence

Is it by chance that a panel of prominent writers recently chose Miguel Cervantes' *Don Quixote* to be the best book of all time? Are not we all a bit like the Man from La Mancha, preferring to live in a world of illusions rather than having to face the harsh realities of our existence? Perhaps we are also like him in the sense that stories pervade our lives; remember that our valiant knight became who he was by virtue of reading too many medieval romances. So do we belong to the sad race of *Homo quixotens?* Or are we rather like the protagonist of Sartre's novel *La Nausée* (*Nausea*), Antonin Roquentin, whose life did not form any narrative unity? Are we *Homo roquentinens*?

I shall only touch lightly questions concerning the nature of the Self in this book, confining my discussion to the *narrativism* that forms the backbone of any idea of a quixotian, narrative Self. We actually already have already a rough idea of how narrativists think owing to my brief presentations of Turner's thoughts on the issue. In this chapter, I shall begin with a discussion of Wilhelm Schapp's narrativism. I shall also include the narrativism of two Canadian philosophers, David Carr and William Dray; their versions of narrativism are somewhat more moderate than Schapp's. I accept theirs and MacIntyre's *implicit* contention that actions have a storied structure and add that thinking and other mental acts have such a structure as well. I then turn to the critics of narrativism, first to theorists like Brian Fay who, despite their critical stance, maintain that there is a grain of truth in narrativism. I continue with an analysis of the criticism of those who reject narrativism out of hand, focusing mainly on Peter Lamarque. I counter his criticism by arguing in favour of my contention that there are spontaneous stories, i.e., stories that in a sense create themselves, for instance, dreams, reveries or scenarios that somehow force themselves upon us. But, generally, I am a cautious, moderate narrativist. Extreme narrativists like Schapp overlook the fact that important aspects of reality escape the grip of stories, for instance, the validity of deductive logic and mathematics.

6.1 Narrativism

If everything we experience, say, think, and do have a storied structure, then the narrativists carry the day. Narrativism has old roots, as the Bard famously told us that life "… is a tale told by an idiot, full of sound and fury, signifying nothing" (Shakespeare 1990: 939). Much later, the literary theorist Wayne C. Booth said, "We all live a large proportion of our lives in a surrender of stories about our lives, and about other possible lives: we live more or less in stories..." (Booth 1988: 14). This sounds like an echo from a German book written twenty-five years earlier, *In Geschichten Verstrickt* (*Entangled in Stories*). Its author was the German philosopher and judge, Wilhelm Schapp. As far as I know, he was the first thinker who articulated the intuitions behind narrativism in a philosophical manner. Schapp was originally a student of Husserl's but then turned to law and worked as a judge for many decades. As a judge, he discovered that there was no such thing as prosecuting, defending or judging a case in any form but a narrative one. Judges, lawyers, and defendants tell endless tales in court. Because of these experiences, he developed a full-fledged narrativistic philosophy:

> Wir Menschen sind immer in Geschichten verstrickt. Zu jeder Geschichte gehört ein darin verstrickter. Geschichte und In-Geschichte-verstrickt-sein gehören so eng zusammen, daß man beides vielleicht nicht einmal in Gedanken trennen kann. (Schapp 1976: 1)
>
> (We humans are always entangled in stories. Every story has someone who is entangled in it. A story and being entangled in story are so intimately connected that we perhaps cannot even disconnect them in thought.)[1]

To be *entangled in stories* means 'being caught up in stories', 'having no way of escaping from them' or more precisely 'being by necessity a part of stories'. I am not only entangled and caught up in the story of my life; I am also co-entangled (*Mitverstrikt*) in other people's stories and they in mine. And both they and I are co-entangled in the stories of our civilisation, our country, our communities, etc. Everything we do, even innocent rounds of chats on the Internet, is a

---

[1] This is my own translation from German. For some mysterious reason, this book has never been translated into English. There is, however, a translation into French.

part of stories. Moreover, the stories are entangled in each other; every story refers to another story about the events leading up to its beginning, and the second story refers to a third one, and so on. Not even the Judeo-Christian myth of creation has a non-ambiguous beginning. After all, the story refers to a potential story of what God did before creating the world (Schapp 1976: 88). In the beginning was the story (at the end the narrative?). It does not make much sense to analyse the story as something being composed by units; a story is an irreducible whole (the kinship with Mink should be obvious). They are not even essentially verbal, even though language can play an important role in them.

It is not by chance that we get to know who a given person is by getting to know the story of his or her life (Schapp 1988: 103). The reason is simply that the story is the only game in town. We are only drops in a sea of stories (Schapp 1959: 4). Our personalities or Selves are only abstractions from the stories in which we are entangled. In the last analysis, there is no such thing as a story-less thing, for the narrative rules and creates the rules. Great minds think alike: in one of his books, American novelist Cormac McCarthy writes: "Things separate from their stories have no meaning" (McCarthy 1994: 142). In a markedly different approach to Schapp's, McCarthy is hardly making a philosophical point. The narrative has some kind of a constitutive function for Schapp, somewhat like it has in the theories of Turner and Ricœur.[2]

According to Schapp, existing (being) means being entangled in stories; in some sense stories are all there is. So, very differently from Mink, the German phenomenologist maintains that stories are not first and foremost something created and told but something in which we discover or find ourselves. Almost by implication, our perceptions, emotions, and thoughts are completely dependent upon stories; they are just as entangled in stories as everything else. But surely we can perceive colours and other sensory qualities without involving stories, someone might say. No, responds Schapp, there is no such thing as experiencing sensory qualities in an isolated form. You do not see a

---

[2] It would be tempting to say that Schapp accords a transcendental function to narratives but that does not square with his descriptive phenomenological approach. Like a good descriptive phenomenologist, he was sceptical of all theorising, including the transcendental kind. He wanted to describe, not to explain (Haas 2002: 36).

colour isolated from everything else you have experienced. In the last analysis your perception only makes sense as something that takes place in a story or is the perception of a storied event, or both. Furthermore, your act of perception takes place at a certain point in your life and your life is a story, entangled in other stories (Schapp 1976: 75). This statement is even clearer when we consider our perception of work-a-day objects (*Wozudinge*), i.e., things that have utility for us. We can only relate to these things as something with a story, things that were in many cases created at given moments for given purposes or things that have broken down at some moment. If you discover that something is broken, you are bound to regard what happened to the thing as a narratable event, or else you would not be able to understand it as broken object (Schapp 1976: 13). Moreover, our relationship to *Wozudinge* constitutes our primary relationship to the world. Schapp is a pragmatist in the same way as Heidegger, who maintained that objects were first 'at hand' (*Zuhanden*) as practical objects before they became 'for hand' (*Vorhanden*), i.e., objects for theoretical reflection. We first relate to the sun as an object that keeps our bodies warm and helps us find our way. This practical relationship gives the sun its identity. Because of this, we can put forth theories about the nature of the sun (Heidegger 1977: 63-113 (§15-27)). In Schapp's view, this means that objects are primarily objects of utility and that such objects only exist in stories or as abstractions from stories. (Schapp would have agreed with Mink on events as being abstractions from stories.)

As the reader might have guessed, Schapp also thought that our relationship to ourselves is primarily of a narrative nature. If we ask ourselves what kind of personal qualities we have, then we cannot answer that question without relating to the stories recounted about these qualities. Needless to say, scrutinising our inner being means analysing our stories (Schapp 1976: 126). Emotions are also of a narrative nature. Emotions such as love or hate are what they are by being entangled in stories (Schapp 1976: 156-157). There is no love without a love story! Think about hate; one cannot hate someone if one is not of the opinion that the object of hate did something bad. There must be a story about that action and its consequences.

Schapp's books make a fascinating reading; they are full of thought-provoking examples from everyday life, besides having a peculiar kind of poetical clarity. They are places where the poetic and the concrete meet. Nevertheless, his analysis is not above criticism. In the first place, he has never defined the concept of a story (just like Turner). According to Stephanie Haas, he thinks that the concept in question cannot be defined successfully (Haas 2002: 36). Perhaps there is a kinship between his view and Mink's contention that plots can only be shown, not said. Be that as it may, one has the feeling that Schapp stretches the concept of a story too thinly and that he assumes *a priori* that everything is a story or is entangled in a host of stories. Secondly, he ignores that the validity of mathematical and deductive logical proofs play an important role in our lives, and it is hard to see how one can reduce this validity to narrativicity, regarding as having nothing but a storied structure. I am not saying that such validity is not context-bound, for instance, to certain cultural practices, but it does not follow that such practices have a storied structure. And it certainly does not follow that a formal logical or mathematical proof has such a structure. Conclusions certainly do not follow from premises in a story-like fashion, as we remember that unpredictability is one of the essential features of stories. The opposite is an essential feature of a logical or mathematical proof, however much its validity might be relative to context.[3] We are rational creatures who partly act on basis of logical and mathematical validity. Need I remind the reader of the important role mathematics and logics play in our technological civilisation, for instance? There is, therefore, a lower degree of narrativicity in our world than Schapp thinks.

Further, Stephanie Haas has a point when she says that Schapp is torn between wanting to focus on concrete individuals and wanting to generalise about humans as beings entangled in stories (Haas 2002: 60). Surely he is busy abstracting from concrete individuals when he is saying that they are all functions of stories.

In short, Schapp saw the whole world through the lenses of narratives and in the process invented the concept of narrativism. His analysis, however, suffers from certain vagueness, and, besides, there are counter-examples (formal logical validity) to his comprehensive narrativism.

---

[3] For arguments in favour of logical reasoning being contextual, see Winch 1958: 55-57.

Another phenomenological argument in favour of narrativism can be found in the works of Canadian philosopher David Carr. His starting point is the phenomenological idea of pre-thematic awareness, and he believes that there are narrative moments in this awareness, which make the activities of historians and other storytellers possible. Narrative structures pervade both our experiences and actions; so in effect, our world is a narrative one (Carr 1986a: 3-9). Carr defends what he calls 'the *continuity* thesis', i.e., the idea that there is continuity between the narrative structure on the pre-thematic level and our actual, articulated narratives. In his view, Mink, White, and even Ricœur are followers of 'the discontinuity thesis', the constructivist idea that actual narratives impose a structure on a chaotic reality. These constructivists think that narratives somehow distort reality or are unable to represent it. But what do they mean by reality? Some ultimate metaphysical reality? Carr argues that they forget that narratives represent the human world, not whatever material reality that might be behind that world. (Carr himself forgets that zoologists and geologists tell stories of the rise and fall of animal species or the story of the earth.) And human reality is structured by stories (Carr 1986a: 16 and Carr 2001: 146).

Inspired by Husserl, Carr regards experience as temporal in the sense that my experience at a given moment – call it M – is only understandable given the background of experiences that I had immediately before M and in the light of our expectations of what kind of experiences I shall have immediately after M. If M is the focus, then the past and the present are the background or the horizon. Husserl called the contribution of the past *retention* and that of the future *protention*. We conserve moments from the past in our experiences, and, at the same time, the experience is only comprehensible in the light of our expectations (projections into the future). Husserl used listening to a melody as an example; every note we hear is only understandable in relationship to both the notes we have heard earlier and the notes we expect to hear in the immediate future; we can even revise our view of the notes we just have heard in consideration of the notes we hear later; maybe we discover that these earlier notes lead to an explosion and not the nice, quite finish we were expecting (Carr 1986a: 25). In this fashion we might grasp in hindsight that the earlier notes were actually the calm lighting of the fuse. Whatever variations there may be, our experiences must necessarily have a beginning (the retention), a climax (M), and an end (the protention), just like a story.

Now, someone might ask whether this analysis is only appropriate for the experience of temporal phenomenon like melodies, but not for non-temporal ones, like stones or furniture. Carr's answer to this question is negative. All our experiences must have this temporal structure (beginning-middle-end) and are always both retentional and protentional. I can use my eyes to analyse a piece of furniture or use my tactile sense to study the surface of a stone, for instance, by stroking it with my hand. In both cases the experience has a temporal structure as well as retentional and protentional aspects. Even simple, momentary experiences as the hearing of high-pitched sound have the same structure. This seems to hold for all possible experiences (Carr 1986a: 47-48).

Our experiences are often more complex than just stroking of a stone or hearing of a high-pitched sound. To watch (and hear) the performance of ballet is a good example. Here, there is a myriad of activity; the prima ballerina is, for instance, executing a pirouette while dancing with her male counterpart. Together these events form a whole. We can analyse this whole in smaller parts, and it requires reflection to understand them as forming a holistic structure (or parts which are fused together). This reflective stance does not play any role in simpler experiences; they are more spontaneous than this stance and are characterised by the experience engulfing us. It is by virtue of this reflective stance that we can take a drink and chat with companions during the break but can nevertheless grasp what happens after the break as a part of what happened earlier. Carr reminds us of the fact that the German expression *sich besinnen* not only means 'to reflect' but also to remind one of where one stands (of what happened earlier in the ballet) and to take stock. Drawing on both Husserl and hermeneutic philosopher Wilhelm Dilthey, the Canadian thinker thinks it is this 'German' kind of reflection that makes our lives coherent (Carr 1986a: 55-57). Carr is aware of the fact that these reflections are not only similar to narrative structures, but also dissimilar to them in some respects. Inspired by Dilthey, Carr maintains that the similarity is that both narratives and reflections on our lives describe events backwards, from an end-point in time. Further, both have in common a temporal relation between part and whole. While reflecting on our lives, we regard different events in our lives as parts of a totality of our lives; in a story, the various events described are parts of the totality. Besides, the person reflecting must regard herself as a spectator of, actor in, and teller of the tale of her own life. One dissimilarity among others is that we can neither experience the beginning nor the end of our lives. My death is a part of my own biography, but I cannot experience it. Because of this, we cannot experience our lives as usual narrative totalities (Carr 1986a: 78-79). This is one of the reasons why many theorists maintain that we cannot see a life as a story. A storyteller can have supreme hindsight; his point of view is not constrained by the limitations of the given moment, in contrast to the one who reflects over her own life. Carr's view on this matter is that,

> …action does involve, indeed quite essentially, the adoption of an anticipated future-retrospective point of view on the present. We know we are in the present and that the unforeseen can happen; but the very essence of action is to strive to overcome that limitation by foreseeing as much as possible (Carr 1986a: 60).

We try by our actions to become storytellers with hindsight. This is quite a compelling argument and seems related to Ricœur's contention that our lives are not stories but that living means searching for stories (Ricœur 1991a: 29).

We still have not seen how Carr argues that actions have a storied structure. He points out that theorists tend to ignore the temporality of action. (Ricœur certainly cannot be accused of that.) Probing into that temporality shows that action has a sort of retentional-protentional structure and by implication a storied structure. Action unfolds in temporal phases like a melody. Consider the case of tennis. The purpose of the tennis player's actions is to hit the ball in certain ways, which are thus the temporal as well as the teleological end of the action. It so happens that the means-end structure of action has a thing or two in common with beginning-middle-end structure of narratives, and so it is no wonder that the temporal and the teleological end overlap in this case. In parallel to a melody, the agent has a kind of prospective and retrospective grasp of the successive phases of the action, both past and future. In the midst of action, the agent does not view the future is not something expected, as in experiences, but something to be brought about by the performance of the action. In action, we focus on the future, because we aim at realising a state in the future. It is in the foreground while past and present form the background. There is something retrospective about action, as if we were located in the future and from this point of view trying to arrange and organise the present (Carr 1986a: 30-40). So the agent is by necessity a time-traveller! If I understand Carr correctly, then the retentional structure shows itself both in the way the agent 'travels to the future' and in the way that the recent actions form a part of the horizon of his actions. The tennis player's swift running towards the ball is a part of the horizon of the very act of hitting the ball. The pro-tential structure is the anticipation of the future and the activity of bringing about a future state.

Now, Carr was a bit puzzled about Ricœur's position on the issue of continuity versus discontinuity. On the one hand, the French philo-sopher appears to think that there is an inchoate narrativity involved in life on the level of prefiguration; on the other, he seems to maintain that whatever structure life has on this level, it is not really a narrative one (Ricœur 1984a: 74). Ricœur insists that the plot unites series of actions and events into larger unity. But Carr thinks we do not need plots for this; we form such unities in everyday life when we engage in complex and long-term endeavours. Something similar holds for Ricœur's contention that the plot brings together goals, means, etc. Again, Carr says, we unite goals and means in ordinary life. As for plots uniting levels of temporality by surmounting the merely sequential with the configurational, Husserl has already shown that time-experience is essentially configurational (Carr 1991: 160-174).

To this Ricœur responded by saying that on the prefigurative level, we grope about seeking a meaning, but we are involved in an ill-wrought history, a history eaten away by discordances, a history badly in need of a transformation into a well-made fiction. Thus we need literature to understand ourselves (Ricœur 1991b: 179-187).[4] (Note that he never mentions fictional movies as vehicles of understanding.) But would it not have been easier for Ricœur to answer by simply pointing out that he has said in no uncertain words that actions can only be understood with the aid of narratives? Would there be any world of acting beings unless they could understand their actions? Does not this point make their narrative understanding an integral part of their world?

---

[4] For a short, pro- Ricœurian overview of this debate, see Venema 2000: 116-121.

Ricœur's former student, the Irishman Richard Kearney, holds that Carr was less than fair to Ricœur. He did not understand that Ricœur's intent was to find a middle way between the continuity thesis and its opposite, the discontinuity thesis. So, the French thinker's swaying between the two is actually a sign of his intent: he is seeking to mediate dialectically between two opposing views. He acknowledges the existence of forms of virtual narrativity at the primordial level of our lived experience, a narrativity not created by fictional or historical texts. Kearney then hints at Carr's going too far in the direction of a univocal and continuist theory of narrative and thereby ignoring important moral as well as epistemological and ontological differences between distinct functions of narratives, i.e., the different functions of narratives in life, history, and fiction. Unfortunately, Kearney does not really elaborate this issue, but he seems to be saying that narrative theory needs pragmatics, not only the virtual semantics Carr provides, which is an excellent point indeed. Instead, Kearney directs some effort towards criticising Carr for an implicit relativism. By arguing for a direct formal continuity between narrative history and lived history, he seems to think that the we who constantly retell and revise history are really a multiplicity of 'we's', constituted by the various communal language-games we play. Telling the story of a community is simply continuing the story-telling at a somewhat more reflective level (Carr 1986a: 177). But does not it follow that the community mentioned here is a plurality of living communities, each with its own particular sense of history? (Kearney 2006: 477-490). Carr's response to these criticisms is not very satisfactory, aside from the fact that he admits having been somewhat unfair towards Ricœur (Carr 1986b: 491-501). Be that as it may, Kearney's accusations of relativism are rather strange. If our experiences and lives already have storied structures before any stories are told about them, how can a possible relativity of story-telling render our knowledge of this storied structure relative to story-telling? According to Carr, the stories are simply out there.

Fellow Canadian William Dray tends to agree with Carr on many issues but criticises him for not having gone far enough in his criticism of the constructivists. Dray's first of three concerns is that Carr is much too cautious in putting forth ontological claims while actually saying that narratives constitute communal life, an ontological claim. It could be added that Carr is also puts forth an ontological claim concerning the narrative constitution of the Self. Dray's second concern is that Carr overemphasises the role of actual narration. Carr, in fact, criticises Schapp and Alasdair MacIntyre for talking as though the narratives that pervade our lives are stories without storytellers, and that is not the case, according to Carr (Carr 1986a: 84). But Dray takes a similar stance as Schapp; the question is not whether there is actual narration taking place but whether the narrative or the story or the story-like structure actually refers to reality. Dray's third point is similar to the second: Carr's three-voice analysis presupposes that there is no narrative without a narrator at the same time as Carr emphasises that there are narrative structures without narrator. Dray is also sceptical of Carr's (implicit?) contention that historical narratives are articulations of storied structures built into experience and action. Historians do tell with the greatest ease the stories of objects, such as the industrial revolution or population trends. To be sure, such objects are the results of experiences and activities, but they themselves are neither experiences nor actions. Even worse for Carr is his insistence that natural scientists tell stories of natural phenomena - the history of the earth, life on earth or the universe, and the like - but we cannot by any stretch of imagination call those phenomena 'products of experience and actions'. One of the problems with Carr's arguments is that he seems to accept the constructivist contention that if narratives are artefacts, that is to say, not natural, then they cannot represent reality. Then Carr tries to show that narratives inhere in something natural, i.e., our actions and experiences. But why should this be the case? Why cannot something artificial represent reality? Further, we can vindicate narrativism without necessarily defending the continuity thesis. We can find narratives retrospectively exemplified in what may not have come narrativised originally. Now, let us assume that something first displays the true temporal succession of elements, secondly ascribes them to a central subject, thirdly relates some of the elements in such a way that they can explain the others, and fourthly shows that the various elements were parts, phases or stages of some developing whole. If an event actually exhibits all of these interrelationships, then it would be difficult to deny that this event exhibits a narrative form. There are actually phenomena that have this form, and some may not have been discovered. Dray raises the notion of 'unknown narrativizable configurations' that are 'tellables', i.e., objects having a narrative form although they may have never been told in an actual story (Dray 2001: 157-179). In my terminology, a tellable is something that possesses a storied structure. The concept of tellable is a fruitful one for my undertaking. But that does not commit me to accept Dray's criticism of Carr in its entirety. He overlooks the possibility that historians and natural scientists only were able to tell the story of, say, the industrial revolution or life on earth, if they project human actions and experiences into these objects, talk like they were acting and experiencing object or products of such object. More importantly he ignores the fact that events are only events under a description, some being narrative, others not. And he also seems un-aware of the fact that the presence of narrative sentences in narratives makes them re-interpretable. In short, Dray is much too objectivistic.

However, Dray and Carr are certainly right about actions having a storied structure (they of course do not use this expression). So the narrativists have several good points. We can strengthen their analysis with the aid of Alasdair MacIntyre's approach. He agrees with the two Canadian theorists that actions have a storied structure, but in contrast to them he focuses on speech acts. They are not are not really under-standable unless we can place them in a narrative context. Imagine that we are waiting for a bus and a woman next to us suddenly says, "The name of the common wild duck is *Histrionicus histrionicus histrionicus*". We should certainly understand the meaning of the sen-tence uttered, but the problem is to understand the point of uttering it. Suppose that the woman utters sentences like this at random intervals, in which case this could possibly be a form of madness. We should render her action of utterance intelligible if, for instance, she has mistaken us for those who approached her in the library some days ago and asked her for the Latin name of the wild duck. We should also understand the action if she mistakenly thought we were her co-spies and she was uttering a code sentence to be decoded by us. In each case, the act of utterance only becomes understandable by being put in a narrative context. Further, personal identities must have a narrative structure. Our actions are episodes in stories, not least our own per-sonal stories. The actions cannot be given an identity unless placed in the agent's biography (MacIntyre 1981: 204-218). I shall not be judge of his theories of personal identities and restrict myself to saying that I think he is right about the speech acts. His analysis shows that we should not be able to understand our own actions without putting them into a narrative context. This adds fuel to both Carr's, Dray's and

Ricœur's contention that actions have something akin to a storied structure.

I want to affix to this some points of my own. I do not believe it is controversial to say that thinking is a mental act. Mental acts are not things that just happen to us but are true-blue actions. In virtue of being such actions, they have a storied structure. This feature at least holds for the process of conscious thought. Of course, we often think in stories, including counterfactual ones. When thinking about how to get to the top of a mountain, I tell myself a counterfactual story about my climbing it. But I am after bigger game: I think there are storied moments in all thinking and, indeed, all mental acts. (a) In the first place, mental acts have a storied structure just like any other action. The fact that they are performed 'inwardly' does not discount them from being actions. (Given the private-language argument, there is no clear dividing line between the inner and the outer anyway.) (b) A thought is *about* something just like a story. (c) A thought is something that begins, has middle, and ends at a certain point in time. In the beginning, the thought is hazy but becomes clearer the moment we see how it all hangs together. What it is all about, what gives it an identity is what I call a *theme*. I might be thinking about Kristin's bad behaviour towards me, for instance. So her bad behaviour is the theme that unifies into one whole all kinds of mental events, which may include vague feelings, inner pictures or sentences 'heard' inwardly. Thus, the theme does the work of the plot.

The concept of the process of a conscious thought obviously satisfies my definition of a storied structure: thoughts have a beginning, middle, and an ending, and form a unified whole. In addition it has something akin that feature of a narrative structure we call 'a plot' (the theme).

Another example could be doubt. If I doubt the existence of the yeti, then my thinking about these issues have the yeti-doubt as a theme. Other mental acts have a similar structure. Willing something begins in time, has middle and ending; the theme of a host of thoughts and feelings are this willing-to-become-nun or willing-to-go-to-China. Actually, the same holds for at least some mental states, including emotional ones. Sorrow has the beginning, middle, end structure and a theme, the sorrow of this or that given kind, for instance because of the death of grandma. These mental states will be discussed in the next section.

Notice that even if actions were not storied or if thinking were not really actions, it does not mean that thinking does not have storied structure. From b) and c), I provide arguments for thinking being storied, independent of any arguments in favour of actions having a storied structure.

Now, if thinking has a storied structure, then that might be an explanation for why we tell stories and tend to see things in storied terms. We cannot help but to see the world in these terms because of the nature of our thoughts. Further, what we call 'stories' are perhaps simply projections of the structure of our thought. To (ab)use the Chomskyian metaphor once again, I speculate that our thinking is like the deep grammar, that the actualisation of that grammar permeate the stories of our lives, and that narratives are like a reworking of this actualisation.

We do not have to be idealists to admit that our thinking decisively colours our world-view. Given that thinking is storied, then the way we see the world must have strong storied traits. This consideration ought to strengthen immensely the narrativist cause, which is indeed my cause.

6.2 Moderate Narrativism

Schapp, Carr, and Dray are obviously among those Brian Fay calls *narrative realists*, those who believe that stories about lives and events are found, not constructed (Fay 1996: 178-190). Such realists maintain that narrative structures exist in the human world itself and not just in the stories people tell about this world. Human lives are already formed into stories before somebody tries to tell them. The task of a raconteur is to tell a story whose beginnings, middles, and endings mirror the actual beginnings, middles, and endings of the events being narrated. After all, a historian did not create the fact that World War I started in 1914 and ended in 1918; her story has to mirror such facts. Fay, however, has misgivings about this view. When does a human life really begin or really end? Maybe we have had a pre-existence and will have a post-existence. If this sounds speculative, then we can ask whether the existence of influential indi-viduals really ended with their death. Must not we also tell the stories of their influence? It could do us a world of good to contemplate how Cheyenne Indians start with the stories of their grandparents when they are asked to tell the story of their lives. For them an individual life is explicitly a part of a greater whole.

Fay maintains that the realists hold both that the identity of a particular act derives from the intention it expressed and that an intention is what it is by virtue of the historical setting into which the agent places it. The act of opening the window is an act of cooling because of the narrative setting: the window was closed, and so I got hot, but if I open the window, the room will be cooler in the future. Each of our lives consists in refashioning the continuous narrative we tell ourselves, adjusting it and our behaviour as time goes by. The basic plot of our lives is the trajectory of this ongoing narrative line. The task of a biographer is to discover this line; therefore, it makes sense to ask what biography is true. But Fay points out that stories comprise not only actions but also the results of these acts and intentions. There is really no such thing as a story if there is no causal connection between events. We see this by looking at the following: X intended a and did y, X intended b and did x, X intended c and did q. There are no connections between these three events, and, therefore, they do not form a story. (Danto might have called this 'a chronicle of sorts'.) But if we make the appropriate causal connections between the events, then we transform 'the chronicle' into a story: X intended a and did y; y produced x and this led X to intend b and so to do q. The causal outcome of actions – here z – provides at least a part of the connective tissue that links together events to form a story. Thus descriptions of y such as 'the cause of z' will abound in narrations about X. Let us consider Thomas Carlyle, for example. After the death of his wife, he discovered that he had made her miserable by his conduct in certain affairs. In light of this discovery, he revised the story of his life; he began to see some of his past actions differently, ones that caused misery.

Due to the fact that the identity of an act or a life is a function of its causal outcomes, there is a fundamental indeterminacy built into their description. The causal repercussions of any act or life can continue indefinitely into the future, even after the death of the agent in question, and these repercussions will strongly influence the nature of the story told about this act or life. There is no such thing, therefore, as the final, definite, narrative of a life. There is no such thing as a life that can be a story in itself, because the stories of our lives are not self-contained. As new causal outcomes resulting from lives emerge, new narratives can be recounted about it. Here, Fay could have added a note on the role of narrative sentences in any biography. Due to their nature, the story a life can always be reinterpreted. In the first years after a soldier fell at the battle of the White Mountain in 1618, nobody could have told his story as 'the story of one the first victims of the Thirty Years war'.

Not only do realists ignore causal outcomes, but also the significance of events. Not every causal outcome matters for biographies or other stories. Consider the following: Fay spoke at January the 5th in 2008 and as a result, he moved numerous air molecules. But surely, this causal outcome has no significance for him or the story of his life. For such a story, only significant intentions, acts, and causal effects matter. Fay defines 'significance' as 'the capacity to advance an emerging narrative pattern'. There is no basic structure that inheres in life. Countless facts, themselves results of interpretations, can be arranged at any number of different ways to form a coherent configuration, which makes life intelligible. Biography, therefore, involves the creative imagination of the biographer, not only the intentions of the biographee. Intelligibility is always the intelligibility of someone, which means that it is relative to some interpreter. The relationship between biographer and the life he is writing about is like the one between translator and what is being translated. Just as there are no definite translations, there are no definite biographies.

This indefinitiveness does not mean that Fay is what he calls *a narrative constructivist*, i.e., someone who believes both that narratives are constructed, not discovered, and that historians impose narrative structures on a formless flow of events (White would be an example). Fay actually thinks that constructivism is as one-sided as realism (Fay 1996: 190-194). Take Charles Dickens' execution of the intentional act of marital separation as an example. That act was in part a function of his coming to re-conceive the story he was telling himself of his marriage. This shows that narratives are in life and not just about it. Intentional agents live within ongoing stories, which they must constantly tell themselves as a condition for being able to perform intentional actions at all. But why is this so? It is because of the peculiar structure of intentional acts. Besides having a temporal character, actions are teleological, i.e., directed towards an end, motivated by and performed for a reason. Having this teleological dimension, actions look towards the future at some possible state of affairs that the act is supposed to bring about. Because they are motivated, actions necessarily are backward-looking, looking to the situation of the agent and how she got there. The moment of acting is precisely the coming together of the agent's sense of his or her past history, present situation, and future possibilities. This temporal dimension has a narrative structure: a beginning (the past), middle (the present), and an ending (the future). This means that activity is itself already narratively structured so that stories are integral to the performance of every act. Moreover, the practices of scientists, legislators or members of religious communities are narratively shaped in the sense that these participants must, perforce, engage in telling themselves and others stories about the nature of their interrelations as a way of continuing their membership in their respective communities. Stories are thus not only about practices but are parts of them.

Narrative constructivism fails to see the ways in which life and story are partly facets of the same structure. Its followers wrongly maintain that narratives and the form of narratives are mere creations imposed on material, which is non-narrational. But there is a grain of truth in it: the narrative account of any life is revisable. There is also a grain of truth in realism: the narrative form is not accidental, not merely a tool we use to represent events but also something that takes part in constituting these events and our identities. But, as we have seen, realism errs in saying that each person's life is just a single enacted narrative. What Fay calls 'narrativism' or I 'moderate narrativism' tries to steer a middle course between realism and constructivism.[5] He points out that the stories we think we are living and the stories others or we come to see ourselves to have been living are not necessarily the same. With hindsight, others or we may come to reassess the nature of the narrative we thought we were living and thereby re-describe the activities in which we were engaged. Look at the marriage of John Stuart Mill and Harriet Taylor. They married and related to each other only because both subscribed to a narrative in

---

[5] Fay's intuitions are a bit like the ones of Ricœur and his followers. Actually, Richard Kearney argues in a similar fashion as Fay (Kearney: 2002)

which they were living in equality. But Taylor dominated Mill, and so this marriage was a complex of at least two narratives, which were contradictory but at the same time intertwined. Something similar holds for historical situations. The participants in the Great War necessarily told themselves that their activities were part of a larger story. Indeed, it is only because they did so that they could wage this war as they did. But later historians or even the participants with hindsight and reflection may have come to retell the story of the war. They may refit it to a narrative of a quite different sort from that of the original participants' (Fay 1996: 94-98).

Fay goes a bit too far in his criticism of the narrative realists. He overlooks the fact that our experiences and thoughts have storied structures. Crucial segments of our lives, actions, and culture have by necessity storied structures, and there is a constant dialectical interaction between what Fay calls 'lived narratives' and 'told narratives'. I prefer to talk about 'lived stories' and 'narratives'; Fay does not, unfortunately, draw the important distinction between narratives and stories. Yet again, I want to invoke the analogy to Kant's thought. If lived stories are like the intuitions, then narratives are like the categories. But this analogy is also misleading, because in Kant's view, the categories do not form the intuitions in any way. In contrast, the narratives are not only the product of the lived stories but also form the stories.

There are stories, however, that are simply found and do not need any dialectical relationship with narratives; stories that, so to speak, force themselves upon us. I call them *spontaneous stories*, they are pure tallbles, being endowed with storied structures. Dreams, daydreams, memories, sexual fantasies, and scenarios of the angst-ridden (or even ordinary people) are stories that happen to us, or even often intrude themselves upon us. We wake up in the morning and remember a dream, which had the form of a story. Of course, it might be that we impose a storied structure upon the dream after we wake up,[6] but the point is that we do not impose the structure willingly. Whether or not we actually dreamt the dream, we certainly did not tell the story,

---

[6] Could it be that dreams really are confabulations that we perform after waking up? To be sure, we have sensory experiences while sleeping but perhaps they are without rhyme or reason. Perhaps the rhyme and reason are the products of confabulation.

unless we maintain that our memory is a storyteller.[7] Our memory provides us with memories in the form of stories, some of which we want to forget, but they keep imposing themselves upon us, without the aid of a conscious narrator. The same holds for the everyday making of scenarios of certain kinds. A person suffering from anxiety experiences all kinds of story-like scenarios in his or her head; the person has a vivid image of the terrible things that would happen if he or she flew on a plane. Usually, this kind of person wants these stories to go away, but they will not. The same holds for the scenarios an ordinary, balanced person experiences on the way home to the spouse after a wet night with the colleagues, that is, if the person is not blessed with oblivion, due to excessive drinking! False memories and confabulations are two more examples of spontaneous stories.

To be sure, sexual fantasies and reveries are not always entirely beyond our control, but usually there is a moment of a lack of control when the fantasies and the daydreams partly happen to us.[8] If they do just happen to us, then they are stories and not narratives, and they certainly are found, not told. They are constructs of the imagination but not of any narrative structure. We can represent these stories in true or false, accurate or inaccurate narratives; they are tellables. They are responsible for the high degree of narrativity of our dreams, daydreams, reveries, fantasies, and scenarios. Owing to spontaneous stories, a large segment of these phenomena (dreams, etc.) have a storied structure.

We also make scenarios consciously, as Carroll indeed pointed out. We ask such questions as "what will happen if we choose strategy A rather than B?" The answers to these questions are often more like narratives than stories, even though it happens that the scenario-story starts to unfold as if automatically. Then the scenario ceases to be a narrative and becomes a story. The same holds for a fantasy that starts as something controlled by a person but then gets out of hand and

---

[7] Experiments show that we become sick if prevented from dreaming. Could it be that we are programmed to crave for stories and get some kind of abstinence symptoms if we do not get these dream-stories? As the Rolling Stones sang in their song *Ruby Tuesday*: "...if you lose your dreams then you lose your mind."

[8] Does becoming mad mean that we lose control over our stories and that they start to control us? Think of the way stories about persecution impose themselves on the mind of the paranoid person.

takes on a life of its own. A narrative is transformed into a story. This shows that there can a thin line between a story and a narrative.

Be that as it may, Fay is oblivious of the existence of the spontaneous stories and, therefore, underestimates the power of narrativism or narrative realism. He is also blind to the storied nature of thought and other mental acts. The fact that he does not differentiate between narratives and stories makes him think wrongly that because we can refashion narratives radically, there must be severe limits to the role stories play out there. But since they are partly independent of narratives, then the fact of radical narrative refashioning does not make them something entirely created by the narrator. He is, however, surely right about there not being any final story of our life. I want to add that outside the dimension of thought and spontaneous stories, there is not much pure storied structure (in Dray's terminology, not too many pure tellables). In other dimensions of human existence stories either arise in complex interplay between storied structures and active narrative imagination or are pure fantasies. It still remains that phenomena in all these dimensions, including that of the spontaneous stories, can only be given identity under a description. And that description must be a narrative one for we cannot successfully describe a storied structure in any other way; a narrative can sort of mirror it. In order to give D identity as a daydream, there must be a way of telling its story, articulating its storied structure narratively. This story must be intersubjecively understandable in order to enable others to check whether the person having D actually was daydreaming and not, say, just dreaming.

A narrative description shapes the identity of the phenomena with a storied structure in a particular way, giving them clearer contours of a story by for instance adding a plot. Further, a narrative description typically consists of a host of narrative sentences, making the narrative re-interpretable in light of facts that occur later in time. So if we articulate narratively a storied structure like that of a spontaneous story or a mental act, their identity is partly shaped by the narrative description of this articulation. The correct narrative description does not exist even though some narratives are blatantly wrong. Bear in mind that a narrative is constituted by aspect-seeing and the correct aspect-seeing does not exist, compare the fact that there is no such thing as the correct way of viewing a duck-rabbit figure.

At the same time, the mental acts we perform in the narrative articulation have a storied structure that in its turn colours the narrative description. So what we have is a complex interplay between objectively existing storied structures and narrative imagining, both shaping each other.

6.3 Lamarque's criticism

Before concluding this chapter, I shall turn to a criticism of narrativism put forth by Peter Lamarque that deserves our attention (Lamarque 2004: 393-408). He reiterates and develops further his and Olsen's views on narratives, the theories that I discussed in II.1 and II.3. He says that it is simply not true that narratives are by necessity fictional; that they create the events or objects they describe, that our Selves are created by narratives; that narratives possess closure (are complete with a beginning, a middle, and an ending); that there are no structures of events independent of narrative; and that narratives distort the reality they describe. Instead, Lamarque proposes four minimal conditions of storytelling: a) stories are told, not found; b) at least two events must be depicted in a narrative; c) there must be some more or less loose, but non-logical, relations between these events; and d) there must be temporal relations between events. We can identify narratives from formal features of individual sentences or sentence strings alone. From such formal identifications we cannot draw any implications about reference, truth, subject matter or discursive ends. Narratives are neutral on such matters; we can infer very little of substance from the premise that a given discourse is a narrative. It does not even have any real explanatory value. Given that a narrative is just the ordering of a sequence of events, including the placing of events in causal sequences, it is a truism that a narrative can be an explanatory device.

Furthermore, it is wrong to conflate history and fiction because historical writing is unavoidably perspectival and selective. In the first place, neither the use of names in historical narratives nor the truth-valuation of individual assertions affects reference by means of proper names or singular descriptions. Secondly, distortion is not an inevitable feature of descriptive narration. To accept the notion of a distorted narrative is to imply that there is an ideal, transparent narrative of sorts that maps facts without any discrimination or weighing. Such an ideal is obviously unwarranted (compare Carroll's criticism of White).

The anti-realists believe in at least two theses: 1) all narration is fiction; and 2) historians create meta-events as a part of narrative structuring. Examples of such meta-events are the Middle Ages and the Cold War. But no general anti-realism about events follows from either 1) or 2). Thus the writing of General Robert E. Lee to the president of the Confederate States, Jefferson Davis, on 25 June 1863, is not a creation of any historian. We should need a general metaphysical and epistemological theory, not necessarily about narratives, to establish that such facts are indeed fictions. This means that 1) is wrong and 2) does not fare any better. When the historians impose a structure on a cluster of events and call the structure 'the Middle Ages', it is a marker of significance, not any invention of facts. Assigning signification within a structure that identifies a beginnings and an end is not creating the very events themselves. We have no reason to believe that the causal sequences of events are creations of narratives.

Not much, then, comes out of studying the semantic or even syntactic features of narratives. Even less comes out of such studies if we consider the fact that a fictional story could be true by pure chance; the story's semantic properties obviously do not make it fictional. An orientation towards the pragmatics of narratives is more worthwhile than a focus on its syntax or semantics. In order to determine the relevance of its structure and semantic properties, we have to know what kind of narrative is involved and in what kind of practices it is involved. As we recall, Lamarque thinks that fiction is a certain practice that aims at creating make-believe, not belief, and, therefore, its truth-value is not really relevant. Biographies and historical narratives have presumably the aim of making us believe that certain propositions are true, implying that their truth-value is highly relevant.

Lamarque's analysis is challenging, but I have some rebuttals. To begin with, he obviously conflates the concepts of story and narrative. Yes, N is only a narrative if it is being told, but S can be a story without being told, as I have indeed shown. As the reader might guess, I disagree vehemently with Lamarque's contention that stories are only told, never found. That spontaneous stories exist and that our experience and thinking have storied structures show that Lamarque is simply wrong.

Secondly, I doubt the importance of the purported fact that the relevance of the semantic properties of a narrative is determined by the practice it is involved in. Surely the same holds for the semantic properties of a scientific treatise. Is not science a particular type of practice? Thirdly, I do not find his deflating claims concerning the explanatory nature of narratives very convincing. Lamarque overlooks the claim made by many narrativists that the epistemological value of narratives is not *that* they give causal explanation, but *how*. We have seen earlier in this book both that narratives do not necessarily make explanations by invoking general laws and that they help us make sense of thing in different way from both logical and nomothetical explanations. Further, Lamarque seems to think that all narrative connections are causal. But I think that Gregory Currie is right in that these connections are not always causal. Saying that narratives can give causal explanation is thus no truism. According to Currie, illusions of connections in a narrative can have two aspects, one external and the other internal. The external aspect is derived from our beliefs about the world outside of the narrative. If in ordinary life, A is believed to be connected to B, then we usually expect the same to hold for a narrative. The internal aspect has to do with what we believe about the nature of narratives. The mere fact that we believe that narratives represent certain events as occurring creates expectation. Take the story of the murder of Mitys. His murderer dies shortly after the statue of Mitys falls on his head, but there is no explanation of which, if any, causal factors were at play. We automatically expect that there is a causal connection between the murder and the death of the murderer because we are used to such connections in a narrative. Also, some of us might believe that there is a higher justice that takes revenge upon the evildoers, and we expect the story to reflect this purported fact. In addition to this, our actions are partly reason-based, and the reasons in question can be represented in a narrative, giving it a non-causal, reason-based set of connections (Currie 2006: 309-316). This analysis I find pretty convincing, not least because I have admittedly interpreted Currie in a way that serves my purposes! I push, so to speak, Currie closer to Georg Henrik von Wright than where he possibly is (von Wright 1971).

This brings us to my second criticism: I do not think that Lamarque is right about narratives not having a special way of representing. A narrative sentence represents in a special fashion because it represents a given event as a function of later events. Thus, in the narrative sentence, "the Thirty Years' War commenced with the Battle of White Mountain", the battle of the White Mountain is represented as a function of a series of events we call 'The Thirty Years' War'. This also means that there is a way in which narrative sentences create events (this does not mean that there is no storied structure out there, only that such sentences can add more such structure or refashion radically that which already exists). It is only in the light of some narrative sentences that the Battle of White Mountain can be given the identity of 'the starting point of the Thirty Years' War'. Remember that actions and events can only be given identities in descriptions (as I said in II.3, Lamarque in his earlier writings subscribed to this view in his earlier writings but seems to have forgotten it in his article from 2004). Some of these descriptions are given in narrative sentences, which can give the events a different identity than a description in non-narrative sentences. A person describing the events at the White Mountain in non-narrative sentences while taking part in the battle could not conceivably give the battle the aforementioned identity. Given that narrative sentences are of great importance in narratives, then this means that we cannot ignore the semantic dimension of narratives, in contrast to what Lamarque thinks.

Certainly, Lamarque is right about there being all kinds of descriptions in a narrative that have no impact on the events described. But narrative sentences abound in narratives and they 'form' or even create events, including by aid of such structures as the Middle Ages. If we see a series of events in view of this structure, surely we can give some events as 'the starting point of the Middle Ages', an identity the events receive owing to our seeing them through the 'stained glass' of this structure. The events acquire this identity under descriptions in which the concept of the Middle Ages plays a decisive role. Thus, concepts like that of the Middle Ages are more than just markers.

6.4 Conclusion

I happily subscribe to narrativism of a somewhat moderate kind. Vastly different premises like the phenomenological one of Schapp and Carr, on the one hand, and Turner's based on cognitive science, on the other - let alone Dray's contribution - support narrativism. At the same time, the counter-arguments do not seem very convincing, at least not Lamarque's arguments. I invoke, then, my principle of counter-induction in arguing in favour of the plausibility of narrativism. But Fay definitely has some good points concerning extreme narrativism. Several factors mitigates my narrativism, for instance my belief that such crucial factors of human existence as formal logical truth do not have a storied structure. However, actions, experiences, thinking and other mental acts certainly do. The same hold for the domain of the spontaneous stories. We shall later see how such spontaneous stories play major role in our emotional life. Our human world, our *Lebenswelt*, is what it is by virtue of being replete with storied structures but usually not in a pure form. However important storied structures might be it does not mean there is nothing but storied structures in our world. Yet again I invoke the analogy to Chomsky: the storied structures function like deep structures in the Chomskyian scheme of things, and they are the deep structure of our thought. These structures are actualised in narration, just as the deep structure of language becomes actualised on the surface level, according to Chomsky. This means that there is a narrative grammar of sorts operating in our human world, a grammar that controls the transformation of the *deep-storied structures* into actual narratives. Just as a linguistic deep structure can be transformed into various modes of surface structure, i.e., different sentences and utterances, a deep-storied structure can be actualised in different stories.

We cannot help but to tell these stories, for we are Quixotian beings after all.

II.7. Notes on Narra-Logic and Summary Of Section II

7.1 The Notes

We have discovered that there is a Svejkian style of reasoning, i.e., a narrative reasoning or narra-logic. In contrast to ana-logic, it is purely methodical and bears but a few important resemblances to logic proper. It concerns the way narratives can be cognitively useful to us. The yardsticks for its correct use are narrative alethetic values; narratives and stories symbolise the world in a somewhat different way from theories and metaphors. For instance, the structure of beginning-middle-end symbolises phenomena differently from a theoretical proposition. The same holds for narrative sentences; they symbolise phenomena in a particular way. Further, if there is such thing as refiguring narratives, then they provide us with a twisted understanding and have the alethetic value of T-correctness.

To understand a tellable, that is, a phenomenon with a storied or narrative structure, or both, requires that we master the techniques of followability. This is a competence that we must posses in order to understand our own lives and the lives of others. The competence in question is a part of that which Ricœur calls 'narrative competence'. Possessing this narrative competence means in the first place that one can formulate narrative sentences and use them in a story, secondly that one knows how to configure events in a narrative whole, thirdly that one has the abilities to emplot and to follow a story (Ricœur 1984a: 175). To this I want to add that a narratively competent person must know how to provide singular causal explanations with the aid of narratives. Further, this person must be able to make sense of certain phenomena by configurating them in a narrative manner. Indeed, explaining phenomena narratively means employing narra-logic. So a narratively competent person must master narra-logic.

Narra-logic shares important features with ana-logic. 1) Like in ana-logic, deduction only plays a minor role in narrative explanation and reasoning; we cannot deduce the end of a story from the rest of it. Furthermore, narrative explanations are not nomological; they cannot be deduced from covering laws. 2) Because of this non-nomological nature of narrative explanations, examples and enthymemes play a major role in them, just like in ana-logic. In all narratives, there is a myriad of unstated premises about human behaviour and other aspects of the world. And when using narratives argumentatively, we give examples in the form of stories, for instance, tales of morality. 3) Polkinghorne points out that narrative validity differs from the validity of formal logic. In the latter, the conclusion follows from the premises, thanks to the rules of logic. But in narrative reasoning, 'validity' means, 'well-grounded conclusion'. Thus, a valid finding in narrative reasoning is a well-grounded conclusion, not a deductive conclusion. The conclusion of narrative reasoning is most often defended by use of informal reasoning (compare what I said earlier about the use of enthymemes and examples). Polkinghorne correctly says that a narrative argument does not produce certainty but likelihood (Polkinghorne 1988: 175). 4) Just like ana-logic, narrative explanation and reasoning operate in a horizontal, synthesising manner, as can be seen in the configurative (aspect-seeing) operations of narratives (remember that aspect-seeing plays a decisive role in ana-logic). Just as in ana-logic, the employment of imagination is of great importance in the synthesising, configurative activity. 5) As Ricœur points out, the historian is bound to use ana-logic, or, more precisely, an analogical approach (though he does not use the expression 'ana-logic'). Ana-logic and narra-logic meet in the works of the historian.

7.2 The Summary

In the first chapter, I discussed narratives and stories in a general manner. I stressed the difference between stories and narratives. I put forth a stipulating a definition of narrative, story, storied structure, and narrative structure.

In the second chapter, I discussed the explanatory power of narratives and their role in reasoning. I endorsed Arthur Danto's view that narratives are explanatory devices and have, therefore, a rational role to play in our cognitive endeavours, like metaphors do in another fashion (their cognitive potential is not necessarily explanatory). At the same time, I criticised Danto for his crypto-positivism. The works of Louis O. Mink offer an antidote for this tendency, especially his idea that narratives are essentially configurating, i.e., constituted by aspect-seeing. But Mink can be criticised for having a somewhat too subjectivistic view of narratives. There is also much we can learn from Jerome Bruner, Donald Polkinghorne, and W. B. Gallie, particularly with regard to understanding the role of narrative in reasoning. Narrative reasoning and explaining constitute narra-logic, a close relative of ana-logic, interacting with it in many ways.

In the third chapter, Hayden White's theory of historical narratives takes the centre stage. I agreed with White that there is fictional moment in historical narratives, but I maintained both that he goes too far in fictionalising narratives and that his theory of tropes has a weak basis. I found Noël Carroll's criticism of White a sensible corrective. But Peter Lamarque and Stein Haugom Olsen go too far in the opposite direction, by reducing narratives to the different stances taken to them. They wrongly think that concepts such as the one of literary narrative can be given an essential definition but I pointed out that these concepts are of the amoebaean kind. There are indicators of literariness but no essence that can be found in all and only literary works.

I focused on Ricœur in the fourth chapter. He agreed with Mink that narratives are constituted by aspect-seeing. At the same time, he analysed the relation between fictional and historical narratives in quite a fascinating way, relating both to our experience of time. Both are in some ways factions. But does his theorising rely on a dubious essentialist notion of the concepts of narratives and fiction? Translating his idiom into mine, I found his refiguring narratives to have the alethic value of T-correctness.

In the fifth chapter, I introduced my idea of the N-Ms, i.e., symbolic structures with traits of both narratives and metaphors. An idea of such a 'hybrid' has been on the tips of the tongues of two vastly different thinkers, Paul Ricœur and Mark Turner. Ricœur said that metaphors and narratives have several things in common: a) both perform a Kantian synthesis; b) both are based on aspect-seeing (seeing-as); c) both have a split reference, which makes them refigurating; d) both create new meaning; e) the narrative discourse is an extended metaphor; and f) historical narratives are true allegories. I agreed with a) and b), suspended judgement on c) but was somewhat sceptical of d) – f).

Ricœur also says that myths are large, refigurating narrative. To this I added that allegories and myths are metaphoric stories. The same holds for a vast number of literary stories.

Turner uses the blending theory of metaphors, which he has developed in association with Gilles Fauconnier. Stories are also blends from mental spaces. An important kind of story is the parable, i.e., a story that is projected into another story. But this is precisely how metaphors work as well. So parables cannot be anything but N-Ms. I also pointed out that there are metaphors with a narrative structure. THE CLOUDS ARE ANGRY can only be understood as a part of a story. There are actually several kinds of N-Ms.

In the last chapter of the section, I introduced my concept of narrativism, i.e., the idea that our lives, world-views, and cognition are constituted or soaked, or both, with stories. They have a high degree of narrativity.

I discussed the theories of Wilhelm Schapp who was arguably the first philosophical narrativist ever. I tried to show that there are certain limitations to the rule of the narrative, in part because the validity of deductive logical inferences plays an ineliminable role in human affairs and it does not have a storied structure. But I agreed with such narrativists as David Carr, William Dray, and Alasdair MacIntyre that actions have a storied structure. The first is right about experience having such a structure. To this I added that thinking and perhaps all mental acts have storied structure.

Further, William Dray has a point when he defends a realistic view of stories; in my terminology the world of action and events has a storied structure. I also discussed both Brian Fay's arguments against extreme narrativism and extreme constructivism. I argued that he is too hard on narrativism in general and that there are spontaneous stories, stories simply found, not related. Finally, I criticised Peter Lamarque's challenging criticism of narrativism. I showed that he and several of the aforementioned thinkers conflate stories with narratives, besides ignoring the existence of spontaneous stories. They do not recognise that both stories and narratives rule the world.

There are stories we live by and stories we live in. Like Sharazad, we ceaselessly relate tales to avoid annihilation.

III. THE POETIC OF EMOTIONS

III.1. Cognitivism, Naturalism, Subjectivism
Theories about Emotions

Until a few decades ago, most philosophers thought that feelings were essentially irrational, subjective experiences, hardly worthy of philosophical attention. However, this has changed; now there is a lively philosophical debate over the nature of emotions. One of the reasons for this renewed interest is due to the so-called cognitivist view of emotions that holds that emotions by necessity have a cognitive content, implying that they can neither be reduced to subjective feelings nor objective processes in the nervous system. In this chapter, the *cognitivism* of Robert C. Solomon plays a major role, mainly because he was one of its founding fathers. Other versions of cognitivism, with the notable exception of Charles Taylor's, tend to be reactions to his position. In general, the cognitivists disagree about the nature of the cognitive content of emotions. Some maintain that judgements constitute the content, others that beliefs do so, and a third group insists that a sort of aspect-seeing is at play. I shall discuss these brands of cognitivism in this chapter and the next one, alongside with its archenemy, scientistic naturalism. Such naturalism claims that emotions are first and foremost events in our nervous system. I shall both criticise scientistic naturalism quite harshly and defend the view that there is typically a subjective moment in emotions. The idea of there being such a moment owes much to Peter Goldie's excellent theorising.

1.1 The Cognitive Import of Emotions

Cognitivists differ over many issues, but they agree that emotions are not necessarily irrational and that they can have cognitive import. As Martha Nussbaum says quite correctly, even though emotions such as love can make us blind, they can also open our eyes. Let us assume that Anne regards her husband John as the most important person in her life. But upon John's death, Anne does not feel any sorrow, only indifference. From her lack of grief she might learn that she perhaps was not honest with herself. Maybe she conned herself into thinking that John was greatly important in her life. Or maybe she does not comprehend the situation or that she is in such a deep state of shock that she has suppressed her grief (Nussbaum 1990: 41).

In my view, we see *emotional alethetic* values at work here. The sorrow symbolises non-sententially the world in a particular emotional way, and this symbolisation can show Anne something important about her emotional life. More precisely, the fact that she is not experiencing certain segments of the world as being thus symbolised is significant. Had she seen the world as being devoid of colour and life because of her sorrow, she would have understood how important her husband was to her. As we will later see, emotions are shot through with meaning, making them virtual symbolic structures and by virtue of being such structures it makes sense to say that they can represent segments of reality. Such a symbolisation can be *E-correct* (*emotionally correct*) or not.

We can get to know that dimension by route of Frank Palmer's analysis of emotions and literary works. He points out that understanding a literary work involves knowing what to feel. Finding *Hamlet* funny would in most cases be an example of lack of understanding of the work, unless one can put forth interesting arguments in favour of interpreting it as some kind of a comedy (preferably tragicomedy). Palmer compares our understanding of literary works with our understanding of persons. Understanding both persons and literary works involves not only cognitive understanding but also learning to feel the appropriate thing towards the appropriate object in the right degree (Palmer 1988: 224).[1]

In my terminology, to find *Hamlet* funny would be to symbolise it wrongly, using inadequate emotional alethetic values. Feeling pity and horror towards the play means symbolising it emotionally more correctly, using more adequate emotional alethetic values for the understanding of the play. Our having the appropriate emotion towards the appropriate object means our having what I call an *E-appropriate* emotion.

There is more than some truth in Palmer's arguments. His reasoning is rather too objectivistic, however (compare what I have said

---

[1] Aristotle said something similar in a different context (i.e., *hexeis*) in *The Nichomachean Ethics*, (e.g., 1106b, 1115b)

earlier about the (weak) Wittgensteinian tendency in that direction). I cannot see any reason how we can show with absolute certainty what *the* appropriate thing to feel towards a literary work is and how we can measure *the* right degree of feeling. Given that there is no such thing as *the* correct interpretation of a literary work, it is quite hard to find exactly the appropriate way of feeling, even though we surely can exclude many inappropriate ways. Maybe there is a very original interpretation of *Hamlet* that would make finding it funny seem to be the correct emotional attitude. I doubt it, but I do not doubt that it does not make any sense to say that we can measure E-appropriateness (or correctness), at least not in this case. But our more or less tacit and intuitive understanding of emotions and situations gives most of us the ability to approximate the right thing when reacting emotionally to literary works of art. There is a huge difference between reasonably appropriate ways of feeling and completely inappropriate ways. Being *emotionally competent* means knowing the rules of thumb for having the appropriate emotions and actually applying them reasonably correctly. The knowledge in question is usually *tacit*; the emotionally incompetent tend either to be oblivious to or mistaken about these implicit rules or to know them only *in abstracto*, needing to grope their way with the crutch of reason to 'measure' the E-appropriateness of emotions. Usually, they fail miserably, just like the person who tries to reason his or her way into doing the job of a carpenter without any practical training.

But let us return to Palmer. We can extend his analysis to both our understanding of other kinds of artworks, besides literary works of art, and to our understanding of other people and ourselves. Does not an understanding of Edvard Munch's painting *The Scream* require feeling a certain horror and even pity with the screaming figure? Does not an understanding of Beethoven's *Symphony No. 5* require a different emotional attitude than an understanding of Bach's *The Well-Tempered Clavier*? And would any emotional involvement help us understanding Mondrian's paintings? Is it not E-appropriate to be horrified at the thought of the Holocaust? Can one really understand it without this feeling? Is one really able to understand the sad fate of a reasonably good person unless one pities the person and feels sad about his or her fate?

Nelson Goodman arrives at a not dissimilar conclusion as Nussbaum and Palmer, but from a very different starting point. He implicitly says that emotions can help us cognise segments of the world in a) our daily life, b) in science, and c) in the art world. a) He points out that in daily life, classification by feeling is often of greater importance than classification by other properties. He says "We are likely to be better off if we are skilled in fearing, wanting, braving or distrusting the right things, animate or inanimate, than if we perceive only their shapes, sizes, weights, etc." (Goodman 1976: 251). Obviously, perceiving the latter group of qualities would certainly not help us discover the danger of tigers, while feeling fear performs the job excellently! Chances are that the tigers would have eaten us before cool reason has proven that the beasts are hazardous to our health.[2] I want to add that seeing a situation as dangerous involves emotions fundamentally; the situation gets its identity *qua* dangerous owing to such emotions as fright. The situation is being symbolised (represented) in a particular manner because of the feeling of fright. The emotion twists the situation into a dangerous one. The alethic value involved cannot be one of logical deduction due to the fact that we do not infer that the situation is dangerous. It cannot be the same as those involved simple non-emotional perception due to the fact that the situation gets twisted. Some kind of T-correctness is obviously involved owing to the twisting power of the emotion. So there are at least some cases when E-correctness implies T-correctness. Whether this holds for all possible kinds of E-correctness, I should not say.

b) Such feelings as excitement and curiosity can play a role in scientific exploration and discovery. c) We apprehend a work of art through the feelings as well as through the senses. Often, one remembers or feels, or both, the movement of dancer rather than the visual patterns. Emotional numbness can disable people's ability to understand art works (Goodman 1976: 248-252). My question is whether an emotionally empty (and by implication emotionally incompetent) person can really understand Munch's *Scream* or Kafka's *Die Verwandlung (Metamorphosis)*. Would not an understanding of these artworks require a great deal of empathy and experience of despair and rejection?

---

[2] This point, or similar points, has been made by several theorists. See for instance Ben-Ze'ev 2003: 151.

Goodman certainly hits the nail on the head when it comes to the role of emotions in the work-a-day world and in our perception of artworks. But he only shows that emotions can play a heuristic role in science, and he does not even discuss the question whether the evaluation of scientific theories has any necessary emotional moments. If it does not, then the role played by emotions in science is miniscule, in contrast to what Goodman seems to think. I do not doubt that emotions can have a heuristic value for science, but there are no scientific alethetic values involved in the emotions he mentions. Besides, it is not clear whether curiosity is really an emotion. It is definitely not a prototypical one. The onus is on anybody who thinks that emotions can play more than a heuristic role in science.

It is quite clear, however, that emotions can have cognitive import, that there are such a things as E-correctness, E-appropriateness and emotional competence.

1.2 The Cognitivist Theory of Emotion

Goodman's analysis of emotions in general is rather crude; unlike Nussbaum, he does not differentiate between emotions and sensations. This differentiation has its roots in the work of Robert Solomon. He discriminates between feelings and passions. 'Passion' ranges over emotions, moods (generalised emotions), and desires. Passions have a cognitive moment; feelings do not (Solomon 1976: 132). Most other cognitivists, however, use *emotion* in roughly the same sense as passion, *sensation* (even 'raw feel') for feeling. They use *feeling* as a common denominator for sensations and emotions. I shall adhere to this ordinary terminology.

Now, what are sensations and emotions? An example of a sensation is an itch, a pain or the feeling of intense well-being. We feel these sensations in our bodies, usually in given parts of them. We feel a pain in our finger, an itch on a part of our skin, and intense well-being everywhere in our body. In contrast to a sensation, an emotion cannot be localised. If I feel fear, it would be wrong to say that I feel fear in a given place in my body, though a sensation in, say, my stomach might arise whenever I feel fear (Kenny 1963: 57-58). Of course, certain parts of the body play a larger role in some emotions than in others; love often involves sensations in certain, unnameable parts of the body. But one can be in love without being sexually aroused; there is no necessary relation between a sensation in a certain body part and the emotion of love. The same holds for other emotions; when frightened, some have pains in the stomach, others in the chest, and others do not have any particular sensation in any given part of the body. Most cognitivists explain this variance by saying either that emotions do not involve sensations at all or that they cannot be reduced to sensations. They add that emotions are in the first place intentional and thus have intentional objects[3]; secondly, they have a propositional content; thirdly, they are about something in the world that can be conceptualised. The upshot of this view is that emotional attitudes are propositional attitudes; our emotions are logically linked to our beliefs.

Let us look at an example: if I am angry, then my anger is directed against someone or something, which is the intentional object of my anger. If I am angry with John for having allegedly stolen my car, then the object of my anger is, as Solomon points out, irreducibly *that-John-stole-my-car*. The object is not the alleged fact that he stole the car since he may not have done so (Solomon 1976: 184). This means that my anger has a propositional content; it is about something in the world, and if not the real one, then at least the world of my fancy. My anger is a propositional attitude (in this case an angry attitude) towards a fact expressed in the proposition "John stole my car". This proposition obviously contains the propositional content of my anger. Note that we cannot have propositional attitudes unless we master certain concepts. In my case, my being angry with John for having stolen my car is not possible unless I master such concepts as 'car' or 'theft'. I want add that this analysis shows that emotions symbolise segments of the world in a particular way. In this case, John-stole-my-car is symbolised in an angry fashion, the emotion having its own alethetic value. If my anger symbolises this segment of the world erroneously, then I am not justified in being angry; my emotion is not E-appropriate.

In contrast to emotions, according to Solomon, we can have a sensation like pain without being able to conceptualise it. Further, a pain does not have an intentional object; it simply is. The same holds

---

[3] Heidegger was actually one of the first thinkers to argue in favour of emotions having intentional objects (Heidegger 1977: 140-142 (§30). Solomon is undoubtly influenced by him.

for other sensations. Knowledge, then, does not play any important role in our sensations. There are more intriguing differences between sensations and emotions. If I wake up after an operation feeling an intense pain in my leg, I do not stop feeling pain by discovering that the surgeons have cut off the leg.

This does not mean, however, that knowledge cannot have any influence on feelings of pain. If my doctor tells me that the pain in my stomach is not due to cancer as I thought but due to some quite harmless cause, it might take my mind off the pain and thereby diminish it. But this is strictly a causal influence; there is no logical contradiction involved in thinking that the doctor's information might have the adverse effect upon me. So there is no logical connection between beliefs and pain, or indeed beliefs and sensations in general.

As Solomon points out, a change in belief typically inspires a change in emotions. I stop being angry with John when I discover that he actually did not steal my car. My anger does not disappear as a matter of cause-and-effect, but as a matter of logic. I simply do not have any reason to be angry with him any more. Similarly, I cannot be embarrassed if I do not believe that my situation is awkward (Solomon 1976: 179). Thus, emotions are logically connected with beliefs (Nussbaum 1990: 41). Solomon and Nussbaum, however, draw different conclusions from this purported logical connection. Nussbaum maintains that for E to be an evaluative judgement about important things is both a necessary and sufficient condition for E being an emotion. In contrast, Solomon says that a judgement is a necessary but insufficient condition for E to be an emotion. There must also be a conative element, a will or desire. In fact, Solomon, influenced by Sartre, thinks that we have free will concerning our emotions.[4] We can be masters of our own emotions. I shall return briefly to these issues later.

In contrast to sensations, we say of our emotions that they are 'reasonable' or 'unreasonable', 'warranted' or 'unwarranted', 'justifiable' or 'unjustifiable'. Had I continued to be angry with John after having discovered that he did not steal my car, my anger would certainly be unjustified, unless I had some other reason for being angry with him. Solomon even maintains that there is no such thing as being

---

[4] Sartre defends this view in several of his writings, including Sartre 1995.

angry or having any other emotion without reasons. Let us assume that Jane shows all signs of being angry at John at the same time as she admits that she has no reason to be angry with him; she is just angry with him. In this case, we must assume that she is lying, deceiving herself or does not know what anger is (Solomon 1976: 184). Maybe she thinks that 'anger' means 'feeling aggressive towards someone" or "having negative thoughts about someone'. This is my addition to Solomon's analysis. Anthony Kenny could have added that she is probably experiencing some kind of an emotional upheaval, but it should not be labelled 'anger', even though she thinks so (Kenny 1963: 68-69).

In stark contrast to emotions, we should never talk about unjustified stomachaches or headaches (Solomon 1976: 162-163). As someone says in the Brigitte Bardot film, *La parisienne,* "one does not prove a migraine" ("on ne preuve pas une migraine"). A migraine is a migraine is a migraine. Thus, while our emotions can be irrational or rational, our sensations cannot. As I see it, we can criticise an emotion for being irrational in the sense of being unwarranted or unjustified, but we cannot prove it to be rational. There is nothing particularly rational about getting angry with someone for stealing my car; I could as well be relieved to get rid of it. Or I might be a person who simply likes being ill-treated and so on. My point is that we can 'falsify' an emotion, but not 'verify' it. Popperian fallibilism obviously has a role to play in emotional life, arguably a bigger one than in science.[5]

Now a perceptive reader might ask how the cognitivists classify gladness and depression. Such feelings are hardly simple sensations, for they cannot be localised in the body. At the same time they do not seem to be *bona fide* emotions since they need not have intentional objects. You can feel depressed or happy without any given reason. Solomon's solution is that they are moods, and moods are, as I said earlier, generalised emotions. A person is glad in a given situation because something nice happened, and the same thing happens to the person again and again. Because of this great frequency of happy occasions, the gladness so to speak liberates itself from the different intentional objects and becomes a state in which the person is in for

---

[5] For Popper's contention that there is an asymmetry between verification and falsification, see Popper 1959: 41.

quite some time, i.e., a mood (Solomon 1976: 132). But is this not an empirical statement? And where is the evidence? The evidence might be forthcoming; I do not doubt that there are cases when frequently experienced emotions turn into moods. I do not think, however, we can exclude the possibility of at least some moods either being rooted in our genes or being caused by the environment. Since moods do not have any objects in Solomon's view, we cannot ignore their causes and simply focus on their reasons. Indeed, he thinks that they are not based on reasons at all because of the lack of objects. So I cannot see that there is any conceptual necessity involved in Solomon's contention. Cognitivists might, however, use arguments from Peter Goldie, even though he does not regard himself as a cognitivist (Goldie 2000: 24)). He has some noteworthy arguments in favour of moods being non-specific emotions, with objects that are hard to pinpoint. He actually thinks that emotions can have non-specific objects too and that there are no clear-cut limits between specific and non-specific objects, or for that matter between moods and emotions (Goldie 2000: 148).[6] The last claim does not concern us but the first certainly does. I should like to append to this the idea that the object of moods is perhaps the world in general or even the person herself, but that neither she nor others clearly perceive the objects. Being proud about your looks has a given, specific object. Being happy maybe expresses a feeling about the state of things in general or about some features of oneself. But, in contrast to the proud person, the happy person is only vaguely aware of these objects. So as I see it, moods have intentional objects of which the persons who have them are not clearly aware. Perhaps the intensity of the sensation involved in moods makes the emoter lose sight of the object. Likewise, others, ignoring the object, tend to focus on the display of strong sensations in the emoter. Perhaps the emoter's knowledge of the object is subconscious. But we shall later see that I am not altogether happy with notion of the subconscious. I only want to suggest that perhaps we are wrong about there being one concept of mood. Maybe there are two distinct kinds of moods, the one based on a non-specific object, the other being an offshoot of emotions. But as we will in the next chapter, there might be a 'seeing-as' way of unifying moods.

---

[6] Like Solomon, he actually thinks that moods can be spin-offs from emotions (Goldie 2000: 149).

Now, one might wonder how on earth it makes sense to say that emotions do not essentially involve sensations, as Solomon did in his earliest phase. Common sense tells us that, at least in the sphere of emotions, subjectivity is truth. But Solomon did not agree. He seems to have had two interwoven arguments against the theory that sensations form the basis of emotions, one empirical and the other conceptual. These arguments are interwoven because he uses the conceptual one to explain a puzzling empirical fact. We must, therefore, examine first the empirical argument, which is based on the results of the so-called Schachter and Singer experiments. These scientists injected test subjects with epinephrine, the adrenal secretion responsible for the most marked sensation of emotion. Then they provided the subjects with different social situations. The scientists discovered that the physiological changes and their accompanying sensations had nothing to do with the differentiation of the emotions. Those subjects who were put in fearful circumstances reported feeling fear, in offensive circumstances anger, and so on (Solomon 1976: 157-158).[7] The injection might be called 'a part of the cause' of the emotions in question, but certainly not the reason for them. It might be shown that sexual deprivation is the ultimate cause of my love for somebody, but my reasons are quite different.[8] The reasons may be that I think that the person I love can make me happy and so on. Note how the concept of a reason and that of an intentional object are woven into one another. My belief about the intentional object of my love functions as a reason in favour of being in love with that particular intentional object.

Solomon believes that the cause of an emotion can never be identical with its object: "The object is always *subjective*, a part of the world as one sees it, whether or not it is in fact the case or not. The cause is always *objective;* it must be the case if it is the cause" (Solomon 1976: 184). This is how Solomon uses a logical argument in

---

[7] Solomon admits that the injection-procedure limits the conclusion that can be drawn about emotions in ordinary-life situations. But he also points out that knowledge of the injection undermines the emotion, and so even in such cases, beliefs influence emotions.

[8] The cause and the reason can contingently be the same. I can, for instance, hate women on the ground that they do not want to have sex with me as the deprivation itself causes the hatred. But the cause and the reason remain logically distinct.

order to explain the strange outcome of the Schachter and Singer experiment.

This example of the injection not only helps us to differentiate between causes of emotions and reasons for having them, but it also strengthens the thesis that it is not possible to discern between our emotions simply by analysing our sensations, more precisely by scrutinising our inner states. In this connection, Solomon asks about the difference in feeling between pairs of emotion like embarrassment and shame. He contemplates two imagined situations. In the first one you are standing in line to board a bus when the crowd behind you suddenly surges forward causing you to bump into an elderly woman, knocking her down into the gutter. In the other, you obey a malicious whim and push her with the same result. Following both incidents you find yourself being confronted by an indignant elderly woman, and you are suffering from an intense feeling, in the first case obviously one of embarrassment, the second of shame. But the feelings involved in these cases are of little use in discriminating between the emotions. Only 'the *logic* of the *situation*' can give us the necessary clues. In the first case, the situation is such that we are not responsible for what happened, even if we do find ourselves in an awkward situation, and, therefore, we feel embarrassment. In the second case, we certainly are responsible, and, therefore, we feel shame. Maybe on closer inspection we can find a relevant difference between our sensations in both cases, but the logic of the situation gives us the information we need (Solomon 1976: 159-162). Notice that the situation is the intentional object in question. This example gives us a clue about how the object 'creates' the emotions. Notice also the intersubjectivist nature of Solomon's logic of situation argument.

The Australian philosopher Paul Griffiths criticises Solomon's use of these experimental findings. He says that it is well established that subjects who are unable to account for their own behavioural or physiological responses will invent an explanation from whatever cues are available and claim that their knowledge results from their direct knowledge of their mental processes. They are in other words engaged in confabulation, and one would expect the subjects of the Schachter and Singer experiments to have been confabulating (Griffiths 1997: 82-83). I confess, however, that, owing to my lack of knowledge of physiology and experimental psychology, I am no position to evaluate Griffiths' and Solomon's interpretations of this experiment.

As hinted at, Solomon has retracted the theory that sensations do not play any necessary role in emotions. He uses shame as an example. Shame is at least in part a feeling of discomfort with other people, a feeling of rejection (Solomon 2003: 16). This is a good move on Solomon's part. For if sensations do not play an essential role, how can we differentiate between emotions and non-emotional evaluative judgements? Is it by chance that humankind has drawn a dividing line between emotions and such phenomena as the evaluative judgements of logical reasoning? The line has been drawn between judgements that necessarily involve sensations and judgements that do not. And indeed, humankind is right! I can judge Chester's logical reasoning as being faulty, and I can be angry with him for this faulty piece of reasoning. That anger certainly involves evaluative judgement, just like my judgement of the quality of his reasoning. Common sense tells us, however, that sensations must be involved in the case of the anger, not the case of the evaluation of the reasoning.

True, I can be said to have been angry at Chester for years even though I do not feel the anger all the time. But does it make sense to say that I was angry at Chester for a long while, but I never felt any wrath? My gut feeling is that the answer must be a resounding "no!" I shall return to the role of sensations in emotion later in this chapter.

Another theory that Solomon should have retracted is his theory that certain emotions do not involve actions and behaviour. Among them are guilt and resentment; they refrain from expression, Solomon says, and this feature belongs to their essence. But if envy and resentment have never been expressed in public, every envious and resentful person could have had his or her own private concept for envy and resentment. And what criteria should we then have had to determine whether they are really envious or resentful and not just imagining that they are in those emotional states? (Compare the private-language argument.) Further, I might believe that I have friendly feelings towards someone, but at the same time my *actions* towards that person and my behavioural pattern in general show that what I mistook for feelings of friendship were actually feelings of paternal-like warmth (i.e., I treat my 'friend' like a child). Chances are that actions can typically give us important clues to the nature of at least some of our emotions. Is not our scrutinising of our actions the best way to find out whether we really love a person or are just infatuated, or even simply fond of that individual? Stanley might sincerely believe that he is in love with Anne while he systematically betrays her, never caresses her, and even beats her now and then. Further, he has clandestine relationships with other women, and when Anne asks him to make a commitment to her, he gets nervous, uneasy, and evasive. Another person could point out to him that his actions contradict his belief. Or he might by analysing his own actions discover that his not really in love with Anne. He might find out that he was only infatuated in her or that he simply wanted to dominate her. In light of these examples it seems plausible that at least some, even all, emotions involve actions and reactions or dispositions to act or react in an essential fashion. I shall return to the issue of emotions and actions later in this book.

1.3 Naturalising Emotions?

To my knowledge, Nussbaum is the sole cognitivist who still defends the view that emotions have no necessary connection with sensations, even though she admits that emotions are typically felt, conscious states (Nussbaum 2001: 62). Well, I think she ought to follow Solomon in retracting this view. One of the reasons for this is that this view actually undermines cognitivism. If conscious experiences (sensations and thoughts) are incidental to emotions, why not go a step further and say that emotions are really just processes in the nervous system? Why should we not just 'naturalise emotions' (my expression), that is, regard beliefs, judgements, feelings, and attitudes as epiphenomena, while the real things (the emotions) are processes in our bodies? I shall now give a short overview over certain naturalistic positions, then discuss briefly Robert Roberts' criticism of naturalism, and at last add my own criticism.

As hinted at, scientistic naturalist maintain that emotions can either be reduced to processes in our bodies or that they are illusions. The first kind are the reductionists, the other one the eliminativists. [9] But

---

[9] There are also non-scientific cognitivist versions of naturalism. The cognitivist Kristján Kristjánsson maintains that emotions are part of our natural endowment, but they nevertheless cannot be reduced to bodily events. For instance Kristjánsson 2002: 48.

let us look at the theories of real life scientistic naturalists and start with the Portuguese neuroscientist Antonio Damasio, then turn to Paul Griffiths. Damasio has made a new version of the so-called James-Lange theory, according to which feelings are the sensory images of the body's inner states, just like we can have visual images of things. Pain is simply the brain's way of sensing that something is wrong in a given part of the body. More advanced emotions are basically complex versions of this kind of sensing. Further, we are not necessarily conscious about our emotions. Nevertheless, there are conscious emotions which Damasio labels 'feelings'. They are reactions to bodily maps, which the brain makes of its own states. The Portuguese scientist maintains that his research confirms this, showing that on occasions when people feel something, activity increases in those areas of the brain that collect information about their bodily states (Damasio 2003: 96-101). But notice that Damasio does not differentiate between emotions and sensations. His theory might very well explain the nature of sensations and whatever moment of sensations there are in emotions, but it hardly explains the complexities of emotions. By having intentional objects, emotions focus on something that neither needs to be a part of our bodies nor be of material nature at all. Understanding the world around us, not only our bodily states, is an important cognitive function of emotions.[10]

Of greater interest for my project are Damasio's studies of the role of emotions in decision-making. They focus on people who have become emotionally dumb due to brain injuries or tumours while retaining intact memories, IQ, linguistic capacities and so on. Damasio's found out that these people had also lost their ability to make rational decisions. They seemed to have become unable to weight the importance and relevance of actions and decisions due to their loss of what I call 'emotional *competence*' (Damasio 1994: 3-79). Even though I cannot judge the quality of Damasio's neurophysiologic research, I find this quite convincing. One of the reasons for this is that it shows how emotions help us understand our surroundings, not only the state of our bodies. We cannot make decisions unless we evaluate

---

However, I shall use 'naturalism' in this book as shorthand for 'scientistic naturalism'.

[10] Unfortunately, Mark Johnson does nothing to rectify this aspect of Damasio's thinking in his attempt to unify it with pragmatism and generative metaphoric (Johnson 2007: 52-68)

segments of the outside world and emotions are often our best evaluative tools.

Griffiths is an excellent example of a naturalist. According to him, 'feeling' is a word we use for disparate phenomena. The cognitivists have not seen this because they rely too heavily on a folk-psychological conception of emotions. This conception is just illusory as the old folk conception that whales are a kind of fish and ought to be replaced with a more rigorous, scientific conception. The concept of emotion is just as empty as the ancient concept of supralunar phenomena, which were wrongly supposed to be of a different nature than things on earth. There is no such thing as a distinct, particular class of supralunar phenomena, and, likewise, there is no such thing as a distinct, particular class of emotions (Griffiths 1997: 1-2). Griffiths holds that there are three types of phenomena, not necessarily connected, that we group together under the heading of emotion. One is *affect program responses*, which are primitive reactions of sorts, swift, and stereotypical. Fear is a good example of such a response. These responses form natural kinds of responses and are a part of our natural endowment.

The two other kinds of phenomena are both higher cognitive emotions. The first class is called *irruptive motivational states*, short-term irrational ways of behaving that are actually long-term rational ways of behaving, being quite beneficial in the in the long run. Shame, jealousy, and loyalty belong to this class. Jealousy is a good example because it is irrational in the short run and disrupts our ability to reach our long-term goals. Othello certainly disrupted his future long-term goals, behaving irrationally in the short run. But jealousy still has a certain long-term pay-off (Griffiths 1997: 118); it does not pay for Othello's wife to flirt with other guys, and this is good for Othello's genes. The long-term pay-off is evolutionary; the genes win even though their bearer loses. This is my own example and I am sure one could construct similar ones for shame and loyalty.

Griffiths' last class is *disclaimed action emotions*, which are social constructs, a kind of an unconscious acting. The best known of these disclaimed actions is love, an emotion that is a fairly recent social construct (Griffiths 1997: 141).

One of the problems with the cognitivists, according to Griffiths, is that they do not know the first thing about the chemistry of emotions. Instead, they focus on conceptual analysis. But that means that they do not do much more than simply clarify the concepts of wrong-headed folk psychology. This is just as unfruitful as clarifying such concepts as that of superlunary objects, make it a bit clearer than it was in ancient times. Unsurprisingly, Griffiths thinks that his own approach is scientific.[11] Understanding beliefs and desires does not help us much when it comes to emotions for the simple reason that both thoughts and feelings are epiphenomena. The real action is in the nervous system; the real emotional processes are events taking place in that system. Our conscious emotions are simply shadows of these material events.

However, Griffiths' arguments are not very convincing. In the first place, Robert C. Roberts has some excellent arguments against Griffiths'. He is critical of what I call Griffiths' 'deconstruction' of emotions. In contrast to Griffiths' claim, fear can have a cognitive moment. Think about the fear a certain professor has when he discovers that there are excellent arguments against his position. This means that there is no divide between the affect program responses and the higher cognitive emotions (Roberts 2003: 24-26). Further, he points out that Griffiths' approach is like saying that music is an epiphenomenon, only vibrations in the air, and a true musical analysis would, therefore, be a physical analysis of the vibrations in the air. But such an analysis of vibrations is not analysis of music; I am analysing music when I classify a certain piece of music as a symphony and analyse its structure. A physical analysis of the material foundations of music cannot be anything but an aid to musical analysis. The reason is that we need musical analysis to give certain physical patterns the identity of a piece of music. Such an analysis is in its turn dependent upon our auditory experiences of music. Analogously, the analysis of the physical foundations of emotions depends upon conceptual analysis of the concepts of emotions. The latter kind of

---

[11] Griffiths is what I call a *neo-scientistic post-analytical philosopher*. In contrast to analytical philosophers of the scientistic persuasion, such a philosopher does not undertake conceptual analysis. They think that the basic role of philosophers is to work in tandem with scientists. In somewhat different manner, scientistic philosophers of the analytical kind think that conceptual analysis has the role of "preparing the way of the Lord", the Lord being nomological science.

analysis is in its turn dependent upon emotional experiences (Roberts 2003: 52-54). I would like to add that materialism is a metaphysical theory and such theories are notoriously difficult to prove or disprove. But Griffiths and other materialists talk like it is either the only game in metaphysical town or simply a non-metaphysical, scientific theory.

Roberts defends the idea of conceptual analysis against Griffiths' criticism. In contrast to Griffiths' claim, Roberts asserts that an analysis of such concepts is only partly an analysis of the actual uses of language. The thinker must also put the concepts in narrative contexts. In such an analysis, it is not enough to collect facts about emotions; the use of imagination is of great importance. Scrutiny of one's own emotions is also central and so is comparison. One has to compare a given emotion with other emotions and the concept of emotions with related concepts, like the concepts of actions and moods (Roberts 2003: 37-38). Roberts is really advocating the use of ana-logic, even though he does not employ that term. The similarity with my idea of analysis as spelled out in the Introduction is obvious; I confess being inspired by Roberts. Our common philosophical ancestor is, of course, Wittgenstein.

1.4 Subjectivity in Emotions

Regardless of Wittgenstein and Roberts, I have made a thought-experiment that ought to show why Griffiths (and for that matter Nussbaum) is wrong. Let us assume that there is a *semi-zombieworld*. The semi-zombies are exactly like us in every physical respect. They also have conscious thoughts and perceptions like us, but unlike us they have no conscious emotional thoughts or perceptions. (They are semi-zombies because, unlike full-fledged zombies, they have a consciousness of sorts.) Despite this lack, they react like us. When they see a semi-zombie tiger coming a-charging, they scream and run away. Exactly the same thing happens in their amagdyla as in ours when we feel frightened. When they see a beautiful person of the other sex (or whatever), they tend to do things that increase the possibility of that person having sex with them, even entering into long-term relationships with them. The only difference between them and us is that they neither feel anything nor have any other subjective attitudes typically involved in feelings. Even when they scream and run, they do not feel frightened. They would 'experience' their reaction in similar way as we 'experience' the involuntary movement of our leg when someone hits a certain spot on our kneecaps. Just like us, they see what is happening and can consciously reflect on it, but they do not feel a thing.

These people would never consciously judge someone who has tricked them out of something as being a 'bastard', a 'mean person' or whatever. But they would behave towards the person exactly like we should react to someone whom we judge in such a manner (our judgement is based upon subjective experiences). Now the question arises: would the people of this semi-zombie world need the concept of a feeling? It would not make any sense for them to say, "I feel frightened" and mean it literally. It would be more informative for them to say, "I am now disposed to behave in frightened manner". They might even not use words like 'fright'. Words like 'bastard' would also have a hollow ring to them. In many cases, emotions do not make us disposed to behave in any particular fashion. A well-disciplined super-Spartan could hide his or her grief and continue to behave in an ordinary fashion. But a semi-zombie super-Spartan would not feel anything and would also go on behaving in an ordinary fashion. Now if all the semi-zombies were super-Spartans in relation to grief, what function would the concept of grief have in their world? My educated guess is that they would not have any need for it, even if the exact same things were occurring in their nervous system as in ours when we feel grief. This shows that our subjective experiences of emotions play an important role in shaping our emotional life. That does not mean that we are bound to have feelings or thoughts whenever we have an emotion. But if we never felt anything and never had any emotional thoughts, then it would be hard to see why we should need the concept of emotion and the concepts of its sub-classes. This means that feeling something whenever one has an emotion must be the rule, not the exception, if the concept of emotion is to be of any use. (The kinship between this argument and my arguments in favour of the heresy thesis is obvious.)

So my conclusion is that the naturalists are wrong and so are those cognitivists who think that sensations are not an essential part of emotions. They are. How exactly sensations and emotions relate to each other I should not say. But we should do well to look to Peter Goldie's approach to analysing emotions. He takes issue with the tendency among philosophers (presumably the cognitivists) both to over-intellectualise emotions and to forget that there is an essential *first-person perspective* involved in emotions. Thus, there is no equivocation in meaning between the first-personal and the third-personal with regard to emotions. There is no equivocation between my reporting about my fear by saying "I feel fear" and my reporting about the fear of others by saying "you feel fear" or "they feel fear" (Goldie 2000: 2-3). There is, therefore, an irreducible moment of subjectivity in emotions.

Instead of differentiating between sensations and emotions, Goldie discriminates between plain bodily feeling and *feelings towards* something. A bodily feeling involves consciousness of the condition of the body (Goldie 2000: 51). Usually there is no intentionality involved in bodily feeling, but there is in feeling towards. We feel grief for someone, we feel towards that someone, but the headache that the grief causes is simply a bodily sensation. Feeling towards is *thinking* of something with feeling, and the feelings are directed towards the object of thought. Feeling disgusted by a hamburger means that the feelings of disgust are directed towards some perceived or imagined property or feature of the hamburger (Goldie 2000: 19 and elsewhere). So feeling towards obviously has a cognitive content even though it is not a belief. We can, for instance, fear something while knowing that it is not dangerous. Secondly, there is a perceptual moment and an imaginative moment in feeling towards that is not necessarily present in beliefs. In the third place, feeling towards is also subject to a decision of will in a way that beliefs are not. We cannot really choose what to believe, but we can work at ridding ourselves of certain feelings, such as the fear of flying. Fourthly, if one believes that something has a certain feature, then one is, *ceteris paribus*, disposed to assent to a question of whether it has this feature. But one can feel an emotion over something that has certain features but at the same time not be disposed to assent to its having these features, because one has the belief that it is inappropriate or disproportionate (Goldie 2000: 72-8).

There is further a difference between feeling towards something and just thinking of it. In the first place, our imagination tends to be less subject to our will in feeling towards than our general way of thinking of things. Our imagination can run wild when we are extremely jealous (in my view, the imagination of the jealous person creates spontaneous stories in the form of scenarios). It is not by chance that, when we give expression to our passions, we are sometimes like passive victims of emotions. In order to understand his second differentiation between feeling towards and thinking of, Goldie asks us to look at the case of a colour-blind person who can reliably pick out red things because someone points them out to him. The colour-blind person can have the thought, "this chair is red". But let us assume that a person who is not colour-blind saw the chair and had a thought expressed by the very same words. The latter's thought would differ in content to the former's thought. *Mutatis mutandis*, the same would hold for feeling towards and plainly thinking of (Goldie 2000: 58-60).

As I said earlier, Goldie thinks that bodily feelings are not always without intentionality. They take on *borrowed intentionality*, presumeably from feeling towards. An example of borrowed intentionality is a pang in the breastbone felt by a grieving person. This pang is not just any bodily feeling, but a pang for the person grieved. Thus the pang 'borrows' intentionality from the feeling of grief towards the person. Indeed, mind and body are usually engaged together in emotional experience; for instance, sexual desire is felt with the whole being (body and soul) for the person desired (Goldie 2000: 55).

The analyses of borrowed intentionality and the holistic nature of emotional experience are fascinating, but need not concern us here. What matters is that he convincingly shows both that we cannot neatly separate sensations and the cognitive moment of emotions and that sensations are of essential importance in emotions. To my mind, emotions are (at least typically) half-cognition, half-sensation (feel), woven into each other (compare Wittgenstein's analysis of aspect-seeing). This web of sensations and cognition has an intentional object; we cognise our enemy John in hateful manner and the sensation of hatred is shaped by the thought and *vice versa*. Call my cousin of Goldie's feeling towards *directed sensation*. In contrast to feeling towards, directed sensation is closely related to aspect-seeing. We shall see later that emotions essentially involve such seeing.

The weight of the moment of cognition and that of sensation varies with both the kind of emotion involved and the circumstances. The cognition might dominate when we are not in the presence of John and the sensation when he is in the vicinity. In pride, the cognition matters more than the sensation, in anger the sensation.

So even though subjectivity is not the entire truth of emotions,[12] it certainly is an ineliminable part of it.

1.5 Conclusion

We have discovered that there is a difference between sensations and emotions, the latter having a cognitive moment. Emotions have alethic values of their own: they can be E-correct or not, E-appropriate or not, and the emotionally competent person can usually judge their correctness and appropriateness. We have seen the weaknesses of scientistic naturalism, that it wrongly thinks feelings can be reduced to processes in our bodies or even eliminated completely. Not only the scientistic naturalists but also the cognitivists tend to underestimate the role of subjectivity of emotions. Due to this, the latter draw a too sharp line between sensations and emotions; they do not see that there are directed sensations.

---

[12] I am alluding to Kierkegaard's contention that subjectivity is truth.

III.2. Towards Hermeneutic Construalism
Roberts, Taylor, Construalism, Hermeneutics and Emotions

I will begin this chapter with criticism of the 'classical' cognitivism of the 'Solomonic' kind, i.e., the kind that thinks emotions are belief- or judgement-based and that we can decide for or against having emotions, thanks to our willpower.

We have already seen that I agree with Roberts' arguments against naturalism. In this chapter I shall try to show that the *construalism* of Robert Roberts and Cheshire Calhoun, i.e., their the seeing-as brand of cognitivism, provides the best understanding of what emotions actually are, but only if fused with aspects of Taylor's hermeneutic approach to emotions and only if it accepts the ineliminability of sensations in emotions. These form the backbone of my *hermeneutic construalism*.

3.1 Construalism and Classical Cognitivism

The classical cognitivism of the 'Solomonic' kind has at least three problems. To begin with, it goes against the grain of common sense to say that we can decide whether or not to have any given emotion. Common sense tells us that there are emotions that we can control, and others that we cannot. Usually, we think that the stronger the emotion, the more difficult it is to control. We also think that some people have greater problems with mastering their emotions than others and that there are situations when anybody would lose control as it were. Common sense also informs us that manic-depressive or schizophrenic persons cannot control their emotions. It further tells us that it is not likely that an ordinary person who has been given LSD or tortured can control his emotions. Now, why do I think it is mandatory for the Solomonic theorist to take common sense seriously? Simply because common sense is the natural ally of cognitivism, as we have indeed already discovered. Naturalists can ignore common sense and get away with it, but cognitivists cannot. Further, my experience and intuition tell me that certain emotions cannot be controlled under certain circumstances and, by implication, that Solomon (and Sartre) is wrong.

Secondly, the Solomonic theorist seems to think that if a belief belongs to the space of reason, then we are somehow free to adopt it. But a belief can be causally produced and at the same time be based on good reasons. My current belief that my computer is in front of me right now is not something I have chosen to believe; it intrudes upon me through my senses, the processes in my brain, and my cultural conditioning. And I have excellent reasons to believe that it is true. The same holds for most of our emotional beliefs; I might not be able to control my anger at John's theft of my car, but I might at the same time have good reasons to be angry with him. Thus the space of reasons is not necessarily in the realm of free will. So even if emotions were belief-based, then it does not follow that we can have voluntary control over them. Solomon is thus plainly wrong about this.

Thirdly, the Solomonic theorist has difficulties in explaining irrational emotions. Consider an example that I call *the case of the Spiderwoman*. The Spiderwoman knows perfectly well that spiders are harmless, but they nevertheless frighten her out of her wits. Certain theorists like Cheshire Calhoun (and, as we have seen, Peter Goldie) think that this shows that beliefs do not play a constitutive role for emotions. To be sure, there is a cognitive component in the Spiderwoman's emotion, but it is not a belief. She sees spiders as being dangerous without believing it. In the same manner, we can see a man's face in a cloud without believing that the cloud contains a picture of a face or indeed anything else (Calhoun 1984: 327-342). Roberts has a similar theory. He does not deny that emotions have a propositional content; in the case of the spider fright it might be, "I see spiders as being dangerous". But the cognitive component of emotions is what he calls a 'construal'. We, or more precisely the Spiderwoman, construe spiders as being dangerous, etc. (Roberts 1988: 183-209).[1] Construing is 'perceptual' in a particular sense of that word. More precisely, it is perceptual in the Wittgensteinian sense of noticing an aspect without having a sensory experience (Wittgenstein 1958: 193). Roberts says that one might see an aspect of the face by *construing* it

---

[1] There are but minor differences between the positions of Roberts and Calhoun. I call both of them *construalists*.

as another face through something like an act of imagination. An example of this in the field of emotions can be a situation in which I feel triumphant. I see or construe myself as being triumphant with the aid of my imagination but without sensory experience (Roberts 2003: 67).

So construals are perceptions of sorts and by implication, emotions are as well (for instance Roberts 2003: 87).[2] Emotions are more precisely *concern-based construals*. In grief, for instance, we construe something very important to us as being irrevocably lost (Roberts 2003: 79). At the same time, the concern is a part of the construing. We see the lost object partly in relation to its great importance to us. In light of this, Roberts would have said that when the Spiderwoman construes the spiders as being dangerous, the concern involved would be her concern for her well-being, even her life.

I find this analysis convincing. But the construalists underestimate both the role of beliefs and sensations in emotions. In order to assay the role of beliefs more adequately, we shall return to the Spider-woman. The construalists ignore the fact that the Spiderwoman must believe that she is seeing a spider when she gets her fits of 'spider-fright'. Consider a case in which she discovers that there was no spider in the room; what she took to be a spider was actually a child's toy. If she goes on fearing the object after she has discovered that she was mistaken it for being a spider, then we cannot call that fear 'spider-fright', and we could possibly call that fear 'child's-toy-fright'. Her beliefs, then, play a constitutive role for her particular emotion. Thus, her 'spider-fright', and other irrational emotions of a similar kind, is partly constituted by beliefs. In a sense, the nature of the beliefs partly determines the species of the emotion but not the genus. The concern-based construal constitutes the genus of fear, not needing the aid of beliefs, in contrast to the species of spider-fright, which beliefs partly determine.

As for the underestimation of sensations, we have already seen that they play an essential role in emotions. I maintain that a concern-

---

[2] We have seen that Goldie also emphasises the perceptual moment in emotions. He is actually quite close to construalism in many ways, as can be seen from how he regards 'thinking of' as being closely related to seeing an aspect and being a moment in emotions (Goldie 2000: 20).

based construal typically involves directed sensations. Thus, the Spiderwoman not only construes the spider as being dangerous, she feels towards the spider in a frightened manner. Remember that I see directed sensation as a sort of seeing-as, being half-sensation, half-cognition. The influence of Wittgensteinian intersubjectivism is undoubtedly one of the reasons why Roberts tends to belittle the role of the subjective in emotions. There is actually a kinship between my defence of the contention that emotions typically have a subjective moment and the qualms I have about Wittgenstein's tendency to treat the subjective solely as an appendage to the intersubjective.

My colleague and countryman Kristján Kristjánsson goes further in his criticism of construalism than I do. He maintains that subconscious beliefs constituted our seemingly irrational, emotional views of things. The upshot of this is that the Spiderwoman subconsciously believes that spiders are dangerous. He also questions the wisdom of operating with an intermediate entity (i.e., construals) between clear perception and vague belief. Here, the Icelandic theorist says, Occam's razor comes in handy (Kristjánsson 2002: 31-33). But Kristjánsson must do better than just invoke the name of Occam. We do have good inductive reasons for maintaining that mental categories tend to be parts of continua. Where exactly does the vague belief end and the clear perception begin in emotions such as jealousy? A child can have a clear perception of a dog but that perception is woven into beliefs about dogs; in the case of very young children such beliefs tend to be pretty vague. From this lack of distinct boundaries, we can say that cognition and feeling, on the one hand, and perception and thinking, on the other, are parts of continua. So why should not vague beliefs and clear perceptions also be parts of a continuum, having all kinds of intermediate entities between them, including construals? I have discussed the difficulties of separating interpretation and sensation in the Introduction. Chances are that the continua discussed there and the one discussed here are of the same kind.

Secondly, Kristjánsson ought to know that the subconscious is a slippery category, and so I should not bet on its existence. In fact, John Searle points out that nobody knows what unconscious thinking is. People talk as if unconscious thinking were like conscious thinking minus the consciousness (Searle 1995: 128). Well, Searle is arguably somewhat unfair here because there are theorists who use the concept in a more cautious manner than those (straw-men?) whom he criticises. Nussbaum is one of these cautious theorists. She points out that we might be said to have subconscious beliefs that guide our actions. Beliefs about causes, actions, and the whereabouts of things are often unconscious and action-guiding. We are repositories of an indefinite number of such beliefs without which we should probably not survive (Nussbaum 2001: 71-72). However, I am sceptical of this argument for two different reasons. The first is that we cannot exclude the possibility that some (even all) of these beliefs are not unconscious but vaguely conscious and that we forget them swiftly as we get along. Daniel Dennett correctly says that much of what we regard as being unconscious perception and intelligent action is really a case of "rolling consciousness with swift memory loss" (Dennett 1991: 137). We drive our car while busily talking to a friend, yet we are somehow aware of what we see on the road and of our actions, but we forget them as we drive along. This could mean that blind rages and suchlike are not emotions without feeling; perhaps when in a state of blind rage we actually feel angry but suffer the kind of swift memory loss Dennett describes. My second reason is that I do not think that we are compelled to dignify everything what Nussbaum calls 'beliefs' with that label. It would not surprise me the least if some (or even all) of them were related to reflexes. My doctor bangs on my kneecap with a hammer, and my foot moves. Nobody would say that I had the subconscious belief that it would be appropriate to move my foot in this fashion. And I do not think it is far-fetched to say that my movements are reflex-like when I open a door without thinking. If that is the case, then my movements are hardly caused by subconscious beliefs. So chances are that some or even all of Nussbaum's unconscious beliefs are either vaguely conscious but easily forgettable ones or that some or even all are more like reflexes than beliefs. Further, could it be that these so-called beliefs only become beliefs upon reflection ("of course I knew perfectly well that I was opening the door") and operate more like, say, construals? Roberts actually seems to think that the act of construing is a subconscious process (Roberts 2003: 178). Perhaps construals are somewhere in-between being beliefs and primitive mental stirrings, caused by reflexes.

Moreover, even if Nussbaum's 'subconscious beliefs' really are beliefs, it does not follow that irrational emotions are based upon subconscious beliefs. Why should I think that the cognitive states and processes involved in fear of flying are of the same kind as the ones involved in automatically opening a door? Maybe the latter involves subconscious beliefs, the former not.

Thirdly, the idea of construals could explain the puzzling character of aesthetic emotions. A scene in a horror movie scares us; despite the fact that we know that there is no real danger. It seems plausible that our perceptions of artworks are construals of some sort and that these construals play an important part in generating aesthetic emotions.[3] We construe a movie non-emotionally and aesthetically as a movie, belonging to the class of horror movies. The act of understanding the artwork as an object of this kind and the act of emoting it as being horrifying seem intertwined. The construals of the artwork and of the emotion are closely connected. We may note that postulating these aesthetic emotions as based on subconscious beliefs is not only speculative but also cumbersome. It is tempting to use Occam's razor to cut away the concept of a subconscious belief.

In the fourth place, Kristjánsson must show how we can do without the concept of a construal. As I said in the Introduction, the concept in question (usually under the name 'seeing-as') has seemed so fruitful in many fields, including aesthetics, the philosophy of science, theories of narratives, and last but not least metaphors. As I have implied, using the concept of seeing-as helps us unify and simplify our picture of the world or at least large chunks of it.

In the fifth place, construalism can explain why animals and very small children seem to have emotions, even though they arguably do not have beliefs or perform judgements. They are seemingly perceiving, sentient beings. They seem to perceive some things as edible, others as dangerous, and so on. It is not far-fetched to believe, then, that a dog consistently showing aggressive behaviour towards a tormentor actually is angry with the person. The anger must be partly created by the dog's perceiving the person as something akin to what we humans would call 'a wrongdoer, deserving punishment'. Actually, Nussbaum seems to think that infants and animals have emotions partly in virtue of being able to see-as. But she is rather unclear on the

---

[3] Richard Wollheim famously used the concept of seeing-as (later another concept, that of seeing-in) to explain our perception of visual artworks (Wollheim 1980: 12-22).

issue. She says in no uncertain words, however, that they can form beliefs and pass judgements, even though they do not possess propositional language. These beliefs and judgements form the core of their emotions (Nussbaum 2001: 89-138 (on seeing-as, Nussbaum 2001: 129). It should not come as any surprise to the reader that I disagree with the last statement but agree on the seeing-as element.

In the sixth place, construalism provides us with a unified picture of emotions and moods. Being in a happy mood means construing the world differently from the way one construes it while depressed. This does not exclude the possibility of there being vastly different kinds of moods, compare what I said earlier about some perhaps being generalised emotions, others being constituted by non-specific objects. In either case, they are construals.

Be that as it may, we have seen that Kristjánsson's criticism of construalism is not altogether satisfying. The strength of construalism is that it gives a plausible, cognitivist explanation of irrational emotions and simplifies our world-picture by being easily integrated with other, well-established theories.

2.2 Taylor's Hermeneutic Cognitivism

Charles Taylor never mentions the cognitivists in his writings despite an obvious kinship between his ideas and theirs. He stresses the cognitive import of emotions but adds a hermeneutic dimension, insisting that emotions must be interpreted.[4] Accordingly, I call his view *hermeneutic cognitivism*. The meaning interpreted in the case of emotions is of a somewhat different nature than the meaning of written texts. It is in some ways closer to the meaning of actions. Actions have what he calls 'an *experiential* meaning'. We are really talking about experiential meaning when we talk as if an action, a situation, a demand or a prospect had a meaning for us. In the first place, such a meaning is for given subjects, even every human subject, but it is never a meaning *in vacuo*. Secondly, it is also of something, an object. We can discriminate between the object as described with regard to both its experiential meaning for someone and its physical

---

[4] Actually, I usually 'translate' Taylor's use of the word 'feeling' into 'emotion'. The reason is that in most cases he uses 'feeling' in the same sense as the followers of the cognitive theory use 'emotion'. In other cases, I do not change his use of 'feeling'.

characteristics. Thirdly, things only have meaning in a field. Being in a field means that an object endowed with experiential meaning is only meaningful in relationship with other objects with different kinds of meaning. An example of such a field of experiential meaning is the range of meaning a subordinate's demeanour can have for us - deferential, respectful, cringing, mildly mocking, ironical, insolent, etc. A field of contrasts establishes the meaning of these terms, just as such fields establish terms of colour. Thus, experiential meaning is for a *subject*, is of *something,* and is in a *field.* Linguistic meaning has all these traits, but, in addition, it is the meaning of signifiers and it is about a world of referents.

Even though Taylor introduces the notion of experiential meaning in connection with actions, it is clearly relevant for the discussion of the meaning of emotions. He says that the language by which we describe our goals, feelings, and desires is also a definition of the meaning they have for us (Taylor 1985c, 22-23). One central concept in his analysis is *import*, i.e., the way in which something can be relevant or significant to the desires or purposes or aspirations or feelings of a subject. Such adjectives as 'humiliating' or 'shameful' define an import. To experience an emotion is to be aware of our situation as humiliating or shameful or dismaying or exhilarating or wonderful and so on. Actually, a given emotion involves experiencing our situation as being of a certain kind or having a certain property. But this property cannot be neutral. We cannot be indifferent to it; if we were, we could not be moved, and being in an emotional state means being moved. Imports are essentially experience-dependent properties because they characterise things in their relevance to our desires or purposes or in our emotional life. Take shame as an example. It is an emotion that a subject experiences in relation to a dimension of his or her existence. A subject can be, say, ashamed of an essential property of himself or herself, and hence Taylor calls them *subject-referring properties.* For instance, even though there is nothing objectively bad about such a property as the shrillness of a voice, John might be ashamed of having such a voice. The reason is that he might experience a voice of this kind as something unmanly. If I have understood Taylor correctly, then the dimension of the subject's existence in this case is the aspiration to be masculine or the like. But it is certain that Taylor thinks that a subject with this aspiration must be capable of experiencing the whole range of imports connected with shame, dignity, and respect. The very account of what shame means involves references to our senses of dignity, of worth, of regard by others, and so forth. These properties are essentially bound up with the life of a subject of experience; they are subject-referring properties. But this subjective aspect does not mean they are somehow illusory. Feeling shame is related to an import-ascription. And to ascribe import is to make a judgement about how things really are, and we cannot simply reduce this judgement to the way we feel about them. I can be rightly or wrongly ashamed, rationally or irrationally ashamed. (Taylor 1985a: 48-55). This argument shows clearly the kinship between Taylor and the cognitivists.

If my reading of Taylor is correct, then our interpretation of the situation can be right or wrong. John might have wrongly interpreted a situation as shameful. John might think, for instance, that his voice sounded shrill while nobody else thought so. It was his inferiority complex that led him to hear his own voice as being shrill. But let us drop my own guessing about what Taylor might be thinking and look at what he actually says. A term of emotion like 'shame' essentially refers to a certain kind of situation, a 'shameful' or 'humiliating' one. Further, it refers to certain modes of response, for instance, hiding oneself or of covering up. This means that it is essential to the identification of this emotion as shame that it is related to the aforementioned type of situations and dispositions to act. At the same time, the situations can only be identified in relation to the emotion it provokes. The same holds for the disposition; the hiding in question is hiding from shame, which is quite different from hiding from an angry bear. We can only understand what 'hiding from shame' means if we know what kind of an emotion and situation we are talking about. Thus, the emotion, the situation, and the dispositions form a hermeneutic circle. The one cannot be understood without reference to the others, and together they form a whole. To be more precise, this circle is wider, for it includes other concepts; I should guess that 'pride' and 'dignity' figure prominently. They, in their turn, cannot be understood without reference to shame. When it all comes down to dust, we can only understand shame with the aid of concepts embedded in a whole language. And the language in its turn is embedded in a certain culture. In some sense, then, the hermeneutic circle of shame is a closed one, limited to given cultures (Taylor 1985c: 23-24). In light of this, it is tempting to say that Taylor has on the tip of his tongue the idea of (at least certain) emotions as being constituted and/or replete with meaning. We shall indeed see that we have even more reasons to believe that this is case. But first we have to take another look at the subject-referring emotions. They incorporate a sense of what it is to be human, what matters to us as human beings. This is intimately connected to how our direct intuitive experience of import is filtered through emotions. Emotions are, therefore, our mode of access to the domain of subject-referring imports. That means that they provide access to what matters to us as subjects or what it is to be human. In light of this, it should not come as a surprise when Taylor says that human life is never without interpreted emotions. The interpretation is constitutive of the emotion, and this means that the emotion is what it is in virtue of the situation it incorporates. But a given sense may presuppose a certain level of *articularity,* i.e., that the subject understands certain terms or distinctions. An emotion cannot, for example, be one of remorse unless there is a sense of the emoter's having done wrong. Some understanding of right and wrong is built into remorse; it is essential to its attributing the import that it does. Thus certain feelings involve a certain level of articulation in the sense that qualities they incorporate require the application of certain terms. But, at the same time, they can admit of further articulation in the sense that things can undergo further clarification. It is quite a common experience to feel remorse without being able to articulate fully what is wrong about what we have done. In such a case, we may seek further understanding. And if we succeed, our emotions may alter. The remorse may dissipate altogether if we come to see that our sense of wrongdoing was unfounded. If we come to understand what is wrong, perhaps then the remorse will intensify as we begin to see how grave the offence was. Perhaps it will lessen as we see how hard it was to avoid.

But what precisely is an articulation in Taylor's view? We can start by saying what it is *not*. It is not something only performed in discursive, verbal language; body language and different artforms can also be means of articulation. It is not the finding of a technical term for a feature of some engine or plant which one can easily identify with some adequate description, e.g., 'The long metal part sticking out on the left'. Although, to my knowledge, Taylor nowhere says it explicitly, articulation is *not* the explication of the meaning of a term with the aid of logical analysis. When I articulate something, I am seeking a language to identify how I feel, to make clear how a thing looks or to locate what was peculiar about certain person's behaviour. A linguistic articulation can make us explicitly aware of phenomena we had previously only sensed implicitly. Taylor appears to view articulation as a process that leads to formulation. By formulating some matter, we bring it to a fuller and clearer consciousness; we identify the matter in question and thereby grasp its contours. An articulated view is one that makes certain distinctions that give a phenomenon certain contours; to focus on it in an articulated fashion is to find an adequate description of it. At the same time, an articulation does not describe things independent of itself (the articulation); its manner of description is not at all like a description such as "this table is brown". An articulation alters the object at hand in a certain way. It shapes and reshapes its object; in some sense it constitutes it but must at the same time be true to it. In the case of a genuine articulation, we can know only by hindsight what it was we tried to identify. What we had sensed implicitly only becomes clear after we have articulated it clearly and can look back on our attempts at articulation (Taylor (1985b), 257-258).

Let us look again at how Taylor regards the role articulation plays in our emotional lives. Articulations are like interpretations in that they are attempts to make clearer the import things have for us. And, as we remember, imports are constitutive for emotions. Further, the way we articulate emotions, at least those that touch essential human concerns, are partly shaped by the way we articulate them. The descriptions we tend to offer of these emotions are not simply external to the reality described but are rather constitutive of it. Thus, when we articulate an emotion in a new fashion, often the emotion itself also changes. Let us say that I am confused over my feelings for a woman. Owing to an articulation, I come to see this feeling as a sign of infatuation and not of the sort of love on which a relationship can flourish. The emotions themselves have become clearer and less fluctuating and have acquired steadier boundaries. Take a person who has felt very guilty about a certain practice, for example, and who has later come to maintain that there is nothing wrong with it. The quality of the feeling of guilt changes; it may even disappear completely. If the feeling does not disappear, it has changed because the person now understands it as a kind of residual reflex from his or her upbringing. The person in question no longer accords to the feeling the same status, that is, a reflection of an unfortunate moral truth about himself or herself (Taylor 1985b: 270-271).

It is hard to understand exactly what Taylor means when he says that articulation constitutes changes of the object while remaining true to it.[5] But it might become clearer if we compare it to what I said earlier about Black's contention that metaphors constitute and reshape objects and in the process deepen our understanding of them (compare my chess metaphor). If the metaphoric transformation is closely related to the reshaping due to articulation, then it does not seem absurd to believe that articulation can give us genuine knowledge. Of course, this does not prove its claim to knowledge, but, frankly, I think that Taylor is on the right track. His theory of articulation is certainly in accordance with my idea of co-authorship, i.e., our interpretation of emotions is a co-author of them. Further, the understanding involved is more than a bit similar to metaphoric understanding; just like metaphors, articulation leads to twisted understanding. It twists emotions but gains a better grip of them owing to the twisting. Just like metaphors, an articulation has the alethic value of T-correctness; it can be T-correct or incorrect, but not true or false. At the same time, articulation has the alethic value of E-correctness, so two kinds of alethic values meet in articulation. It would be even better to think of articulation as possessing an alethic value of its own that contains elements of both T- and E-correctness.

Now Richard Moran criticises Taylor for not seeing that only beliefs can have the transformative power Taylor attributes to articulations. Interpretations and redescriptions of emotions cannot do the job unless believed in (Moran (2001): 36-65). If true, then I would be wrong about articulations not necessarily having the alethic value of truth. But think again of the person who felt guilty and let us assume that she started to believe that the feeling of guilt is nothing but a residue of upbringing. Would not the feeling simply disappear due to this belief rather than be transformed? Now, let us assume that she never thought about the possibility that the guilt could be such a residue but all of a sudden discovers it. She does really know whether it is true that her guilt is such a residue but she starts to view her guilt

---

[5] The kinship between Taylor's 'articulation' and Ricœur's 'refiguration' ought to be obvious.

in the light of this possibility. The guilt would hardly disappear but it certainly would change in virtue of being seen as a residue. So beliefs might simply destroy the emotion, while seeing-as articulates it, transforms it but nevertheless preserves it. But Moran might be justified in doubting that it holds for all emotions that they can be constituted and shaped through articulation and suchlike.[6] However, it suffices for my purposes that transformation through articulation is an important part of our emotional life. Without them our emotional life would be simpler, even impoverished, even changed beyond recognition.

I shall return to Taylor's concept of articulation later in this section. Now it is time to return to the subject-referring emotions. One of the basic reasons why such emotions are essentially interpretable is that they are shaped by language, since experiencing such emotions essentially involves seeing that certain descriptions apply to it (compare Taylor's examples above). Even if baboons had some kind of dignity, it must be totally different from our sense of dignity because ours is shaped by language. But there are emotions that are neither subject-referring nor constituted by language. Fear is a case in point. The import of physical danger is language-independent in that different descriptions and understanding of the danger do not fundamentally alter for us the imports of bodily integrity or life. But language can enter in because we might need to be apprised of the danger through language. Not even our pre-articulated sense of our feelings is completely language-independent. For they are the feelings of language-beings who can say something about them. An emoter can say, for example, that he feels something disturbing or perplexing to which he cannot give a name. We experience our pre-articulated emotions as perplexing, prompting the raising of questions. This experience no non-language animal can have (Taylor 1985a: 60-74). Animals with language would experience pains or fears differently than non-language animals.

I think that this analysis shows that the differentiation between sensations and emotions is not refined enough. Simple, primitive, 'instinctual' fear does not seem to have much to do with ratiocination. The same holds for blind, spontaneous rage. Non-subject-referring

---

[6] He definitely has a point when he says that it is not clear whether Taylor thinks that the process is solely constitutive or also causal.

emotions like these are somewhere in between sensations and emotions proper, i.e., subject-referring emotions. But as we have seen, Taylor does not use the conceptual apparatus of cognitive theory. Moreover, in possible contrast to him, I think there are fears and rages that are subject-referring. Think about the fear of atomic war or the rage felt because of a perceived insult, and contrast those with the instinctual fear you would feel as the target of a charging tiger. The fear of the charging tiger is obviously not subject-referring; perhaps it 'object-referring' since it concerns our care for our body.

Regardless, my analysis requires assistance from Taylor's comprehensive hermeneutics of emotions. Propositional content and attitudes do not alone constitute the meaning of emotions and texts. These contents and attitudes only exist as parts of situations, languages, and forms of life.

Actually, I do not see any essential opposition between my view and Taylor's. On the contrary, I think they mutually strengthen each other. Considering that I think that seeing-as is semi-interpretative, there is no gulf between Taylor's interpretative approach and the construalist approach I favour. A concern-based construal is a semi-interpretation, because it is a seeing-as. It is no wonder, then, that I call my own position *hermeneutic construalism*.

But just as I put forth critical comments to traditional contrualism, I have certain critical comments on Taylor's hermeneutic theorising. In the first place, his concept of interpretation needs differentiation, most notably between interpretation proper and that of semi-interpretation, i.e., aspect-seeing. If he gave room for the latter, then there would be space for construals in his way of approaching emotions. Secondly, it remains unclear what, if any, role sensations play in his conception of emotions.

We have discovered that, according to Taylor, a) emotions essentially involve import; b) some emotions have subject-referring properties; c) understanding such emotions requires moving in a hermeneutic circle; d) as a part that movement articulation is essential; e) these emotions are constituted by articulation and interpretation.

By fusing Taylor's theorising with the cognitive theory, we can discriminate between: a) *subject-referring emotions*; b) *other* emotions; and c) *plain (bodily?) sensations*. In my view, a mixture of

construalism, my Goldie-inspired idea of there being directed sensations, and Taylor's hermeneutic approach is the most fruitful way of
understanding emotions. Thus, a) and b) are concern-based construals,
both typically involving a web of directed sensations.

In the following chapters we shall discover that emotions have still
more hermeneutic and construalist aspects, not least metaphoric,
narrativist, and textual ones. But before concluding this chapter I want
to introduce two interrelated concepts that will play a major role in the
rest of the book.

a) *Emotive structure.* A phenomenon P has an emotive
    structure if and only if P would not be P without emotions or
    would not have come into existence without emotions or is
    shaped by emotions in an important way.

b) *Emotivity.* I am not going to define this concept here but
    only say that many diverse things can have the quality of
    emotivity. If something is permeated with emotions, it has a
    high degree of emotivity. An emotion has obviously a maxi-
    mum degree of emotivity; by contrast, a mathematical proof
    has zero degree of emotivity, even though the process of
    understanding it might contain some moments of emotivity.
    If you are in state of intense fright, then your state of mind
    has the quality of emotivity to a high degree. But a work of
    serial music has a low degree of this quality. The more emo-
    tive structure there is in this world and the more important
    they are the higher degree of emotivity there is. But in
    keeping with what I have said earlier, I warn against thinking
    that 'degree of emotivity' can be measured in any ordinary
    way.

2.3 Conclusion

In this chapter I have criticised Solomonic cognitivism while trying
to add some support to construalism, agreeing with the construalist
contention that emotions are structured by aspect-seeing. We have
found out that it is advantageous to fuse construalism with Taylor's
hermeneutic cognitivism, adding to it a dash of Goldie's ideas. This
has lead to me to the conclusion that there are three basic kinds of
feelings: sensations, ordinary emotions, and subject-referring emotions. These are the basic tenets of hermeneutic construalism. At the

same time, I have introduced the concepts of emotivity and emotive structure. It remains to be seen whether emotive structures abound and consequently, whether the human world is imbued with emotivity.

III.3. Emotions and Narrations

Is it by chance that we often tell stories when we talk about feelings? I do not think so, anymore than I think it was by chance that the first great narrative in the West, Homer's *Iliad*, is about an emotion, the wrath of Achilles and its consequences.

In this chapter I want to show first that emotions have a storied and a narrative structure, besides being shaped by stories and narratives in other ways. Secondly, I want to demonstrate that narratives play a decisive role in the justification, identification, explanation, and understanding of emotions. Thirdly, I shall add a short discussion on the issue of whether stories and narratives as such are constituted by emotions.

3.1 The Storied Structure of Emotions

We have already discovered that Wilhelm Schapp said, over fifty years ago, that emotions are constituted by narratives. Alas, his treatment of the relationship between narrations and emotions remained sketchy. The same holds for Martha Nussbaum's analysis. She presumes that there is an important link between narratives and emotions without invoking any empirical evidence that we learn to emote with the aid of stories (Nussbaum 1990: 287). William Gallie also said something similar four decades ago (Gallie (1968): 48). But, just like Nussbaum, Gallie never elaborated this idea. Yet British-Canadian philosopher Ronald de Sousa has. According to de Sousa, our emotional vocabulary is made familiar to us by association with *paradigm scenarios*. They are first drawn from daily life, later reinforced by stories and fairy tales, and then supplemented and refined by literature and art. A paradigm scenario involves two aspects: first, a paradigmatic situation providing the characteristic *objects* of an emotion, and second, the scenario provides us with characteristic *responses* to the situation. More than this, the role of scenarios in relation to emotions is analogous to the ostensive definition of a common noun. Unfortunately, even though extremely absorbing, de Sousa's theory is somewhat limited in scope; it only focuses on the way emotions are taught. Further, his theory is strictly empirical, although it certainly can inspire analyses of emotional concepts (de Sousa 1987: 181-184). Despite it being empirical, de Sousa just like Nussbaum does not invoke any empirical evidence in favour of it. Until that evidence is provided, I cannot take stance upon the theory.[1]

Peter Goldie has, however, analysed the relationship between emotions and narrations in depth. I shall, therefore, devote considerable space to a discussion of his analysis.

I myself maintain that E cannot count as an emotion unless it does have a storied structure or is constituted by narratives in other ways. An emotion is a mental state and as such it has a beginning, middle and ending. And like other mental states it has a plot-like theme that organises sensations, perceptions, actions etc. into one whole. Being angry-at-John for having stolen my car is the theme of a certain emotion and certainly unfolds in time like a story. This is the main thesis of this chapter. But I shall vindicate this thesis by route of vindicating my other thesis. The second thesis is as follows: emotions are (at least typically) embedded in narratives in such a manner that the way they are embedded is crucial to their *identification, justification, explanation,* and *understanding.*

I am not saying that it is a necessary condition for E to be an emotion that it has to be embedded in all these ways, even though that might very well be the case. There might be emotions that are neither, say, explainable or justifiable narratively. But I find it hard to imagine that there is an (at least human) emotion, which is *neither* narratively explainable, identifiable *nor* understandable.

In order to show that this is the case, I want to argue in favour of the following: narratives can function i) as indispensable tools for the identification of emotions; ii) as part of reasoning in favour of person P being justified in having E (call such narratives 'justificatory

---

[1] As for the empirical aspect of emotions, I dearly want to know how spontaneous stories function in certain emotions like anxiety, hatred, and anger. The anxious, hateful, and angry often seem to be enthralled by recurring scenarios. I do not exclude the possibility that the experience of such recurring spontaneous stories is an essential part of some brands of hatred, anxiety, anger, and other similar emotions. But now I am indulging in possibilology, yet again!

narratives'); iii) by taking part in the *constitution* of emotions; d) as explanations for the fact that person P has emotion E (those are 'explanatory narratives'); and iv) as an important tool for P in his examination and understanding of his own emotions (notice that, broadly understood, explanation ranges over understanding). I shall discuss i) - iv) in that order, and then I shall distil from this treatment a proof for my main thesis.

i) *Identifying emotions*: In order to show that we need narratives to identify emotions, we must seek guidance from Peter Goldie. But before we can turn to the question of identification, it is best to give a general outline of his theory about the narrative structure of emotions. According to him an emotion is typically complex, episodic, dynamic, and structured. The complex in question involves episodes of emotional experience, including perceptions, thoughts, and feelings of various types. Further, it involves bodily changes and dispositions, including the dispositions to experience further emotional thoughts and feelings and to act in certain ways. Emotions are neither static nor given; they tend to change; the elements in them can come and go or wax and wane. An emotion is structured in that it constitutes a part of a narrative in which the emotion is embedded. The narrative unites the different elements and thus moulds them into a coherent whole, which we call 'an emotion' (Goldie 2000: 12-13). Note that what Goldie calls 'narrative structure' is the same as my storied structure since emotions do not need an narrator in order to exist, even though a narrative is needed for the identification of emotions. Note further that, if this is true, it follows that emotions must have a storied structure, regardless of whether the emotions are reason-based or not.

Perhaps it would be productive if one could link Goldie's arguments to Ricœur's contention that narratives perform a kind of Kantian synthesis with the aid of the plot. Similarly, Goldie thinks that the narrative structure unifies feelings, beliefs, actions, and personal traits in a single emotional whole. Let us call these 'Ricœurian-Goldian' narratives 'synthesising narratives'. They are narratives that *constitute* emotions. We could also link these arguments to my arguments about emotions having plot-like themes.

Be that as it may, we can hardly explain the emotions of a given individual without invoking narratives of important parts of his or her life, which in most cases are pretty complex stories. Ultimately,

emotions must be embedded in the narratives of lives, in the biographies of individuals and even societies. Goldie gives an example of
a boy who is brought up by extremely timorous parents. As a result of
this upbringing, he tends to fear things excessively, even in adulthood.
In order for us to understand an episode when he reacts with great
fright at the sight of a wasp, the story of his upbringing must be told
(Goldie 2000: 35).

Now it is high time to show more precisely how Goldie thinks that
we identify emotions. He maintains that for each sort of emotional
experience there is a paradigmatic narrative structure, meaning that
such emotions as anger and jealousy have their own paradigmatic narrative structure. The narrative structures contain paradigmatic recognitional thoughts and paradigmatic responses involving motivational
thoughts and feelings and so on. He sees connections between this
idea and James Russell's theory about different emotions having different 'scripts'. If we know the scripts, then we can identify the emotions. The script of anger looks like this:

1. The person is offended; the offence is intentional and harmful.
The person is innocent. An injustice has been done.
2. The person glares and scowls at the offender.
3. The person feels internal tension and agitation, as if heat and
pressure were rapidly mounting inside. He feels his heart pounding
and his muscles tightening.
4. The person desires retribution.
5. The person loses control, and strikes out, harming the offender
(Russell 1991: 39).

Goldie maintains that these five 'steps' can be related to his own
idea of a paradigmatic narrative structure in the following fashion:
   Step 1: paradigmatic recognitional element involved in anger;
   Step 2: paradigmatic facial expression for anger;
   Step 3: paradigmatic bodily changes and feeling of these changes;
   Step 4: paradigmatic motivational response involved in anger;
   Step 5: paradigmatic action out of anger (Goldie 2000: 93-94).

One can recognise when other people are having given types of
emotional experience on the strength of knowing the paradigmatic
narrative structures (Goldie 2000: 33). If I understand Goldie correctly, then knowing this kind of narrative structure is a precondition for

the identifying of emotions, at least from the third-person perspective. (Let us call narratives of the type implicit in Russell's script an 'identifying narrative').

I think that Goldie's arguments are convincing. In the first place, he shows that synthesising narratives at least partly constitute emotions, giving them a storied structure. Secondly, he correctly states that knowing narratives is the precondition for identifying emotions, at least from the third-person perspective. This holds for both non-irrational and irrational emotions.

ii) *The justification of emotions*: Let us leave Goldie for a while and return to my own theorising. It is important to bear in mind that I am talking about vindication of beliefs, woven into certain emotions, when I talk about 'justification of emotions'. I am not discussing the moral aspects of emotions. Further, I am definitely not saying that all emotions need justification, but only those emotions where beliefs or judgements play a constitutive role.

Let us scrutinise an example of such a justification. Someone asks Jill "Why are you angry at John?" Jill answers (S) "I am angry at John because he stole my car". But (S) hardly makes sense unless it can be embedded in some kind of narrative. It does not make sense to say that (S1) "John stole my car, but he did not commence the operation, since there is no moment in the process that can be called its 'beginning' and neither is there a 'middle part' (let alone climax or reversal) nor did the operation stop at any given time". If there is no tellable essentially involved, then S1 makes sense. But it does not.

Further, there is a sort of description of the acts of an agent in (S) and the reaction of another agent (Jill) to these acts. Now, stories are typically recounted by storytellers and they typically are about the acts of agents. It does not seem far-fetched to call Jill 'the story-teller' and to add that she is also one of the two protagonists of the tale, the other being John. (She would remain the story-teller, with her and John as the protagonists, even if she only 'said' (S) in her own mind.) Furthermore, S would not count as a description of a theft if there was no way it could be embedded in a more elaborated narrative about how John presumably broke into the car, started the engine, drove down the main street, etc. This elaborated, full narrative must give an answer to the question of whether the operation being described qualifies as a theft, in contrast to, say, an innocent practical joke. It must, as it were, emplot the events as 'theft-events', by containing a sub-story that shows that John had no right to drive the car, for instance. Another sub-story about John's earlier thefts might be decisive for making plausible his stealing of the car.

Even though generalisations about such phenomena as 'theft-events' play an important part in many narratives, they are typically about unique events, and an emotional event tends to have indivi-duating aspects. We can safely say that every emotion is to a certain extent unique. An important part of Jill's anger with John is that it is Jill's particular wrath directed to a particular person in a given situa-tion. Do not forget that emotions tend to have a subjective component, i.e., a component of sensation; obviously, only a given individual has a given sensation at a given time in a given sensation. This component of sensation is an important element in the particularity of emotions, their *Einmaligkeit*.

Now to the main point, that of justification. The narrative can also function as part of a justification of the emotion in question. If I ask, "Are you really justified in being angry with John?" Jill can answer "I certainly am! John stole my car". I can ask "Are you sure?" Jill, then, must be able to relate the story of the theft, i.e., to provide a justi-ficatory narrative, if I am to be able to evaluate whether or not Jill is justified in being angry. (I must, of course, also have access to the empirical evidence concerning the alleged theft.) Further, I must be in the position to evaluate whether Jill should be relieved that the old battered car is now off her hands, whether it would be in Jill's and everybody else's interests for her to become more stoical about unpleasant events, etc. It seems fairly obvious that narratives play an important role in such an evaluation. It is important to note that this narrative justification does not need to be an intersubjective affair; it could very well be a part of Jill's own reasoning, only taking place in her head. She must be able to tell herself stories in order to be able to justify her own emotions.

We can connect my idea of justification with the idea of a narrative script. In order to justify an emotion, one tacitly supposes the validity of a narrative 'script' of an emotion. Furthermore, one must be able to show that the events were in accordance with the script. Jill must be able to show both that John took her car without her permission and that she is completely innocent in the affair. She, for instance, did not pay him to take it in order to fool the insurance company. In this case, the events are in accordance with step 1. But unless Jill believes in the validity of the script for anger, she cannot be justified in being angry with him, i.e., she is not justified in moving from step 1 to step 5. Usually, we do not have to recount the script, because it is a part of the background knowledge of our interlocutors.[2] So it suffices to say "I am angry with John because he stole my car", and then to proceed to prove that he is the culprit. Further, more elaborate narratives are very often required in order to justify an emotion. There are cases when I have to tell a long story about my relationship with a person in order to justify that certain actions that she performed made me terribly mad or very glad. Maybe the action in itself was not very important, but it was the umpteenth time the person in question annoyed me, and so I was justified in losing my patience and becoming extremely angry.

Be that as it may, we can obviously reconstruct Jill's justification in the following manner:

Premise (1): Everyone is justified in being angry if his or her property is stolen.

Premise (2): A description of the reason for anger (and other emotions) makes sense if and only if it is a part of a narrative that is about an actual instance of the possibility mentioned in the if-clause in premise (1).

Premise (3) (the description of a reason for anger):

John stole my (Jill's) car.

Premise (4): The description in premise 3 is a part of a narrative that is about an actual instance of the possibility mentioned in the if-clause in premise (1).

Conclusion: I (Jill) am justified in being angry with John.

Remember that (3) does not make sense outside of a narrative, and therefore, (4) must be postulated.[3] As I have hinted at, the narrative in

---

[2] If they had belonged to another culture, a telling of the script's tale could have been necessary in many cases. The scripts too might vary from culture to culture.
[3] Mark Turner would certainly say that a sentence like 3) is a small narrative unto itself (Turner 1986: 61).

our example would be about what happened when John stole Jill's car. That event was obviously an actualisation of the possibility mentioned in the if-clause of premise (1).

Let us recall the Spiderwoman from an earlier chapter. Would she tell tales in order to justify that what made her frightened was actually a spider? Would it not suffice to cite non-narrative evidence that a spider was indeed present? Regardless, in order to justify the claim that it is true that the Spiderwoman had a fit of spider-fright, then someone must be able show that her emotional reaction was in accordance with a spider-fright script. Thanks to this script, narrativity plays a necessary role for the justification of this emotion.

iii) *Explanation of emotions*: We have already seen Goldie's convincing example of a narrative explanation. We can add that I can explain Jill's anger with John by telling my interlocutor(s) about John's theft of the car. As we remember, Danto showed that narratives play an explanatory role. It would not make sense to say that the story of the theft and its consequences only describes the events but does not explain them. Add the script to the story, and we have a reasonably good explanation of the emotion in question.

Consider also that our emotional reactions tend to have some idio-syncratic moments. This means that, in many cases, an explanation of an emotion requires telling the story of an individual's life or of the emotion, as we saw in the example of the boy and the wasp.

To this someone might respond by saying that narratives only give a superficial explanation of emotions. A true understanding of them requires a non-narrative explanation. We can, for example, explain emotions in a truly scientific way by invoking social and biological causes in a non-narrative fashion. "If person P has genetic disposition D and has lived in circumstances C, then P will get angry if P's car gets stolen". I see no reason to believe that such nomological explanations are of a narrative nature until someone proves otherwise. Be that as it may, we may consider the following points. First, narrative explanations are usually sufficient. Telling the story of how the Spiderwoman came to abhor spiders in such an irrational manner is in most cases sufficient in order to explain her plight. To be sure, explaining with the aid of a story requires background knowledge, including the knowledge of natural and possibly psychological laws. No story is an island, and the same holds for theories. A nomological theory with great explanatory power also requires background knowledge, but that does not mean that it is really the background knowledge that has the explanatory power, not the nomological theory. *Mutatis mutandis*, the same holds for the relationship between the story and its background knowledge, including such knowledge that is embedded in nomological theories. Secondly, and most importantly, an individual experiences emotions as an integral part of his or her *individual* life (compare what I said about the *Einmaligkeit* of emotions). Abhorrence is always *someone's experience* of an abhorrence of something. As we have seen earlier, a typical emotion has a unique aspect by being felt by someone in a given situation at a given time. This fact limits the role of nomological explanations; they must be supplemented by some kind of idiographic explanation of which narratives provide good examples. To understand Jill's *particular* anger or the Spiderwoman's particular fright, there must be a story told about *each of them*. Any explanation must invoke an individual case history. This means that the explanation of emotions must at least partly be narrative.

iv) *Our understanding of our own emotions*: In order to show that our understanding of our own emotions has a necessary narrative component, we must take another look at the role of actions and behaviour in our emotional life. Remember the story about the jerk who thought he was in love with Anne, but his actions and behaviour showed that he was not? How can we identify this complex of actions, behavioural patterns, and emotions unless we know its story of Stanley's behaviour and actions towards Anne? Can Stanley himself, or we for that matter, identify the emotions in question without knowing the story of his actions? Can we really understand his emotions without knowing this story?

Notice that this realisation strengthens the arguments in favour of narratives as indispensable tools for both the identification and the understanding of emotions. By studying the narratives of his own behaviour and actions, Stanley can correctly identify his own emotion. Indeed, he can examine his own emotional life with the aid of narratives.[4] And so can we all. This possibility means that narratives are important tools in our examination of our emotional life.

From my treatment of i) - iv), we can see that my conditions for something having a storied structure are obtained by emotions. In the first place, emotions essentially unfold in time; there is no such thing as an emotion that does not have some kind of beginning, middle, and end. Secondly, we have seen that emotions form a unified whole in their unfolding in time. John's love of Jane certainly changes in the course of time, but it could not be given the identity of John's love of Jane unless there is a unifying thread of a certain attitudes and actions towards Anne.

Moreover, emotions also have a narrative structure[5], which we can see by distilling the essence out of my treatment of i) - iv). Given that Jill's emotion was non-irrational, then the narrative justification is an indispensable part of the constitution of her emotion. This theory does not get any weaker if we add the fact that emotions have a plot-like theme.

At the same time, emotions have a storied structure. The script is a story, not necessarily narrated, and it is a necessary part in the constitution of both non-irrational and irrational emotions. The script simply is the structure of emotions. As I said earlier, all emotions are partly constituted by synthesising narratives, providing them with storied structure in the process. Having both narrative and storied structures gives emotions a high degree of narrativity.

I mentioned in an earlier chapter that metaphors and narratives have meeting places. Myths figure prominently among them. Now, Robert C. Solomon had a point when he said that emotions are myths or mythologies consisting of metaphors and images (Solomon 1976: 202-211 and elsewhere). The mythologies or mythic stories of the emotions synthesise and dramatise the judgements, which are built into the emotions.[6] Here we see yet another example of a theory related to Ricœur's theories about the synthesising nature of metaphors and narratives.

---

[4] I am alluding to Ricœur's contention that the examined life is a life examined by narratives (Ricœur 1985b: 444 and Ricœur 1988: 247).
[5] In my sense of the word, not Goldie's, he conflates narrative and storied structure.
[6] Solomon maintains that emotions in general are judgements (Solomon 1976: 185).

Solomon thinks that emotions form our view of the world in a subjective fashion, just as mythologies do. We make individuals heroes or villains in our emotional narratives, which takes the shape of a heroic tale or a myth (Solomon 1976: 276-279).[7] (In my view, the heroes can be seen as metaphors for the good, the villains for the bad.) Every emotion has its own mythology. The mythology of wrath is the Olympian mythology of the courtroom. The angry person is legislator, judge, and representative of moral values; the object of the anger is the defendant. Notice how the wrath dramatises reality (compare what I said earlier about the dramatisation of judgements) (Solomon 1976: 286). In fact, Solomon does not explain why this mythology is Olympian. Perhaps he is thinking of the fact that Zeus was judge, legislator, and upholder of morality, all rolled in one. He was also a hot-tempered deity!

Despising has a different mythology. If we despise someone, we regard him or her as a despicable individual. In such a mythology, a host of metaphors, both dead and alive, play a certain role. We often call people we despise 'cockroaches' or 'dirt' (Solomon 1976: 292).

Solomon's idea is useful, even though he seems both to regard mythologies as ideological systems and to ignore the fact that they are stories. After all, 'plot' and 'story' were some of the original meanings of 'myth'. More importantly, how can Solomon's mythology of wrath be what it is without stories? We cannot call certain event 'legislation' unless we talking about a process with narrative characteristics, i.e., beginning, climax, and end, as well as a plot. The same holds for other emotions and their mythologies. If emotions such as wrath dramatise reality, then it is pretty clear that they are somehow related to stories, since dramatising something means giving it a storied structure. The mythical stories of emotions are among the stories or myths we live by. Given my sketch of the idea of ur-stories we live by, we could imagine that our raw-feel dispositions and the nature of our culture somehow filter our experience of raw feelings, creating abstract patterns of emotional ur-stories that then contribute to the constitution of emotions proper. The ur-stories function as deep structures, activated in various ways depending on the circumstances.

---

7 This theory seems to have been inspired by Sartre, who says that emotions endow things with magical properties. If you are scared of spiders, your fright transforms a little spider into a magical monster (Sartre 1948: 62 and elsewhere).

Once again, I remind the reader of the speculative character of this idea.

It is pretty clear that emotions have storied and narrative structures and metaphoric moments that meet in the mythologies. I shall elaborate upon the metaphoric moments in the next chapter.

3.2 Hogan on the Emotive Structure of Stories

Hitherto, we have only discussed the way emotions are narratively structured; now it is time to look at the possible emotive structure of narratives. American literary theorist Patrick Colm Hogan has developed an engaging theory about emotions and narratives. Emotions are narratively structured and narratives emotionally structured.[8] More precisely, narratives are prototypically elaborated versions of micro-narratives, which constitute emotions. He is quite taken by the idea of the prototypical and maintains that we can only define the concepts of emotions and narratives in the terms of *prototypicality*. Thus, he borrows Anna Wierzibicka's contention that we can only identify emotions by standard situations and thus the meaning of 'emotion terms' has this general form: 'X feels emotional = X feels as one does when…' More substantially: 'X feels sad = X feels as one does when one thinks that what one has desired to happen has not happened and will not happen'. Hogan points out that de Sousa's idea of paradigm scenarios is not dissimilar to Wierzibicka's theory (Hogan 2003: 82). This leads us to Hogan's first hypothesis (of four): Emotion terms are prototype-based in both eliciting conditions and expressive and actional consequences Situations (Wierzibicka's term) and paradigm scenarios should be regarded as specific in the way that the prototype of birds is. Thus, when we judge someone to have a certain emotion, we do so by comparing his or her situation with prototypical situations and his or her response with prototypical responses. For example, our lexical entry for 'sad' would not include a Wierzbicka-like abstract equation but rather something like 'What you feel when someone you

---

[8] He is inspired by Keith Oatley and Philip Johnson-Laird who have argued that emotion is the product of an agent's evaluation of his or her successes and failures in achieving particular goals within a narrative structure (Hogan 2003: 76). No mentioning of Peter Goldie, whatsoever.

love dies and what you express through weeping' (Hogan 2003: 82).[9] The concreteness of prototypes of emotion has to do with them being bound up with implicit stories.[10] Stories in their turn should be regarded in relation to prototypicality. Now, what does it mean to say that some narratives are prototypical while others are not? It means that our mental lexicon includes prototypes for narratives and that we judge narratives - including what is and what is not a narrative - by reference to prototypes (Hogan 2003: 87). As strongly suggested, some narratives are more typical than others. The story of young lovers overcoming obstacles is more typical than the story of furnace (Hogan 2003: 86) But what characterises prototypical narratives? One important property is emotional interest. Surely, a story of lovers engages emotions but hardly that of a furnace. Actually, the standard goal of literary storytelling is emotional appeal. When the purpose of our storytelling is in part emotive, which it is in prototypical story-telling, that story-telling will be bound up with prototypes of emotion. These emotion prototypes will help guide our decisions of what sort of story is tellable, what is of interest, what is valid, and what is effective and engaging. This is true when the narrative is fictional biographical or historical, set in the form of an epic a drama or a novel. In each of these cases, owing to the emotive purpose of the tale, emotion prototypes will provide central structural principles for the story, partly guiding its overall shape and outcome, its tone, and so on. At the same time, the stories play an important role in the shaping of our emotions. We may feel badly for a character who is weeping, but our response is given depth and intensity only through an understanding of

---

[9] He admits that he is not the only one to use a prototypical model of emotions. George Lakoff and Zoltan Köveces are among the adherents of such prototypical approach. But Hogan stresses that theirs is different from his model because it treats a much broader sequence of a more abstractly prototypical cultural model of anger. This model has five stages: cause of anger, existence of anger, attempt at control, loss of control, retribution. He points out that this model is a model of scripted emotions He actually doubts that there are scripts of the Lakoff -Köveces sort. Rather he suspects that their findings are a residue of our separate ideas about the causes of emotions and the justification of emotions (Hogan (2003): 84-85). I shall return briefly to Lakoff and Köveces in the next chapter.

[10] Hogan also stresses that emotions have other dimensions, including phenol-menological tones (raw feel), the actional and expressive outcome of emotions (for example, flight in case of fear), vague principles of justification, (variable) norms bearing on the self-conscious evaluation, and control of emotional impulses (Hogan (2003): 85).

what has led to this expression of sorrow, i.e., by our knowing its story.

This leads us to Hogan's second hypothesis. Prototypical narratives are generated largely from the prototype *eliciting* conditions for emotions. Put differently, our prototypical stories are expansions of the micro-narratives that define our emotive terms (Hogan 2003: 88). But for forming the backbone of a prototypical narrative, not any old emotion will do. Certainly, every emotion has its narrative; we tell tales in order to provoke fear, anger, and disgust. But these emotions do not form the backbone of prototypical narratives even though fear, anger, and disgust may play a certain role in such narratives. Instead, such emotions as happiness and sorrow form that backbone. We actually evaluate anger and disgust in relationship to happiness and sorrow. Fear is fear of what would lead to sorrow or to diminished happiness. The threesome is punctual emotions, prototypically elicited by temporally *thin* events, for instance, a momentary attack by an animal. Happiness and sorrow, on the other hand, arise typically out of temporally *thick* conditions. The route to happiness is usually winding and takes a long time to travel. Happiness and sorrow are emotions of outcome because they define the enduring feelings we prototypically consider to be the final evaluation points for junctural emotions like the threesome. Indeed, insofar as narratives prototypically recount pursuits of goals and by implication actions, then they are necessarily organised by reference to the eliciting conditions of happiness. After all, happiness is the aim of action. Moreover, we do not pursue undifferentiated happiness (Hogan 2003: 92). This leads to Hogan's third hypothesis: *Romantic* union and social or political *power* is the prototypical outcome from which our prototypical narratives are generated. Romantic union and power are the goals sought by protagonists in prototypical narratives. The corresponding prototypes for sorrow are death of the beloved and the complete loss of social and political power, typically through social or political exclusion either within society (imprisonment) or outside society (exile) (Hogan 2003: 94). Hogan's fourth and final hypothesis is that, cross-culturally, there are two prominent structures of literary narratives, romantic and heroic tragi-comedy, derived respectively from personal and social prototypes for happiness (Hogan 2003: 98). The typical heroic tragi-comedy has the following kind of plot: the rightful leader of society is displaced from rule or prevented from assuming rule, most often by close relative. He or she is exiled or imprisoned. However, such a plot is not as common as the ones of romantic tragi-comedy. The most common plot structure across different traditions is almost certainly romantic tragi-comedy, the story of the union, separation, and ultimate reunion of lovers. The importance of the separation in such plots leads Hogan to an extension of the third hypothesis: the construction of a plot leading to prototype eliciting conditions for happiness must necessarily develop through a period when these conditions do not obtain. This is the Aristotelian middle; this middle is prototypically assimilated to the correlated prototype eliciting conditions for sorrow (Hogan 2003: 102-109). Here my concepts of emotive structure and of emotivity come into the picture: a narrative, which is structured in the manner described by Hogan, has such a structure. It has a fair degree of emotivity.

Hogan's analysis is daring and inspiring, even if a bit far-fetched. But he nowhere takes up the challenges against the concept of emotions as being prototypical. Kristján Kristjánsson is one of those challengers, criticising Aaron Ben-Ze'ev's idea of prototypicality. Ben-Ze'ev claims both that emotions constitute prototypical categories and that the degree of similarity to the most typical cases determines their inclusion in them. But Kristjánsson asks how we can find out which cases are the most typical. Ben-Ze'ev maintains that the prototypical example is the one that exhibits the most significant features of the given emotional category and has but a few distinctive features that are not shared by category members. We can determine which features are significant by asking people to describe typical cases and through conceptual analysis (Ben-Ze'ev 2003). To this Kristjánsson replies that people tend to disagree about such cases. More fundamentally, Ben-Ze'ev is faced by a dilemma: *either* the prototypical example yielded by conceptual analysis is prototypical because it best captures the natural point of the category, in which case the concept itself and not only the particular example should be explicated, *or* it is the best example for another reason, in which case mere reference to conceptual analysis does not tell much how we can find the example (Kristjánsson 2002: 23-24). To this I have a few comments. The first is that the Icelandic philosopher simply assumes that people do not agree about which cases are typical. Where is the evidence? The second comment is that by saying that categories have natural points, Kristjánsson treats them as though they *must* have one given essence or one given point. If he wants to refute the idea of prototypicality, then he is just begging the question. If the concept of emotions is a prototypical one, then it makes no sense to say that it has one given point; rather, it has some interrelated points with unclear boundaries to whatever points related concepts might have. I think that is the case. What is the common point of being frightened of a charging tiger, being frightened of speaking in public or being frightened of a future ecological catastrophe? My conclusion is that Kristjánsson has not refuted the idea of the prototypicality of emotions. I do not exclude the possibility that the concepts of emotions and its sub-concepts are prototypical concepts. Yet, I do not rule out the possibility that Kristjánsson might be right about emotions as being open-textured concepts rather than being prototypical ones (Kristján Kristjánsson (2002): 21-22). My basic point is simply that he has not shown that they *cannot* be prototypical concepts or any other sort of amoebaean concept. Maybe Amélie Rorty is right when she says that the concept of emotion cannot be defined and does not form a natural class (Rorty 1980: 105). Griffiths seems to be making a similar point, albeit from very different perspective. However, I think Robert Roberts has an excellent point when he says that Rorty gives up too early in trying to find a fundamental conception of emotions (Roberts 2003: 64). Griffiths ought also to take heed of this criticism. I certainly do; for all I know it might turn out that the concept of emotion is some kind of an essentialist one, even though my intuitions point in the direction of it being an amoebaean concept.

Regardless of whether I am right or not, it might be more promising to concentrate on the possible emotional constitution of subclasses of narratives and to define the concepts of these subclasses in an essentialist or open-textured fashion.[11] Thus comedies might be essentially extensions of the micro-narratives, which constitute mirth, and tragedies essentially extensions of micro-narratives, which constitute sorrow and so on. In this manner, we could draw from Hogan's ideas as we suspend judgment on his sweeping generalisations about emotions and narratives.

---

[11] In fact, Aristotle provides us with such a definition of the kind of narrative we call 'tragedy' (Aristotle 1965: 47-49 (Chapter 13)). We can reconstruct it in the following fashion: T is a tragedy if and only if T is capable of eliciting pity and fear in the audience.

3.3 Conclusion

We have seen that emotions have storied and narrative structures and are shaped by narratives in various ways and that narratives and stories in their turn might be constituted by emotions. Further, narratives play indispensable roles in the identification, justification, explanation, and examination of emotions. Emotions are narrations indeed, and narrations might, for all we know, have an emotional structure.

We have discovered some interesting arguments in favour of emotion concepts being prototypical concepts, but I have suspended judgement on whether it is true, even though my intuition tells me that it is some kind of an amoebaean concept.

III.4. Emotions and Meaning

It has been à la mode in Paris for quite some time to say that this or that is really a text. It is well-known that Jacques Lacan maintained that the subconscious is structured like a text. I am certainly no Lacanian, nor am I passionately fascinated by fashions of Parisian provenance. So I will resist whatever temptation I might feel for calling emotions 'texts' or 'text-analogues'. Instead I want to show that emotions are imbued with and constituted by meaning. Let us see how: 1) In the first place, one (or, more precisely, two) of the moments which make emotions meaningful are their metaphoric and narrativist structures. Narratives and metaphors are meaningful entities and partly constituted by interpretations and semi-interpretations. Seeing-as means semi-interpreting as; the metaphoric (seeing-as) moment in emotions is thus constituted by semi-interpretations. We have already discussed the narrative nature of emotions but not their metaphoric nature, so it will be my first theme in this chapter. 2) Secondly, the propositional contents of emotions have a constitutive role for them. That such contents are meaningful is obvious. 3) Thirdly, emotions have illocutionary aspects, which are obviously meaningful, and thus contribute to their meaningfulness. 4) Further, emotions often (even always) are by necessity connected to actions, and actions are meaningful entities, to be interpreted and often constituted by interpretation. Thus in one interpretation moving of one's hand can be the action of offending the gods, a sacrilege, in another interpretation waving to a friend. 5) There is also something akin to an emotional meaning, that which I call *experiential emotional meaning* (*Ex.Em.M*). 6) Moreover, we very often have to interpret our emotions in order to find out what emotions we or others really have. (This, of course, does not show that interpretations are essential to emotions.) It almost goes without saying that an interpretation can only be an interpretation of something meaningful. 7) The final reason is that emotions are partly constituted by interpretations, as Taylor has indeed shown. Being thus constituted means being constituted by meaning. I have already discussed the last reason, and so I shall in this chapter concentrate on

1-7. I place the greatest emphasis on 1) because of the role metaphors play in this book.

4.1 Emotions and Metaphors

(1) Roberts only discusses metaphors in connection with moods. Moods are characterised by metaphors; we say, "he is gloomy" or "his mood was grey". Emotions have moods; joy is bright while grief is dark and heavy. But metaphors do not play any great role in his theorising. Fluency in metaphors can enrich our ability to recognise, experience, and discriminate moods (and by implication emotions). Nevertheless, they can never become substitutes for direct acquaintances (Roberts 2003: 112-113). While this is undoubtedly true, Roberts underestimates the role of metaphors in emotional life. He does not see that we can regard concern-based construals as having a metaphoric nature. If metaphors are seeing-as, then they are construals, which could be, but are not necessarily, concern-based. According to Roberts, construals involve 'in-terms-of-relationships' (Roberts 2003: 76). But as we have already seen, so do metaphors according to Black and Lakoff. Notice that being a construal must mean having a metaphoric structure or something akin to it, given my definition of such a structure. Further, we remember that Roberts correctly thinks that construing in an emotive way means synthesising various elements. But we also remember that this is precisely what metaphors do, according to Paul Ricœur. And we certainly have not forgotten that they are constituted by aspect-seeing, in accordance to Ricœur's and Black's arguments; the same holds for emotions in Roberts' view. I have also mentioned that Glicksohn and Goodblatt convincingly argue in favour of metaphors being Gestalts. This brings us back to emotions because Ronald de Sousa calls emotions 'perceptual gestalts'. Emotions are somewhat like Kuhnian paradigms; we see the world through them (de Sousa 1980: 127-151). In contrast, Roberts maintains that emotions are far more complex than Gestalt figures (Roberts 2003: 81). But if emotions are construals, then they are close relatives of Gestalts; they may have an ineliminable Gestalt-moment. The upshot of this is that if these theorists are right (which I believe they are), then metaphors and emotions have some important things in common. Both are construals and have Gestalt-like qualities.

Now it is time to redeem my promise of showing how emotions transfigure or transform reality and thus act as co-authors of our reality-text. I think it is easy to see that construals transform reality but do not necessarily create new realities. I construe the tiger as fearful, and this construction 'colours' my whole understanding of a certain situation. But chances are that the tiger is real and dangerous to my health. In that case, I do not create fearfulness of the beast *ex nihilo*. This is quite like the way the chess metaphor for war transforms the object but does not create it out of nothing.

To this we could add some parts of Jean-Paul Sartre's valuable analysis of emotions. He says that an emotion is a transformation of the world (Sartre 1948: 48). We can only experience an object as frightful, saddening, irritating, and suchlike on the basis of a total alteration of the world. This alteration or transformation has, metaphorically speaking, a magical nature. This means that whenever we see things in an emotional manner, we do not see them as obeying natural laws but as magical objects. In fear, we act as though we use magic instruments to make fearful things disappear. And when joyful, we sing and dance like shamans performing a rite.

We get a better grip on this idea by looking at Sartre's analysis of the horrible. In order that an object might appear as something horrible, it must manifest itself as an immediate and magical presence, face-to-face with consciousness. The face that appears four meters away from me in the window frame must be experienced as being immediately present to me in its menacing way. The distance is not experienced as one that must be physically traversed in contrast to what natural laws require. It is perceived as the unitary basis of the horrible. The window is not perceived as something that must be opened in order for the menacing thing to crawl in. It is perceived as the frame of the horrible face (Sartre 1948: 87-88). The kinship with the seeing-as mode of thinking ought to be obvious; Sartre's analysis strengthens my conviction that emotions transform their objects, as metaphors do. But I do not agree with Sartre's contention that emotions are necessarily magical or illusory, even though irrational emotions certainly are. (Sartre's analysis gave an excellent insight into the phenomenology of irrational emotions, while he mistakenly thought that he was studying emotions in general.) We have already seen that they have a cognitive component, for instance, by showing us in a flash that certain objects are dangerous. We have also seen that metaphors have such a cognitive component; one of the reasons that metaphors can give us insights is that the metaphoric transformations make certain sides of reality salient. The same holds for transformations due to emotions. As I said earlier, the metaphoric transformations make certain sides of reality salient. Ronald de Sousa has pointed out that emotions are one of the mechanisms we use to make features of reality salient (de Sousa 1987: xv). Regardless of de Sousa's analysis, I think that, for instance, the transformation of perceived features of a situation due to fear makes those features salient, which we feel to be threatening our well-being. An emotion cannot be E-correct unless it makes the 'right' features salient; in order to be E-correct fear must make the features of danger to our wellbeing salient. Irrational fear makes features salient that are not really dangerous, therefore it is not E-correct.

This squares well with Damasio's empirical studies of patients who lost their ability to judge the relevance and salience of phenomena owing to emotional impairment. Maybe de Sousa's analysis of argumentation and emotions can fortify Damasio's conclusions. De Sousa says that emotions can endow one set of supporting considerations with more salience than others and thus break a deadlock in argumentation when reason cannot help us to make up our mind between alternatives (de Sousa 1987: 16 and elsewhere). Chances are that people with 'Damasioan' brain injuries lose the ability to endow some supporting consideration with more salience than others due to loss of emotional competence. As a consequence, they cannot make rational decisions.

Before concluding point 1), I might as well admit that I am under a certain influence from the Lakoffian School. Heavily inspired by Lakoff and Johnson, the Hungarian linguist Zoltán Kövecses maintains that emotions have a metaphoric structure. In a typical Lakoffian manner, he maintains that the sources of emotional metaphors tend to be bodily experiences. We experience emotions non-metaphorically as being embodied, and our bodies metaphorically as being containers. Therefore, we tend to regard emotions metaphorically as being inside containers. We talk about our (our containers) bursting with anger and so on.

But Köveces uses the expression 'metaphoric structure' in a way that differs from mine. There are certainly no construals involved in his scheme of things (Köveces 2000). However, we certainly agree that emotions are somehow metaphorically structured. Even though the Lakoffians probably overestimate the role of the corporeal in the creation of emotional (and other) metaphors, I do not doubt that the corporeal plays a vital role in the creation of a host of such metaphors. After all, emotions have much to do with bodily reactions, and so it is no wonder that many of our metaphors for emotions have such reactions as their source. But, as I said in my earlier criticism of the Lakoffians, we have no reasons to believe that all our basic metaphors are of corporeal provenance. And the Lakoffians certainly lack the seeing-as perspective, when it comes to both metaphors and emotions.

We have seen that metaphors and emotions have much in common. Metaphors and emotions are construals, even Gestalts, which unify different elements into wholes. In the process they transform, as it were, their objects and make certain features of these objects salient. This way of making features salient is one of the ways both metaphors and emotions can give us cognitive insights.

Emotions can be subsumed under my notion of a metaphoric structure because there would not be any emotions if certain phenomena were not understood through certain other phenomena, certain concepts seen in the terms of other concepts. To be sure, there would be sensations, on the one hand, and thoughts, on the other, but never the twain should have met.

Without metaphoring, no emoting.

4.2 Propositional Contents and Illocutionary Aspects

(2) I can have different attitudes towards the propositional content of an emotion; I can have an emotion even though I do not believe in its propositional content. A case in point is fear of flying. I know that flying is not particularly dangerous; nevertheless, flying scares me out of my wits. Notice that my attitude towards the propositional content is a necessary part of giving the emotion an identity as irrational fear. My attitude, alongside with the propositional content, endows this emotion with meaning, and thus contributes decisively to its con-stitution. In such an emotion there is a contradiction involved, bet-ween my belief that flying is not dangerous and the emotion I am

actually having (call this an *emotional contradiction*). It is somewhat like believing that flying is both not dangerous and dangerous simultaneously. However, it is even more like a performative contradiction. If I seriously say, "I do not exist", then my act of maintaining it contradicts the proposition I utter. The speech-act I am performing cannot but fail. Performative or not, being contradictory is a quality that only meaningful entities can have. If emotions can possess this quality then they surely are meaningful entities.

(3) It is well-known that utterances involve by necessity illocutionary acts, for instance assertions, warnings, promises and threats. That an utterance is a meaningful entity goes without saying. Emotions have something in common with utterances, 'illocutionary' traits. Robert C. Solomon has a point when he says that emotions are preverbal analogues of Austin's performatives. Emotions are judgements that do something rather than simply describe or evaluate states of affairs. In anger, we judge someone's behaviour to be offensive, but that anger is not just a report or reaction to an offence. The anger *declares* that the comment is an offence in the same way as a magistrate declares that someone is guilty (Solomon 1976: 195). This means that anger has an (quasi-?) illocutionary aspect (it would be going a bit too far to say that an emotion has a full-fledged illocutionary aspect; after all illocution is typically an aspect of speech-acts).

As the reader may already have guessed, I do not agree with Solomon's contentions that emotions are always based on judgments. Nevertheless, I think he is right about there being a declarative or even quasi-declarative moment in emotions. I cannot be angry unless I am disposed to declare something as offensive, even though I do not really believe it. (There is a quasi-declarative moment in my anger.) I am like the judge who declares someone guilty even though I know that most of the evidence points in the direction of the person's innocence, but in my heart of hearts I do not really believe it. The same holds for other irrational emotions.

Norwegian philosopher Petter Nafstad quite correctly points out that articulated emotions have illocutionary aspects (maybe he should have said 'quasi-illocutionary aspects'). The articulation of real anger and hatred will be taken as a potential threat to the objects of these emotions (for threatening is obviously an illocutionary act). Taking it as something else would mean that the articulation was interpreted as another kind of emotion. If someone's actions were taken as acts of vengeance and it later turned out that the actor was not angry at all, then we have reason to suspect that the action had been given a wrong description. Further, the actor must have a disposition to act in a way originally connected with the anger, for instance, in a vengeful way (Nafstad 2001).

Now, illocutionary acts are actions, and, therefore, there are some logical connection between actions and least certain classes of emotions. Further, many 'ordinary' actions have illocutionary traits. Promising is a good example. Actions of a certain sort, for example, the raising of a hand when volunteers are called for, can, in the appropriate context, count as a promise no less than a verbal pledge can.[1]

As I showed earlier in this book, there are cases when understanding actions is our only way to understand our own or other's emotions. Actions by definition are meaningful and must typically be interpreted. Both Ricœur and Taylor think that actions are text-analogues (Ricœur 1981: 197-220).[2] I am not going to discuss this contention, but only mention that, according to Taylor; the meaning of the text-analogues called 'action' is an experiential one. We do not have to believe in the text-analogue part in order to see the idea of actions having an experiential meaning is fruitful. Taylor says that our actions are ordinarily characterised by the purposes sought and explained by desires and emotions. And the language we use to describe our goals, emotions, and desires also defines the meaning things have for us (Taylor (1985): 23). We see how the experiential meaning of actions and emotions are interwoven. This adds yet another bridge between actions and emotions.

(4) Inspired by Taylor's idea of experiential meaning, I want to show that there is something we can call 'emotional meaning', given a broad understanding of 'meaning'.

Let us say someone thinks that a given object is terrifying while another finds the object attractive. Obviously these things have a different experiential meaning for these two subjects. It seems to me that such a meaning is partly value or import; we often say "this means a

---

[1] I borrowed the last example from Bernard Dauenhauer (Dauenhauer (2002).
[2] In this article, the French philosopher says that all actions have illocutionary traits.

lot to me" or "she is my significant other". At the same time, the connotations of terms form a part of experiential meaning. The import constrains the connotations; experiencing something as truly terrifying foregrounds the most negative and dramatic connotations of the term, while seeing a terrifying scene in a fictional movie would foreground less negative connotations. But the connotations also constrain the import. Let us imagine a person for whom the only connotations the term 'terrifying' has are those of the ordinary moviegoers. Further, he or she possesses no roughly equivalent expression and no expression with the aforementioned negative and dramatic connotations. That person might have a hard time conceptualising an experience most people would find truly terrifying.

This analysis is my own way of developing Taylor's idea; I am talking about my *Em.Ex.M.* This analysis indicates that there is a particular emotional meaning somewhat like there is a particular metaphoric meaning. The understanding of metaphors has the understanding of connotations as a precondition[3], and the same holds for the Em.Ex.M. And just as T-correctness is of utmost importance for the understanding of meaning, E-correctness and E-appropriateness are decisive for the understanding of emotions. Knowing the both conditions for the E-correctness and the E-appropriateness of any given emotion is one of the conditions for knowing what it is. This means that in order to understand an emotion, it is vital that we know a) how the emotion represents reality, b) when it is appropriate to have that emotion, at least in a given culture. These are necessary but not sufficient conditions for knowing what emotions are, knowing their meaning.

However, there are some important differences between the understanding of emotions and that of metaphors. The latter has nothing to do with the understanding of import even though metaphors might help us get a grip of imports. The meaningfulness of narratives is closer to the Em.Ex.M because narratives help make sense of things and help us explicate our feeling of the import of things by explaining

---

[3] This does not mean that I am giving up my theory of metaphoric understanding, only admitting that Black is right about the understanding of connotations as a part of understanding metaphors. But he wrongly thought that understanding connotations were what understanding metaphors is all about. See my discussion of Black in the first chapter.

them narratively. So when it comes to meaning in a very broad sense of that word, the Em.Ex.M. is somewhere in between narratives and metaphors.

(5) Utterances and other meaningful objects can, even must, be interpreted. The same holds for emotions. It often takes interpretation to find out what the propositional content of a given emotion is and the same holds for the attitude involved.[4] (I think it is pretty uncontroversial that attempts to uncover meaning are interpretations. I actually use 'interpretation' in this chapter strictly in this sense.) The reason is that emotions are complex webs of desires, actions, reactions, feelings, and thoughts. Finding the propositional content and the attitude in these webs is not always an easy task. As I said earlier, the meaning to be grasped in emotions is largely constituted by their propositional content and propositional attitudes. (We shall later discover why I say 'largely'.) Something similar holds for written texts and oral utterances. What make them meaningful are basically their propositional content and the intentions (attitudes) of writers and speakers, and even readers and listeners. Like understanding other meaningful objects, understanding emotions requires understanding signs. Some of the signs involved in emotions are carriers of meaning; they stand for something else. Think about certain symbolic gestures with hands or fingers. Thoughts matter too, both our own and others, and thoughts are structured like languages or other systems of meaning-carriers. (There are notorious difficulties involved in drawing a sharp dividing line between thought and the employment of some kind of symbols.)[5] I find myself thinking again and again, "Anne is so lovely", and this indicates that I might be in love with her.[6] Understanding our own thoughts and guessing what others are thinking are also important parts of the grasping of emotions. Again and again,

---

[4] A propositional attitude is a meaningful entity because it is constituted by language and possibly by other systems of carriers of meaning. It is hard to see how one may discern between having such attitudes as believing or disbelieving and the content of such expressions as "I believe X/I do not believe X" which a person with an attitude forms in his mind or even says aloud.

[5] I mentioned in the Introduction to this book that Wittgenstein pointed out that we have criteria for translation between languages, but not between non-lingual thought and language. I agree, provided that 'language' is interpreted as 'system of all meaning-carriers', including sign language and symbolic pictures.

[6] Notice that this thought is expressed in words, and chances are that the meaning of the sentence and the thought coincide.

John experiences spontaneous stories about his wife's cheating on him or at least showering a great deal of attention on other men. He does not want to experience these scenarios but nevertheless he does. And they are meaningful to him because he interprets them in certain ways. The interpretations and the way these stories force themselves on him make him (or his shrink or a friend) understand that he is frightfully jealous.

Take my recurring thoughts about Anne as a case in point. I have a vivid image of Anne in my mind which I keep 'seeing' again and again, sometimes even in my dreams. This image is meaningful: it is what it is in virtue of referring to, even symbolising, Anne. It must, at least in certain cases, be interpreted. There might be, for instance, cases where I must find out whether the image is really of Anne and not her younger sister. Besides, both the vividness of the image and its recurrence can point in the direction of my being in love with Anne. It is not clear, however, whether the vividness and the recurrence really belong to the realm of the meaningful. They might be borderline cases. Indeed, understanding emotions has aspects, which have no-thing to do with carriers of meaning. In the first place, some of the signs involved are telltale signs of emotions, such as a face red with shame, signs that are indexical. They are, strictly speaking, not meaningful but as we have seen earlier, we can talk about indexical interpretation in cases where understanding indices is part of inter-preting something meaningful. Our knowledge of indexes is fallible, just like our understanding of meaningful carriers, which, in at least important cases, stand in need of interpretation. I thought she blushed but actually she was catching a cold.[7] Secondly, the sensations involved in emotions are not meaningful. Feeling a thrill when I see Anne can be an indication that I am falling in love with her, yet the thrill itself is not meaningful. And feeling a chill while seeing her cer-tainly is neither meaningful nor an indicator of my being in love with her! But these are tell-tale signs, indexes which must be understood in order to gain understanding of something replete with meaning, i.e., my emotions. In actual fact, understanding *bona fide* meaningful entities also involves knowledge derived from sensory experience, which does not involve the understanding of meaning-carriers. In oral

---

[7] Some indexical signs are symbolic entities. I can consciously exaggerate my stern look in order to send a message about my anger.

discourses, one has to be able to hear sounds. (If one discourses with the aid of sign language, then seeing movements of limbs is a prerequisite for understanding.) Besides, a part of understanding what an interlocutor says can comprise observing involuntary reactions such as blushing or the trembling of hands. And in reading written texts, one has to sense the shape and size of letters. In some cases, thrills or fears felt while reading may be parts of understanding a text. Feeling fear when reading a novel can lead the reader to understand it as a horror story. Anyway, emotions are, as we have discovered, meaningful entities, and the road towards understanding them goes by, among others, the route of interpreting signs.

Before I stop (for the time being) talking about the interpretation of emotions, I want to explicate what I hitherto have been hinting at, namely that we do not only interpret the emotions of others but also our own emotions. Remember all the indications that led me to conclude that I was falling in love with Anne.

An excellent description of emotional self-interpretation can be found in Jane Austen's *Pride and Prejudice*, when Elizabeth Bennet finds out that she is not really in love with Mr. Wickham. One of the reasons is that she is not upset when she finds out that he has turned his gaze upon another woman. (Compare what I said earlier about the role that the understanding of actions and reactions plays in our understanding of emotions.) We can, of course, misunderstand both our emotions and the emotions of others. (Compare my earlier examples of persons who thought they were in love, but were actually just infatuated.) A good example of how we can misunderstand the emotions of others can be found in Austen's novel. Mr. Darcy wrongly supposed that Jane Bennet was not really in love with Mr. Bingley, which resulted in dramatic consequences for several people. In fact, our knowledge about the propositional content of emotions is fallible. We cannot even be certain about the content of our own emotions; not even our sensations give us any certainty. Robert Roberts has an example of this: Zack has a test coming up and feels quite anxious; after all, he has a stomach-ache; but this ache is due to a flu which is just coming on but has not yet declared itself. His 'anxiety' has the following propositional content: *This test is vaguely a threat to my standing as a bright student*. Then with the progress of the disease he realises what is causing his stomachache. Owing to this realisation, he finds his feeling of anxiety disappears. The evidence that he is not anxious, despite feeling that way, might be the following: first, he is not in the habit of getting anxious about tests; secondly, he is not currently displaying any behaviour typical of such anxiety; and thirdly, he ceases to feel anxious when he discovers that he is sick (Roberts 2003: 315). Roberts is actually trying to prove a different point than I am. Nevertheless, I take the liberty of using this example as evidence in favour of my theory that our beliefs about our own emotions are fallible. The fact of this fallibility and the fact of the meaningfulness of emotions show interpretations are of great importance in emotional life. We should not need interpretations if our understanding were infallible. Further, the fallibility of our beliefs about our own emotions gives other people important roles to play in our emotional lives. As we have seen, others can correct our mistaken beliefs about our own emotions.

Fallible or not, we typically need to interpret emotions and the narratives and other symbolic structures that constitute them. And symbolic structures such as metaphor are partly constituted by interpretations. By implication, emotions must be so constituted being in their turn partly constituted metaphorically. This analysis of the role of interpretation in emotional life ought to add fuel to my hermeneutic construalism. More fuel will be added in the next chapter where I will discuss how emotions can be disclosed; disclosure is either a sort of interpretation or a close relative.

4.4 Conclusion

In this chapter (and an earlier one) we have discovered that a) emotions have a metaphoric structure; (b) they are constituted by propositional contents and attitudes towards them. Therefore, they can be contradictory like utterances and sentences; c) like utterances, emotions have illocutionary aspects; (d) actions are meaningful and some of them are internal to at least some emotions are and therefore interpretable; (e) like utterances and other meaningful entities, emotions can, even must, be interpreted; (f) understanding emotions is a complex process, involving both understanding of meaning and sensory perception; (g) the understanding of emotions is fallible; and (h) emotions have a peculiar kind of meaning, emotional-experiential meaning. Being thus permeated with meaning makes emotions virtual symbolic structures that can be said to represent segments of reality.

The conclusion of this part of the chapter is, of course, that emotions are constituted by meaning. This weakens both subjectivist and materialist reductionism concerning emotions still further, while strengthening my hermeneutic approach to them. Meaning is public and if emotions are shot through with meaning, then they cannot be reduced to something entirely subjective. Further, meaning cannot be reduced to material objects or processes, by implication, emotions can neither.

III.5. The Maieutics of Ana-Logic
On poetic metaphors, similes, emotions, and tacit knowledge

In this chapter I want to show that the employment of ana-logics can help us disclose the tacit aspects of our knowledge about emotions. Poetic metaphors, similes, and analogies (and some other poetic devices) help us bear forth the knowledge we are pregnant with; like Socrates, they are our spiritual midwives, there is a midwifery of poetry. The employment of the three poetic devices and other such devices do not necessarily increase our knowledge but rather help us articulate the tacit knowledge we already possess. (There is a sense in which that kind of knowledge possesses us!) At the same time, they perform their *disclosive* function best as parts of literary works.

I think that this theory explicates the widespread intuition that poetry and lyrical prose tend to deal with some kind of intuitive knowledge, knowledge that cannot be adequately expressed in non-literary, prosaic ways. Among those who have had this intuition was the Norwegian romantic poet Johann Sebastian Welhaven, who said that poetry expresses the ineffable.[1] And certainly, Ricœur tried to explicate this intuition in his theory of parables, discussed in the last section. Further, the very idea of metaphors as vehicles for expression of that which is not directly expressible seems to be an attempt to explicate the same or similar intuition.

Let us briefly outline the themes of this chapter. The first theme is tacit knowledge, yet again. The second theme is the question of whether our knowledge of emotions tends to have tacit sides, a question that I answer in the affirmative. The discussion about the second theme is woven into an attempt to show how poetic metaphors and its siblings can make us aware of our tacit knowledge of emotions. This attempt is my third and most important theme.

---

[1] This is my own translation. There is a somewhat misleading English translation of this line by Charles Wharton Stork (Welhaven 1990: 187).

5.1 Tacit Knowledge Once Again

Not only shall I revisit tacit knowledge now but also the concept of disclosure. Just like Wittgenstein, Heidegger never used any expression remotely resembling 'tacit knowledge' but had it on the tip of his tongue. The carpenter discloses the hammer as a tool in virtue of not thinking about it (compare Polanyi's analysis of the absence of thinking in tacit knowledge). The carpenter's knowledge is tacit.

The richest vein of Heidegger's analysis is his implicit contention that tacit knowledge is something to be disclosed, not something that can be adequately grasped in propositions. But the kind of disclosure discussed in this chapter is of a less practical nature than Heidegger's example. Moreover, I am not talking about disclosure as some kind of a revelation or epiphany in a deep or high-strung spiritual sense, like a sudden revelation of the interconnectedness of Being. Rather, what I call 'disclosure' is a revelation of the ordinary, the emotions or the thoughts we have always had but not really understood. We see them in a new, more fruitful way thanks to disclosure.[2] However, there is also a pretty straightforward Heideggarian way of talking about disclosure that suits my project admirably. Heidegger writes about emotions as though they have a disclosive function (Heidegger 1977: 134-139 (§29). It is common knowledge that our moods and emotional states make the world or segments of it appear in different shades. Sometimes this seeing of the world in different emotional ways can help us understand segments of the world. Our fear of the charging tiger, for instance, *discloses* the tiger as being dangerous, or our disgust at the foul deeds of the child molester discloses him as being morally reprehensible. The yardsticks for the legitimacy of such emotions are emotional alethic values, different from the alethic values of a description of the tiger as a part of an ecological system or the child molester as a biological entity or a swarm of atoms. It is either E-correct or not E-correct that the tiger is a threat.

---

[2] There might be some affinities between poetic disclosure and Taylor's conception of epiphany, i.e., the idea of a work of art as being a locus of a manifestation of something that is otherwise inaccessible, something which is of great spiritual significance. This manifestation defines or completes something, even as it reveals (Taylor 1989: 419. and elsewhere). The difference between epiphany and disclosure is that the latter does not have to disclose something of great spiritual significance; it can be the down-to-earth truths of our emotional lives.

Not only Heidegger's theory of disclosure but also Johannessen's idea of knowledge by familiarity (KF) plays a certain role in my idea that poetry is disclosive of tacit knowledge. Hinting at or articulating KF with the aid of poetic metaphors, analogies, similes, and so on is a poetic way of disclosing tacit knowledge.

KF has a cousin called 'know-what', a brain-child of Frank Palmer. 'Know-what' is a third type of tacit knowledge, alongside know-how and KF. According to Palmer, our knowledge of emotions is what he terms 'knowing what', which differs from 'knowing that'. We can know *that* sadness is caused by too little serotonin in the brain, but at the same time have no inkling about what it feels like to be sad. In order really to know, we must, of course, experience sadness. Such knowledge is not necessarily propositional for it does not involve the ability to provide descriptions. Rather, it involves the capability to recall, or even imagine, experience. Propositional knowledge has the form 'know that p' and the object of knowledge is a true proposition. But if we have 'know-what' about a phenomenon, then the object of knowledge is an experience, not a proposition. It does not really make sense to equate the mere experience of depression with knowing what the experience is like. It seems absurd to maintain that there is equivalence between "I am depressed" and "I am knowing depression". However, there is no such absurdity involved in equating "I have experienced depression" and "I have known depression". That the present-perfect statements are equivalent suggests that this type of knowledge requires a certain distance. If I understand Palmer correctly, then this is the reason why literary works can express know-what; whatever the nature of such a literary expression is, it is not the same as the subjective experience of emotions. A book has no feelings and can, therefore, provide us with a distance to our own emotions. I think this is quite correct and I want to add that the tools of ana-logic might do a better job in articulating the tacit knowledge of our emotions when used in literary works, since such works give us this distance to our emotions.

Palmer says that Shakespeare would not have been able to write *Hamlet*, nor could the readers understand the play, if there was no way of getting into the mind of a depressed person and seeing the world through his or her eyes. Indeed, even though know-what is non-propositional, it is not entirely ineffable (consider Johannessen's analysis).

The ability to say it amounts to 'showing', and 'showing' requires talent and imagination. As I said earlier, Palmer contrasts 'showing' with 'telling', the latter being a simple description of states of affairs like "I am not feeling very well; my wife has left me". Poems worth their salt do not just contain the poet's descriptions of his state of mind but rather show it with the aid of images, metaphors, and poetic devices like rhythm. (He seems to be using 'showing' in the sense of 'disclosing', a most use indeed.) In order to show what love or sadness is, we need something akin to the condition of poetry (Palmer 1988: 190). In Palmer's view, imaginative literature helps us to imagine what it means to experience such emotions, and thus know what they are (Palmer 1988: 205-207). It does not require great imagination to see that Palmer's know-what is a kind of tacit knowledge, a third kind alongside know-how and KF. It is closely related to KF, but perhaps somewhat closer to propositional knowledge than KF. The reason is that know-what comprises the classification of phenomena (e.g., "this is depression"), just as propositional knowledge often is (e.g., "this is a table"). In contrast, KF does not give us classificatory knowledge. But the nature of the know-what classifications is obviously different from the propositional ones. Propositional knowledge is often knowledge of that which is somehow tangible, or objective, for instance, tables. (It can also be knowledge of that which is objective, but not tangible, for instance, mathematical theorems.) In contrast to this, know-what can only be knowledge of the subjective. Further, it goes almost without saying that we know propositional and know-what classifications in different ways. Be that as it may, I think that Palmer's contentions are by and large correct and that they are in harmony with those of Johannessen, whose contentions I have also mainly endorsed.

As I have already hinted at, Johannessen does not explicate the concept of articulation. Perhaps we can get some help from Charles Taylor, not because he necessarily uses the term in the same sense as the Norwegian philosopher, but because his concept of articulation is useful for my undertaking, both because he sees art as means of articulation and because he regards articulation as a means for making implicit (tacit?) knowledge explicit. I think that poetic metaphors, similes, and other literary devices can help us articulate our emotions and at the same time shape, reshape, and partly constitute them. So presumably, these devices can reshape our knowledge of familiarity while articulating it. I shall later give a concrete example of this in connection with my analysis of some well-known Shakespearean metaphors and similes as well as a poem by August Stramm.

Notice that the 'Taylorian articulation' is an articulation of a person's *own feelings*. We shall see that the 'Johannessenian articulation' is an articulation of our knowledge by familiarity of emotions, regardless of whether they are our own or others. Moreover, whatever cognitive insights Taylorian articulation can lead to, it cannot be a know-what of emotions since know-what has to do with the nature of a given emotion (the 'whatness' of, say, wrath). However, I think that know-what and Taylorian articulation are mutually dependent. In order to acquire know-what of emotion E, we must be able to experience it, and that experience would be impoverished if it were not an articulated experience. Articulation can help us to understand what given emotions really are. I, for instance, gain a clearer under-standing of the nature of true love versus infatuation, thanks to my articulation of my feelings towards a certain lady. To be sure, in order for us to be able to articulate in a Taylorian fashion, we must have know-what of at least some emotions. (Obviously, we cannot arti-culate a feeling as being the feeling of depression unless we know the 'whatness' of depression or some related emotions.)

We shall discover later in this chapter why knowledge by fami-liarity is essential for our emotional knowledge. In that context we shall see how Taylorian articulation and know-what can be harmonised with the idea of knowledge by familiarity. We shall also see that the devices embedded in literary works can be useful when we acquire know-what, articulate our own emotions, and articulate our KF of the emotional world.

I shall return to Palmer's theories later and use them to analyse a certain literary work. We shall see that literature can be useful both when we acquire know-what of emotions and when we articulate our KF of the emotional world. But in order to prepare this part of the chapter, I shall briefly discuss the concept of imaginative literature. I have not much to add to what I said earlier about literary narratives. I want to remind the reader that poeticality and stylicity are indicators of a work being imaginative literature. This means that the greater role the three devices and stylistic tools play in a work, the higher degree of literariness it possesses. Besides the stylistic tools mentioned earlier, I want to add the tool of *Verfremdung* (estrangement), which is supposed to create *Verfremdungseffekt*, i.e., the effect of estrangement.

Now, we have learned from Palmer that imaginative literature can give us a unique, productive *distance* to things. Some of the devices strengthen this distancing function of imaginative literature, most notably the device of *Verfremdung*. To use one of Victor Shklovsky's examples, Tolstoy estranges our work-a-day world and our particular society by describing it through the eyes of a horse in a short story, thereby making the readers aware of things they previously took for granted (Shklovsky 1965: 5-24). Estrangement creates a distance to the subject of the work of literature. Creative poetic metaphors also increase the distancing effect; they actually often have an effect of estrangement. Take for instance Shakespeare's creative poetic metaphors in Macbeth's famous monologue "Life's but a walking shadow, a poor player, that struts and frets his hour upon the stage and then is heard no more; it is a tale told by an idiot, full of sound and fury, signifying nothing" (Shakespeare 1990: 939). These words estrange life, disclose it anew, and make us look at it with new eyes owing to their displacing us from our usual bearings. (That the distance is productive can be seen from its producing new ways of seeing life). This increases the distance we already have to the subject owing to the fact that these are the words of a fictive person, not a statement put forth by a living individual making truth-claims. If the latter were the case, then we might immerse ourselves in evaluating the claims or explain the motivations of the maker of this claim or make fun of him and so on. In none of these cases do we gain any productive distance to the text, a distance that lies in between myopic immersion and hyperopic explanation.

Now, the borders of imaginative literature are porous, as can be seen from the fact that the devices are used outside of these borders. There are poetic modes of expressing oneself in daily life or in political speeches, or even in scientific discourses. However, even though there are creative poetic metaphors found outside the realm of imaginative literature, they do not have this particular effect of lengthening productive distance. After all, is not imaginative literature the true realm of *creative poetic* metaphors? Such metaphors (and the other devices) as organic parts of works of imaginative literature can disclose the tacit dimension but can hardly disclose the know-how. As far as I know, nobody has ever learned to swim by reading poetry. We are left with the 'know-what' of KF or even some hitherto unknown type of tacit knowledge. I shall try to demonstrate that literature can help the articulation of KF and know-what.

5.2 Disclosing Emotions

Johannessen quite correctly says that our mastery of emotional concepts tends to be tacit; our knowledge of emotions is to a large extent KF. In order to show this aspect, Johannessen once again seeks Wittgenstein's support. Wittgenstein was right about there being more consensus concerning our judgements about colours than our judgements about emotions. To be sure, we learn to employ both types of concepts in a similar fashion, i.e., with the aid of examples. The difference lies in the observation that the situations in which we learn how to master emotional concepts are much more complex and less amenable to perspicuity than situations involving most other kinds of concepts. The situations in question are difficult circumstances of human existence in which other people are involved. In such situations an experienced person with a keen understanding of other people can teach someone less experienced by giving him the correct hints. The experienced person can, for instance, ask his or her less experienced friend to notice the fact that a man in their presence is shifty-eyed and his hands shake every time a stranger is present. Now, the experienced one can point out to his or her inexperienced friend that the man's body language (including his facial expressions) can mean different things, depending upon the context. If the man in question has been apprehended for shoplifting, his body language may be thought to express his fear of the consequences. We can also think of a context in which he reveals to us the secret of his unrequited love for a certain lady, which allows us to infer that his body language expresses his unhappiness. Then again we can think of a situation in which our nervous friend is waiting for a person whom he does not want us to meet. In that case, we can interpret his body language as expressing uneasiness. So we see that the correct use of emotional concepts is a function of the understanding of the complex interaction between bodily expressions, on the one hand, and the nature of the situation, on the other. But this we cannot grasp this complexity with the aid of rules that have no exceptions. Understanding other people can, therefore, only be acquired with the aid of correct judgements, as Wittgenstein says (Wittgenstein 1958: 227-229). This means that our understanding of other humans is determined by paradigmatic coup-lings of types of situations and emotional expressions. The person who knows the working of the human mind operates very much like a judge who works within the framework of a common-law judicial sys-tem whereby the case-law principle dominates. In such a system, certain rulings set precedents while the paragraphs of the law book play a lesser role (what Wittgenstein calls 'judgements' are analogous to the judgements passed in courts of this type.) The world of emo-tions is a world where case law rules, since our knowledge of emo-tions is KF. Contrast this to our propositional knowledge of the physiccal world; it can be grasped in propositions about iron laws that admit of no exceptions.

However, this Wittgensteinian analysis has at least two shortcomings. In the first place, it all but ignores the subjective side of emotions. Johannessen could have strengthened his contention that emotions have a tacit side by using his own analysis of the tacit side of sensations. Because I agree with that analysis at the same time as I think sensations are typically involved in emotions, I believe that our understanding of the subjective moment in emotions is tacit. Second-ly, this analysis disregards the cognitive component of emotions.

Both my earlier criticism of Solomon and the strength of the Wittgensteinian analysis show that there are at least some important cases where observing and analysing actions in a given context play an important role for the understanding of emotions. Here is where my analysis of imaginative literature comes into the picture. I maintain that literature can give us insights into the peculiarities of the aforementioned contexts. Literature often describes unique situations, in contrast to the generalisation of nomological science. We tend to feel that great literature provides us with unique descriptions of the unique (!) and that the value of literature lies, among other things, in this descriptive ability. Let us look at the following quotation from Virginia Woolf's *To the Lighthouse*:

> Never did anybody look so sad. Bitter and black, half-way down, in the darkness, in the shaft from the sunlight to the depths, perhaps a tear formed; a tear fell; the waters swayed this way and that, received it, and were at rest. Never did anybody look so sad (Woolf 1977: 31).

Janet Martin Soskice has a point when she says that the sorrow, thematised in this quotation, is a private, particular sorrow, which must be illuminated the aid of *this* particular metaphor, and not any old metaphor (Soskice 1987: 47-48). This also illustrates the personal aspect of emotions, the fact that an emotion is something that only a given person can have, an aspect that no analysis of emotions in general can forget but which is nonetheless hard to incorporate in analysis. The particular ability of imaginative literature to disclose the unique, not least the uniquely personal, comes in handy here.

We find some good descriptions of Wittgensteinian contexts in *Egil's Saga,* one of the greatest Icelandic sagas of the Middle Ages. Its chief protagonist, the Viking and bard Egill Skallagrímsson, was at one point a mercenary in the forces of the Anglo-Saxon king Athelstan. Egill's brother was also at the Anglo-Saxon court and was killed in a battle. The saga contains a marvellous description of the mighty warrior's reactions to the death of his brother. Egill sits down in front of the Anglo-Saxon king with his head bowed. He draws the sword in and out of the sheath, implying that he is contemplating whether or not to slay the king. At the same time, he lets one eyebrow sink down right to the cheek and lifts the other up to the roots of his hair. This masterful description of the great warrior's actions, facial expressions, and body language is then tied to a description of his temper and looks.[3] The interplay between these elements helps us to understand that he expresses both wrath and sorrow. Indeed, I think that the saga's description magnifies our insight into what it means to express feelings with the aid of gestures, facial expressions, and suchlike. Examples of this kind show us the fact that gestures and facial expressions are context-dependent, especially because the writer does not force us to accept one particular interpretation. As readers, we have to interpret Egill's gestures and facial expressions in the light of the description of the situation and the character. Further, the saga does not provide us with any new information about emotions - at least not with information we could not have gathered either from experience or from non-narrative and non-literary sources. What the saga can do is to articulate our KF about certain emotions, in this case

---

[3] This description is to be found in the 55th chapter of the saga. For instance, *Egil's Saga* 1976: 128.

anger and sorrow. It does this articulation with the aid of a concrete and unique example of the way such emotions can be expressed (compare the role of examples in the articulation of KF). Moreover, it gives us an opportunity to become conscious of the fact that there are no formulas for our interpretation of other people's emotional behaviour. In practice, most of us do not apply any formulas in such cases, but we almost never think about that fact until we are confronted by a great literary work like *Egil's Saga*.[4] Being a story, something that is not a part of our lives, gives us the necessary distance to these issues, a distance that helps us to take a reflective stance to them (compare Palmer's analysis). Thus, imaginative literature awakens us from our dogmatic slumbers.

Let us see how the use of similes can articulate our gentle, cosy feeling of warmth in a snowy landscape. This is how Swiss writer Robert Walser does it:

> Und warm ist es in all dem dichten weichen
>
> Schnee, so warm wie in einem heimeligen
>
> Wohnzimmer, wo friedfertige Menschen zu
>
> irgendeinem feinen lieben Vergnügen versammelt
>
> sind (Walser 1971: 254-255).

In my rough translation:

> And it is warm in all this thick soft snow, as warm as a cosy room where peaceful people are gathered for some fine, sweet entertainment.

Walser's simile is very apt; it really fits the feeling of tranquillity we often have in such a snowy landscape, but which we usually lack the words to describe adequately. Notice that he discloses something intangible (the feeling of tranquillity in a snowy landscape) by comparing it to something more concrete, i.e., the doings of peaceful people in their homes. Notice also that we are dealing with the tacit side of a sensation, not of behaviour or actions connected to feelings.

---

[4] Obviously, there is nothing against reading the saga as a fictional work, i.e., a work of literary imagination, even though it might originally have been something different.

I just want to mention that Walser's text fits nicely into the Lakoffian scheme of things because it likens a certain emotion to something physical. And even though Walser uses the marker 'wie' (as) which indicates a simile, Lakoff would probably designate it a metaphor. After all, Lakoff rejects the notion that metaphors are primarily linguistic and thinks that they can be expressed with the aid of similes (Lakoff 1993: 208-209 and elsewhere).

It is common knowledge that metaphors are even more important than similes in literature. As we remember, Johannessen correctly assigns metaphors a key role in the articulation of KF, or at least some kinds of it. He emphasises that they are crucial in the articulation of our knowledge of emotions, due to the tacit nature of that knowledge. This can be connected to Lakoff's and Turner's contention that poetic metaphors develop and extend conventional metaphors. "Death is a dream" can be a poetic extension of the conventional metaphor DEATH IS SLEEP (Lakoff and Turner 1989: 71). This is quite an intriguing theory, especially when stripped of its cognitive science clothing (compare my earlier criticism of Lakoffian scientism). We can support it with an example from the writings of prize-winning Icelandic author Einar Már Guðmundsson. He shows us how we can make a poetic extension of the conventional metaphor (and oxymoron) of 'deafening silence', which indeed is a (dead?) metaphor for a certain emotion:

> The silence.
>   It is a blind man with a stick. It plays a drum solo by the kitchen sink, flushes the toilet and turns the raindrops, lashing against the windowpanes into speakers with pulpits like humps on their backs, continually raising their voices.
>   Louder, louder, louder, until they end up sounding like a male voice choir singing part-song, so overpowering that floor cloths cover up their ears (Guðmundsson 1994: 32).

The author uses striking and original metaphors to articulate our intuitive understanding of this emotion, the feeling of an over-whelming, 'loud' silence. We could say in a Lakoffian fashion that the author develops an everyday metaphor ('deafening silence') by creating new metaphors on the basis of it. Notice also that he uses concrete phenomena (the sound of a toilet flushing, the sound of raindrops on windowpanes, and so on) as means for disclosing something abstract and intangible, i.e., the emotion in question. Further, he uses one of literature's noblest tools, the time-honoured *Verfremdung*. Now, the effect of estrangement is supposed make us aware of things that we take for granted, and we certainly do take our tacit knowledge for granted. This includes, of course, our tacit knowledge of the feelings of deafening silence. Chances are that the Icelandic author's use of *Verfremdung* can make us aware of this knowledge.

Anyway, we have learned earlier from Lakoff and his colleagues that metaphors provide us with an indispensable and indirect understanding of such slippery phenomena as love. Furthermore, Johannessen is right that we need metaphors because of the tacit nature of emotional knowledge.[5] So it is no coincidence that literature is full of metaphors for emotions. Think about that very gospel of love, *Romeo and Juliet*. The play brims over with metaphors of love; need I remind my learned readership of "...Juliet is the sun"? (Shakespeare 1990: 835). Does not this metaphor articulate the feeling we have that the loved one somehow shines and is at the centre of our universe?[6] Does not the great Bard articulate a similar feeling in his famous *Sonnet XVIII* "Shall I compare thee to a summer's day? Thou art more lovely and more temperate..."? (Shakespeare 1990: 1201). Both in this and in Romeo's metaphor, Shakespeare gives us an opportunity to see something intangible, the feeling of loving admiration, through something more physical, the weather of a summer's day and the sun. This, of course, is in accordance with Lakoff's analysis. Moreover, these metaphors can help us articulate our emotions in the Taylorian sense of articulation. I might, for instance, articulate my own love for a certain lady with the aid of Shakespeare's beautiful metaphors while at the same time my emotion slightly changes. I might connect the emotion (my love) to the sun and summer days so that whenever I feel my love for the lady I also feel the warmth of a nice summer's day. I did not have that feeling before the articulation, so the emotion is not exactly as it used to be. And my understanding of the emotion has deepened; I know now that there is a distant relationship between the happiness I feel whenever I am with my lady and the blissfulness I felt

---

[5] Notice that we often say, "I cannot express how much I love you". Is it because our emotional knowledge is tacit?

[6] Notice that I use the metaphoric expression 'centre of our universe' in my attempt to give a sketch of Shakespeare's metaphor. It can hardly ever be fully explicated.

as a child on beautiful sunny days. (I come from a country where the sun hardly ever shines!)

My educated guess is that such poetic metaphors and similes help us to articulate our tacit emotional knowledge. There must be a reason why poetic metaphors for emotions are so widely used, both in ordinary discourse and in imaginative literature.[7] My theory could be an explanation for this. Further, the theory of the productive distance, provided by literature, can explain why we often feel that poetic metaphors for emotions in literary works tend to articulate emotions far better than such metaphors used in other contexts.

I have still not given any example of how a literary work can, as a whole, help our articulation of KF. Such an example can be found in Robert Frost's poem *The Road not Taken*. The speaker in the poem says that he was once faced with having to choose between two paths in "a yellow forest". In the last lines of the poem he says:

> Two roads diverged in a wood, and I—
> I took the one less travelled by,
> And that has made all the difference.[8]

This poem is usually interpreted as being in its entirety a metaphor for the choices we make in life. Life is metaphorically seen as a journey, and the speaker in the poem has chosen to live a different life from those of ordinary people. The poem has a bittersweet quality; it seemingly expresses that strange ambivalent feeling we often have when we contemplate the existential choices we have made. We might feel that we have by and large made the correct choices, but there is a slight sadness in us, as though we also mourn the moments lost irrevocably by our choosing other paths. Frost helps us clarify these feelings by presenting us with a vivid, concrete picture of a wanderer in a wood. More precisely, he helps us articulate our KF of these emotions, knowledge we already possess and which possesses us, but which we have not been able to articulate. Frost provides us with

---

[7] Could it be the case that we can mirror the metaphoric structure of emotions in metaphors? Could that be the reason that metaphors often are our best tools for disclosing emotions? An answer to this question belongs to possibilology, but perhaps only for the time being.

[8] From the *The Robert Frost Web Page*, http://www.robertfrost.org/indexgood.html. Retrieved 10 July 2008.

tirelessly fresh poetic metaphors, one of the best instruments for articulating our KF of this and other emotions. His poem is very much like a midwife, aiding our nascent knowledge of the emotions connected to existential choices.

Let us probe the realms of feelings still further. Sorrow has a cousin called 'depression', and depression is a mood. Let us look at August Stramm's expressionistic poem *Depression* (*Schwermut*).

> Schreiten Streben
> Leben sehnt
> Schauern Stehen
> Blicke suchen
> Sterben wächst
> Das Kommen
> Schreit!
> Tief
> Stummen
> Wir (Stramm 1957: 392).

In my translation:

> Striding striving.
> Life yearns.
> Shuddering standing.
> Looks seek.
> Dying grows.
> The Coming
> Screams!
> Deep down
> Dumbified
> We.

Actually, this poem is hardly translatable because the poet uses the peculiarities of German language for all it is worth, while creating a language of his own at the same time. Perhaps moods like depression can only be expressed in new language ('dumbified'), far removed from everyday chitchat. By breaking up the syntax, Stramm hints at the broken down, chaotic inner world of the sad person. Note also the *Verfremdungseffekt* caused by the nominalisation of verbs. In our case we suddenly understand that the world of the sad one is frozen like the verbs, which are frozen into nouns. The suggestive rhythm of the poem is also of utmost importance. One can almost hear the fast heartbeat of the unhappy one and the rhythmic march of his dark thoughts through his brain. "The world of the happy", Wittgenstein says, "is quite another than the world of the unhappy" (Wittgenstein 1922: 185 (§6.43)). Stramm's poem is a message from the unhappy world to the world of the blissful.

But poetic words about messages and unhappy worlds cannot help us to understand the cognitive import of Stramm's poem. That help can be found in the theories of Palmer. Because of Stramm's and our ability to see the world through the eyes of a depressed person, Stramm could write the poem and we could understand it (compare Palmer's analysis of *Hamlet*). Remember also Palmer's contention that such literary devices as the use of rhythm can help a writer to show states of mind. This is exactly what Stramm does with the agitated rhythm of his poem. We can safely say that the poem gives us know-what about depression. It shows rather than tells us about this mood, which is one of the reasons why it aids us in articulating a tacit knowledge of it. The main means the poet uses for that end is once again the *Verfremdung*. As we have seen, there are ways in which the *Verfremdung* can help us articulate our KF of emotions. This fact ought to strengthen our belief that KF and know-what share certain things in common. Literary works can help articulate our KF and know-what of emotions. The tools used for attaining these goals are my three devices plus such stylistic devices as the *Verfremdung*. I think that the other examples I have used are also examples of articulations of know-what about emotions. We get a better grip on what the feeling of warmth and cosiness is by reading Walser, and Guðmundsson helps us to understand what deafening silence is. At the same time these literary works articulate our knowledge through our familiarity of the emotions and moods in question. Indeed, Stramm's poem does that as well because it helps us articulate knowledge of a mood most of us have felt without being able to say much about it. Further, they (at least Stramm's poem) aid us in Taylorian articulations. Stramm's *Schwermut* might, for instance, help me to articulate an ongoing depression in such a way that I start to see it as having moments of *Angst*, since, after all, the poem is replete with anxiety ("Das Kommen schreit!", "The Coming Screams!"). In the light of this, I understand this depression differently while it somehow changes; my depressive feelings acquire a distinct 'flavour' of anxiety. Maybe the depression was, at bottom, caused by repressed *Angst*.

The poem has been my midwife, helping me to deliver these monstrous Siamese twins, depression and angst.

5.3 Disclosure and Possible Rejoinders

We have discovered in this chapter that the kind of insight we get thanks to the disclosive power of literature and metaphors is akin to KF and knowing-what. As I said earlier in this book, disclosing means showing, not saying, just as Guðmundsson shows what deafening silence is. We also remember that disclosing means grasping something intuitively and holistically, as when Stramm provides us with a total vision of depression, a vision that helps us to understand depression intuitively, an understanding in stark contrast to a scientific, analytic understanding. Further, we have seen that disclosing often is like seeing something *as* something else, for instance, when a poetic metaphor shows a beloved lady as the sun. Moreover, the results of a Taylorian articulation can hardly be called anything but 'disclosure'.

Let us now turn to some possible objections against my analysis. The first objection is as follows: we do not need literary works for such an articulation. We can use apt metaphors and concrete examples in everyday life or in imaginative theoretical discourses. Furthermore, meaningful gestures (one of the means of articulation) certainly have no role to play in literature, except perhaps in plays.

Well, I quite agree, but I want to add that I have never said that literary works monopolise the articulation. As I said earlier, my three devices can be means for such an articulation, but this does not imply that they have to be a part of a literary work in order to perform that task. Yes, a philosophical or religious text containing several poetic metaphors can be an instrument of articulation. But texts of imaginative literature tend to be even better tools for that endeavour, since imaginative literature gives us a productive distance to our feelings. The same does not hold for religious and philosophical texts, unless they are read as literary works. If we do not read them as literary works but as texts with straightforward truth-claims, then we are faced with a dilemma. Either we believe or disbelieve the claims or analyse them otherwise and thus immerse ourselves in them, focusing solely on the information that the text is supposed to give. Or we seek causal explanations for the truth-claims, wondering, for instance, whether the writer was schizophrenic, and thereby moving far away from the text

(Compare what I said earlier about persons using poetic metaphors in everyday settings.) In neither case do we get any productive distance from content of text. The productive distance can only be reached by reading the text *qua* a work of literary imagination, in so far as one can focus solely on it that way (the inspiration from Ricœur is obvious, Ricœur 1986: 113-149). I am not contradicting what I said earlier about the difficulties of focusing on a literary work in a purely aesthetic way. Focusing on a text *qua* a work of literary imagination does not mean that the focus is solely aesthetic; it can also be very personal and emotional. And as I have implied, there is always a blurred line between different focuses on literary works, for instance aesthetic, ethical, or emotional focuses.

The second possible criticism is the following: The author of this book has already admitted that there is no such thing as *the* correct interpretation of literary works. So why accepting his interpretations of the works cited in this chapter? To this I want to reply that I have already argued in favour of interpretation being not entirely subjective. I take my chances that my interpretations are somehow acceptable, i.e., adequate or fruitful, or both. The same applies to my analysis in general; I know I am treading on slippery ground when I maintain that literature can give insights into tacit knowledge. It is hard to see how we can verify such a theory with absolute certainty. (What philosophical or scientific theory can be thus verified?) But bear in mind that we cannot be 100% sure that physics is not a sham, even though we have good reasons to think that this not the case. I simply hope that I have put forth reasonable arguments in favour of literature's power to articulate tacit knowledge, arguments that might provide an inspiration for other scholars. Further, it is important to connect the analysis in this chapter with my earlier analysis of metaphors. If metaphors have cognitive import, then that fact ought to strengthen my theory of their ability to disclose or articulate tacit knowledge of emotions. My metaphoric and poetic examples certainly twist reality: strictly speaking, silence is not a man with a stick, Juliet is not the sun, and dying does not grow. Nevertheless, they facilitate our understanding of certain segments of reality, and the understanding in question is, of course, twisted. Thus my contention is that the metaphoric and poetic examples discussed in this chapter are candidates for T-correctness; Guðmundsson offers us description of deafening silence that is a hot candidate for such correctness.

The third possible criticism is perhaps the most challenging. A critic might say that there simply is no such thing as tacit knowledge. Saying that X is an object that we have tacit knowledge of and, therefore, we cannot describe adequately in words is absurd. By saying that we cannot describe X is actually to describe it. To this objection I say that this can only mean that there are no degrees of 'describability', and that this rejection of nuance or adoption of all-or-nothingness flies in the face of common sense. Our experience tells us that some things are easy to describe while others are very difficult to describe, and that there are several gradations between the two. Some seem only to be describable in rough outlines, others in details. This does not mean that things are in themselves easy or difficult to describe. They are easy or difficult relative to our practical purposes and our cognitive capabilities. It is often urgent for us to be able to describe our feelings in detail, but words often seem to fail; we admit such failures when we say (and seriously mean!) "I cannot express how much I love you". But it is usually not important for us to be able to describe tables in details, for neither practical nor aesthetic uses of tables require minute descriptions. It would not surprise me at all if a person with Asperger's syndrome never found it important to describe emotions in detail while describing tables in detail always were.

5.4 Conclusion

We have seen in this chapter that our knowledge of emotions tends to be tacit. But this knowledge is not entirely ineffable, and poetic metaphors and related devices, poetry and poetic texts can play a major role in articulating and disclosing it. (At the same time, emotions have disclosive functions.) Poetic devices and imaginative literature do not necessarily provide us with new information. What they do best is to give us insight into the (tacit) knowledge we already possess. Thus the poets and the makers of metaphors are midwives, helping us to deliver, soothing us in our birth pangs.

III.6. Notes on Enal and Emo-Logic & Summary of Section III

6.1 The Notes

Blaise Pascal famously said that "Le cœur a ses raisons, que la raison ne connaît pas" ("The heart has its reasons of which reason knows nothing") (Pascal 2000: 467). But is it really true that the reasons of heart have nothing to do with reason itself? We have seen in this Section that we do not have any reason to believe that there is a gap between emotions and reason.

I believe that there is an emo-logic similar to ana-logic and narra-logic. Correctly employing the rules of thumb involved in emotional behaviour and thinking means being emo-logical. Being emo-logical is the hallmark of the emotionally competent person; one of the virtues of such a person is a reasonably high EQ. But my hunch is that emo-logic would be even farther away from logic proper than narra-logic. It would also be less of a methodology than narra-logic is. Perhaps it would be somehow akin to Lakoff's and Johnson's metaphoric reasoning. Emotions have implications just like metaphors. Even though emotions such as anger are not necessarily based upon beliefs, there is a method to its madness. From the fact that I despise John, it follows that I have a low opinion of him. That opinion, of course, is among the factors that cause me to despise him, but, nevertheless, "I have a low opinion of John" follows from "I despise John". Of course, ordinary deductive logic plays a role in such deductions, but the employment of the rules requires a tacit, intuitive grasp of the peculiarities of situations. The combination of deduction and the grasping of the tacit is one of the cornerstones of emo-logic.[1] Further, we need emo-logic to evaluate the ways emotional alethetic values symbolise reality. An important part of such an evaluation is the ability to feel in the appropriate way towards the appropriate object in the appropriate degree, i.e., knowing the E-appropriateness of the emotions. The hallmark of highly emotionally competent persons is precisely this ability, plus knowledge of the conditions for the E-correctness of emotions and an ability to empathise and understand one's own feelings. However, there is also a minimal emotional competence that we must have in order to determine the salience and relevance of phenomena and on basis of that make decisions (compare Damasio's examples). The same holds for our ability to break argumentative deadlock with the aid of emotions (compare de Sousa's analysis).

We saw in the last chapter that ana-logic and emotions meet in imaginative literature. To this it we must add that there is meeting place for ana-logic, narra-logic, and emotional cognition that I call *emo-narra-analogic* (ENAL). Let us look at an example: From 'reading' certain cues, I understand that a given person is very unhappy. My emotional intelligence is essential for this interpretation of cues. I also discover that this person had a traumatic experience in his youth. Telling the story of that incident and the person's reaction constitutes an adequate explanation of his unhappiness, even if there might be nomological explanations as well. To understand his unhappiness, I should need a good deal of empathy, and, in order to get a grip on his state of mind; I also need a host of apt metaphors, analogies, and similes. I employ ana-logic in my effort to understand him; I might conclude, for instance, that his past is his present; he cannot get away from the past incident. I also note that his memories cut like knives. Others, including this unhappy person, can then check the aptness of these metaphors and similes. There is no doubt

---

[1] Mark Johnson has rejuvenated William James' old theory that logic is emotional and embodied. Qualifying a thought with a 'but' is really an expression of feeling of hesitation and an if-thought creates an expectation of a then-thought, the expectation being a feeling that makes hypothetical thinking possible (Johnson 2007: 86-110). But his version is very sketchy and hampered by Damasioian lack of differentiation between sensations and emotions. By ignoring the fact that emotions have intentional objects, it is easy to see whatever logical emotions there might be as something locked in our bodies.

whatsoever that this approach to the unhappy one is rational in its own way. It can be supplemented by more scientistic nomological theories, but it would not surprise me at all if the best way to identify and understand (at least in a preliminary fashion) unhappiness would be this combination of the employment of emotional intelligence, narrative explanations, and apt metaphors. This combination can be used in other areas as well. The understanding of artworks often requires a combination of the threesome. I understand the terror of Munch's *Scream* because of my emotionality; I partly explain it narratively by situating it in the story of art and the biography of Munch; and I try to understand it ana-logically: "It represents the lost soul of modern Man". The metaphor can be criticised for being too abstract to be apt, which means that it can be evaluated rationally and perhaps replaced with more concrete and more apt metaphors. Be that as it may, this is how the emo-narra-ana-logic works; we actually employ it in the course of our everyday lives when we try to come to grips with our inner lives, art works, social situations, and so on.

It is worthwhile to note that high-functioning autists, i.e., people who suffer from Asperger's syndrome, have an impaired emotional competence and lack subject-referring emotions in addition to having both difficulties in understanding the non-literal usage of language and but little narrative competence. I think that their lack of ability to follow a story makes it difficult for them to understand themselves and others, given that Selves and lives have storied structure. The limits to their emotional competence further decrease their understanding of themselves and others. They are not known for their social intelligence, and their lack of narrative competence could be a part of the explanation for their low social IQ. Further, taking decisions and making plans based on a judgment of salience and relevance is not their strong point, further vindicating Damasio's and de Sousa's theories.

Despite these shortcomings, they usual have no lack of ability to reason in a paradigmatic fashion; some of them actually excel in logico-mathematical reasoning while being at the same time expert fact-collectors.[2] This observation would not be interesting if high

---

[2] On Asperger's syndrome, see for instance Gerland 1999. On the difficulties of high-functioning autists to handle narratives and the difficulties it creates for them in understanding emotions, see Losh and Capps 2003: 239-251.

functioning autists were masters of metaphors while being low on emotional IQ and having no talent for narra-logic. Nor would it be interesting if they were not good at paradigmatic reasoning because it would be tempting say that their lack of ENAL was due to lack of general intelligence. Yet, they do not master any of the three dimensions of ENAL while they are quite capable in the paradigmatic field. These findings concerning high functioning autists could thus be regarded as corroboration of my hypothesis about ENAL.

Now, just how pervasive are emotions in our world? Do emotive structures abound? Should we be emotionalists (compare metaphorists and narrativists)? My answer is that we have good reasons to adopt at least a moderate version of emotionalism. In the first place, there are phenomena with emotive structure; a given painting P that has the identity of sad painting has this identity due to emotive structure. Without the more or less metaphoric sadness, this painting would not be P-the-sad-painting. *Mutatis mutandis*, something similar holds for a host of artworks. Giving artworks identities in this fashion is closely related to how we confer identities upon ourselves and others. John can only have the identity of a happy fellow thanks to an emotive structure. John-the-happy-fellow is constituted by this structure.

Further, we have seen that our reason has by necessity some emotive streaks. This means that emotive structures take part in constituting our reason. We can see this from the following: if there was no emotivity in our world, then we could not evaluate the relevance, even not the salience, of phenomena and therefore hardly understand much of our world, let alone find our way around it. We would have problems understanding ourselves and other people, not to speak of artworks. In fact, there would not be much to understand in a world without emotions because we could not exist without them. I am not saying that there could not be minded beings without emotions but they would act, think and perceive so differently from us that their world would be for all intents and purposes another world. The conclusion is that emotivity abounds.

Be that as it may, we can learn from my notes on ana-logic, narra-logic, emo-logic, and ENAL that the concept of reasoning is broader than we Platonist-Cartesians tend to believe. Reason has narrative, emotive, and metaphoric sides.

6.2 The Summary

The basic theme of section III is my conviction that we need a poetic of emotions of two reasons. First, because the concept of emotion is dependent upon those of narrative and metaphor and they belong to the sphere of poetic. Second, emotions are constituted, made in many ways and are therefore products of poeisis in the original Greek sense. But they are not made *ex nihilo* any more than sculptures; to 'create' emotions raw materials are required, among them brain processes, subjectivity, thoughts, actions and language.

In the first two chapters, I introduced some modern views of emotions and developed my own views on basis of them. I said that emotions give twisted understanding of reality and that they can be E-correct or not. They can also be E-appropriate; the emotionally competent person knows when to have a given emotion and in what way.

I endorsed major parts of the construalist version of the cognitive theory of emotions, i.e., Robert Roberts' and Cheshire Calhoun's idea that emotions are concern-based construals. Consequently, I accepted most of Roberts' criticisms against both traditional cognitivism (Solomon) and naturalism (Griffiths). I think, however, that sensations play a more important role in emotions than most cognitivists admit. In a world without sensations, there would be no need for a concept of emotion. At the same time I expressed agreement with Peter Goldie's contention that emotions typically involve our feeling towards something. On basis of his idea, I developed my theory of directed sensation.

I also think that Charles Taylor is on the right track when he says that emotions are partly constituted by interpretation and that there are subject-referring emotions. I used this idea to develop a more finely grained classification of feelings than the ordinary cognitivist one; differentiating between sensations, ordinary emotions and subject-referring ones, the two latter being imbued with directed sensations.

I tried to unify Taylor's hermeneutic cognitivism with construalism, calling my own position 'hermeneutic construalism'.

In the third chapter, I defended the thesis that emotions are narrations. I agree with Peter Goldie's contention that an emotion is structured in such a way that it constitutes a part of a narrative in which the emotion is embedded. The narrative, Goldie says, unites different elements and thus moulds them into a coherent whole, which we call 'an emotion'. As I see it, emotions have a storied structure. I added certain things to the narrativist concept of emotions, one of them being a variation of a theme from Robert Solomon that says that emotions are myths. In my view, myths are metaphors moving in narrated space, and the same holds for emotions. Further, I discussed Patrick Colm Hogan's original theory about narratives' having an essential emotive structure. While being critical of certain aspects of his analysis, I maintained that he is heading in the right direction.

In the fourth chapter, I considered the relationship between emotions and metaphors. I said that the constructed context (the seeing-as) of emotions is metaphoric, giving emotions a metaphoric structure. Both metaphors and emotions can 'transform' their objects in cognitively productive ways. This transformation can show us the salience of phenomena and thus be cognitively productive.

I said that I am inspired by George Lakoff's and Zoltan Köveces' theory about emotions (or at least an important class of them) being constituted by metaphors. I then added that the Lakoffian theory of metaphors has a number of weaknesses, among them that the theory is extremely hard to test. I tried to argue in favour of the contention that my way of linking metaphors and emotions is more fruitful than the one of the Lakoff School.

Narrations and metaphors are meaningful entities and by having a constitutive role for emotions help making them meaningful entities. There are other reasons for regarding them as being meaniful: a) emotions are constituted by propositional contents and attitudes towards them; b) like written texts and utterances, they can be contradictory; c) like other meaningful entities, they can, even must, be interpreted; d) understanding emotions is a complex process, involving both understanding of meaning and sensory perception; e) the understanding of emotions is fallible; f) like utterances, emotions have illocutionary aspects; g) there is an experiential emotional meaning, having E-correctness and E-appropriateness as two of its yardsticks. Finally, as Taylor points out, there are emotions that are constituted by articulation or interpretation, or both (h).

In the fifth chapter, I said that it is not by chance that we use the tools of ana-logics, not least poetical metaphors, as instruments for expressing and describing our emotions. One of the reasons for this is that the tools of ana-logic can be devices for the disclosure of inexpressible, tacit knowledge. (At the same time, emotions have disclosive functions.) At least a certain portion of our knowledge of emotions has tacit aspects. I employed several examples, both from daily life and from works of imaginative literature to support my point.

We have seen, then, that the concept of emotion is very complex one, having many dimensions that intersect in various ways: a physical one, a subjective one, a cognitive-construalist one, a narrative one, a metaphoric one, a meaningful one, a tacit one, a action-related one, and so on. Whether it is an amoebaean, an open-textured concept or even an essentialist one I should not say. But defining it is no easy task. It is, however, easy to see that our world was born of emotions and will remain their slave forever.

Conclusion of The Book, Or the (Un) Holy Trinity

Let us start this conclusion by summing up my basic findings in the different Sections. But before listing them, I want to remind the reader that I used some space in the Introduction to argue in favour of there being a multitude of alethetic or truth-like values. I also declared my self as being a philosophical opportunist, somewhere in-between analytical and Continental philosophy, with flair for Wittgenstein and Ricœur. Later, I said that I wanted to develop a cautious form of philosophical poetic, this is the conclusion of the first part of that poetic, and indeed this book is that part.

The following are my basic findings in Section I:
1. In metaphors we see one thing in terms of another thing; metaphors are constituted by seeing-as.
2. In order for M to be a metaphor, there is typically an interaction at an abstract level in M's background. In the foreground there is not necessarily any interaction, usually only fuzzy, tacit ways that the topic relates to the vehicle.
3. Metaphors have a cognitive content, more precisely, truth-like or alethetic values.
4. The alethetic value of metaphors is T-correctness, i.e., transformative correctness. To be T-correct, M must give a twisted understanding of N.
5. M gives a twisted understanding *iff* M transforms reality and by transforming it gives better understanding of it.
6. Metaphors disclose; i.e., they show rather than say.
7. We understand metaphors *iff* we know under what conditions they would be T-correct and know the kind of indirect understanding they can give.
8. There is no clear-cut separation between literal and metaphoric language.
9. Metaphors play a necessary role in our cognition and our existence in general. There is much metaphoric structure around, a fair amount of metaphoricity.

10. There is an ana-logic, i.e., an imaginative, metaphorical, tropological rationality.
11. Being metaphorically competent means being able to use ana-logic.
12. Being highly metaphorically competent means being able to create new, original metaphors.
13. Typically, neither metaphors nor poems can be paraphrased.
14. We can discriminate between adequate and inadequate interpretations of literary works.
15. But such interpretation do not have truth values, instead they can be T-correct or incorrect.

In Section II, I concluded that:

1. Stories are like Kantian intuitions, narratives being like the categories.
2. Both stories and narratives are constituted by aspect-seeing.
3. Actions and experiences, among others, have a storied structure or even a narrative structure.
4. Narratives are explanatory devices.
5. Narra-logic is closely related to ana-logic.
6. Being able to employ narra-logic means possessing narrative competence.
7. Narratives can be rationally evaluated.
8. There are typically aesthetic moments in narratives.
9. Narratives often have metaphoric structures.
10. Refiguring narratives provide us with twisted understanding; the yardstick for their correctness is T-correctness.
11. The concept of literature is an amoebaean concept.
12. There are indicators of literariness; the more of them a text possesses, the better reason we have to call it a 'literary work'.
13. There are hybrids of narratives and metaphors, i.e., metaphoric stories and suchlike.
14. There are stories we live by.
15. There are stories out there, not least spontaneous stories (daydreams, scenarios, dreams, etc).
16. Our thinking, and other mental acts and states, have a storied structure.

17. Due to 12 and 13, among others, there is a more than a grain of truth in narrativism; our human world has a high degree of narrativicity.
18. But S is only a storied structure under a description in a narrative.
19. The narrative moulds the structure but is in its own turn being shaped by the mental storied structures of the narrator.

These are the main points of Section III:

1. Emotions can have cognitive import.
2. They help us evaluate the relevance and salience of phenomena and owing this, help us in our decision-making.
3. They have their own emotional alethetic values.
4. The yardstick for them is E-correctness, which sometimes implies T-correctness.
5. E-appropriateness is also of vital importance for emotional life.
6. Emotions are concern-based construals.
7. Emotions have subjective and bodily aspects; the subjective aspect I call 'directed sensation'.
8. There are three kinds of feelings: a) bodily sensations, b) ordinary emotions, c) subject-referring emotions. The latter two involve directed sensations.
9. Emotions have a metaphoric and storied structure.
10. There are emotional myths we live by.
11. Emotions are meaningful entities.
12. There is a special emotional meaning, E-correctness and E-appropriateness being two of its most important yardsticks.
13. My own position I call 'hermeneutic construalism'.
14. Emotions tend to be woven into our actions and vice versa.
15. Emotions can have disclosive functions.
16. Metaphors and poetical texts can help us disclose tacit aspects of our emotions.
17. Being emotionally competent means being able to use emo-logic.
18. There is a way of reasoning that I call 'ENAL', i.e., Emotional, Narra- and Ana-Logical reasoning.
19. Our world is imbued with emotivity, emotive structures abound.

The upshot of all this is that the concepts of narratives, metaphors, and emotions *interact* in the sense of being logically dependent on each other, besides being siblings. They are all constituted by aspect-seeing. Further, they are cognitive tools, even though there is no such thing as a non-metaphorically true emotion, narrative or metaphor. They have related cognitive functions; they help make salient vital features and grasp the concrete, the individual, i.e., that which cannot easily be subsumed under laws. They are at the same time meaningful entities and entities that endow other phenomena with meaning.

That metaphors, narratives, and emotions have particular alethic values increases their claim to some kind of rationality, though not necessarily exactly the same rationality that is operative in the realm of literal, non-narrative propositions with truth-claims, a realm ruled by whatever passes for cool reason. Using Wittgensteinian language, you might say that these types of rationality have family resemblances. And you might add, using the same jargon, that metaphors, narratives, and emotions are parts of language-games, separated from the language-games of cool reason but tied to it by the aforementioned kind of resemblances.

Metaphors, emotions, stories and narratives permeate our lives in various ways. It is not easy to compare the degree of this permeation, but stories and narratives are even more all pervasive than metaphors and emotions due to the fact that our thinking (and most probably other mental acts) have storied, even narrative, structures. These structures constitute and shape a big portion of the world we live in. To be sure, metaphors and emotions are also of great importance; our language and culture certainly are shot through with metaphors, and our lives with emotions. But neither metaphors nor emotions are as dominant as stories and narratives.

Dominant or not, they are a part of an (un) holy trinity that bears sway over the world of humanity.

Bibliography

Aristotle. 1965. *On the Art of Poetry* in Aristotle, Horace, Longinus *Classical Literary Criticism*. (tr. T.S. Dorsch) (Penguin Classics) Harmondsworth: Penguin.

Barthes, Roland. 1977. *Image, Music, Text*. (tr.Stephen Heath) London: Fontana Paperbacks.

Baudelaire, Charles. 1962. *Flowers of Evil*. (tr. Florence Louie Friedman). London: Elek Books.

Baudelaire, Charles. 1975. *Baudelaire. Selected Poems* .(tr. Joanna Richardson) Harmondsworth: Penguin.

Beardsley, Monroe. 1962. 'The Metaphorical Twist' in *Philosophy and Phenomenological Research* XXII (3): 293-307.

Beardsley; Monroe. 1981. *Aesthetics (2nd Edition)*. Indianapolis: Hackett.

Beer, Gillian. 1996. *Open Field: Science in Cultural Encounter*. Oxford: Clarendon Press.

Ben-Ze'ev, Aaron. 2003. 'The Logic of Emotions' in Hatzimoysis, Anthony (ed.) *Philosophy and the Emotions*. Cambridge: Cambridge University Press: 147-162.

Best, David. 1985. *Feeling and Reason in the Arts*. London: Allen & Unwin.

Best, David. 1992. *The Rationality of Feeling. Understanding the Arts in Education*. London and Washington, DC: The Falmer Press.

Black, Max. 1962. *Models and Metaphors*. Ithaca: Cornell University Press.

Black, Max. 1993. 'More about Metaphors' in Ortony, Andrew (ed.): *Metaphor and Thought. 2nd Edition*. Cambridge: Cambridge University Press: 19-41.

Blamey, Kathleen. 1995. 'From the Ego to the Self' in Hahn, L.E. (ed.) *The Philosophy of Paul Ricoeur*. Chicago and LaSalle: Open Court: 571-603.

Blumenberg, Hans. 1996. *Paradigmen zur einer Metaphorologie*. Frankfurt: Suhrkamp.

Booth, Wayne. 1988. *The Company we keep*. Berkeley: University of California Press.

Bremond, Claude. 1996. 'The Logic of Narrative Possibilities' (tr. Elaine D. Cancalon) in Onega, Susana and García, José Angel (eds.) *Narratology: An Introduction*. London and New York: Longman: 61-75.

Brooks, Cleanth. 1968. *The Well-Wrought Urn*. London: Dennis Dobson.

Brooks, Peter. 1996. 'Reading for the Plot' in Onega, Susana and García, José Angel (eds.) *Narratology: An Introduction*. London and New York: Longman: 251-261.

Bruner, Jerome. 1986. *Actual Minds, Possible Worlds*. Cambridge, Mass and London, England: Harvard University Press.

Caldwell; Mark. 1997. 'The Science of Fiction' *Discover Magazine,* (online http://markturner.org/discover.html, consulted 10.09.2005)

Calhoun, Cheshire. 1984. 'Cognitive Emotions?' in Calhoun, Cheshire and Solomon, Robert (eds.) *What is an Emotion*? New York and Oxford: Oxford University Press : 327-342.

Carlsson, Anna-Lena. 2005. *"...is hunger or superabundance that has become creative?" Nietzsche on Creativity in Arts and Life*. PhD thesis. University of Uppsala, Sweden.

Carroll, Noël. 1988. *Mystifying Movies. Fads and Fallacies in Contemporary Film Theory*. New York: Columbia University Press.

Carroll, Noël. 1998. 'Art, Narrative and Moral Understanding' in Levinson, Jerrold (ed.): *Aesthetics and Ethics. Essays at the Intersection* Cambridge: Cambridge University Press: 126-160.

Carroll, Noël. 1999. *Philosophy of Art*. London and New York: Routledge.

Carroll, Noël. 2001. 'Interpretation, History, and Narrative' in Roberts, Geoffrey (ed.): *History and Narrative Reader*. Florence KY: Routledge: 246-265.

Carr, David. 1986a. *Time, Narrative, and History*. Bloomington/Indianapolis: Indiana University Press.

Carr, David. 1986b. 'Response to Casey, Crowell and Kearney' in *Human Studies*, 29 (special issue 'Scholars Symposium: The Work of David Carr'): 491-501.

Carr, David. 1991. 'Discussion. Ricoeur on Narrative' In Wood, David (ed.) *On Paul Ricoeur: Narrative and Interpretation*. London: Routledge & Kegan Paul: 160-174.

Carr, David. 2001. 'Narrative and the Real World. An Argument for Continuity' in Roberts, Geoffrey (ed.) *The History and Narrative Reader*. London: Routledge: 143-156.

Cassirer, Ernst. 1969. *Wesen und Wirkung des Symbolbegriffs*. Darmstadt: Wissenscahftliche Buchgesellschaft.

Cavell, Stanley. 1969. *Must We Mean What We Say?* Cambridge: Cambridge UP.

Cavell, Stanley. 1979. *The Claim of Reason. Wittgenstein, Skepticism, Morality and Tragedy*. New York and Oxford: Oxford University Press.

Chiappe, Dan. 2003. Review of Glucksberg (2001) in *Metaphor and Symbol* 18 (1): 55-61.

Chomsky, Noam. 1968. *Language and Mind*. New York: Hartcourt

Cooper, David.1986. *Metaphor*. Blackwell: Oxford.

Cotterel, Arthur et al (eds.). 2002: *Encyclopedia of World Mythology*. Bath, UK: Paragon.

Culler, Jonathan. 1983. *On Deconstruction. Theory and Criticism after Structuralism*. London: Routledge.

Currie, Gregory. 2006. 'Narrative Representation of Causes' in *Journal of Aesthetics and Art Criticism,* 64 (3): 309-316.

Czerny, Robert. 1977. 'Translator's Introduction' in Ricœur 1977: vii-viii.

Damasio, Antonio. 1994. *Descartes' Error. Emotion, Reason and the Human Brain*. London: Papermac.

Damasio, Antonio 2003. *Looking for Spinoza*. London: Vintage.

Dannenberg, Hilary P. 2005. 'Plot' in Herman, David, Jahn, Manfred and Ryan, Marie-Louise (eds.): *Routledge Encyclopedia of Narrative Theory*. London: Routledge: 435-439.

Danto, Arthur. 1964. 'The Artworld' in *The Journal of Philosophy* 61 (19): 571-584.

Danto, Arthur. 1981. *The Transfiguration of the Commonplace. A Philosophy of Art*. Cambridge, Massachusetts and London, England: Harvard University Press.

Danto, Arthur C. 1985. *Narration and Knowledge*. New York: Columbia University Press.

Dauenhauer, Bernhard. 2002. 'Paul Ricouer'. *Stanford Encyclopaedia of Philosophy.* Online at: http://plato.stanford.edu/entries/ricoeur/ (consulted 25.04.2006).

Davidson, Donald. 1984. *Inquiries into Truth and Interpretation*, Oxford: Clarendon Press.

Davies, Paul. 2006. 'That Mysterious Flow' in *Scientific American* 16 (1): 6-11.

Dennett, Daniel. 1991. *Consciousness Explained.* New York: Little, Brown and Co.

Derrida, Jacques. 1974. 'White Mythology. Metaphor in the Text of Philosophy' (tr. Alan Bass) in *New Literary History* 6: 5-74.

Derrida, Jacques. 1978. 'The Retrait of Metaphor' (tr. Peggy Kamuf), in *Enclitic*: 1-44.

Derrida, Jacques. 1991: (tr. Alan Bass and Peggy Kamuf) (ed. Kamuf, Peggy). New York etc.: Harvester Wheatsheaf.

Dickie, George. 1974. *Art and the Aesthetics. An Institutional Analysis.* Ithaca: Cornell University Press.

Dickie, George. 1995. 'The New Institutional Theory of Art' in Neill, Alex and Ridley, Aaron (eds.): *The Philosophy of Art. Readings Ancient and Modern.* McGraw-Hill: Boston: 213-223.

Dornisch, Loretta. 1975. 'Symbolic Systems and the Interpretation of Scripture: An Introduction to the Work of Paul Ricoeur' in *Semeia* 4: 1-21.

Dray, William. 2001. 'Narrative and Historical Realism' in Roberts, Geoffrey (ed.) *The History and Narrative Reader.* London: Routledge: 157-179.

Evans, Gareth. 1982. *The Varieties of Reference* (John McDowell ed.). Oxford: Clarendon Press.

Farrell, Frank.1987. 'Metaphor and Davidsonian Theories of Meaning' in *Canadian Journal of Philosophy* 17 (3): 625-642.

Fay, Brian 1996: *Contemporary Philosophy of Social Science.* Oxford: Blackwell.

Fauconnier; Gilles. 1997. *Mappings in Thought and Language.* Cambridge UP: Cambridge.

Fauconnier, Gilles and Turner, Mark. 1998. 'Conceptual Integration Networks' in *Cognitive Science* 22 (2): 133-187 (I quote an expanded web-version from 2001, online at http://markturner.org/cin.web/cin.html. Consulted 20.06.2006)

Fauconnier, Gilles and Turner, Mark. 2000. 'Metaphor, Metonymy and Binding' in Barcelona, Antonio (ed.) *Metonymy and Metaphor.* Berlin and New York: Walter de Gruyter: 133-145.

Fauconnier, Gilles and Turner, Mark. 2002. *The Way We Think. Conceptual Blending and the Mind's Hidden Complexities,* New York: Basic Books.

Fauconnier, Gilles and Turner; Mark. 2008. 'The Origin of Language as a Product of the Evolution of Modern Cognition' in Bernard Laks et al (eds.) *Origin and Evolution of Languages: Approaches, Models, Paradigms.* London: Equinox (PDF-file without page numbers, online at: http://markturner.org/., consulted 09.07.2008).

Feyerabend, Paul. 1975. *Against Method.* London: NLB.

Fishelov, David. 1993. 'Poetic and Non-Poetic Simile: Structure, Semantics and Rhetorics' in *Poetics Today* 14 (1): 1-23.

Foucault, Michel (1970): *The Order of Things. An Archeology of the Human Sciences* (tr. unknown) New York: Vintage Books.

Frost, Robert. *The Road not taken.* Online at (consulted 26.05. 2006): http://www.robertfrost.org/indexgood.html.

Gadamer, Hans Georg. 1990. *Wahrheit und Methode. 6 Auflage.* Tübingen: J.C.B. Mohr.

Gallie, William. 1968. *Philosophy and the Historical Understanding.* New York: Shocken Books.

Gallie, William. 2001. 'Narrative and Historical Understanding' in Roberts, Geoffrey (ed.) *History and Narrative Reader.* Florence, KY, USA: Routledge: 40-51.

Genette, Gérard. 1980. *Narrative Discourse* (tr. Jane E. Lewin). Basil Blackwell: Oxford.

Gerland, Gunilla. 1999. *Finding out about Asperger Syndrome, High Functioning Autism, and PDD.* London and Philadelphia: Jessica Kingsley Publishers.

Gibbs, Ray. 1993. 'Making Sense of Tropes' in A. Ortony, Andrew (ed.): *Metaphor and Thought* (*2nd Edition*). Cambridge: Cambridge University Press: 271-275.

Gibbs, Ray. 1994. *The Poetics of Mind. Figurative Thought, Language and Understanding.* Cambridge: Cambridge University Press.

Giddens, Anthony. 1982. 'Reason without Revolution? Habermas's Theorie des Kommunikativen Handelns' in *Praxis International* 2 (3): 318-338.

Glicksohn, Joseph and Goodblatt, Chanita. 1993. 'Metaphor and Gestalt: Interaction Theory Revisited' in *Poetics Today* 14 (1): 83-97.

Glock, Hans-Johann. 1996. *A Wittgenstein Dictionary.* Oxford UK and Cambridge, Mass: Blackwell.

Glucksberg, Sam. 2001. *Understanding Figurative Language.* Oxford: Oxford University Press.

Glucksberg, Sam and Boaz Kayser. 1993. 'How Metaphors Work' in Ortony, Andrew (ed.) *Metaphor and Thought, Cambridge*: Cambridge University Press: 401-424.

Goldie, Peter. 2000. *The Emotions. A Philosophical Exploration.* Oxford: Clarendon Press.

Gombrich, Ernst. 1977. *Art and Illusion.* London: Phaidon Press.

Goodman, Nelson. 1976. *Languages of Art. Second Edition.* Indianapolis: Hackett.

Goodman, Nelson. 1978a. *The Ways of Worldmaking.* Indianapolis: Hackett.

Goodman, Nelson. 1978b. 'Metaphor as Moonlighting' in Sacks, Sheldon (ed.) *On Metaphor.* Chicago and London: The University of Chicago Press: 175-180.

Greimas, Algirdas. 1983. *Structural Semantics. An Attempt at a Method* (tr. Danielle McDowell). Lincoln: University of Nebraska Press.

Grice, Paul. 1968. 'Utterer's Meaning, Sentence Meaning, and Word-Meaning' in *Foundations of Language* 4: 225-42.

Griffiths, Paul. 1997. *What Emotions Really Are.* Chicago and London: University of Chicago Press.

Guðmundsson, Einar Már. 1994. *The Epilogue of the Raindrops* (tr. B. Scudder). London: Scud Thames Books.

Guttenplan, Samuel. 2005. *Objects of Metaphor.* Oxford: Clarendon Press.

Haas, Stephanie. 2002. *Keine Selbst ohne Geschichten.* Zürich/New York: Georg Olms Verlag Hildesheim.

Habermas, Jürgen. 1977. *Zur Logik der Sozialwissenschaften.* Frankfurt a.M.: Suhrkamp.

Hanson, Norwood Russell.1958. *Patterns of Discovery.* Cambridge: Cambridge University Press.

Harré, Rom. 1990. 'Some Narrative Conventions of Scientific Discourse' in C. Nash Christopher (ed.) *Narrative in Culture. The Uses of Storytelling in the Sciences, Philosophy and Literature.* London and New York: Routledge: 81-101.

Harward, Donald W. 1976. *Wittgenstein's Saying and Showing Themes.* Bonn: Bouvier Herbert Grundmann.

Hawking, Stephen W. 1988. *A Brief History of Time. From the Big Bang to Black Holes.* London: Bantam Books.

Heidegger, Martin. 1954. *Vom Wesen der Wahrheit.* Frankfurt a.M.: Vittorio Klosterman.

Heidegger, Martin. 1977. *Sein und Zeit.* Tübingen: Max Niemeyer Verlag.

Heidegger.Martin. 1950. *Der Ursprung des Kunstwerkes.* Frankfurt a.M.: Vittorio Klostermann.

Hesse, Mary. 1966. *Models and Analogies in Science.* Notre Dame: University of Notre Dame Press.

Hesse, Mary. 1988a. 'The Cognitive Claim of Metaphor' in *The Journal of Speculative Philosophy,* II (1): 1-16.

Hesse, Mary. 1988b. 'Family Resemblance and Analogy' in Helman, D.H. (ed.) *Analogical Reasoning.* Dodrecht: Kluwer Academic Publisher: 317-340.

Hesse, Mary. 1993. 'Models, Metaphors, and Truth' in Ankersmit; F.R. and Mooji, J.J.A. (eds.) *Knowledge and Language. Volume III,* Dodrecht: Kluwer Academic Publishers: 49-65.

Hogan, Patrick Colm. 2003. *The Mind and its Stories. Narrative Universals and Human Emotions.* Cambridge: Cambridge University Press.

Honderich; Ted (ed.). 1995. *The Oxford Companion to Philosophy.* Oxford and New York: Oxford University Press.

Husserl, Edmund. 1962. *Die Krisis der europäischen Wissenschaften und die Transzendentale Phänomenologie.* Haag: Martinus Nijhoff.

Jakobson, Roman. 1971. 'Two Aspects of Language and Two Types of Aphasic Disorder' in *Selected Writings II: Words and Language.* The Hague: Mouton: 239-259.

Johannessen, Kjell S. 1981. 'Language, Art and Aesthetic Practice', in Johannessen; Kjell and Nordenstam, Tore (eds.) *Wittgenstein-Aesthetics and Transcendental Philosophy.* Vienna-Hölder-Pichler-Tempsky: 108-126.

Johannessen, Kjell S. 1994. 'Philosophy, Art and Intransitive Understanding' in Johannessen, Kjell S, Åmås, Knut Olav and Larsen, Rolf (eds.) *Wittgenstein and Norway.* Oslo: Solum: 217-250.

Johannessen, Kjell S. 2004. 'Praksis, kunnnskapssyn og analogisk tenkning' ('Practice, views of Knowledge and Analogical Thought'), in Guldbrandsen, Arild (ed.) *Om skapande yrkesutøvelse. En nyskaping innen academi (On Creative Practices in Professional Life).* Bergen, Trondheim, Stockholm: Sky skrift nr. 1-04: 77-96.

Johannessen, Kjell S. 2006. 'Knowledge and Reflective Practice'', in Göranzon, Bo, Hammarén, Maria and Ennals, Richard (eds.) *Dialogue, Skills and Tacit Knowledge.* Chichester, England: John Wiley & Sons, Ltd: 229-242.

Johnson, Mark. 1983. 'Metaphorical Reasoning' in *The Southern Journal of Philosophy,* 21 (3): 371-389.

Johnson, Mark. 2007. *The Meaning of the Body. Aesthetics of Human Understanding.* Chicago & London: The University of Chicago Press.

Kant, Immanuel. 1963. *Kritik der Urteilskraft*. Stuttgart: Reclam (originally published in 1781).

Kant, Immanuel. 1996. *Kritik der reinen Vernunft*. Stuttgart: Reclam (originally published in 1790).

Kearney, Richard. 1989. 'Paul Ricoeur and the Hermeneutic Imagination' in Kemp, Peter and Rasmussen; David (eds.) *The Narrative Path: The Later Works of Paul Ricoeur*. Cambridge Mass and London, England: The MT Press: 1-31.

Kearney, Richard. 2002. *On Stories*. London and New York: Routledge.

Kearney, Richard. 2006. 'Parsing Narrative-Story, History Life' in *Human Studies*, 29 (special issue 'Scholars Symposium: The Work of David Carr'): 477-490.

Kennedy, John and Vervaeke, John. 1996. 'Metaphors and Language of Thought: Falsification and Multiple Meaning' in *Metaphors and Symbolic Activity* 11 (4): 273-284.

Kenny, Anthony. 1963. *Actions, Emotions and Will*. London: Routledge and Kegan Paul.

Kittay, Eva Feder. 1987. *Metaphor: Its Cognitive Force and Linguistic Structure*. Clarendon: Oxford.

Kittay, Eva Feder. 1995. 'Metaphors as Rearranging the Furniture of the Mind: A Reply to Donald Davidson's 'What Metaphors Mean' ', in Radman, Zdrako (ed.) *From a Metaphorical Point of View: A Multidisciplinary Approach to the Cognitive Content of Metaphor*. Berlin/New York: Walter de Gruyter: 72-116.

Kockelmans, Joseph J. 1967. 'Husserl's Transcendental Idealism' in Kockelmans, Joseph J. (ed.): *Phenomenology. The Philosophy of Husserl and its Interpretation*. Garden City, N.Y.: Doubleday & Company, Inc.

Kövecses, Zoltán. 2000. *Metaphor and Emotion. Language, Culture, and Body in Human Feeling*. Cambridge: Cambridge University Press.

Kristjánsson, Kristján. 2002. *Justifying Emotions*. London and New York: Routledge.

Kuhn, Thomas 1970. *The Structure of Scientific Revolutions (2nd Edition)*. Chicago and London: Chicago University Press.

LaCapra, Dominick. 1983. *Rethinking Intellectual History*. Ithaca and London: Cornell University Press.

Lakatos, Imre. 1970. 'Falsification and the Methodology of Scientific Research Programmes' in Lakatos, Imre and Musgrave, Alan (eds.) *Criticism and the Growth of Knowledge*. Cambridge: Cambridge University Press: 91-196.

Lakoff, George and Johnson, Mark. 1980. *Metaphors We Live By*. Chicago and London: The University of Chicago Press.

Lakoff, George and Turner, Mark. 1989. *More than Cool Reason*. Chicago and London: The University of Chicago Press.

Lakoff, George. 1993.'The Contemporary Theory of Metaphor' in Ortony, Andrew (ed.) *Metaphor and Thought. Second. Edition*. Cambridge: Cambridge University Press: 202-251.

Lakoff, George and Johnson, Mark 1999: *Philosophy in the Flesh*. New York: Basic Books.

Lamarque, Peter. 1979. 'Review of *The Structure of Literary Understanding*' in *Philosophical Review* 88: 468-471.

Lamarque, Peter. 1990. 'Narrative and Invention: The Limits of Fictionality' in Nash, Christopher (ed.) *Narrative in Culture*. London and New York: Routledge: 131-153.

Lamarque, Peter and Olsen Stein Haugom. 1994. *Truth, Fiction, and Literature*. Clarendon Press: Oxford.

Lamarque, Peter. 2004. 'On not expecting too much from Narrative' *Mind & Language* 19 (4): 393-408.

Lawlor, Lawrence. 1992. *Imagination and Chance. The Difference between the Thought of Ricoeur and Derrida*. New York: State University of New York Press.

Levin, Samuel. 1993. 'Language, Concepts and Worlds' , in Ortony, Andrew (ed.) *Metaphor and Thought (2nd Edition)*. Cambridge: Cambridge University Press: 112-123.

Levinson, Jerrold. 2001. 'Who's Afraid of a Paraphrase?' *Theoria* 67 (1): 7-23.

Livingston, Paisley. 2001. 'Narrative' in Gaut, Berys and McIver Lopes, Dominic (eds.) The *Routledge Companion Aesthetics*. London: Routledge: 275-284.

Losh, Molly and Capps, Lisa 2003: 'Narrative Ability in High-Functioning Children with Autism or Asperger's Syndrome', *Journal of Autism and Developmental Disorders*, Vol. 33, No. 3, June: 239-251.

MacCormac, Earle. 1985. *A Cognitive Theory of Metaphor*. Cambridge Mass: Cambridge University Press.

MacIntyre, Alasdair. 1981. After *Virtue*. London: Duckworth.

MacLeish, Archibald. 1964. *Ars Poetica*, in Moore, Geoffrey (ed.) *American Literature*. London: Faber & Faber.

de Man, Paul. 1979. 'The Epistemology of Metaphor' in Sacks, Sheldon (ed.) *On Metaphor*. Chicago and London: The University of Chicago Press: 11-28.

Mandelbaum, Maurice. 1965. 'Family Resemblances and Generalization Concerning the Arts' in *American Philosophical Quarterly* 2 (3): 219-228.

Margolis, Joseph. 1991. *The Truth about Relativism*. Oxford and Cambridge: Blackwell.

McCarthy, Cormac. 1994. *The Crossing*, New York: Alfred A Knopf.

McClone, Matthew S. 2001. 'Concepts as Metaphors' in Glucksberg, Samuel *Understanding Figurative Language*. Oxford: Oxford University Press: 90-107.

McDowell, John. 1989. 'One Strand in the Private Language Argument' in *Grazer Philosophische Studien* 33/34: 285-303.

Merriam-Webster Online Dictionary. Omnline at: http://www.m-w.com/dictionary/ (consulted 10.06. 2008).

Mink, Louis. 1987. 'Modes of Comprehension and the Unity of Knowledge' in Fay, Brian et al (eds.): *Historical Understanding*. Ithaca and London: Cornell University Press: 35-41.

Mink, Louis. 2001. 'Narrative Form as Cognitive Instrument' in Roberts, Geoffrey (ed.) *History and Narrative Reader*. Florence, KY, USA: Routledge: 211-220.

de Mul, Jos. 1984. 'Images without Origin: On Nietzsche's Transcendental Metaphor' in McCormick, Peter J (ed.) *The Reasons of Art*. Ottawa: University of Ottawa: 273-284.

de Mul, Jos. 1999. *Romantic Desire In (Post)Modern Art & Philosophy*. New York: State University of New York Press.

Moran, Richard (2001): *Authority and Estrangement. An Essay on Self-Knowledge*. Princeton and Oxford: Princeton University Press.

Mulhall, Stephen. 1990. *On Being in the World. Wittgenstein and Heidegger on Seeing Aspects*. London and New York: Routledge.

Mukengebantu, Paul. 1990. 'L'unité de l'œuvre philosophique de Paul Ricœur' in *Laval théologique et philosophique* 46 (2): 209-222.

Nafstad, Petter. 2001. *Some Aspect of the Human Emotions*. Tromsø, Norway: The University of Tromsø.

Nietzsche, Friedrich. 1966. Von Wahrheit und Lüge in Aussermoralischen Sinn' in Schlechta, Karl (ed.) *Werke im drei Bändern. Band III*, Munich: Carl Hanser Verlag: 309-322.

Nietzsche, Friedrich. 1976. *Jenseits von Gut und Bös*e. Stuttgart: Kröner.

Novitz, David. 1985. 'Metaphor, Derrida, and Davidson' in *Journal of Aesthetics and Art Criticism* 43: 101-114.

Nussbaum, Martha. 1990. *Love's Knowledge*. Oxford: Oxford University Press.

Nussbaum, Martha. 2001. *Upheavals of Thought. The Intelligence of Emotions*. Cambridge: Cambridge University Press.

Oatley, Keith. 2008. 'The Science of Fiction', *New Scientist, Vol. 198, Issue 2662*, 42-43.

Ortony, Andrew. 1993. 'The Role of Similarity in Similes and Metaphors' in Ortony, Andrew (Ed.): *Metaphor and Thought*. 2nd Edition. Cambridge: Cambridge University Press: 342-356.

Palmer, Frank. 1992. *Literature and Moral Understanding*. Oxford: Clarendon Press.

Pascal, Blaise (2000): *Pensées*. Paris: Le livre de poche classique.

Peirce, Charles Sanders 1992. 'Deduction, Induction and Hypothesis' in Houser; Nathan and Kloesel, Christian J. W. (eds.) *The Essential Peirce, Selected Philosophical Writings, Volume 1 (1867–1893)*, Bloomington and Indianapolis, IN: Indiana University Press: 186-199.

Pepper, Stephen. 1942. *World Hypothesis. A Study in Evidence*. Berkeley: University of California Press.

Polanyi, Michael. 1958. *Personal Knowledge. Towards a Post-Critical Philosophy*. Chicago: University of Chicago Press.

Polanyi, Michael. 1966. *The Tacit Dimension*. Garden City; NY: Doubleday.

Polkinghorne, Donald. 1988. *Narrative Knowing and the Human Sciences*. New York: State University of New York Press.

Popper, Karl 1959. *The Logic of Scientific Discovery*. New York: Harper Torchbooks.

Pound, Ezra. 1975. *The Cantos*. London: Faber&Faber.

Prince Gerald. 1982. *Narratology. The Form and Functioning of Narrative*. Berlin, New York and Amsterdam: Mouton Publishers.

Prince, Gerald. 1987. *Dictionary of Narratology*. Aldershot: Scolar Press.

Ramachandran, V.S. 2004. *A Brief Tour of Human Consciousness*. New York: P.I. Press.

Richards, I.A. 1936. *The Philosophy of Rhetorics*. Oxford: Oxford University Press.

Ricœur, Paul. 1969. 'La structure, le mot, l'événement' in *Le conflit des interprétations: essais d'herméneutique*, Paris: Seuil : 80-97.

Ricœur, Paul. 1972. 'La métaphore et le problème central de l'herméneutique' in *Revue philosophique de Louvain*, 70 : 93-112.

Ricœur, Paul. 1975. "Biblical Hermeneutics" *Semeia* 4: 29-148.

Ricœur, Paul. 1976. *Interpretation Theory: Theory of Discourse and the Surplus of Meaning*. Fort Worth, Texas: The Texas Christian University Press.

Ricœur, Paul. 1977. *The Rule of Metaphor. Multi-Disciplinary Studies in the Creation of Meaning*. (tr. Robert Czerny). London: Routledge.

Ricœur, Paul. 1979. 'The Metaphorical Process as Cognition, Imagination and Feeling' in Sacks, Sheldon (ed.) *On Metaphor*. Chicago: University of Chicago Press: 141-157.

Ricœur, Paul. 1981a. '*Hermeneutics and the Human Sciences. Essays on Language, Action and Interpretation*. (tr. John B. Thompson), Cambridge: Cambridge University Press.

Ricœur, Paul. 1981b. 'Narrative Time' in W.J.T. Mitchell (ed.) *On Narrative*. Chicago: University of Chicago Press: 165-186.

Ricœur, Paul 1984 a. *Time and Narrative. Volume I* (tr. Kathleen McLaughlin and David Pellauer). Chicago & London: Chicago University Press.

Ricœur, Paul. 1984b. 'Le temps raconté' in *Revue de métaphysique et de la morale* 4 : 436-452.

Ricœur, Paul. 1985a. *Time and Narrative. Volume II* (tr. Kathleen McLauglin and David Pellauer) Chicago: Chicago University Press.

Ricœur, Paul. 1985b. *Temps et récit. Tome III: Le temps raconté*. Paris: Éditions du Seuil.

Ricœur, Paul.. 1986. *Du texte à l'action*. Éditions du Seuil: Paris.

Ricœur, Paul. 1988. *Time and Narrative. Volume III* (tr. Kathleen Blamey and David Pellauer). Chicago and London: University of Chicago Press.

Ricœur, Paul. 1991a. 'Life in a Quest for Narrative' (tr. David Wood) in Wood, David (ed.) *On Paul Ricoeur: Narrative and Interpretation*. London: Routledge & Kegan Paul: 20-33.

Ricœur, Paul. 1991b 'Discussion. Ricoeur on Narrative' in Wood, David (ed.) *On Paul Ricoeur: Narrative and Interpretation*. London: Routledge & Kegan Paul: 179-187.

Ricœur, Paul. 1992. *Oneself as Another* (tr. Kathleen Blamey). Chicago and London: Chicago University Press.

Ricœur, Paul. 1995. 'Comment' in Hahn, L.E. (ed.) *The Philosophy of Paul Ricoeur*. Chicago and LaSalle: Open Court: 257.

Ricœur, Paul. 'Synthèse panoramique'. Online at (consulted 30.06. 2007): http://www.balzan.it/premiati.aspx?lang=it&Codice=470&from=465&show=1

Riessman, Catherine Kohler. 2008. *Narrative Methods for the Human Sciences*. LA, London, New Dehli, Singapore: Sage Publications.

Roberts, Robert C.. 1988. 'What an Emotion is: A Sketch', *The Philosophical Review* XCVII (2): 183-209.

Roberts, Robert C. 2003. *Emotions: An Essay in Aid of Moral Psychology*. Cambridge: Cambridge University Press.

Rorty, Amélie Oksenberg. 1980. 'Explaining Emotions' in Rorty, Amélie Oksenberg (ed.) *Explaining Emotions*. Berkeley: University of California Press: 103-126.

Rosch, Eleanor. 1973. 'On the Internal Structure of Perceptual and Semantic Categories' in Moore, Timothy (ed.): *Cognitive Development and the Acquisition of Language*. New York and London: Academic Press: 111-144.

Ross, Stephanie. 1992. 'Caricature' in Alperson, Phil (ed.) *The Philosophy of the Visual Arts*. Oxford University Press: New York and Oxford: 114-118.

Russell, James. 1991. 'In Defence of a Prototype Approach to Emotion Concepts' un *Journal of Personality and Social Psychology* 60 (1): 37-47.

Ryan, Marie-Laure. 2005. 'Narrative' in Herman, David, Jahn, Manfred and Ryan, Marie-Louise (eds.) *Routledge Encyclopedia of Narrative Theory*. London: Routledge: 344-348.

Sartre, Jean-Paul. 1995. *Esquisse d'une théorie des émotions*. Paris: Hermann (originally published 1939)

Sartre, Jean-Paul. 1948. *The Emotions. Outline of a Theory* (tr. Bernard Frechtman). New York: The Philosophical Library.

Schapp, Wilhelm. 1976. *In Geschichten Verstrickt. Zum Sein von Mensch und Ding*. Wiesbaden: B. Heymann (originally published in 1953).

Schapp, Wilhelm. 1959. *Philosophie der Geschichten*. Leer/Ostfriesland: Verlag Gerhard Rautenberg.

Searle, John. 1979. 'On Metaphor' in Ortony, Andrew (ed.): *Metaphor and Thought*. Cambridge: Cambridge University Press: 83-111.

Searle, John. 1995. *The Construction of Social Reality*. New York: The Free Press.

Shakespeare, William. 1990. *The Complete Works of William Shakespeare* (ed. T.W. Craig) London: Henry Pordes.

Shen, Dan. 2005. 'Story-Discourse Distinction' in Herman, David, Jahn, Manfred and Ryan, Marie-Louise (eds.): *Routledge Encyclopedia of Narrative Theory*. London: Routledge: 566-568.

Shusterman, Richard. 2002. *Surface and Depth*. Ithaca: Cornell University Press.

Shklovsky, Victor. 1965. 'Art as Technique', in Lemon, L.T. and Reis, M.J. (eds.) *Russian Formalist Criticism. Four Essays*. Lincoln, Nebraska: University of Nebraska Press, 1965: 5-24.

Skilleås, Ole Martin. 1988. *Stein Haugom Olsen's Institutional Theory of Literature: A Critical Assessment* (MA-thesis). Trondheim: University of Trondheim.

Skilleås, Ole Martin. 1995. *Literature and the Value of Interpretation*. Bergen, Norway: Department of Philosophy.

Skilleås, Ole Martin. 2006. 'Knowledge and Imagination in Fiction and Autobiography' in *Metaphilosophy*, 37 (2): 259-276.

Skúlason, Páll. 2001. *Le cercle du sujet dans la philosophie de Paul Ricœur*. Paris: L'Harmattan.

de Sousa, Ronald. 1980. 'The Rationality of Emotions', Rorty, Amélie Oksenberg (ed.) *Explaining Emotions*. Berkeley: University of California Press: 127-151.

de Sousa, Ronald. 1987. *The Rationality of Emotions*, Cambridge, Mass & London, England: MIT Press.

Solomon, Robert C. 1976. *The Passions*. Garden City, New York: Doubleday.

Solomon, Robert C. 2003. 'Emotions, Thoughts, and Feelings: What is a 'Cognitive Theory' of Emotions and Does it Neglect Affectivity?' in Hatzimoysis, Anthony (ed.) *Philosophy and the Emotions*. Cambridge: Cambridge University Press: 1-18.

Sørensen, Øystein. 2004. *Historien om det som ikke skjedde. Kontrafaktisk historie* (*The Story about what did not happen. Counterfactual History*). Oslo: Aschehoug.

Soskice, Janet Martin. 1987. *Metaphor in Religious Language*. Oxford: Clarendon.

Sovran, Tamar. 1993. 'Metaphor as Reconciliation: The Logical-Semantic Basis of Metaphorical Juxtaposition' in *Poetics Today* 14 (1): 25-48.

Statkiewicz, Max. 2003. 'Live Metaphor in the Age of Cognitivist Reduction' in *Monatshefte*, 95 (4): 546-552.

Sterelny, Kim. 2001. *Dawkins vs. Gould*. Cambridge, UK: Icon Books/Totem Books.

Stern, J.P. 1978. 'Nietzsche and the Idea of Metaphor' in Paisley, M. (ed.) *Nietzsche: Imagery and Thought*. London: Methuen: 64-82.

Stramm, August. 1957. *Schwermut*, in *The Penguin Book of German Verse* (ed. L. Forster). Harmondsworth: Penguin Books: 392.

Taylor, Charles. 1985a. 'Self-Interpreting Animals' in *Human Agency and Language. Philosophical Papers. Vol. 1*. Cambridge: Cambridge University Press: 45-76.

Taylor, Charles. 1985b. 'Theories of Meaning' in *Human Agency and Language. Philosophical Papers. Vol. 1*. Cambridge: Cambridge University Press: 248-292.

Taylor, Charles. 1985c. 'Interpretation and the Sciences of Man' in *Philosophy and the Human Sciences. Philosophical Papers. Vol. 2*. Cambridge: Cambridge University Press: 15-57.

Taylor, Charles. 1985d. 'What is Human Agency?' in *Philosophy and the Human Sciences. Philosophical Papers 1*. Cambridge: Cambridge University Press: 15-44.

Turner; Mark. 1995. 'Cognitive Science and Literary Theory', *Stanford Humanities Review, 4 (1): Bridging the Gap* (online at: http://www.stanford.edu/group/SHR/4-1/text/turner.commentary.html. (Consulted 25.11.2006).

Turner, Mark. 1996. *The Literary Mind*. Oxford: Oxford University Press.

Turner, Mark. 2004. 'The Origin of Selkies' in *Journal of Consciousness Studies*, 11 (5-6): 90-115. Turner, Mark. 2007. 'The Way We Imagine' in Roth, Ilona (ed.) *Imaginative Minds*. London: British Academy and Oxford University Press: 213-236.

Unknown. 1976. *Egil's Saga* (tr. Hermann Pálsson) Harmondsworth: Penguin Books.

Unknown. *1979. The New Bantam English Dictionary*. New York: Bantam Books.

Unknown. 1990. Concise English Dictionary. London: Tophi Books.

Vaihinger, Hans. 1924. *Die Philosophie des Als Ob*. Leipzig: Verlag von Felix Meiner.

Venema, Henry Isaac 2000. *Identifying Selfhood*. New York: State University of New York Press.

Vico, Giambattista. 1984. *The New Science of Giambattista Vico* (tr. Thomas Goddard Bergin and Max Harold Fisch). Ithaca: Cornell University Press (originally published in 1744).

Waisman, Friedrich. 1951. 'Verifiability' in Flew, Anthony (ed.) *Essays on Logic and Language*. New York: Philosophical Library: 117-144.

Way, Eileen Cornell. 1991. *Knowledge Representation and Reality*. Dordrecht: Kluwer.

Way, Eileen Cornell. 1995. 'An Artificial Intelligence Approach to Models and Metaphors' in Radman, Zdrako (ed.) *From a Metaphorical Point of View: A Multidisciplinary Approach to the Cognitive Content of Metaphors*. Berlin and New York: Walter de Gruyter: 165-197.

Walser, Robert. 1971. *Kleine Dichtungen, Prosastücken, Kleine Prosa. Das Gesamtwerk. Bind II*. Genève and Hamburg: Kossodo.

Weinsheimer, Joel. 1982. 'The Heresy of Metaphrase' in *Criticism: A Quarterly for Literature* 4: 309-326

Weitz; Morris. 1956. 'The Role of Theory in Aesthetics' in *The Journal of Aesthetics and Art Criticism* XV: 27-35.

Welhaven, Johann Sebastian. 1990. *The Soul of Poetry (translated by* Charles Wharton Stork), in Aarnes, Asbjørn and Paul Grøtvedt, Paul (eds.). 1990. *Demringens tolker. En essaysamling om Johann Sebastian Welhaven (The Interpreter of Dusk. A Collection of Essays on Johann Sebastian Welhaven)* Oslo: Aventura.

White, Hayden. 1973. *Metahistory. The Historical Imagination in Nineteenth-Century Europe.* Baltimore and London: The John Hopkins University Press.

White, Hayden. 1978. *Tropics of Discourse. Essays in Cultural Criticism.* Baltimore and London: The John Hopkins University Press.

White, Hayden. 1986. 'The Metaphysics of Narrativity' in David Wood (ed.) *On Paul Ricoeur: Narrative and Interpretation.* London: Routledge & Kegan Paul: 140-159.

White, Hayden. 1987. *The Content of the Form. Narrative Discourse and Historical Representation.* Baltimore and London: The John Hopkins University Press.

White, Hayden. 2001. 'Emplotment and the Problem of Truth', in Roberts, Geoffrey (ed.) *History and Narrative Reader.* Florence, KY, USA: Routledge: 375-389.

Williams, William Carlos. 1985. *Selected Poems.* New York: New Directions Publishing Company.

Winch, Peter. 1958. *The Idea of a Social Science and its Relation to Philosophy.* London: Routledge & Kegan Paul.

Winters, Yvor. 1959. *In Defense of Reason.* Denver: Alan Swallow (originally published in 1938).

Wittgenstein, Ludwig. 1922. *Tractactus Logico-Philosophicus.* London: Routledge & Kegan Paul.

Wittgenstein, Ludwig. 1958. *Philosophical Investigations* (tr. Elizabeth Anscombe). Oxford: Blackwell.

Wittgenstein, Ludwig. 1979. *On Certainty/Über Gewissheit.* Oxford: Blackwell.

Wollheim, Richard. 1980. *Art and its Object. 2nd Edition With Six Supplementary Essays.* Cambridge: Cambridge University Press.

Woolf, Virgina. 1977. *To the Lighthouse.* London: Grafton Books.

Worth, Saul. 1974. 'Seeing Metaphor as Caricature' in *New Literary History* VI (1): 195-209.

von Wright, Georg Henrik. 1971. *Explanation and Understanding.* Ithaca: Cornell University Press.

Index of names